READING FROM THE INSIDE OUT

INCREASING YOUR COMPREHENSION AND ENJOYMENT OF COLLEGE READING

DEBORAH SILVEY
DIABLO VALLEY COLLEGE

Longman

New York • San Francisco • Boston
London • Toronto • Sydney • Tokyo • Singapore • Madrid
Mexico City • Munich • Paris • Cape Town • Hong Kong • Montreal

In loving memory of my parents,

Herbert and Margretta Noble

Vice President and Publisher: Joseph Terry
Senior Acquisitions Editor: Steven Rigolosi
Associate Editor: Barbara Santoro
Senior Marketing Manager: Melanie Craig
Senior Supplements Editor: Donna Campion
Production Manager: Joseph Vella
Project Coordination, Text Design, Photo Research,
    and Electronic Page Makeup: Thompson Steele, Inc.
Cover Design Manager: Wendy A. Fredericks
Cover Designer: Joseph DePinho
Cover Credit: © Digital Vision
Senior Manufacturing Buyer: Dennis J. Para
Printer and Binder: Courier Corporation
Cover Printer: The Lehigh Press

For permission to use copyrighted material, grateful acknowledgment is made to the copyright holders on pp. 509–513, which are hereby made part of this copyright page.

Library of Congress Cataloging-in-Publication Data

Silvey, Deborah.
    Reading from the inside out : increasing your comprehension and enjoyment of college reading / by Deborah Silvey.
        p. cm.
    Includes bibliographical references and index.
    ISBN 0-321-08580-9 (alk. paper)
    1. College readers. 2. Reading comprehension. I. Title.
    PE1122 .S48 2002
    428.6--dc21

                                                        2002031523

Copyright © 2003 by Pearson Education, Inc.

Please visit our Web site at http://www.ablongman.com

ISBN 0-321-08580-9

1 2 3 4 5 6 7 8 9 10—CRW—05 04 03 02

BRIEF CONTENTS

CONTENTS

* * *

✳ ✳ ✳

TO THE INSTRUCTOR

Reading from the Inside Out teaches traditional reading skills using a new focus: the reading process as interaction between reader and writer. The approach encourages students to consider their own feelings and ideas about what a writer is saying, so reading becomes a space for self-discovery as well as for gaining information. Each part of the book is linked to a theme that provides a unifying context for personally involving materials and more academic readings.

The text also fosters metacognitive processes, since students monitor their own thinking as they move from purely personal reactions to more objective analysis. This progress comes from learning a sequence of reading strategies—starting with ways of connecting to the writer's ideas and then moving through a logical but flexible progression for comprehending, interpreting, analyzing, and evaluating the ideas in a reading.

The book shows students how strategies build on one another, so they incorporate what they've already practiced along with each new strategy. They learn how to combine strategies and, eventually, how to choose appropriate strategies for a reading. Each strategy is introduced as a way to find meaning in a complete reading on a theme. This integration of instruction with thematically linked readings increases students' interest and motivation for learning strategies. You have several choices of readings to assign for practice, with many readings linked to more than one theme.

In addition to comprehension questions and vocabulary exercises for each reading, a range of writing, reflecting, and discussion activities helps students refine their thinking. Collaborative activities also help students develop the connection between reading, thinking, talking, and writing.

Organization: Reading Strategies and Themes

Each of the 14 chapters in *Reading from the Inside Out* introduces a new reading strategy and provides one or two appropriate readings to practice the strategy. More readings are provided at the end of each part, and you can choose from them for additional or substitute material. An optional study skills supplement called "Time Out for You" follows several of the book's chapters. You may assign any or all of these supplements, but students can also use them on their own.

The progression of strategies builds logically from easy intuitive responses to challenging analytical techniques. And students are reminded of strategies they've already learned in the context of each new reading.

The book is also organized thematically, with each part containing readings that follow a different theme.

- In Part I, "You and the Author," students learn to **check in, respond,** and **work with new words,** using readings about *the reading process* itself.

- In Part II, "Predicting and Questioning," the strategies—**get an overview** and **ask questions**—are presented with selections on the theme of *childhood and family.*

- In Part III, "Comprehending Main Ideas," students learn to **find and mark main ideas, look for patterns of thought,** and **make inferences,** using readings on the theme of *learning for yourself.*

- In Part IV, "Summarizing in Your Own Words," the strategies taught are **mapping main ideas** and **writing a summary,** and the theme of the readings is *understanding others.*

- In Part V, "Interpreting Language and Purpose," the strategies are **finding meaning in metaphor** and **determining the writer's purpose,** in the context of material about *nature's adventures and challenges.*

- In Part VI, "Analyzing and Evaluating," students are taught to **analyze the information** and **make an evaluation,** with readings on *popular culture and everyday life.*

Special Features

Reading from the Inside Out begins with students' interests and their responses to readings. It contains several features to emphasize this student-centered approach:

- A focus on reading as an interaction between reader and writer

- Support for metacognitive processes, from response to analysis to evaluation

- Thematic arrangement of readings, to interest students and hone critical thinking

- Complete readings to practice each reading strategy

- Consistent presentation of each strategy, with introductory outline, step-by-step demonstration, and follow-up practice

- Clear, flexible sequence of reading strategies

- Writing activities for each reading

- Choice of readings for teaching each strategy

- Collaborative activities

- Vocabulary development for each reading

- Additional questions in a multiple-choice format for assessing comprehension and vocabulary

Teaching and Learning Package

A complete **Instructor's Manual** is available to accompany *Reading from the Inside Out* (ISBN: 0-321-08582-5). In addition, a series of other valuable ancillaries is available.

Electronic and Online Offerings

[NEW WEB VERSION] Longman Reading Road Trip Multimedia Software, CD Version and Web/Course Compass Version. This innovative and exciting multimedia reading software is available either on CD-ROM format or on the Web. The package takes students on a tour of 15 cities and landmarks throughout the United States. Each of the 15 modules corresponds to a reading or study skill (for example, finding the main idea, understanding patterns of organization, and thinking critically). All modules contain a tour of the location, instruction and tutorial, exercises, interactive feedback, and mastery tests. To shrinkwrap the CD or the access code to the Web site with this textbook, please consult your Longman sales representative.

[NEW] Longman Vocabulary Website. For additional vocabulary-related resources, visit our free Vocabulary Web site at **http://www.ablongman.com/vocabulary.**

The Longman Electronic Newsletter. Twice a month during the spring and fall, instructors who have subscribed receive a free copy of the Longman Developmental English Newsletter in their e-mailbox. Written by experienced classroom instructors, the newsletter offers teaching tips, classroom activities, book reviews, and more. To subscribe, visit the Longman Basic Skills Web site at **http://www.ablongman.com/basicskills,** or send an e-mail to BasicSkills@ablongman.com.

For Additional Reading and Reference

The Dictionary Deal. Two dictionaries can be shrinkwrapped with *Reading from the Inside Out* at a nominal fee. *The New American Webster Handy College Dictionary* is a paperback reference text with more than 100,000 entries. *Merriam Webster's Collegiate Dictionary,* tenth edition, is a hardback reference with a citation file of more than 14.5 million examples of English words drawn from actual use. For more information on how to shrinkwrap a dictionary with your text, please contact your Longman sales representative.

Penguin Quality Paperback Titles. A series of Penguin paperbacks is available at a significant discount when shrinkwrapped with any Longman Basic Skills title. Some titles available are Toni Morrison's *Beloved,* Julia Alvarez's *How the Garcia Girls Lost Their Accents,* Mark Twain's *Huckleberry Finn, Narrative of the Life of Frederick Douglass,* Harriet Beecher Stowe's *Uncle Tom's Cabin,* Dr. Martin Luther King, Jr.'s *Why We Can't Wait,* and plays by Shakespeare, Miller, and Albee. For a complete list of titles or more information, please contact your Longman sales consultant.

Newsweek Alliance. Instructors may choose to shrinkwrap a 12-week subscription to *Newsweek* with any Longman text. The price of the subscription is 59 cents per issue (a total of $7.08 for the subscription). Available with the subscription is a free "Interactive Guide to *Newsweek*"—a workbook for students who are using the text. In addition, *Newsweek* provides a wide variety of instructor supplements free to teachers, including maps, Skills Builders, and weekly quizzes. For more information on the Newsweek program, please contact your Longman sales representative.

For Instructors

Electronic Test Bank for Reading. This electronic test bank offers more than 3,000 questions in all areas of reading, including vocabulary, main idea, supporting details, patterns of organization, language, critical thinking, analytical reasoning, inference, point of view, visual aids, and textbook reading. With this easy-to-use CD-ROM, instructors simply choose questions from the electronic test bank, then print out the completed test for distribution (CD-ROM: ISBN: 0-321-08179-X, Print version: ISBN: 0-321-08596-5).

CLAST Test Package, Fourth Edition. These two 40-item objective tests evaluate students' readiness for the CLAST exams. Strategies for teaching CLAST preparedness are included. Free with any Longman English title (Reproducible sheets: ISBN: 0-321-01950-4, Computerized IBM version: ISBN: 0-321-01982-2, Computerized Mac version: ISBN: 0-321-01983-0).

TASP Test Package, Third Edition. These 12 practice pre-tests and post-tests assess the same reading and writing skills covered in the TASP examination. Free with any Longman English title (Reproducible sheets: ISBN: 0-321-01959-8, Computerized IBM version: ISBN: 0-321-01985-7, Computerized Mac version: ISBN: 0-321-01984-9).

Teaching Online: Internet Research, Conversation, and Composition, **Second Edition.** Ideal for instructors who have never surfed the Net, this easy-to-follow guide offers basic definitions, numerous examples, and step-by-step information about finding and using Internet sources. Free to adopters (ISBN: 0-321-01957-1).

The Longman Guide to Classroom Management is the first in a series of monographs for developmental educators. Written by Joannis Flatley of St. Philip's College, it focuses on issues of classroom etiquette, providing guidance on dealing with unruly, unengaged, disruptive, or uncooperative students (ISBN: 0-321-09246-5).

The Longman Instructor's Planner is an all-in-one resource for instructors. It includes monthly and weekly planning sheets, to-do lists, student contact forms, attendance rosters, a gradebook, an address/phone book, and a mini almanac. It is free upon request (ISBN: 0-321-09247-3).

For Students

The Longman Reader's Journal, by Kathleen T. McWhorter. This reader's journal offers students a space to record their questions about, reactions to, and summaries of materials they've read. Also included is a personal vocabulary log, as well as ample space for free writing. For an examination copy, contact your Longman sales representative (ISBN: 0-321-08843-3).

[NEW] The Longman Reader's Portfolio. This unique supplement provides students with a space to plan, think about, and present their work. The portfolio includes a diagnostic area (including a learning style questionnaire), a working area (including calendars, vocabulary logs, reading response sheets, book club tips, and other valuable materials), and a display area (including a progress chart, a final table of contents, and a final assessment). Ask your Longman sales representative for ISBN 0-321-10766-7.

Researching Online, **Fifth Edition.** A perfect companion for a new age, this indispensable new supplement helps students navigate the Internet. Adapted from *Teaching Online,* the instructor's Internet guide, *Researching Online* speaks directly to students, giving them detailed, step-by-step instructions for performing electronic searches. Available free when shrinkwrapped with this text (ISBN: 0-321-09277-5).

Ten Practices of Highly Successful Students. This popular supplement helps students learn crucial study skills, offering concise tips for a successful career in college. Topics include time management, test-taking, reading critically, stress, and motivation (ISBN: 0-205-30769-8).

[**FOR FLORIDA ADOPTERS**] *Thinking Through the Test,* by D. J. Henry. This special workbook, prepared specially for students in Florida, offers ample skill and practice exercises to help students prep for the Florida State Exit Exam. To shrinkwrap this workbook free with your textbook, please contact your Longman sales representative. Available in two versions: with answers and without answers. Also available: Two laminated grids (one for reading, one for writing) that can serve as handy references for students preparing for the Florida State Exit Exam.

The Longman Planner. This free planner helps students organize a business life. Ask your Longman sales representative for an examination copy (ISBN: 0-321-04573-4).

Acknowledgments

The contributions of many people helped make this book a reality, and I'd like to thank them all.

My students and colleagues at Diablo Valley College gave me important insights about how to help students read better and with greater pleasure. Judy Myers and Sharon Pastori provided many helpful suggestions. I am especially grateful to Sue Shattuck for using an early version of the book in her courses and generously sharing many ideas for improvement.

The editorial staff of Longman Publishers gave invaluable support to this project. Senior editor Steven Rigolosi saw the possibilities in a thematic, student-centered book and encouraged me throughout its development. Ann Hofstra Grogg, my developmental editor, engaged me in an intense, creative dialogue. Her unusual sensitivity to the goals of this book sharpened and clarified my ideas.

Several reading teachers reviewed earlier drafts, and I am grateful for their suggestions and ideas:

Carol Brenner, Pellissippi State Technical Community College

Kathleen S. Britton, Florence–Darlington Technical College

Janice Buchner, Suffolk Community College

Leslie Cappiello, Brookhaven College

Beverly Carpenter, Brookhaven College

Denise G. Chambers, Normandale Community College

Carolyn Conners, Wor-Wic Community College

Carol Copenheffer, Central Ohio Technical College

Janet Curtis, Fullerton College

Denise Davis, St. Louis Community College at Florissant Valley

Kathleen Dixon, University of North Dakota

Robert S. Mann, Des Moines Area Community College

Alice Perrey, St. Charles Community College

Dee Pruitt, Florence–Darlington Technical College

Ilene Rutan, Brookdale Community College

Deborah Schaum, Cisco Junior College

Stacy Waddoups, Utah Valley State College

Susan Wickham, Des Moines Area Community College

My family—Chris, Rachel, Dylan, Carla, Lerryn, Tim, and Devon—deserve great thanks for their ideas, their patience, and their support. Many friends deserve the same thanks, especially Kent and Patricia Daniels. Finally, my deepest gratitude goes to my husband, Robert, who gives me inspiration and assistance always.

—*Deborah Silvey*
Berkeley, California

TO THE STUDENT

WELCOME TO *READING FROM THE INSIDE OUT*

This book was written to help you understand and enjoy what you read in college. A major purpose is to show you ways to relate what you read to your own life, so reading will be meaningful to you. Readings in this book are grouped around specific *themes*—general subjects—to encourage you to think about your own experiences. Each theme is a part, and the book has six parts, each with two or three chapters.

Part I: You and the Author

Part II: Childhood and Family

Part III: Learning for Yourself

Part IV: Understanding Others

Part V: Nature's Adventures and Challenges

Part VI: Popular Culture and Everyday Life

Another major purpose of *Reading from the Inside Out* is to teach you reading strategies—clear plans or methods for working your way efficiently through your college reading assignments. Each chapter of the book introduces a new reading strategy, such as finding patterns or marking a text. You will practice using these strategies with the kinds of reading assigned in your college courses, such as textbooks and journal articles, along with some stories and poems. Eventually you will develop a system for using strategies that will work well for you in a variety of reading situations. A feature following some chapters, called "Time Out for You," gives you further advice to help you study. Your instructor may assign these "Time Outs," but you can also use them on your own to improve your reading skills and your chances for success in college.

Finally, this book encourages you to *collaborate*—to work in cooperation with others—to increase your understanding of what you read. Joining with other readers shows you that instead of being an isolated activity, reading can benefit from group investigations and discussions. This symbol 👥 before a question or activity indicates it is especially suited to group work.

As you progress through this book, you will practice ways of reading that increase your ability:

- to discover more about yourself

- to get the information you need for your college courses

- to collaborate effectively with other students

- to *enjoy* reading!

PART I

YOU AND THE AUTHOR

WITH READINGS ON
THE READING PROCESS

When you pick up a book or a magazine, you probably don't think about what a strange activity reading is. But it is unlike anything else you do. You look at a piece of paper with a variety of squiggles on it and suddenly you're seeing—thinking, feeling—the author's ideas. Your head is filled with someone else's ideas, whether they were typed into a computer yesterday or written by hand, with pen and ink, 500 years ago. Writers can speak to you from any time or any place.

Writers can tell you about anything you can imagine as well as things you have never imagined. They can anger you, cheer you up, inform you. Of course they can communicate to you only if the basic conditions for reading are met. First, the squiggles they use must represent the words you speak. Second, you must know the system for decoding the squiggles.

But these are only the basic conditions. You're not really reading unless the words you've read spark an understanding of the writer's message in you and get you to respond in some way. Successful reading is a dialogue between the writer and the reader. A writer puts down his or her ideas as clearly as possible. As the reader, you take in those ideas and say—in your mind—what you think about them.

Unfortunately, communication between the writer and the reader sometimes breaks down. Writers don't always communicate as clearly as they should. Readers don't always give their full attention to what they read. But when reading works the way it is intended to work, it is a *two-way process,* with you, the reader, just as involved as the writer.

The title of this book, *Reading from the Inside Out,* suggests that reading is a two-way process.

- The *Inside* refers to what goes on inside of you as you read. It reinforces the idea that you're not really reading unless the words on the page make something happen in your mind.

- The *Out* refers to what's *outside* you as you read—the writer's words. Some books—mystery novels, for example—get and keep your attention so easily that you need to make no special effort to connect to the ideas in them. But in other cases, especially for the reading you'll do in college, you need to take special steps to make a *connection* with the writer.

- *Inside Out* reminds you that the two-way process in reading always begins with and comes back to you, the reader. This book shows how becoming more aware of yourself as a reader can make reading a much better experience for you. It also shows you how to strengthen the connection between you and the writer.

Making a connection doesn't necessarily mean agreeing with the writer. You may disagree violently. What connecting does mean is paying full attention to what you're reading. To make the connection, you always need to start where *you* are—with your own experience and interests. Then you're ready to use what you know and care about to consider carefully what the writer is saying.

But reading from the inside out is not a single movement away from the self and toward the writer. Rather, it's a continuous process. You reach *outside*—to the words on the page—so you can bring the writer's ideas back *inside*—to your mind. In your mind, you respond in some way to these ideas—relating them to your own experience, or asking questions, or disagreeing. Then you go back to the writer for more. You'll find that the more you read with this continuous inside-out, back-and-forth process, the more involved with the reading you'll be. In other words, you'll be doing the kind of reading that means something to you.

Part I of this book, "You and the Author," focuses on how an awareness of yourself as a reader can help you find reading a more meaningful experience. The reading strategy introduced in Chapter 1 shows you how to get involved in a reading; the strategy in Chapter 2 helps you stay involved with the reading and think about what you've read. Chapter 3 then introduces another essential strategy—a process for understanding the unfamiliar words you find in college reading.

CHAPTER

1

PUT YOURSELF
IN THE READING PROCESS:
CHECK IN

When you begin reading, you instantly become as important in the reading process as the writer and the writer's words. Many others may have read those words before you. But when *you* read, the writer's message will be filtered through *your* mind, and no one else's. So, as you read, your mind, with all its unique experiences, not only takes in the writer's words, but also shapes their meaning.

Introduction to the New Strategy: Check In

Because you bring all of your experiences with you as you read, the reading process begins as soon as you know something about the reading. That often starts with the title or some other clue about the subject. Strategy 1—check in—reminds you to look inside yourself to see what ideas and experiences you already have that will help you connect to the reading. This strategy doesn't take much time—with practice only a few seconds. But those few seconds can give you a stronger *purpose* for reading—an intention, for example, to compare the writer's ideas to your own or to add new information to what you already know.

STRATEGY 1: CHECK IN

1 Get a quick, first impression of the subject.

2 Look inside for any feelings you have—good, bad, or in between—that you bring to the subject.

3 Look inside for any ideas, knowledge, and experience you bring to the subject.

Use this strategy to **check in** before reading the first part of a poem, "The Voice You Hear When You Read Silently," below.

The Title and the Subject

1 Get a quick, first impression of the subject.

The *subject* is what the reading is about. It is the focus for all of the ideas. Often you can get an idea of the subject from the title. The title of this poem shows that the subject is *silent reading*.

Your Feelings

2 Look inside for any feelings you have—good, bad, or in between—that you bring to the subject.

Do you have mainly positive or at least neutral feelings about reading? What about poetry? If you have any negative feelings either about reading or about poetry, don't let them get in your way. Try to put them aside for the moment.

Your Experiences

3 Look inside for any ideas, knowledge, and experience you bring to the subject.

Here are some suggestions for using your own ideas and experience to connect with the subject of this poem:

- *Question:* "What could the writer mean by 'the *voice* you hear'? What could be heard as you read *silently?*"

- *Predict:* "Maybe he means the voice I hear in my own head."

- *Comment:* "Hearing a voice when reading silently? Strange idea!"

- *Remember:* "I remember the sound of my mother's voice reading to me."

Involving your mind before starting to read prepares you to connect with the reading. Even if the writer explores the subject in a different way from what you were expecting, you've awakened your curiosity, and staying curious is the best way to open up to new ideas.

Now, try reading the first part of the poem.

THE VOICE YOU HEAR WHEN YOU READ SILENTLY

is not silent, it is a speaking   1
out-loud voice in your head: it is *spoken,*
a voice is *saying* it
as you read. It's the writer's words,
of course, in a literary sense   5
his or her "voice" but the sound
of that voice is the sound of *your* voice.
Not the sound your friends know

or the sound of a tape played back
but your voice   10
caught in the dark cathedral
of your skull, your voice heard
by an internal ear informed by internal abstracts°
and what you know by feeling,
having felt.   15

informed by internal abstracts: influenced by what you have in your mind that you've *abstracted,* or taken out of, your experience.

First Impressions   These lines answer the question about what the title of the poem means. It is your own voice that you hear in your mind as you read, bringing your own awareness of what the writer's words mean as you say them. From what we see so far, the poem gives a glimpse of reading from the inside out. We see reading being made as much inside the reader as outside the reader. Reading, the poet reminds us here, is always finally yours—your experience. ∎

Try the New Strategy: Check In

Now that you've been introduced to Strategy 1, try **checking in** with Reading 1, "I Do Not Like to Read—Sam-I-Am!"

The Title and the Subject

1 Get a quick, first impression of the subject.

If the title of a reading doesn't give you enough information about the subject, look at the first lines or paragraph to get a sense of what the reading is about. For example, by glancing ahead at this reading, you can see that the subject of "I Do Not Like to Read—Sam-I-Am!" is *learning to read.* You may not understand the last part of the title, "Sam-I-Am," but you now have enough information to think about your feelings and experience on the subject.

Your Feelings

2 Look inside for any feelings you have—good, bad, or in between—that you bring to the subject.

What are your feelings about your early experiences with reading? If you notice negative feelings about the subject, put them aside for the moment.

Your Experiences

3 Look inside for any ideas, knowledge, and experience you bring to the subject.

Here are two samples of ideas or experience that connect with the subject:

- *Comment:* "The title seems childish, almost like the words in a child's book."

- *Remember:* "I wasn't read to very much as a child. My parents were just too busy most of the time."

Think of your own comments, memories, questions, or predictions.

Now that you've **checked in,** read "I Do Not Like to Read—Sam-I-Am!" As you read, pause wherever you feel the author is saying something that relates to your own early reading experiences. Keep noticing both the similarities and the differences between her experience and yours.

I DO NOT LIKE TO READ—SAM-I-AM!

REBECCA GRABINER

Rebecca Grabiner is an alumna of the University of Chicago. She wrote about learning to read for the University of Chicago Magazine, *in 1997 toward the end of her senior year. In this reading, she talks about a very popular book for young children,* Green Eggs and Ham *by Theodore Geisel, known throughout the world as Dr. Seuss. "Sam" is a character in the book.*

I never knew how to read until I was forced to learn in school, in the   1
first grade. It wasn't that I didn't like books. On the contrary, I looked forward eagerly to the time every night when I sat in my father's lap, and he read me stories and rhymes. . . . I just didn't feel any pressing need to see for myself that the words actually said what my parents told me they did. I was a very trusting child.

The summer before I turned 6, when I had completed kindergarten at   2
my small, friendly, neighborhood elementary school, my father's sabbatical took us halfway across the country to Indiana. Now, my kindergarten education was by no means bad, but my school had certain revolutionary ideas: It thought children should enjoy learning. The early grades moved slowly. Lessons always seemed more like games than work, and we were never graded. At almost 6, I was a proficient finger-painter; I could draw a turkey by tracing either my right or left hand; I could count to a hundred; and I knew the alphabet, but only in capital letters.

At Child's School in Bloomington, Indiana, I quickly discovered that, in   3
spite of my two-handed turkey-drawing ability, I was very much behind the other children. My classmates laughed when they saw me carefully printing my name all in uppercase, when I thought that the more Elmer's glue you used the better it stuck, and when I didn't know the Pledge of Allegiance, even though it was printed on the inside of my pencil-box lid.

I was put in the lowest reading group, which had only two other mem-   4
bers: a girl who had been left back the year before and a boy everyone feared because he had a chipped front tooth. Every day, I had to stay in at recess because I couldn't finish my phonics assignments in time.

When my father read to me at home and tried to help me by pointing   5
out the letters as he read, I squeezed my eyes shut until he stopped, refusing to look at anything but the pictures. I couldn't bear to think that the

books I enjoyed so much at home could have anything in common with that dreadful Dick and Jane and their horrid dog, Spot.

I liked listening to stories and looking at the pictures, but that wasn't what I thought of when someone mentioned reading. Reading was getting bad grades and being laughed at. It was sitting next to the boy with the chipped tooth and spending 30 minutes of hard work only to find out that Dick and Jane had gone to the market and bought apples, pears, and bananas, but that they could not buy cucumbers because the shopkeeper was out of cucumbers.   6

When I got home that day, I was almost surprised to see a cucumber in our refrigerator and thought how stupid Dick and Jane were to go to that dumb shopkeeper when they should have gone to the supermarket like my mother did. That night, my mother was going to read to me because my father was out of town for a math conference, so I went to the shelf to pick out a book while she did homework for her computer-programming class. I chose *Green Eggs and Ham,* recognizing it by the color of its binding, and squinting so my vision blurred and I couldn't see the letters on the spine.   7

My mother was taking forever to finish her work, so I began to flip through the pages, looking for my favorite picture, the one with the goat in it. What happened next was really an accident. . . . Almost without realizing it, I found myself reading the entire page, and liking it.   8

"I would not, could not, on a boat. I would not, could not, with a goat." And I found out that the words on the page were the same as the ones that my parents said, and I could read them.   9

I was reading and I wasn't bored. I was reading to myself and I could do it as quickly or as slowly as I wanted, without my name being written on the board, without check marks, and without staying in at recess. I could even read the same sentence more than once if I wanted to.   10

"I DO NOT LIKE GREEN EGGS AND HAM. I DO NOT LIKE THEM. SAM-I-AM!" I read, shouting now. I read it twice, then three times, at the top of my voice. My mother looked up from her work.   11

"I'll read it to you in just a second," she said.   12

"No! I'll read it to you!" I yelled. And I did.   13

Activities   After you've finished reading, use these questions to respond to "I Do Not Like to Read—Sam-I-Am!" You may write out your answers in your own words or prepare them in your mind to discuss in class.

1. What were the similarities and differences you noticed between Grabiner's experience and your own? For example, were you put off by reading lessons in school as she was? Did a favorite book suddenly change your attitude in the way that *Green Eggs and Ham* got Grabiner excited about

reading? In a small discussion group, share with others what you would like to say about your early experiences with reading.

2. How did Grabiner try to keep herself from learning to read? Do you ever remember trying actively to *not* learn something?

3. Choose a part of the reading you particularly liked or didn't like. Explain your choice.

4. Discuss with others what recommendations you would make about how to make early reading experiences as positive as they can be. Use your own experiences and Grabiner's to determine what works well and what should be avoided.

5. Because of some bad experiences, Grabiner put up mental barriers to stop herself from reading. Discuss with others the barriers that get in your way as you try to connect with a reading (see Figure 1.1). ■

Apply the New Strategy: Check In

Checking in helped you make a connection with the ideas in the excerpt from the poem, "The Voice You Hear When You Read Silently." The strategy also prepared you to connect with the ideas in "I Don't Like to Read—Sam-I-Am." Now, come back to "The Voice You Hear . . ." to see how the strategy adds to your understanding of the entire poem. As you **check in** again, look

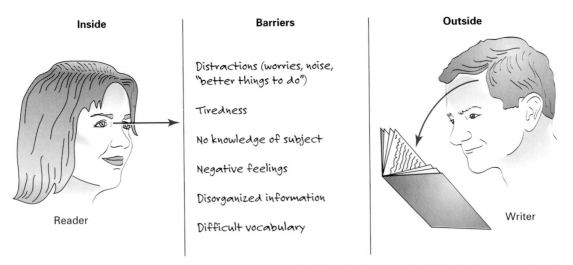

Figure 1.1   Barriers that get in the way of the inside-outside (reader-writer) connection. What barriers come from the reader? What barriers come from the writer's text? What other barriers would you add?

inside for more ideas, memories, and questions to get you involved in the reading.

As you read the poem, stop where it feels natural to do so. Keep in mind the *layout* of the poem—the end of a line doesn't necessarily signal the end of a sentence. These brief stops give you a chance to see how the poem answers your questions or relates to your experience.

At each stopping point, think about what catches your attention:

1. Is there an idea to consider? Do you agree or disagree? Or do you need to read more to figure out what Lux is saying here?

2. Is there an *image*—a picture the words create in your head?

3. Do you feel impatient or frustrated at any point in the poem?

READING 2   **THE VOICE YOU HEAR WHEN YOU READ SILENTLY**

THOMAS LUX

Thomas Lux is an award-winning poet and author of several books of poetry. He currently teaches at Sarah Lawrence College in New York. "The Voice You Hear When You Read Silently" first appeared in a 1997 issue of the New Yorker *magazine.*

THE VOICE YOU HEAR WHEN YOU READ SILENTLY

is not silent, it is a speaking   1
out-loud voice in your head: it is *spoken,*
a voice is *saying* it
as you read. It's the writer's words,
of course, in a literary sense   5
his or her "voice" but the sound
of that voice is the sound of *your* voice.
Not the sound your friends know
or the sound of a tape played back
but your voice   10
caught in the dark cathedral
of your skull, your voice heard
by an internal ear informed by internal abstracts
and what you know by feeling,
having felt. It is your voice   15
saying, for example, the word "barn"
that the writer wrote
but the "barn" you say
is a barn you know or knew. The voice

in your head, speaking as you read,   20
never says anything neutrally—some people
hated the barn they know,
some people love the barn they know
so you hear the word loaded
and a sensory constellation°   25
is lit: horse-gnawed stalls,
hayloft, black heat tape wrapping
a water pipe, a slippery
spilled *chirrr*° of oats from a split sack,
the bony, filthy haunches of cows.   30
And "barn" is only a noun—no verb
or subject has entered into the sentence yet!
The voice you hear when you read to yourself
is the clearest voice: you speak it
speaking to you.   35

a sensory constellation/is lit: the collection (*constellation*) of associations we have with a word because of what we have *sensed*—seen, smelled, heard—in relation to it.

chirrr: the sound the oats make as they spill from the sack.

Activities   Just as the reading process begins before you begin reading, it continues after you've read the last word. For example, once you've carefully read this poem, you get more ideas about what it means to you.

Here are some activities that can help you think more about the poem.

1. What does the "voice" in the poem finally mean to you?

2. Pick the part that means most to you and say why.

3. The poem shows how each of us has different associations with a word by using the example of *barn*. But you may not have a strong association with that word if you didn't grow up in the country. In a small group, compare the different associations each of you have with another word for a place, such as *kitchen* or *yard* or *beach*.

4. How does this poem demonstrate the importance of the reader in the reading process?

Chapter 1 Summary

How does Strategy 1 help you *read from the inside out?*

Reading from the inside out describes how you continually look inside at your own experience to connect what you think and feel to the outside—the writer's ideas. **Checking in** reminds you to look inside to find your own associations with a subject before you start to read.

How does the *checking-in* strategy work?

To **check in,** you use the title and first lines or paragraph to identify the subject of the reading. Then you look inside to see what feelings and experience you have in connection with the subject.

STRATEGY 1: CHECK IN

1 Get a quick, first impression of the subject.

2 Look inside for any feelings you have—good, bad, or in between—that you bring to the reading.

3 Look inside for any ideas, knowledge, and experience you bring to the subject.

Are you familiar with the meaning of these terms?

subject: what the reading is about; the focus for all the ideas

purpose: what you intend to get out of a reading

How is the strategy working for you so far?

1. Which parts of the **check-in** have you found most helpful in the readings you've practiced with? Which have been least helpful?

2. How successful were you at using the title and first lines or paragraph to find the subject? Were you able to think of connections between your experience and the subject? If not, what would make the strategy more useful to you?

3. Have you tried this strategy for readings in other courses? If not, what courses could you imagine using this strategy in?

4. What did you appreciate about using this strategy? What did you dislike?

**For more practice with *checking in,*
use the Reading Road Trip CD-ROM or Web site.**

TIME OUT FOR YOU

What's Been Your Experience of Reading?

You've now had the chance to see that **checking in** with your own ideas and experience before reading can help you connect to the writer's ideas. But if you're like most students, the idea that reading involves talking back to the writing on the page will still seem strange. You may also think it's too time consuming to stop and think about what a writer is saying. So, before going further in this book, take some time to consider yourself as a reader. How do you read when you get to choose books or articles for your own entertainment? Then think about why learning an additional way of reading can help you comprehend and enjoy more types of reading, especially the types of reading you'll do in college.

Whatever you read for pure pleasure—whether it's a Stephen King suspense novel, a Danielle Steele romance, or a car magazine—you don't have to think about stopping to interact with the writer. You just begin, go through the reading, and come to the end. In fact, you may get so involved you forget you're reading! Getting lost in reading in this way is something readers look forward to.

But what happens when a book or article doesn't capture your attention? Do you read challenging material, like a textbook chapter, the same way you would read a longtime favorite writer—just starting at the beginning and reading straight through without stopping? If so, you've probably found it was a waste of your time. You may have been able to get through the reading quickly, but you have no understanding of what you've read. This kind of "being lost" is very different from "losing yourself" in a favorite book, and it's a frustrating experience all readers have had at one time or another.

When you're trying to read challenging writings—as you are in your college courses—you need another way of reading that helps you stay aware of your response. Instead of reading straight through, pause now and then. Talk back to the writer to clarify for yourself what you agree with or disagree with, what you find confusing, and what you understand. Reading challenging material in this way takes longer but will give you the satisfaction of understanding what you read.

By the time you're done with *Reading from the Inside Out,* you'll have the strategies to know how to enjoy many different kinds of reading experiences and to make sure you learn from what you read.

Answer the following questions so you will know yourself as a reader. That's the first step to becoming a better reader.

1. What sorts of things do you enjoy reading most?

   _____

   _____

   _____

2. If you haven't done much reading outside of school, what kinds of readings have you enjoyed most for your classes?

   _____

   _____

   _____

3. How often do you have the experience of getting hooked by what you're reading, so you can't put the book or magazine down? What gets you hooked?

   _____

   _____

   _____

4. If you've had any problems with reading in the past, how have you dealt with them? What kinds of approaches have worked best for getting around these problems?

   _____

   _____

   _____

5. What kind of challenging writing have you read during the last year? Did you do this reading for school? For some other reason? Can you list some of the books or articles you would call challenging?

   _____

   _____

   _____

6. How well could you concentrate while reading challenging writing? How much did you remember of what you read? Were you aware of responding—positively or negatively—to what you were reading?

_____

_____

_____

7. Which of your courses this college term will increase your need to read challenging material?

_____

_____

_____

CHAPTER

2

STAY INVOLVED IN THE READING PROCESS: RESPOND

"Reading from the inside out" is a reminder that reading starts with you, the reader. It begins when you **check in.** You find the subject, and then you pause to see what you think and feel about it before you begin to read. Then, you read. Now the reading process involves you and the writer. As you read what the writer has to say, you come back to what *you* think. What do you understand? What is your opinion about the writer's ideas?

In other words, you *respond.*

Try the New Strategy: Respond

Check In, Strategy 1, gets you involved before you actually read. Strategy 2, **Respond,** keeps you involved in the process as you read. By talking back to the writer as you read, you stay in touch with what *you* think.

STRATEGY 2: RESPOND

1 Respond while you're reading and after you've finished reading.

2 Make a place or space to respond.

3 Ask questions and say what you think of the writer's ideas.

4 Link ideas from other readings or sources.

5 Talk with others.

Try reading "Forbidden Reading" by Alberto Manguel. As you do, respond: agree or disagree, find things you like and don't like, connect Manguel's ideas to things you already know. Get ready to talk about the reading with others. As you read, stop when it feels natural to do so, so you can *notice* how you are responding.

| READING 3 | FORBIDDEN READING |

ALBERTO MANGUEL

Alberto Manguel is a writer, translator, and editor, with a wide-ranging knowledge of literatures of the world. Born in Buenos Aires, Argentina, Manguel is now a citizen of Canada. In his book A History of Reading *(1990), he explores what has drawn people throughout history to want to read, even when, as in this excerpt, they are forbidden to.*

STRATEGY 1: CHECK IN
- What could the title of this reading mean? Were you ever forbidden to read something?
- The first sentence hints at the subject. What do you already know about this subject?
- Be aware of any strong feelings you might have about the subject.

For centuries, Afro-American slaves learned to read against extraordinary odds, risking their lives in a process that, because of the difficulties set in their way, sometimes took several years. The accounts of their learning are many and heroic. Ninety-year-old Belle Myers Carothers—interviewed by the Federal Writers' Project, a commission set up in the 1930s to record, among other things, the personal narratives of former slaves—recalled that she had learned her letters while looking after the plantation owner's baby, who was playing with alphabet blocks. The owner, seeing what she was doing, kicked her with his boots. Myers persisted, secretly studying the child's letters as well as a few words in a speller she had found. One day, she said, "I found a hymn book . . .° and spelled out `When I Can Read My Title Clear.'° I was so happy when I saw that I could really read, that I ran around telling all the other slaves." Leonard Black's master once found him with a book and whipped him so severely "that he overcame my thirst for knowledge, and I relinquished its pursuit until after I absconded.°" Doc Daniel Dowdy recalled that "the first time you was caught trying to read or write you was whipped with a cow-hide, the next time with a cat-o-nine-tails° and the third time they cut the first joint off your forefinger." Throughout the South, it was common for plantation owners to hang any slave who tried to teach the others how to spell.

. . . : a series of dots shows some words have been left out.

"When I Can Read My Title Clear": *title* here means a deed showing ownership.

absconded: ran away and hid.

cat-o-nine tails: whip made with nine knotted cords.

Under these circumstances, slaves who wanted to be literate were forced to find devious° methods of learning, either from other slaves or from sympathetic white teachers, or by inventing devices that allowed them to study unobserved. The American writer Frederick Douglass, who was born into slavery and became one of the most eloquent abolitionists° of his day, as well as founder of several political journals, recalled in his autobiography: "The frequent hearing of my mistress reading the Bible aloud . . . awakened my curiosity in respect to this mystery of reading, and roused in me the desire to learn. Up to this time I had known nothing whatever of this wonderful art, and my ignorance and inexperience of what it

devious: sly, indirect.

abolitionist: someone who campaigned to do away with slavery.

1

2

could do for me, as well as my confidence in my mistress, emboldened me to ask her to teach me to read. . . . In an incredibly short time, by her kind assistance, I had mastered the alphabet and could spell words of three or four letters. . . . [My master] forbade her to give me any further instruction . . . [but] the determination which he expressed to keep me in ignorance only rendered me the more resolute° to seek intelligence. In learning to read, therefore, I am not sure that I do not owe quite as much to the opposition of my master as to the kindly assistance of my amiable mistress." Thomas Johnson, a slave who later became a well-known missionary preacher in England, explained that he had learned to read by studying the letters in a Bible he had stolen. Since his master read aloud a chapter from the New Testament every night, Johnson would coax him to read the same chapter over and over, until he knew it by heart and was able to find the same words on the printed page. Also, when the master's son was studying, Johnson would suggest that the boy read part of his lesson out loud. "Lor's over me," Johnson would say to encourage him, "read that again," which the boy often did, believing that Johnson was admiring his performance. Through repetition, he learned enough to be able to read the newspapers by the time the Civil War broke out, and later set up a school of his own to teach others to read.

Learning to read was, for slaves, not an immediate passport to freedom 3 but rather a way of gaining access to one of the powerful instruments of their oppressors: the book. The slave-owners (like dictators, tyrants, absolute monarchs and other illicit° holders of power) were strong believers in the power of the written word. They knew, far better than some readers, that reading is a strength that requires barely a few first words to become overwhelming. Someone able to read one sentence is able to read all; more important, that reader has now the possibility of reflecting upon the sentence, of acting upon it, of giving it a meaning.

"rendered me the more resolute": made me more determined.

illicit: illegitimate, unlawful.

Get a Close-Up of the New Strategy: Respond

Remember that reading is a conversation between you (the reader) and the writer. The conversation begins as you **check in,** continues as you read, and goes on after you've read, as you think about what the writer said.

Time for Responding

1 *Respond while you're reading and after you've finished reading.*

As you read, pause and think about what you've just read. Ask questions, or notice things you like or don't like. Depending on the reading, you will pause at different points. Sometimes you might stop after each sentence. Other times you'll read a group of paragraphs before pausing.

Once you come to the last sentence, don't stop responding. Carry on the conversation with the writer by asking more questions, making more comments, or looking back to make sure you have the main ideas.

Space for Responding

2 *Make a place or space to respond.*

It's helpful to have different places for responding during and after you read. Your choice will depend on your own preferences and your instructor's guidelines.

Your own mind. The conversation between you and the writer takes place in your own mind. While you read and after you've finished reading, give your mind the space to **respond** with your own thoughts about what the writer has said.

Margin notes. Mark places in the margin where you find yourself responding. Just put a pencil mark next to the sentence or paragraph you responded to. Or, if what you read puzzles you, put a question mark. If it amazes you, put an exclamation point (!). Or make a smiley face or a frown. Later we'll cover other ways to mark ideas.

Journal or log. A journal or reading log is useful for jotting down responses as you go along and after you've finished reading. Some people divide a notebook into two columns, one column for writing a few words from the reading and the other column for a personal response to them.

Reading partner. It is sometimes helpful to read with a partner. In a "joint reading" you each read the same text silently. After each paragraph you pause to say how each of you responds. Then, you read the next paragraph, and so on. This technique is especially useful for difficult readings.

Questions and Comments

3 *Ask questions and say what you think of the writer's ideas.*

Questions. As in a conversation, you sometimes need to ask questions to make sure you haven't misunderstood. You can often find the answer to a question just by looking more closely at what you've read. If you can't, don't get discouraged. Keep in mind what you *do* understand, and identify what other information you need. You can work on these questions or get help with them later.

Agreements and disagreements. Connecting with the writer doesn't mean you have to agree with what the writer is saying. Notice when you agree or disagree. For example, after reading "Forbidden Reading," do you agree with what Manguel says about the power of reading?

Likes and dislikes. This reading is a good one for noticing your likes and dislikes. Manguel describes cruelty experienced by slaves, so you probably didn't like what he says. But you might like learning about the slaves' cleverness in figuring out secret ways to learn to read. You might find some examples interesting, but you might be frustrated by the old-fashioned language in statements by former slaves. What specific things did you like in this reading? What didn't you like?

Connections with Other Ideas

4 *Link ideas from other readings or sources.*

Compare the information a writer gives with what you know from other sources—from seeing a film or TV program on the subject or from another reading. Seeing relationships between ideas helps you identify what different writers have in common as well as what makes each writer's ideas unique.

For example, Grabiner (Reading 1) and Manguel each describe the process of learning to read. But how are the readings different? What is Grabiner's purpose? What is Manguel's purpose?

Talking with Others

5 *Talk with others.*

Throughout this book you'll find ways of moving beyond your one-on-one conversation with the writer. Writers *want* you to talk back to them, but they also want you to talk about their ideas with other readers. A writer's ideas really come to life in the discussions readers have about what they've read.

Readers also find that a reading means much more after they've talked about it with others. Even when readers have different opinions, they help each other to get more out of the reading.

Follow-Up Activities Throughout This Book

Reading from the Inside Out is set up so you always have a chance to **respond** after reading. Beginning with this chapter, there is a section of Follow-Up Activities for each reading. The following types of questions are always included:

- *Grab your first impressions.* What do you feel and think immediately after you've finished reading?

- *Ask and answer questions.* See if you can answer questions that are provided for you about the reading. Then, try to ask and answer your own questions.

- *Form your final thoughts.* After you're sure you've understood the writer, decide what you think of the reading.

These questions may be answered in a variety of ways, depending on your instructor's guidelines. You may:

- Prepare them in your mind to discuss in a small group or with the class.

- Work with classmates to prepare your answers. Questions with the icon are especially good for discussion with fellow classmates.

- Write out your answers either in a reading journal (or log) or as a separate written assignment. When writing answers, be sure to use your own words (don't just copy from the reading).

Follow-Up Activities   After you've finished reading, use these activities to respond to "Forbidden Reading." You may write your answers or prepare them in your mind to discuss in class.

Grab your first impressions.

1. What surprised you most about this reading? What did you find most meaningful?

2. What about the reading did you like? What didn't you like? Explain your choices.

Ask and answer questions.

1. How did plantation owners try to keep slaves from learning to read?

2. How can people teach themselves to read whole books just by learning the alphabet and a few words?

3. What two things motivated Frederick Douglass to learn to read?

4. Why did plantation owners want to keep slaves from reading?

 ### Ask and answer your own question.

Write a question of your own. Share your question with others and collaborate on an answer. Or, imagine that you're able to talk to the author of this reading. What part of the history of slaves learning to read would you like to know more about?

Form your final thoughts.

1. Share your ideas about the reading with someone else or with a group. What similarities and differences do you find in your responses?

2. Now that you've thought more about "Forbidden Reading" and discussed it, what is your opinion about it? How did your response change from your first impressions?   ■

Apply the New Strategy: Respond

Now that you understand Strategy 2, put it into practice with Reading 4, "'See Spot Run': Teaching My Grandmother to Read." **Respond**—in your mind, on paper, or in discussion with others. **Respond** by asking questions, saying what you like or don't like, and agreeing or disagreeing with the writer's ideas. Link ideas from this reading with others you've read about the subject.

READING 4   ## "SEE SPOT RUN": TEACHING MY GRANDMOTHER TO READ

ELLEN TASHIE FRISINA

Ellen Tashie Frisina is a journalism professor at Hofstra University in Hempstead, New York. In this reading she remembers herself as a young teenager following an unusual desire: to teach the basics of reading to her grandmother, who never had the opportunity to learn when she was young.

STRATEGY 1: CHECK IN
- Have you known any adults who could not read? What do you imagine it would be like to live in today's society without knowing how to read?
- What kind of relationship have you had with grand-parents? Can you imagine teaching a grandparent or other older relative how to read or do some other basic skill?
- What feelings—positive or negative—do you bring to this subject?

stealthily: secretly.

monosyllabic: having only one syllable.

When I was 14 years old, and very impressed with my teenage status (looking forward to all the rewards it would bring), I set for myself a very special goal—a goal that so differentiated me from my friends that I don't believe I told a single one. As a teenager, I was expected to have deep, dark secrets, but I was not supposed to keep them from my friends.   1

My secret was a project that I undertook every day after school for several months. It began when I stealthily° made my way into the local elementary school—horror of horrors should I be seen; I was now in junior high. I identified myself as a graduate of the elementary school, and being taken under wing by a favorite fifth grade teacher, I was given a small bundle from a locked storeroom—a bundle that I quickly dropped into a bag, lest anyone see me walking home with something from the "little kids" school.   2

I brought the bundle home—proudly now, for within the confines of my home, I was proud of my project. I walked into the living room, and one by one, emptied the bag of basic reading books. They were thin books with colorful covers and large print. The words were monosyllabic° and repetitive. I sat down to the secret task at hand.   3

"All right," I said authoritatively to my 70-year-old grandmother, "today we begin our first reading lesson."   4

For weeks afterward, my grandmother and I sat patiently side by side—roles reversed as she, with a bit of difficulty, sounded out every word, then   5

STRATEGY 2: RESPOND

1 Respond while you're reading and after you've finished reading.

2 Make a place or space to respond.

3 Ask questions and say what you think of the writer's ideas.

4 Link ideas from other readings or sources.

5 Talk with others.

read them again, piece by piece, until she understood the short sentences. When she slowly repeated the full sentence, we both would smile and clap our hands—I felt so proud, so grown up.

My grandmother was born in Kalamata, Greece, in a rocky little   6
farming village where nothing much grew. She never had the time to go to school. As the oldest child, she was expected to take care of her brother and sister, as well as the house and meals, while her mother tended to the gardens, and her father scratched out what little he could from the soil.

So, for my grandmother, schooling was out. But she had big plans for   7
herself. She had heard about America. About how rich you could be. How people on the streets would offer you a dollar just to smell the flower you were carrying. About how everyone lived in nice houses—not stone huts on the sides of mountains—and had nice clothes and time for school.

So my grandmother made a decision at 14—just a child, I realize now—   8
to take a long and sickening 30-day sea voyage alone to the United States. After lying about her age to the passport officials, who would shake their heads vehemently at anyone under 16 leaving her family, and after giving her favorite gold earrings to her cousin, saying, "In America, I will have all the gold I want," my young grandmother put herself on a ship. She landed in New York in 1916.

No need to repeat the story of how it went for years. The streets were   9
not made of gold. People weren't interested in smelling flowers held by strangers. My grandmother was a foreigner. Alone. A young girl who worked hard doing piecework to earn enough money for meals. No leisure time, no new gold earrings—and no school.

She learned only enough English to help her in her daily business as   10
she traveled about Brooklyn. Socially, the "foreigners" stayed in neighborhoods where they didn't feel like foreigners. English came slowly.

My grandmother had never learned to read. She could make out a   11
menu, but not a newspaper. She could read a street sign, but not a shop directory. She could read only what she needed to read as, through the years, she married, had five daughters, and helped my grandfather with his restaurant.

So when I was 14—the same age that my grandmother was when she   12
left her family, her country, and everything she knew—I took it upon myself to teach my grandmother something, something I already knew how to do. Something with which I could give back to her some of the things she had taught me.

And it was slight repayment for all she taught me. How to cover the fig   13
tree in tar paper so it could survive the winter. How to cultivate rose bushes and magnolia trees that thrived on her little piece of property. How to make

baklava: pastry made of many layers of paper-thin dough with a filling of ground nuts and honey.

baklava,° and other Greek delights, working from her memory. ("Now we add some milk." "How much?" "Until we have enough.") Best of all, she had taught me my ethnic heritage.

First, we phonetically sounded out the alphabet. Then, we talked about vowels—English is such a difficult language to learn. I hadn't even begun to explain the different sounds "gh" could make. We were still at the basics. 14

afghan: type of blanket or shawl.

Every afternoon, we would sit in the living room, my grandmother with an afghan° covering her knees, giving up her crocheting for her reading lesson. I, with the patience that can come only from love, slowly coached her from the basic reader to the second-grade reader, giving up my telephone gossiping. 15

Years later, my grandmother still hadn't learned quite enough to sit comfortably with a newspaper or magazine, but it felt awfully good to see her try. How we used to laugh at her pronunciation mistakes. She laughed more heartily than I. I never knew whether I should laugh. Here was this old woman slowly and carefully sounding out each word, moving her lips, not saying anything aloud until she was absolutely sure, and then, loudly, proudly, happily saying, "Look at Spot. See Spot run." 16

When my grandmother died and we faced the sad task of emptying her home, I was going through her night-table drawer and came upon the basic readers. I turned the pages slowly, remembering. I put them in a paper bag, and the next day returned them to the "little kids" school. Maybe someday, some teenager will request them again, for the same task. It will make for a lifetime of memories. 17

Follow-Up Activities   After you've finished reading, use these activities to respond to "'See Spot Run': Teaching My Grandmother to Read." You may write your answers or prepare them in your mind to discuss in class.

Grab your first impressions.

1. What about the reading did you like? What didn't you like? Explain your choices.

2. Do you think many teenagers would want to do what Frisina did? Why or why not?

Ask and answer questions.

1. Why did Frisina's grandmother want to come to the United States all by herself at such a young age?

2. Frisina suggests that her grandmother's difficulties upon arriving in this country were typical for most immigrants. What were these difficulties?

3. What had the grandmother taught the author that inspired the author to want to teach her in return?

4. How did these reading lessons affect the relationship between the author and her grandmother? Why do you think the lessons seemed so important to both of them?

 Ask and answer your own questions.

Write a question of your own. Share your question with others and collaborate on an answer. Or, imagine that you're able to talk to the author of this reading. What part of her story would you like to know more about?

 Form your final thoughts.

1. What does this reading show about what it is like to be an immigrant or a member of an immigrant family? Compare what you learned to what you already knew about the immigrant experience.

2. Now that you've thought more about "'See Spot Run': Teaching My Grandmother to Read," what is your opinion about it? Of the four readings in Chapters 1 and 2, which one appealed to you the most? Why? ■

Chapter 2 Summary

How does Strategy 2 help you *read from the inside out?*

Reading from the inside out means connecting the inside—what you think and feel—to the outside—the writer's ideas. When you **check in,** you prepare yourself to make that connection. As you read and after you've finished reading, you continue making that connection by **responding** with your own questions, comments, and ideas.

How does the *respond* strategy work?

The **respond** strategy reminds you to keep the conversation going between you and the writer. Here are the five reminders for Strategy 2.

STRATEGY 2: RESPOND

1 Respond while you're reading and after you've finished reading.

2 Make a place or space to respond.

3 Ask questions and say what you think of the writer's ideas.

> 4 Link ideas from other readings or sources.
>
> 5 Talk with others.

Are you familiar with the meaning of these terms?

margin notes: marks or very brief notes in the margin showing your response

journal or reading log: a place for writing your personal responses to a reading

linking ideas: seeing relationships between ideas in different readings or other sources

How is the strategy working for you so far?

1. Which ways of **responding** have you found most helpful while you are reading the material? Which have been least helpful?

2. Which ways of **responding** have you found most helpful after you've finished reading?

3. Have you tried this strategy for readings in other courses—especially for textbook reading? If so, how well did it work? If not, in what courses could you imagine using this strategy?

4. What did you appreciate about using this strategy? What did you dislike?

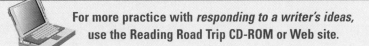

For more practice with *responding to a writer's ideas,* use the Reading Road Trip CD-ROM or Web site.

TIME OUT FOR YOU

What Do You Want Out of College?

The approach in this book puts the focus on you, the reader, because without your active involvement, no real reading takes place. In just the same way, you are the only person who can really decide what you want to accomplish as a college student. Success in college depends on having a strong sense of your own direction or purpose. Without direction, you can easily get distracted or discouraged. Take some time now to think about what you want out of college.

Perhaps you've already chosen a career. If you have, that will help you face challenges in your courses, especially in courses you might not have taken on your own. For example, if you know you want to be a dental technician, it's easier to put in the hours studying for the required anatomy course even if anatomy is not your favorite subject.

But what if you're not sure what you want? If you haven't yet come up with clear-cut goals for yourself, don't worry—you're not alone! A majority of first-year college students have not chosen their majors, and many students change their majors, sometimes more than once.

Every campus has resources that can help you choose majors and careers. These include:

- Orientation to college and study skills courses

- Individual counseling appointments at the counseling center

- Transfer counseling (for students wanting to transfer from 2-year to 4-year schools)

- Career information center or job placement center

- Courses and tests for assessing career interests

- Career development courses (for exploring careers in many different fields)

- Apprenticeship programs

But don't wait until you've chosen a career or even a definite major to look at the direction you're going as a college student. One of the most important things you can do at any point of your college life is to see how much you're guided by *external direction* and how much by your own *internal direction*.

External Direction

People guided primarily by external direction feel driven by the expectations of others—perhaps parents, teachers, or friends. Because those expectations are sometimes in conflict with one another, they feel like pressure and often lead to frustration. Here are some sample statements students in this category often make:

- My father made me take these courses; I have no interest in them.

- My professor gives so much work, I can't possibly get it done.

- My friends keep me out late partying, so I can't get any studying done.

- I messed up on the first test, so I'm sure I'll fail the midterm for this class.

Internal Direction

People guided primarily by internal direction feel more in control of their lives, even as they face the same kinds of external pressures expressed in the four statements just cited. Students who rely more on internal direction can deal more easily with the problems and conflicts that inevitably arise. Here are the same statements expressed by someone with stronger internal direction. Each statement is completed in two possible ways in order to show that the more inner control you feel, the more flexibility you have to deal with each situation.

- My father advised me to take these courses,
  . . . so I'm going to give them a try, although I've never had an interest in them before.
  or
  . . . but I did some research to show him that I should try some other courses first.

- My professor gives so much work,
  . . . I've had to cut back a couple of hours at my job.
  or
  . . . I got a study group together so we can help each other with the work.

- My friends keep me out late partying,
  . . . so I make sure we only go out together on the weekend.
  or
  . . . but I've convinced one of them to study with me a couple of nights a week instead.

- I messed up on the first test,
  . . . so I'm going to talk to the professor about how to interpret her test questions.

or

. . . so I'm going to go to the tutoring center to get a clearer understanding of the questions that will be on the midterm.

Finding Your Internal Voice

Notice that students in the first group allow each situation to be determined by others. They see it as something they can't change. In contrast, students in the second group see the same situations as challenges that they can find some way of handling. The first group is limited to reacting; the second group is able to act in a productive way. Clearly, the more you can rely on your own inner direction, the more satisfying and successful you will be not only in college but throughout your life.

Answer the following questions to get a stronger sense of your own direction:

1. Why do I want to be in college? What will it do for me now? What about in a year's time? In five years' time?

   _____

   _____

   _____

2. As I begin new courses, how can I take time to explore possibilities and be open to new things, taking something for myself from every course?

   _____

   _____

   _____

3. What do I really want from my relationships? How can I have a good social life and also do well in my courses?

   _____

   _____

   _____

4. How can I respond positively when I get grades that are lower than I want? What can I do to get better grades?

   _____

   _____

   _____

3

UNDERSTAND THE LANGUAGE: WORK WITH NEW WORDS

Check In, Strategy 1, and **Respond,** Strategy 2, help you be *involved* in a reading. But when you're in the middle of reading something for a college course, every other word may seem unfamiliar to you. Difficult vocabulary can get in the way of your **responding** to the writer. Strategy 3, **Work with New Words,** gives you a process for dealing with unfamiliar words so you can stay in contact with what the writer is saying.

Try the New Strategy: Work with New Words

Working with new words helps you understand unfamiliar vocabulary, so you can remove language barriers between the writer and you. The strategy gives you three ways to figure out word meanings. It also shows you how to develop your own system for expanding your vocabulary.

STRATEGY 3: WORK WITH NEW WORDS

1 Get what you can from the context.

2 Make the dictionary work for you.

3 Use word parts to figure out words and build vocabulary.

4 Create a system for learning new words.

Try reading "Where English Words Come From." You'll find a few words in italics that are probably unfamiliar to you. As you read, notice that for each of these words a margin box gives you a way to figure out its meaning.

READING 5   WHERE ENGLISH WORDS COME FROM

DEBORAH SILVEY

Textbooks and academic writers give credit for material borrowed or quoted from others. Parentheses point you to a full credit at the end of the reading, called "Works Cited" or "References."

unabridged: complete (*abridged* means shortened).

profusion: great quantity. Notice the nearby references to *great quantity,* which help give you the meaning of the word.

quotidian: everyday. Notice that all the examples—*wake, eat, drink,* and so on—are things we do every day.

As author of this textbook, I have relied on experiences that have worked well for many years with students in my reading and English classes at Diablo Valley College in California. Students in my classes have enjoyed knowing a little bit about how events in the past helped make English the way it is today. This reading presents that information as an introduction to **working with new words.**

Snail mail, whazzup, chill, e-commerce—these are just a few of the newcomers that *lexicographers*—the people who compile dictionaries—added to the 2000 edition of *Merriam-Webster's Collegiate Dictionary.* These words join past years' new entries, such as *chain smoker* (1930s), *desegregation* (1950s), *yuck* (1960s), and *heavy metal* (1970s) (Wright 37). Although some words fall out of use—and therefore out of dictionaries—English speakers show no sign of losing their enthusiasm for using a great wealth of words.   1

Over its long history, the English language developed an unusual facility for incorporating new words. By now *unabridged°* dictionaries contain from 450,000 to 600,000 words, far more than are in other languages. There is a special word to express almost anything. Although it makes English extremely flexible, this *profusion°* of possibilities may seem like an overabundance when you're confronted with so many new words.   2

Where did all of these words come from? A brief glance at the history of English will provide some answers.   3

TALKING WITH AN ENGLISHMAN FROM THE YEAR 1000

The English language developed among the Germanic tribes who invaded England centuries before the first millennium. By around the year 1000, the inhabitants of England were speaking what we now call Old English. With its Germanic roots, Old English would seem like a foreign language to us. For a modern English speaker, trying to talk with an Englishman of the year 1000 would be pretty frustrating.   4

But if you stuck to the basic words of everyday life, you and the Englishman might do all right. A hundred or so of our most frequently used words have been around for at least a thousand years. These include many of our words for family relationships, such as *mother, father, husband, wife, child, brother,* and *sister,* as well as many words for our *quotidian°* activities, such as *wake, eat, drink, fight, love,* and *sleep.* You and the man from 1000 would also understand the same basic function words: *to, for, but, and, in,* and so on. But your conversation would be limited. Apart from these basic words, you would find little in common between today's English and Old English. What happened to change the language so drastically?   5

THE BATTLE THAT TRANSFORMED ENGLISH

STRATEGY 2: RESPOND

echelons: level. Notice the word *but*, which suggests that the lower classes—the peasants—were the opposite of the upper echelons.

The biggest transformation in English came as a result of a French victory over England in 1066. For the next several generations, French became the language of the court and the upper *echelons*° of society, but the lower classes—the peasants—"continued to eat, drink, work, sleep, and play in English" (Bryson 54). Thus English acquired a vast new collection of French words but held on to many Old English words for the basics of everyday life.   6

In many cases English doubled its vocabulary—using both an Old English word and a French word for almost the same thing. One of the clearest examples of how this doubling added a helpful distinction can be seen in the words for farm animals and the meat they provide. The animals tended by the peasants kept their English names (*sheep, cow, calf*), whereas the meats served to the upper classes were given the French names (*mutton, beef, veal*). English gained that distinction, but French did not.   7

A BORROWING LANGUAGE

upheaval: a complete change. Notice that the word *transformed* is in the previous heading; *transformation* is in the first sentence under that heading. Notice also that the word contains two parts: *heave* and *up*.

The English language never went through such an *upheaval*° again. Believe it or not, the English of Shakespeare's time—the sixteenth century—is considered modern English, because the changes that have occurred since that time have been so minor compared to the earlier transformations in the language.   8

But English never stopped adding new words from other languages. Wherever English people have traveled and traded and colonized, they have taken in new words. From Native American languages came *moccasin* and *raccoon;* from India came *pajamas* and *shampoo;* and from the Tagalog language of the Philippines came *boondocks.*   9

BORROWING FROM THE PAST: GREEK AND LATIN WORD PARTS

The largest number of new words have been borrowed from two ancient languages—Latin and Greek. Latin word parts (prefixes, roots, and suffixes) came into English by way of French, itself a direct descendant of Latin. But right up to the present, English has gone on making up words with Latin and Greek word parts. Why?   10

The answer is in part that for hundreds of years these were the languages of scholarship and learning. Scholars throughout Europe communicated with one another in Greek or Latin. Even up until the beginning of the twentieth century, students at a university were supposed to know Greek and Latin.   11

For this reason, these languages have been the basis for words to   12
name hundreds of discoveries, inventions, or new ideas. For example,
when space travel was first considered more than just a fantasy, scientists
needed a name for the people who would do the traveling. The term *astro-
naut* was coined from *astro,* Latin for "star" and *naut,* Latin for "sailor."
Although "star sailor" might have done just as well to name an explorer of
space, to some it would have seemed too fanciful, whereas the Latin-based
word sounded sufficiently technical.

Because so many new words in English have come from Latin and   13
Greek, learning the most common word parts from these languages is a
good way to expand your vocabulary.

WHAT'S THE FUTURE OF ENGLISH?

As you can see, English has always embraced new words to commu-   14
nicate both new ideas and slight variations of old ideas. And our society is
now changing so fast that we can expect an even greater increase of new
words to express the changes in our lives.

These words won't necessarily be borrowed from other languages.   15
New words like those we started off with—*whazzup, chill, snail mail,
e-commerce*—are now often derived from homegrown slang or from new
technologies.

Where will the new English words come from? Just listen (and read)!   16
If enough people use a word enough times—whether it comes from street
slang, the computer business, or the Brazilian dance scene—you can be
sure the lexicographers will be on to it. Watch to see which ones make it
into the next *Merriam-Webster's Collegiate.*

Works Cited

Bryson, Bill. *Mother Tongue: English and How It Got That Way.* New York:
    William Morrow, 1990.
Wright, Karen. "Keepers of Words." *Discover* Mar. 2000: 37–39.

Follow-Up Activities   After you've finished reading "Where English Words
Come From," use these activities to think about the reading and Strategy 3. You
may write out your answers or prepare them in your mind to discuss in class.

Grab your first impressions.

1. What parts of "Where English Words Come From" did you like or not like?
   Explain your choices.

2. What was most surprising to you about how English developed?

Ask and answer questions.

1. What kinds of words do we still use today that are basically the same as the ones used in Old English? What are some examples of these words?

2. How did the French language influence English after the French victory in 1066?

3. Why are so many of the new words you find in college textbooks derived from Greek or Latin?

4. What context clues can you use in order to get meaning from the context?

5. How can you make the dictionary work for you?

6. Why does it make sense to learn some common prefixes, roots, and suffixes?

 Ask and answer your own question.

Write a question of your own. Collaborate with others on an answer.

Form your final thoughts.

1. What new slang word, word from technology, or word from another language do you hear being used more and more often? Is it in the dictionary yet? Bring the word to class to discuss where it comes from and how you use it.

2. If you know another language, compare it to English. What words has it borrowed from English?

---

1 *Get what you can from the context.*

2 *Make the dictionary work for you.*

3 *Use word parts to figure out words and build vocabulary.*

4 *Create a system for learning new words.*

Get a Close-Up of the New Strategy: Work with New Words

The notes in the margins of "Where English Words Come From" suggested ways to understand new vocabulary. Now get a close look at four ways to figure out new words.

Context Clues

1 *Get what you can from the context.*

The word *context* refers to the surroundings. Surrounding words and ideas give clues about word meanings. The meaning of *upheaval* is suggested by its context, as the margin box explains.

Your use of the context will be most effective if you learn to recognize four different types of context clues: logic, example, contrast, and definition.

Logic clues. You can often guess the meaning of a word just from "the sense of the sentence," or from the logic of the rest of the sentence and perhaps the sentences around it. The meanings of *upheaval* and *profusion* are suggested by logic clues.

Signals for Examples

for example
for instance
to illustrate
such as
included are
like the following

Example clues. Sometimes the context gives specific examples that provide clues. Notice how the examples helped you understand that *quotidian* means *everyday,* or *common.* Phrases that signal an example is coming are listed in the margin.

Contrast clues. Sometimes a contrast between a word you already know and one you don't know will tell you that one is the opposite of the other. For example, note the contrast clues that indicate the meaning of *deciduous* in this sentence: "Deciduous trees turn color in the fall, but evergreen trees stay green all year long." The word *but* points to a contrast, and the sentence shows that *deciduous* means the opposite of *evergreen.*

Signals for Contrast

on the other hand
however
while
whereas
but
on the contrary
instead
although (or even though)

See how contrast clues help define *echelons.* The word *but* signals a contrast. The other contrast clue is found in the opposite words *lower* and *upper.* Because the contrast is between *lower classes* and *upper echelons,* you can assume *echelons* is another word for the *class* of a society.

Contrast clues are probably the least obvious clues. For this reason, learning them can make the biggest improvement in finding meaning from the context.

Signals for Definition

Punctuation clues: dashes
and parentheses
Words or phrases
or
that is
in other words

Definition clues. Sometimes words are obviously defined, as is *lexicographers.* A word might also be defined with a *synonym,* a word that means the same thing. The synonym *everyday* defines *quotidian* in this sentence: "Eating and sleeping are *quotidian,* or everyday, activities." Punctuation clues and certain phrases signal that a definition is coming.

The Dictionary

2 *Make the dictionary work for you.*

Make sure you have a desk or collegiate dictionary. Pocket dictionaries can be useful for looking up a word where and when you want to, but they have too few words and limited information about each word. *Merriam Webster's Collegiate Dictionary, The American Heritage Dictionary,* and *The Random House Dictionary* are three widely used collegiate dictionaries.

When to look up a word. You may occasionally need to look up a new word while you are reading. But usually you won't want to interrupt your response to the writer's ideas. As you read, keep track of unknown words. Underline them or make a list. After reading, look them up so you can understand the reading.

Dictionary entries. Dictionary entries are packed with information. Study the sample dictionary entry for *afghan,* a word from Reading 4, "'See Spot Run': Teaching My Grandmother to Read," to see what it can tell you.

The right definition for the context. Many words have multiple meanings, so you need to depend on the context to choose the one that fits. In Reading 4, *afghan* was used in this context: "we would sit in the living room, my grandmother with an afghan covering her knees."

The sample entry (Figure 3.1) gives four definitions. In this case, the context makes it fairly easy to determine. We can be sure *afghan* is a noun, because it is a thing covering her knees.

1. *A native of Afghanistan?* Unlikely!

2. *Pashto,* we know from the etymology (language history), is a language, so we can eliminate that one.

3. *A coverlet of wool, knitted or crocheted.* This definition makes the most sense. Notice, too, that this version of the word is not capitalized, matching the way the word is used in the reading.

4. *An afghan hound?* Not impossible, but there would probably be other references to a dog besides that mention.

Word Parts

3 *Use word parts to figure out words and build vocabulary.*

Sometimes a long word contains a familiar little word that gives clues to the long word's meaning. You could guess the meaning of *upheaval* from the two smaller words that make up the longer one: *up* and *heave.*

Latin and Greek word parts, known as *prefixes, roots,* and *suffixes,* are the building blocks for thousands of English words. By learning some of these word parts, you greatly increase the number of words you know.

Prefixes. Prefixes come at the beginning of a word. Some prefixes add meanings such as *in, out, back, before, across,* or *not.* Others add a number or an amount. Here are some common examples:

pre (before): preview, pretest

re (back; again): return, review

un (not): unhappy, unabridged

tri (three): tricycle, triangle

Knowing just a few prefixes gives you a head start on understanding hundreds of new words.

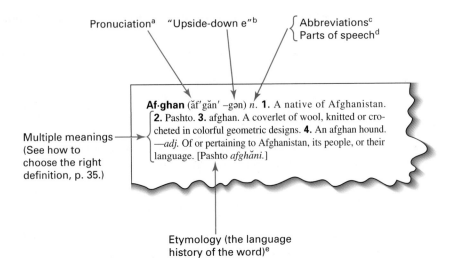

a. **Pronunciation**—sometimes two possibilities are given. If so, the first is "preferred"; the second is acceptable. The pronunciation key is always given at the bottom of the page.

b. **Upside-down e symbol**—appears repeatedly as the unaccented vowel like **a** in *alone* or **o** in *gallop*.

c. **Abbreviations**—used to save space. Get to know a few common ones like *L* for *Latin, OE* for *Old English,* or *usu.* for *usually.* You'll find a key to abbreviations at the beginning of the dictionary.

d. **Parts of speech**—*n.* for *noun,* *v.* for *verb,* *adj.* for *adjective,* etc. Look also for plurals of some nouns and tenses for irregular verbs.

e. **Etymology**—in brackets, gives you the origins of the word, including what language it came from. Now at least you know that Pashto is a language. This part can also give you a word part like **–logy** in *etymology* (meaning *the study of*) that helps you with the word's meaning.

Many dictionary entries also include a *synonym*—a word that has the same, or close to the same, meaning as the entry word. Examples of synonyms are: *contented* for happy; *automobile* for car; *argue* for fight.

ă pat / ā pay / âr care / ä father / b bib / ch church / d deed / ĕ pet / ē be / f fife / g gag / h hat / hw which / ĭ pit / ī pie / îr pier / j judge / k kick / l lid, needle / m mum / n no, sudden / ng thing / ŏ pot / ō toe / ô paw, for / oi noise / ou out / o͝o look / o͞o boot / p pop / r roar / s sauce / sh ship, dish / t tight / th thin, path / th this, bathe / ŭ cut / ûr urge / v valve / w with / y yes / z zebra, size / zh vision /ə about, item, edible, gallon, circus / œ *Fr.* feu, *Ger.* schön / ü *Fr.* tu, *Ger.* über / кн *Ger.* ich, *Scot.* loch / N *Fr.* bon.

Figure 3.1   Sample Dictionary Entry

Roots. The root of a word gives its core meaning. The root can often produce a clear picture in your mind, especially if you recognize it from a familiar word. For example, *lexicographers* contains the root *graph*, meaning "writing." *Graph* is the root for familiar words such as *autograph* and *biography*.

A word's *etymology*—its origin and history—is given in the dictionary entry. Look there to see if a Greek or Latin root makes the word's meaning clearer. Here are two more common roots:

port (carry): <u>port</u>able = able to be carried; ex<u>port</u> = carry out; <u>port</u> = place where ships carry things in and out

dict (say, speak): pre<u>dict</u> = say before; <u>dict</u>ion = style of speaking; <u>dict</u>ate = tell someone what to do or to write

Suffixes. Suffixes, which come at the end of words, tell you how the word is used, whether it is a noun, verb, adjective, or adverb. Here are some common suffixes:

–ize shows action: criticize, sanitize, baptize

–ist indicates a person who does something: artist or violinist

–ful indicates an adjective: colorful, helpful, grateful

–ly is the usual suffix for adverbs

See the charts on pages 45–48 for lists of common prefixes, roots, and suffixes.

A System for Learning New Words

4 Create a system for learning new words.

Words don't become part of your vocabulary until you make them your own. Here's a system for doing that.

Deciding what words to learn. Your instructor may assign vocabulary lists for you to learn, but you can also choose new words to learn:

- words you've run into several times
- words you are likely to find again in your reading or you can imagine using in writing or conversation
- words relating to subjects that interest you

Vocabulary cards for studying words. On the front of a 3 x 5 index card, write the word in context (plus pronunciation symbols if needed). On the back, write the definition, along with other helpful information such as you see on

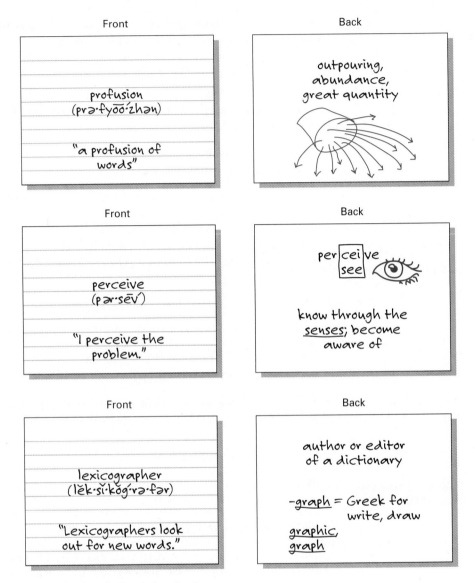

Figure 3.2   **Sample Vocabulary Cards**

the sample cards in Figure 3.2: simple drawings or diagrams (*profusion*), associations with the sound of the word (*perceive*), or word parts that connect it to related words (*lexicographer*).

What are the advantages of using cards over lists in a notebook?

- It's easier to test yourself without cheating when the definition of the word is on the back of the card.

- You can carry a pack of these cards with you to look over whenever you have a free moment or are stuck waiting in a line.

- You don't waste time going over words you've already learned. Once you know the word on a card, you put it aside.

- You don't become dependent on learning words in a set order, as you do with a list of words in a notebook.

Apply the New Strategy: Work with New Words

Now that you understand Strategy 3, put it into practice with the following exercises for reviewing context clues, the dictionary, and word parts. Write out your answers. Work with classmates to prepare your answers if your instructor tells you to do so.

Context Clues

Before doing the exercises for context clues, read these examples.

Logic clues. Use the meaning of the sentence to figure out what a word means.

> *Example:* Oscar had been known to *prevaricate* so often that no one ever believed him anymore; his word was simply not trustworthy.

The sentence shows that Oscar doesn't tell the truth, so you can guess that *prevaricate* means "to lie."

Example clues. Use examples given to figure out what a word means.

> *Example:* The inn has added new *amenities* (an exercise room, a sauna, a whirlpool, and new lounge chairs on the balcony).

All the words in the parentheses are examples of something that would bring a guest more comfort, so *amenities* would probably refer to "comforts" or "features."

Contrast clues. Use opposing ideas to figure out what a word means.

> *Example:* Dad gave *credence* to my story, but Mom's reaction was one of total disbelief.

The opposing ideas here suggest that *credence* must have to do with "believing," because the opposite idea is "disbelief." The word *but* also signals the contrast.

Definition clues. Take advantage of supplied definitions.

Example: He was known for his performance of the *fado*—a type of Portuguese folk song—and gained fame throughout the early part of this century.

Look for context clues.

For each of the following sentences, look for the context clues that can suggest the meaning of the italicized word. Then state what kind of context clue you used: logic, example, contrast, or definition. Don't use the dictionary!

EXAMPLE: He was a *landlubber,* whereas his companion had <u>grown up on boats and knew all about the sea.</u>

someone who knows nothing about being on boats or at sea

clue: contrast

1. The effects over time of too much alcohol can be extremely *deleterious*: there can be a steep drop in job performance, an increase in health risks, and a gradual onset of deep depression.

   _____

   clue: _____

2. The *novice* scuba diver knew he might need help in the water because this was his first time diving.

   _____

   clue: _____

3. He tried to *ingratiate* himself (make himself pleasing to us), but to no avail.

   _____

   clue: _____

4. The professor's *nefarious* activities became well known to the public; whereas his brother's excellent and helpful works went unnoticed.

   _____

   clue: _____

5. The parents *munificently* rewarded the child for any good behavior, giving her expensive presents and large amounts of spending money.

_____

clue: _____

6. She grew frightened at the *insouciance* of the tourists who allowed their children to climb high on the rocks without seeming to notice the danger of falling.

_____

clue: _____

7. Some people express their thoughts using few words; others are *verbose*.

_____

clue: _____

8. Some instances of the *harrowing* experiences faced by all parents are losing a child in a crowded store, finding her playing with matches, or suddenly seeing her at the top of a tall tree.

_____

clue: _____

9. After the long drought all the crops died and there was a *dearth* of food for the inhabitants of that land.

_____

clue: _____

10. Although the priceless vase seemed to be in a *precarious* position near the edge of the mantel, it was actually made quite secure by the special wax on the bottom that held it in place.

_____

clue: _____

11. Her entire speech was made up of one *bromide* (trite saying) after another.

_____

clue: _____

12. Ben is fearless, but his brother Jim never tries anything and is as *timorous* as can be.

_____

clue: _____

Choose the right definition.

Read this paragraph and see which definition of *assimilation* best fits the context.

EXAMPLE: Americans have always welcomed some immigrants more readily than others. Not surprisingly, those have been the immigrants who have been most easily *assimilated* into this country's culture. Others, those who have not had that same kind of warm greeting, are especially resistant to the notion of America as a kind of melting pot.

as·sim·i·late (ə-sĭm′ə-lāt′) *v.* -lat·ed, -lat·ing, -lates. —*tr.* **1.** *Physiol.* **a.** To consume and incorporate into the body; digest. **b.** To transform (food) into living tissue; metabolize constructively. **2.** To absorb and incorporate (knowledge, for example) into the mind. **3.** To make similar; cause to assume a resemblance. **4.** *Ling.* To alter (a sound) by assimilation. **5.** To absorb (an immigrant or culturally distince group) into the prevailing culture. —*intr.* To become assimilated. [ME *assimilation* < Lat. *assimilare,* to make similar to : *ad-*, to + *similis,* like.] —as·sim′i·la′tor *n.*

Definition 5 is the best definition because it clarifies the special use of *assimilate* in relation to immigrants and thus makes the best choice out of the five definitions.

Now check the following entries from *The American Heritage Dictionary, College Edition,* for the meaning of these words from Reading 5. Choose the definition that fits the way the word was used.

1. profusion _____

   1. The state of being profuse; abundance.
   2. Lavish or unrestrained expense.

2. quotidian _____

   1. Recurring daily.
   2. Everyday; commonplace.

3. upheaval _____

   1. The process or instance of growing upward.
   2. A sudden and violent disruption or upset: "The psychic upheaval caused by war" (Wallace Fowlie).
   3. *Geol.* A lifting up of the earth's crust by the movement of stratified or other rocks.

Now read another paragraph about the experience of elderly immigrants coming to this country. After you've read the paragraph, choose the correct definition for each italicized word as it is used in this context.

Elderly parents who are brought here by their immigrant children may sometimes seem *recalcitrant* about learning the ways of American culture, preferring instead to *steep* themselves in memories of their homeland. In reality, they *pine* for the home and friends they left behind. They miss what they were used to, such as the special bread, pastry, or other *delicacy* that they could find in any small shop back home. The foods they find at our supermarkets are an *affront* to their taste buds. To make matters worse, many of these older people are not *fluent* in English, and their difficulty in communicating adds to the impression they give of being unfriendly and *remote*.

1. recalcitrant _____

    1. *adj.* Stubbornly resistant to authority, domination, or guidance, refractory.
    2. *n.* A recalcitrant person.

2. steep_____

    1. To soak in liquid in order to cleanse, soften, or extract a given property from.
    2. To infuse or subject thoroughly to.

3. pine_____

    1. To suffer intense longing or yearning: *pined for her family.*
    2. To wither or waste away from longing or grief: *pined away and died.*

4. delicacy _____

    1. Something pleasing and appealing, esp. a choice food.
    2. Exquisite fineness or daintiness of appearance or structure.
    3. Frailty of bodily constitution or health.

5. affront _____

    1. *v.* To insult intentionally, esp. openly.
    2. *n.* An open or intentional slight, or offense.

6. fluent _____

    1. Having facility in the use of language: *fluent in three languages.*
    2. a. Flowing effortlessly; polished. b. Flowing smoothly; graceful: *fluent curves.*

7. remote _____

    1. Located far away; relatively distant in space.
    2. Distant in time: *the remote past.*
    3. Distant in manner; aloof.

Use prefixes and roots to find meaning.

A. The following are real words. Try to figure out their meanings by analyzing their prefixes and roots, using the charts on pages 45–48.

1. Give the meaning of each word part.

2. Say what the whole word means.

> *EXAMPLE:* synchronize <u>*syn* = "together or with" and *chron* = time; word means "to check to see that you have the *same time.*"</u>

1. retrospect _____

2. intervene _____

3. apathy _____

4. graphology _____

5. fusion _____

6. circumvent _____

7. pseudonym _____

8. monotheism _____

9. biocide _____

10. telepathy _____

B. The following words are not real words, but they are made up of commonly used prefixes and roots that *do* have real meanings. With your knowledge of these word parts, give the meaning of the made-up words:

> *EXAMPLE:* telecide <u>*-cide* = kill and *tele-* = far; word would mean "kill from far away."</u>

1. mortology _____

2. prespect _____

3. postdict _____

4. malport _____

5. rechronize _____

6. anthropophobia _____

7. eupsychology _____

8. hypercredible _____

9. transvene _____

10. mononym _____

C. Using the charts, combine prefixes and roots to come up with five more "new words" like the ones in Part B, and say what they would mean given their parts. Be innovative, but be accurate!

D. To each of the following roots, add a suffix from the chart of suffixes that shows the correct part of speech.

> *EXAMPLES:* If you set the time, you might *chronize* (or *chronate* or *chronify*).
>
> We might describe someone who can see well as *spective* (or *spectful*).

1. Someone who feels might be a path_____.

2. If you believe, you might cred_____.

3. If you look, you might spect_____.

4. We might describe someone who says a lot as dict_____.

5. Someone who blends things together would be a fus_____. ■

Common Latin and Greek Prefixes

Latin Prefix	Sample Words
a (or *ab*): without or not	*a*moral (without morals); *ab*normal (not normal)
anti: against	*anti*freeze (against freezing)
circ (or *circum*): round or around	*circ*le (round shape); *circum*ference (boundary around)
co (or *con*): together or with	*co*operate (work together); *con*join (join together)
de: down or showing a reversal	*de*grade (downgrade); *de*activate (make inactive)
dis: not	*dis*agree (not agree)
ex (or *e*): out or out of	*ex*port (take out of the country); *e*ject (throw out)

in (or *il*, *im*, *ir*): in or not	*in*spect (look into); *il*legal (not legal); *im*moderate (not moderate); *ir*regular (not regular)
inter: between or among	*inter*mediate (placed in between); *inter*national (among nations)
mal: bad	*mal*nutrition (bad nutrition)
pre: before	*pre*marital (before marriage)
post: after	*post*date (date after)
pro: forward	*pro*gress (move forward)
re: again or back	*re*do (do again); *re*ject (throw back)
retro: backward or earlier	*retro*active (active as of earlier date)
sub: under	*sub*marine (boat for under water)
trans: across	*trans*port (carry across)
Greek Prefix*	**Sample Words**
eu: happy	*eu*phoria (great happiness)
hyper: over	*hyper*active (overactive)
mono: one	*mono*tone (one tone)
pseudo: false	*pseudo*science (false science)
syn (or *sym*): with or together	*syn*chronize (set the same time); *sym*phony (instruments playing together)
tele: far	*tele*scope (instrument for far sight)

*Greek word parts are some of the most unusual spellings in English.

Common Latin and Greek Roots

Latin Roots	Sample Words
-cide: kill (always at end of word)	insecti*cide* (kill insects)
cred: belief	*cred*ible (able to be believed)
dict: word; say	*dict*ionary (book of words); pre*dict* (say beforehand)
fus: pour or blend as if by melting	in*fus*e (pour into); *fus*e (verb meaning blend together)

log; logy: knowledge, record, or study of	cata*log* (record of knowledge); zoo*logy* (study of animals)
mort: death or dying	*mort*ician (one who prepares the dead for burial); im*mort*al (not dying)
port: carry	trans*port* (carry across)
spec (or *spect*): look or see	in*spect* (look inside)
ven (or *vent*): come	con*vent*ion (coming together)
Greek Roots	**Sample Words**
anthropo: human	*anthropo*logy (study of humans)
auto: self	*auto*biography (writing about yourself)
bio: life	*bio*logy (study of life)
chron: time	*chron*ic (continuing a long time)
graph (or *graphy*): writing or drawing	bio*graphy* (writing about someone's life); *graph* (drawing that diagrams information)
-onym: word or name (always at end of word)	syn*onym* (word with same meaning); pseud*onym* (false name)
path: feeling or suffering	sym*path*y (feeling with someone)
phobia: irrational fear of	claustro*phobia* (fear of enclosed spaces)
psych (or *psycho*): mind	*psycho*analysis (analysis of the mind)
theo: God or gods	*theo*logy (the study of religion or God)

Common Suffixes

Suffixes for Verbs	Sample Words
-ate	initi*ate*, gener*ate*
-ify	just*ify*, simpl*ify*
-ize	critic*ize*, symbol*ize*
Suffixes for Nouns (Person)	**Sample Words**
-er, -or	teach*er*, doct*or*
-ist	dent*ist*, real*ist*

Suffixes for Nouns (Quality or Condition)	Sample Words
-ance, -ence	assist*ance*, refer*ence*
-ation	imagin*ation*, realiz*ation*
-ion	act*ion*, tens*ion*
-ism	pessim*ism*, real*ism*
-ity	activ*ity*, human*ity*
Suffixes for Adjectives	**Sample Words**
-able, -ible	stretch*able*, sens*ible*
-ful	color*ful*, beauti*ful*
-ive	act*ive*, destruct*ive*

Chapter 3 Summary

How does Strategy 3 help you *read from the inside out*?

By **checking in** and **responding,** you connect the *inside*—what you think and feel—to the *outside*—the writer's ideas. But that connection may get interrupted when you run into too many new words. Strategy 3, **Work with New Words,** gives you ways to understand unfamiliar words so you can continue to stay involved with what the writer is saying.

How does the *work with new words* strategy work?

Strategy 3 gives you methods for figuring out meanings of words during and after reading and for expanding your vocabulary over the long term. Here are the four methods for this strategy.

STRATEGY 3: WORK WITH NEW WORDS

1 Get what you can from the context.

2 Make the dictionary work for you.

3 Use word parts to figure out words and build vocabulary.

4 Create a system for learning new words.

Are you familiar with the meaning of these terms?

> *context:* surroundings in which you find a word
>
> *synonym:* word that has the same meaning
>
> *etymology:* origin and history of a word
>
> *prefix:* word part that comes at the beginning of a word; it shows such information as direction (in, out, under) and number
>
> *root:* word part that gives the core meaning of a word
>
> *suffix:* word part that comes at the end of a word: it shows the word's part of speech (verb, noun, adjective, adverb)

How is the strategy working for you so far?

1. Which methods have you found most useful in figuring out word meanings during and after reading? Context clues? Word parts? Or the dictionary? How might these methods work better for you?

2. Which methods have you found most useful in expanding your vocabulary? Which have been least helpful?

3. Have you tried this strategy for readings in other courses, especially for textbook reading? If so, how well did it work? If not, what courses could you imagine using this strategy in?

4. What did you appreciate about using this strategy? What did you dislike?

For more practice with *working with new words*, use the Reading Road Trip CD-ROM or Web site.

TIME OUT FOR YOU

WHAT MATTERS TO YOU?

The Time Out for You in Chapter 2 showed you the importance of finding your own direction in order to get what you want out of college. You can develop your inner direction by defining personal goals. Having goals then helps you schedule your time so you can focus on your own priorities, the things that matter most to you. Take some time now to think about your goals and priorities.

Long-Term Goals

A *goal* is a definite objective you direct yourself toward. A *long-term goal* is a bigger vision of what or where you hope to be. It may take years to accomplish a long-term goal. Becoming a nurse or starting your own small business or being the first person in your family to get a college degree—any of these are long-term goals.

Answer the following questions to help you think about your long-term goals.

1. If you have you decided on a major or a specific career path, how are your present courses related to this goal?

   _____

   _____

   _____

2. If you are unsure of your major, what can you do now to explore your interests and begin to see possible career paths?

   _____

   _____

   _____

3. If you are starting college by "getting requirements out of the way," what can you find in each course that will contribute to your future employment—as well as your future enjoyment?

_____

_____

_____

4. If you haven't yet begun planning for your future after college, how can you stay committed toward the goal of doing well in your courses *this* term?

_____

_____

_____

Short-Term Goals

Short-term goals are the steps you take that lead you toward your long-term goals. Completing a math assignment, taking a test for assessing career interests, reading a textbook chapter—these are all short-term goals that help you reach a long-term goal.

Look at the following examples to see how one student created meaningful short-term goals that led to her long-term goals:

- *Assignment:* Introduction to Business—read pp. 34–56 in textbook.

  Short-Term Goal: Understand ideas in the textbook about managing a small office.

  Long-Term Goal: I'm thinking about having my own business some day.

- *Assignment:* Biology—a test next time on the structure of the cell.

  Short-Term Goal: Make it to my biology study group to help me get a B on the test.

  Long-Term Goal: I want to be the first in my family to graduate from college, and I need to pass biology to complete my science requirement for my degree.

- *Assignment:* American History—read the chapter on late-19th-century immigration.

  Short-Term Goal: Find out what life was like for my mother's great-grandparents (immigrants from eastern Europe) and my father's great-grandfather (a Chinese laborer for the railroad).

  Long-Term Goal: I want to understand more about how my family and I have participated in the history of this country.

Look at your class assignments for the next few days. Try turning each of these assignments into short-term and long-term goals, steps that move you toward what you want for yourself.

*Assignment:*_____

Short-Term Goal: _____

Long-Term Goal: _____

*Assignment:*_____

Short-Term Goal: _____

Long-Term Goal: _____

*Assignment:*_____

Short-Term Goal: _____

Long-Term Goal: _____

*Assignment:*_____

Short-Term Goal: _____

Long-Term Goal: _____

Set Priorities

With short- and long-term goals in mind, you're ready to find time for the things that really matter to you. These are your *priorities*.

For example, suppose you have a long-term goal of becoming a physical education instructor. Your short-term goals might involve passing a difficult anatomy course needed for your major. Studying for anatomy would become one of your priorities. You might then have to choose between extra study time for that course and going to a Saturday football game. Or, if you chose to go to the game, you'd look for another spot in your schedule for the additional studying. When your schedule is based on your own priorities, you're more likely to want to keep to it.

Making a schedule that really works for you isn't easy. It can't be too rigid or you won't be able to keep to it. However, you need to plan it in enough detail to make it useful. Start by using the blank schedule on page 53. Make several photocopies of it, so you can make adjustments. On the schedule, fill in your set times—your college courses, your hours for work, and any personal time commitments you aren't likely to change. (Look at the sample on page 54.)

Also, remember that a reasonable schedule has to include enough time for sleep, food, and fun! After considering your long- and short-term goals, decide

Weekly Schedule

Hour	Sunday	Monday	Tuesday	Wednesday	Thursday	Friday	Saturday
7:00							
8:00							
9:00							
10:00							
11:00							
12:00							
1:00							
2:00							
3:00							
4:00							
5:00							
6:00							
7:00							
8:00							
9:00							
10:00							
11:00							
12:00							

Weekly Schedule: Student Sample

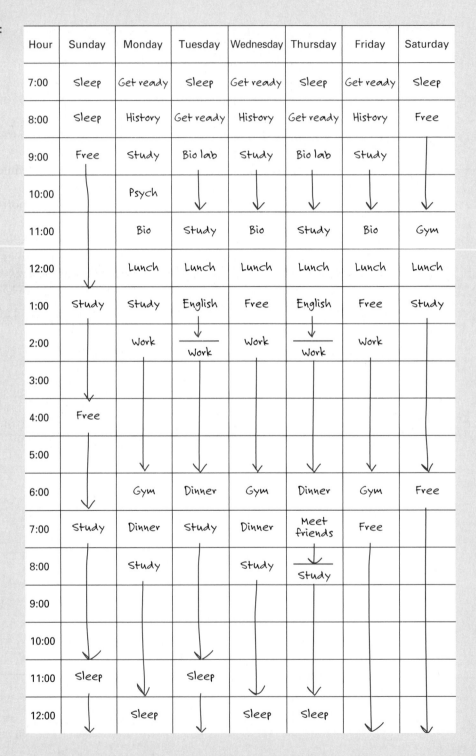

Hour	Sunday	Monday	Tuesday	Wednesday	Thursday	Friday	Saturday
7:00	Sleep	Get ready	Sleep	Get ready	Sleep	Get ready	Sleep
8:00	Sleep	History	Get ready	History	Get ready	History	Free
9:00	Free	Study	Bio lab	Study	Bio lab	Study	
10:00		Psych	↓	↓	↓	↓	↓
11:00		Bio	Study	Bio	Study	Bio	Gym
12:00		Lunch	Lunch	Lunch	Lunch	Lunch	Lunch
1:00	Study	Study	English	Free	English	Free	Study
2:00		Work	↓ Work	Work	↓ Work	Work	
3:00							
4:00	Free						
5:00		↓	↓	↓	↓	↓	↓
6:00	↓	Gym	Dinner	Gym	Dinner	Gym	Free
7:00	Study	Dinner	Study	Dinner	Meet friends	Free	
8:00		Study		Study	↓ Study		
9:00							
10:00	↓		↓				
11:00	Sleep	↓	Sleep	↓	↓		
12:00	↓	Sleep	↓	Sleep	Sleep	↓	↓

on your priorities for the next week, and fill in your flexible times with what you plan to do. If you're not sure how much study time to include, follow this general rule: study at least two hours for every one hour that you're in class.

Then, for the week that starts today—right now!—take another copy of your schedule and write in what you *actually* do during the next week. (See the sample on page 53.) Compare what you planned to do with what you actually did. Did you spend time on things that are not priorities? How can you make better use of those times? Were there priorities that you forgot to include in the schedule? Where will they fit in your next schedule? At the end of a week, compare your ideal schedule with what you actually did. Determine what adjustments you need to make to achieve your short-term, and eventually your long-term, goals.

Then, a week from now, make a new schedule based on what you learned from keeping track of your time. Post it so you can be reminded of your overall plan. But keep in mind that schedules are guides. You don't have to follow them perfectly for them to be useful. To work, a schedule needs to build direction, not frustration.

PART I REVIEW

You and the Author

Now that you've completed Part I, think over the ideas in the readings. Recall that each one relates to the reading process. Then review the three strategies introduced in this part, and think about how they work throughout the reading process.

Linking Ideas on the Theme: The Reading Process

 Respond to the readings in Part I by linking ideas on the theme of exploring the "Reading Process." Answer these questions in writing or in discussion with others.

1. What similarities do you see between the ideas about reading expressed in "The Voice You Hear When You Read Silently" and the ideas about reading described in "Reading as a Two-Way Process" (pp. 1–2)? How do the first two strategies, **Check In** and **Respond,** relate to these ideas?

2. Choose two writers who discuss the process of learning to read. What are the different purposes of each writer? What are the important differences in the situations they describe?

3. Compare the ideas about reading in any of these readings to other sources—other books or a movie or TV program.

4. Choose your favorite reading so far. Did your choice depend on previous interest in the subject? Or did you especially like the way the writer expressed the ideas? Discuss the reasons for your choice with others. Get a feeling for the variety in people's tastes in reading.

Using Strategies Throughout the Reading Process

Strategy 1: **Check In**

Strategy 2: **Respond**

Strategy 3: **Work with New Words**

Like any process, reading has a beginning, middle, and end. But, as we've seen, the reading process begins sooner than you might have thought. In the first stage, you *get started* as soon as you **check in.** The title (or other clues) triggers a response in you, and you begin making a connection with the writer's ideas. In the next stage, you *read.* As you do, you **respond,** making a stronger connection with the writer. But the connection doesn't stop with the last word of the last paragraph. It continues as you *follow up,* thinking over what you've read. You interpret the writer's language by **working with new words** and looking closely at the ideas, so you can be sure you've understood

GET STARTED   Begin with strategies that help you think about the subject and find out about what the writer will say.

- Check in

READ   Use strategies that help you read with greater understanding, interpret the language, and respond with your own questions and ideas.

- Respond
- Work with new words

FOLLOW UP   End with strategies that help you look more closely at the language and ideas in the reading, assess your understanding, and respond in a thoughtful way.

- Work with new words
- Respond

them. Finally, you follow up by **responding** with your own thoughts, once you're sure you've understood the writer. By using these three strategies, you move more easily through each stage of the process.

Use the chart as a reminder of how a particular strategy helps you at each of the three stages: *Get Started, Read, Follow Up.*

How Are the Strategies Working for You?

Answer the following questions to help you evaluate what you have learned. Then, compare your answers with other students', and ask your instructor for ideas on how to get more out of the strategies.

1. At what stage of the reading process—*Getting Started, Reading,* or *Follow Up*—have the strategies been most helpful to you? Why?

   _____

   _____

   _____

2. How much time are these strategies taking? Remember that all strategies take more time while you're learning them, but because they will help you understand more easily, they will save you time.

   _____

   _____

   _____

3. Overall, how helpful have the strategies been in increasing your concentration, understanding, and/or enjoyment of what you read?

   _____

   _____

   _____

4. What can you do to make the strategies work better for you?

   _____

   _____

   _____

PART II

PREDICTING AND QUESTIONING

WITH READINGS ON
CHILDHOOD AND FAMILY

Summer
Summer is golden,
Summer is green,
The freshly cut grass,
Down, down, down, we go, from the peak of the hill,
ROLLING.

Gillian Sellers, age 9

Being Nobody
Have you ever felt like nobody?
Just a tiny speck of air.
When everyone's around you,
And you are just not there.

Karen Crawford, age 9
From Richard Lewis, *Miracles*

Can you remember what it felt like to be 9 years old? Maybe these poems by two young girls will stir your own memories. If so, they'll give you practice in reading from the inside out. You can connect what's inside you to what they say, feeling both the joy of playing and the loneliness of "being nobody." All the readings in Part II will give you practice in relating your own experiences of childhood to new ideas and information about various aspects of growth and development.

Here are some questions to keep in mind as you think about this theme.

■ What things helped you grow as a child? What things got in the way of your development?

■ What joyful times do you particularly remember? What painful times?

- How do children's needs and ideas about the world differ from those of adults?

- If and when you have children, how would your parenting be the same and how would it be different from the parenting you received from your own mother and father?

The strategies in Part II, "Predicting and Questioning," continue to help you read from the inside out. Strategy 4, **Get an Overview,** tells you what to expect from the reading ahead of time. Then, when you start to read, you're ready to be involved in a conversation with the writer. Strategy 5, **Ask Questions,** shows how you can keep that conversation lively as you read to answer your own questions.

CHAPTER

4

KNOW WHERE YOU'RE GOING: GET AN OVERVIEW

When you **check in,** you look at the title and first paragraph and consider what feelings and ideas you have about the subject. Strategy 4—Get an Overview—lets you predict what the writer considers important about the subject. Because you know better what the reading will be about, you're ready to **respond**—to participate more fully in the dialogue between you and the writer.

Try the New Strategy: Get an Overview

Getting an overview of something means looking at the big picture so you don't get lost in the details. It's the kind of view you get from a skyscraper, when you look down over an entire city. You don't see each neighborhood. Instead you get a general—or overall—sense of all the major locations in the area. In the same way, an **overview** gives you a general sense of the entire reading. You're then able to predict what will be meaningful and important, so you get involved in the reading right from the start and can follow the writer's ideas more easily.

STRATEGY 4: GET AN OVERVIEW

1 Use the title as a key to finding the subject.

2 Flip through pages to learn more about the subject.

3 Skim paragraphs if you need more information.

4 Predict what the writer will say.

Try this strategy with the next reading, "What Deprived Children Tell Us about Human Nature," which begins on page 65. Turn to it now. **Check**

in, and then try **getting an overview** of the reading. See what the title says about the subject, and keep the title in mind as you flip through the pages to find more information. If you need to know more, skim through paragraphs. Then, based on what you find, try to predict what the writer will say about the subject.

The Title: The Author's Key to the Subject

1 *Use the title as a key to finding the subject. Look at the title first.*

The title indicates the subject of the reading. Everything in the reading will be about that subject. When you **check in,** you look at the title to think about what that subject might mean to you. But when you **get an overview,** you use the title as a key for finding what the writer will say about the subject. When you start looking through the reading for more information, be sure you see how it is related to, or connected to, the information you get from the title.

For example, the title of Reading 6 is "What Deprived Children Tell Us about Human Nature." The subject of the reading involves both deprived children and human nature. The title shows that the writer's main concern is to explain what we can learn from deprived children about what makes us human—our human nature.

Other Important Cues

2 *Flip through the pages to learn more about the subject. What else do you find?*

Take some time before reading to flip through the pages looking for other important cues about the reading. Various parts of the reading will direct your attention to the writer's ideas. These parts include the introduction, illustrations, and the conclusion.

The time you'll need to flip through the pages will vary. Complex material that you will be tested on may require several minutes. Easier or more familiar material may take just a few seconds. But the **overview** saves you time later, since it helps you concentrate and understand the reading.

Here are the cues you are likely to find in many different kinds of writing.

Headnotes. Notes that appear before the reading, often in books made up of a collection of readings, like this textbook, are called *headnotes.* Headnotes give helpful information about the author and often tell you what to expect in the reading. For example, the headnote for Reading 6 suggests that the social aspects of human nature will be discussed, since the reading comes from a chapter entitled "Socialization" in a sociology textbook.

Headings. In Reading 6, headings tell you that both isolated and institutionalized children will be discussed. Deprived animals will be discussed, too. You might predict that deprived children will be compared to deprived animals so we can understand what makes us human.

What to Look For in an Overview

What	Where	Why
Title	Just before the reading	Tells (or suggests) subject of entire reading
Headnotes	Usually before the reading (mainly in magazines or collections of readings by many authors)	Gives information about the author and the reading
Headings	Spaced throughout a reading	Tells the subject of a specific section of the reading
Introduction	The first paragraph (or first few paragraphs)	1. Gets your interest and/or 2. Lets you know the overall point
Conclusion	The last paragraph (or last few paragraphs)	1. Gives a final example or comment and/or 2. Sums up the information
Visual features (illustration, photos, charts, tables, maps)	Usually near a relevant piece of information	Shows examples to help you picture ideas; adds interest
Captions for visual features	Under or beside the feature	Explains visual feature; often adds important pieces of information

Introduction. Look at the first few sentences or paragraphs of Reading 6. The shocking example of Isabelle suggests what happens when a child is isolated. You can expect the reading to tell you more about what happened to Isabelle under the heading "Isolated Children."

How does this example relate to the word *deprived* in the title? What was this child deprived of?

Conclusion. The final paragraph (paragraph 20), following the heading "In Sum," gives a summary of the ideas in the reading. How does the summary relate to the title and the other information you have already gained from the headings and the introduction?

Illustrations. In many types of writing—especially in textbooks—authors use visual information to illustrate their ideas. Look for drawings or photographs.

They can stimulate your interest and clarify the subject. In textbooks, look for charts and tables that help you visualize information. (See, for example, the table on page 63 about what to look for in an **overview.**)

Don't forget the captions under the illustrations. They often add important pieces of information.

In this reading, what does the photograph of the monkey (Figure 4.1 on page 69) tell you about this subject? What has the monkey been deprived of? How does the information in the caption relate to what you discovered from the rest of your **overview?**

Skimming

3 Skim paragraphs if you need more information.

Skimming is the high-speed reading you do when you skip over many words and sentences—even paragraphs—in order to grasp the broad outlines of a reading. For your **overview,** you may need to skim the paragraphs in a reading to get more information. Here are some guidelines for efficient skimming.

- Look for information related to the title and subject.

- Read some first and/or last sentences, where the main idea of the paragraph is often given.

- Skip most sentences, even paragraphs.

- Set a time limit; don't turn skimming into reading.

Skimming Reading 6 can help you find out what happens to a child who is isolated. You might skim until you come to the first paragraph under "Isolated Children." There you learn that children like Isabelle are unable to speak.

Predicting

4 Predict what the writer will say.

Putting together the title and other cues. Once you've become familiar with the reading's organization and various parts, you can make a good prediction about what the reading will cover. Use the title as the key to what is most important. For example, from our **overview,** here are some ideas that connect to the title, "What Deprived Children Tell Us about Human Nature."

- The isolated child, Isabelle, had no contact with other human beings.

- Isolated children don't know how to interact with others and have no language.

- Institutionalized children are also discussed. Probably they have similar problems because of little or no human contact.

- Baby animals deprived of contact with their mothers can't interact with others.

- Humans need contact with others as they grow up in order to develop normally.

The overall point. By putting together the ideas in the title and the information from your **overview,** you can predict the writer's overall point about the subject. The *overall point* of a reading is the writer's most important message. Just as an overview looks over a whole area or subject, the overall point goes over all the other ideas in the reading, meaning that it covers—or includes—all those ideas. It can be summed up in a general statement about the subject.

Predict the overall point in one or two sentences. Try using your own words, as if you were talking to a friend. For Reading 6 you could predict the overall point in this way:

> If children don't have contact with other people, they don't learn how to talk or to relate to others. Deprived children show that what makes us human—our human nature—has to be learned from other people.

READING 6   **WHAT DEPRIVED CHILDREN TELL US ABOUT HUMAN NATURE**

JAMES M. HENSLIN

STRATEGY 1: CHECK IN
- If children are described as *deprived,* what does that mean? What do children need that they could be deprived of?
- What gives us our "human" nature? What makes us different from animals?
- What feelings does this subject bring up for you?

STRATEGY 2: RESPOND

STRATEGY 3: WORK WITH NEW WORDS

James M. Henslin is a sociology professor at Southern Illinois University. This reading comes from the chapter entitled "Socialization" in his textbook The Essentials of Sociology *(2000). In this section from the chapter, the author uses specific cases of deprived children to investigate what people need in order to become truly human.*

The old man was horrified when he found out. Life never had been good since his daughter lost her hearing when she was just two years old. She couldn't even talk—just fluttered her hands around trying to tell him things. Over the years, he had gotten used to that. But now he shuddered at the thought of her being pregnant. No one would be willing to marry her, he knew that. And the neighbors, their tongues would never stop wagging. Everywhere he went, he could hear people talking behind his back.   1

If only his wife were still alive, maybe she could come up with something. What should he do? He couldn't just kick his daughter out into the street.   2

After the baby was born, the old man tried to shake his feelings, but they wouldn't let loose. Isabelle was a pretty name, but every time he looked at the baby he felt sick to his stomach.   3

He hated doing it, but there was no way out. His daughter and her baby   4
would have to live in the attic.

. . . Unfortunately, this is a true story. Isabelle was discovered in Ohio   5
in 1938 when she was about 6½ years old, living in a dark room with her
deaf-mute mother. Isabelle couldn't talk, but she did use gestures to communicate with her mother. An inadequate diet and lack of sunshine had
given Isabelle a disease called *rickets.* Her legs

> were so bowed that as she stood erect the soles of her shoes came
> nearly flat together, and she got about with a skittering gait. Her
> behavior toward strangers, especially men, was almost that of a wild
> animal, manifesting much fear and hostility. In lieu of speech she made
> only a strange croaking sound. (Davis 1940/1999:138)

When the newspapers reported this case, sociologist Kingsley Davis   6
decided to find out what happened to Isabelle after her discovery. We'll
come back to that later, but first let's use the case of Isabelle to gain some
insight into human nature.

WHAT IS HUMAN NATURE?

For centuries, people have been intrigued with the question of what is   7
human about human nature. How much of people's characteristics comes
from "nature" (heredity) and how much from "nurture" (the *social environment,* contact with others)? One way to answer this question is to study
identical twins who have been reared apart. . . . Another way is to study children who have had little human contact. Let's begin with the case of Isabelle.

Isolated Children

Cases like Isabelle's surface from time to time. What can they tell us   8
about human nature? We certainly can conclude that humans have no natural language, for Isabelle, and others like her, are unable to speak.

But maybe Isabelle was not normal. This is what people first thought,   9
for she scored practically zero on an intelligence test. But in a few months,
after intensive language training, Isabelle was able to speak in short sentences. In about a year, she could write a few words, do simple addition,
and retell stories after hearing them. Seven months later, she had a vocabulary of almost 2,000 words. It took only two years for Isabelle to reach the
normal intellectual level for her age. She then went on to school, where she
was "bright, cheerful, energetic . . . and participated in all school activities
as normally as other children." (Davis 1940/1999:139)

Institutionalized Children

But what besides language is required if a child is to develop into what   10
we consider a healthy, balanced, intelligent human being? We find part of

the answer in an interesting experiment from the 1930s. Back then, orphanages dotted the United States, and children reared in orphanages tended to have difficulty establishing close bonds with others—and to have lower IQs. "Common sense" (which . . . is unreliable) told everyone that the cause of mental retardation is biological ("They're just born that way"). Two psychologists, H. M. Skeels and H. B. Dye (1939), however, began to suspect another cause. For background on their experiment, Skeels (1966) provides this account of a "good" orphanage in Iowa during the 1930s, where he and Dye were consultants:

> Until about six months, they were cared for in the infant nursery. The babies were kept in standard hospital cribs that often had protective sheeting on the sides, thus effectively limiting visual stimulation; no toys or other objects were hung in the infants' lines of vision. Human interactions were limited to busy nurses who, with the speed born of practice and necessity, changed diapers or bedding, bathed and medicated the infants, and fed them efficiently with propped bottles.

Perhaps, thought Skeels and Dye, the absence of stimulating social interaction was the basic problem, not some biological incapacity on the part of the children. To test their controversial idea, they placed thirteen infants whose mental retardation was so obvious that no one wanted to adopt them in an institution for the mentally retarded. Each infant, then about 19 months old, was assigned to a separate ward of women ranging in mental age from 5 to 12 and in chronological age from 18 to 50. The women were pleased with this arrangement. They not only did a good job taking care of the infants' basic physical needs—diapering, feeding, and so on—but also they loved to play with the children, to cuddle them, and to shower them with attention. They even competed to see which ward would have "its baby" walking or talking first. Each child had one woman who became

> particularly attached to him [or her] and figuratively "adopted" him [or her]. As a consequence, an intense one-to-one adult–child relationship developed, which was supplemented by the less intense but frequent interactions with the other adults in the environment. Each child had some one person with whom he [or she] was identified and who was particularly interested in him [or her] and his [or her] achievements. (Skeels 1966)

The researchers left a control group of twelve infants at the orphanage. These infants also were retarded but were higher in intelligence than the other thirteen. They received the usual care. Two and a half years later, Skeels and Dye tested all the children's intelligence. Their findings were startling: Those assigned to the retarded women had gained on an average of 28 IQ points while those who remained in the orphanage had lost 30 points.

What happened after these children were grown? Did these initial dif-   13
ferences matter? Twenty-one years later, Skeels and Dye did a follow-up
study. Those in the control group who had remained in the orphanage had,
on average, less than a third grade education. Four still lived in state insti-
tutions, while the others held low-level jobs. Only two had married. In contrast, the average level of education for the thirteen individuals in the
experimental group was twelve grades (about normal for that period). Five
had completed one or more years of college. One had not only earned a
B.A. but had also gone on to graduate school. Eleven had married. All thirteen were self-supporting and had higher-status jobs or were homemakers
(Skeels 1966). Apparently, then, one characteristic we take for granted as
being a basic "human" trait—high intelligence—depends on early close
relations with other humans.

Let's consider one other case, the story of Genie: 14

> In 1970, California authorities found Genie, a 13-year-old girl who
> had been kept locked in a small room and tied to a chair since she was
> 20 months old. Apparently her 70-year-old father hated children, and
> had probably caused the death of two of Genie's siblings. Her 50-year-
> old mother was partially blind and was frightened of her husband.
> Genie could not speak, did not know how to chew, and was unable to
> stand upright. On intelligence tests, she scored at the level of a 1-year-
> old. After intensive training, Genie learned to walk and use simple
> sentences (although they were garbled). As she grew up, her lan-
> guage remained primitive, she took anyone's property if it appealed to
> her, and she went to the bathroom wherever she wanted. At the age
> of 21, Genie went to live in a home for adults who cannot live alone.
> (Pines 1981)

From this pathetic story, we can conclude that not only intelligence but   15
also the ability to establish close bonds with others depends on early interaction. In addition, apparently there is a period prior to age 13 in which
language and human bonding must occur for humans to develop high
intelligence and the ability to be sociable and follow social norms.

Deprived Animals

A final lesson can be learned by looking at animals that have been   16
deprived of normal interaction. In a series of experiments with rhesus monkeys, psychologists Harry and Margaret Harlow demonstrated the importance of early learning. The Harlows (1962) raised baby monkeys in
isolation. They gave each monkey two artificial mothers, shown in the photograph on the next page. One "mother" was only a wire frame with a
wooden head, but it did have a nipple from which the baby could nurse. The
frame of the other "mother," which had no bottle, was covered with soft
terrycloth. To obtain food, the baby monkeys nursed at the wire frame.

Figure 4.1   Like humans, monkeys also need interaction to thrive. Those raised in isolation are unable to interact satisfactorily with others. In this photograph, we see one of the monkeys described in the text. Purposefully frightened by the experimenter, the monkey has taken refuge in the soft terrycloth draped over an artificial "mother."

When the Harlows (1965) frightened them with a mechanical bear or dog, the babies did not run to the wire frame "mother." Instead, they clung pathetically to their terrycloth "mother." The Harlows concluded that infant–mother bonding is due not to feeding but, rather, to what they termed "intimate physical contact." To most of us, this phrase means cuddling.   17

In one of their many experiments, the Harlows isolated baby monkeys for different lengths of time. They found that when monkeys were isolated for short periods (about three months), they were able to overcome the effects of their isolation. When they were isolated for six months or more, however, they were unable to adjust to normal monkey life. They could not play or engage in pretend fights, and the other monkeys rejected them. In other words, as in the case of Genie, the longer the isolation, the more difficult it is to overcome its effects. In addition, a critical learning stage may exist; if that stage is missed, it may be impossible to compensate for what has been lost.   18

Because humans are not monkeys, we must always be careful about extrapolating from animal studies to human behavior. The Harlow experiments, however, strongly support what we know about children who are reared in isolation.   19

In Sum

Society makes us human.   Apparently, babies do not develop "naturally" into human adults. Although their bodies grow, if raised in isolation they become little more than big animals. Without the concept of language, they can't experience or even grasp relations between people (the connections we call brother, sister, parent, friend, teacher, and so on). And without warm, friendly interaction, they aren't "friendly" in the accepted sense of the term; nor do they cooperate with others. In short, it is through human contact that people learn to be members of the human community. This process by which we learn the ways of society (or of particular groups), called *socialization,* is what sociologists have in mind when they say "Society makes us human."   20

References

Davis, Kingsley. "Extreme Social Isolation of a Child." *American Journal of Sociology,* 45, 4 Jan. 1940: 554–565.

Harlow, Harry F., and Margaret K. Harlow. "Social Deprivation in Monkeys."
    Scientific American, 207, 1962: 137–147.

Harlow, Harry F., and Margaret K. Harlow. "The Affectional Systems." In
    Behavior of Nonhuman Primates: Modern Research Trends, Vol. 2,
    Allan M. Schrier, Harry F. Harlow, and Fred Stollnitz, eds. New York:
    Academic Press, 1965: 287–334.

Pines, Maya. "The Civilizing of Genie." *Psychology Today,* 15, September
    1981: 28–34.

Skeels, H. M., and H. B. Dye. "A Study of the Effects of Differential Stimula-
    tion on Mentally Retarded Children." *Proceedings and Addresses of
    the American Association on Mental Deficiency,* 44, 1939: 114–136.

Skeels, H. M. "Adult Status of Children with Contrasting Early Life Experi-
    ences: A Follow-Up Study." *Monograph of the Society for Research in
    Child Development,* 31, 3, 1966.

Follow-Up Activities   After you've finished reading, use these questions to
respond to "What Deprived Children Tell Us about Human Nature." You may
write out your answers or prepare them in your mind to discuss in class.

Grab your first impressions.

1. How did you respond to these stories of deprived children? What did they
   show you about what we need as human beings?

2. What parts of the reading did you find interesting? What was least interesting? Explain your choices.

Work with new words.

Some words in this reading may be unfamiliar to you. Use the methods
of Strategy 3 to explain what the listed words mean.

1. Use context clues.

   a. nature; nurture (paragraph 7) _____
      These words are defined for you in parentheses, but you may also
      come to understand what they mean through *contrast,* too. What is the
      special meaning of each of these words?

   b. trait (paragraph 13)_____
      Use logic clues and the example clue of one kind of trait—high intelli-
      gence.

2. Use word parts.

   a. controversial (paragraph 11) _____
      Note that *contra,* meaning "against," may be spelled *contro* in some
      words. Use the meaning of that prefix along with logic clues.

   b. norms (paragraph 15)_____

Norm is the root word for the word *normal.* Use that familiar word to understand norm.

3. Use the dictionary.

   Choose the correct definition of these words as they are used in the context of this reading.

   a. gait (paragraph 5) _____

   b. bond; bonding (paragraphs 15 and 17)_____

   c. compensate (paragraph 18) _____

4. List here additional words you're unsure of from the reading. Use one of the methods of Strategy 3 to discover their meaning.

   _____   _____

   _____   _____

   _____   _____

Ask and answer questions.

1. Why was Isabelle able to catch up with her peers in her intellectual and social development, whereas Genie remained severely limited both intellectually and socially?

2. What was the "commonsense" idea in the 1930s about the reason for orphanage children's low intelligence and poor social skills?

3. What did the women in the institution for the mentally retarded provide for the babies that the standard orphanages did not? What effect did this different treatment have on the babies' later development?

4. Why did the baby monkeys prefer the "mother" covered with terrycloth even though the wire-covered "mother" was the one with the food? How does this animal experiment seem related to the other ideas in this reading about human children's needs?

5. Paragraph 7 asks, "How much of people's characteristics comes from 'nature' (heredity) and how much from 'nurture' (the *social environment,* contact with others)?" What do the cases of deprived children tell us about the role of nurture in developing the characteristics that make us most human?

 ### *Ask and answer your own question.*

Write a question of your own. Share your question with others and collaborate on an answer.

Form your final thoughts.

1. Did this reading change your ideas about what children need in order to become fully developed human beings? Explain why or why not.

2. Henslin concludes by saying, "Society makes us human." How does this reading support that statement?   ■

Apply the New Strategy: Get an Overview

1 *Use the title as a key to finding the subject.*

2 *Flip through pages to learn more about the subject.*

3 *Skim paragraphs if you need more information.*

4 *Predict what the writer will say.*

Now that you understand Strategy 4, put it into practice with Reading 7, "The Good Person" (or with one of the Additional Readings at the end of Part II, selected by your instructor).

Before reading "The Good Person," Reading 7, **check in** and **get an overview.**

Skimming should be a part of your **overview** this time, since the meaning of the headings in Reading 7 is not as obvious as in Reading 6. For example, a quick skimming of the first page will give you the following pieces of information that relate to the title:

■ Children were discussing what makes a good person.

■ These were children in an elementary school where the author taught.

■ He used a story called "Starry Time" to think about "goodness."

■ The story has to do with there being no stars in the sky.

Now put together information from skimming and the rest of your **overview** to see what Coles will say about the subject. Try using your own words to predict the overall point of the reading.

READING 7   ## THE GOOD PERSON

ROBERT COLES

STRATEGY 1: CHECK IN

• How would you define "a good person"?

• How did you learn about being "a good person" as a child? What kind of moral lessons did you get at home, at school, or with your friends?

• What feelings do you have about the whole idea of teaching children to be "good"?

Robert Coles, a professor of psychiatry at Harvard Medical School, writes frequently about child psychology. This reading comes from The Moral Intelligence of Children *(1997), in which Coles analyzes the ways children develop their ideas about moral behavior.*

For many years I have been asking children to tell me their ideas about   1
what makes for a good person. Rather obviously, those children have varied in their responsive definitions, some emphasizing a person's interest in reaching out to and assisting others, some putting stress on a person's religious beliefs, some pointing out the importance of certain secular values

STRATEGY 2: RESPOND

STRATEGY 3: WORK
WITH NEW WORDS

such as independence of mind, civic responsibility, commitment to work, to a solid family life.

In an elementary school class I taught, twenty-eight children sat before me, their desks lined up row upon row; I remember how they reacted when we had a discussion of "goodness." We exchanged moral scenarios. At one point I told the children a story; it had been written by a college student of mine, Howie Axelrod, a young man of great intelligence and heart, both. The story, a moral fable, if you will, was called "Starry Time," and it went like this: 2

Once upon a time, there were no stars in the sky.

Only the lonely moon shone at night. And since it was sad and alone, it gave off very little light.

One person had all the stars. He was not a powerful king. And she was not an evil witch. But a little girl named Stella. When Stella's mother turned off her lights at night, Stella's ceiling turned into sparkles brighter than any Christmas tree.

Sometimes she felt as though she was looking down from an airplane over a city of lights.

Stella loved falling asleep under her starry ceiling. She always had bright and wonderful dreams. One day in school, she overheard some boys and girls talking. One boy said, "I can't sleep at night. My room is very dark and I get scared."

A girl agreed, "Me too. That sad old moon doesn't do any good. My room is as dark as a closet."

Stella felt bad. She hadn't known that she was the only one with stars in her room.

That night, when her mother turned off the lights, her ceiling lit up like the lights of a city. But Stella could not sleep. She thought about all of the boys and girls who were lying awake in the dark, and she felt sad.

She climbed out of bed, and opened her window. The moon hung sadly in the sky.

"Moon, why don't you give off more light?" Stella asked.

"Because I am lonely. I have to spend the whole night out here by myself. Sometimes I get scared."

"I'm sorry," Stella said. She was surprised that something as big and beautiful as the moon could get scared just like little boys and girls.

"Plus, I get tired," said the moon. "It's a big job to light the whole sky."

Stella thought for a while.

"Moon," she said, "Would my stars help to keep you company?"

"Yes," said the moon.

"And would they make the sky brighter?"

"Yes, and they would make me happy."

Stella stood back from her window. She looked up at her stars.

"You should go and help the moon," she said. "I will miss you, but every night I will look out my window and see you in the sky." She wiped a tear from her eye. "Now, go."

With that, the stars burst from her ceiling and whirled around with a dazzling glow until they gained enough speed to shoot towards the moon. They streamed out of her window, and fanned out across the sky. It was the most beautiful sight Stella had ever seen.

From then on, the nights were brighter. The moon had many friends, and he beamed with happiness.

And with the light of the new night sky, grandmothers and grandfathers sat outside on their porches telling stories about the old days. And young couples strolled hand in hand along the streets.

And best of all, Stella could sit outside with a friend, and they could watch the stars together.

The children were enchanted. They wanted to hear the story again. 3 They wanted me to make copies of the story, so that they could take it home, read it to their parents, or ask their parents to read it aloud to them. They were anxious to discuss the story, glean from it a message, a line of thinking. Most of all, they were touched by Stella's gesture, and by her capacity, her willingness, to think of others, and more than that, to give of her world so that the world of others would be brighter. Stella's generosity prompted them to marvel at their own humanity. A girl said, "She was being—she was being good. It was natural—it's what you'd want to do, if you could." Another girl took immediate issue, wondered whether "natural" is quite the word to use, since, she observed, "Lots of people wouldn't want to share those stars with anyone else, probably." In no time, these ten-year-olds were having a spirited discussion of the extent and limits of generosity, an aspect of the subject of "goodness" that we had been exploring with some considerable and (for all of us, I thought) quite instructive determination.

Moreover, I soon learned, "Starry Time," starring Stella, had a stirring 4 life in home after home for several weeks. Parents read it, read it to their children, and talked of it, so that when we addressed it once more (I asked several children to divide it up and read aloud to us their chosen segments), their exchanges were even more lively, knowing, at times passionate. These children began to think of what *they* had in their closets (in their lives, really), that they might want to share with others—and, also very important, of what the consequences would be of so doing.

WORDS INTO ACTION

That last word, "consequences," needless to say, was quite important: 5 it is one thing to make a list of qualities that in their sum make for a good person or child; it is something else to try to picture oneself enacting this or that virtue, to live it out in daily life—to turn nouns such as generosity, kindness, thoughtfulness, sensitivity, compassion into verbs, words of action.

When that class was over, I thought I'd finally stumbled into some old-fashioned "advice" that I could offer to the parents of children I teach or work with as a doctor—and all of us parents have our moments of hungry eagerness for such advice. Take those nouns that denote good moral traits, and with the help of your sons and daughters try to convert them into verbs: tasks to accomplish, plans for action, to be followed by the actual work of doing. An imagined plan or plot is a mere prelude to a life's day-to-day behavior, yet over the long run of things, the sum of imagined plans turned into action becomes one's "character." With imagined scenarios we are quite possibly setting the stage for later actions, whereas lists of good qualities, of values and virtues, can be rather quickly forgotten, as quickly as they are memorized.

At one point in the discussion of "Starry Time" a boy wondered whether the story might help us figure out how to describe a "good child"—as I've mentioned, I'd been pressing those children and others for some time to help me come up with some useful specifications. "If you read the story," the boy declared, "and you go give something to someone, and it's a good thing you've done—you've given the world a star, and that means you're better than you were before. But you could fall back and forget about the next guy, so you have to keep sharing with others, or you'll be good for one day, and then the next, you're not doing what's good, and that's a missed chance, my mom said." As I listened I thought of the myth of Sisyphus in Greek mythology—with its image of a man condemned to rolling a heavy rock up a hill, only to have it fall down each time, just as he nears the top, and its reminder of the constant struggle to lift up ourselves, as it were, with backsliding an ever-present possibility. And I thought of Emerson's notion of each day as a god, his way of emphasizing the enormous moral possibilities a given span of time can offer. All of that worked into a child's worried, yet vigorously demanding ethical speculation.

A GOOD PERSON

Good children are boys and girls who in the first place have learned to take seriously the very notion, the desirability, of goodness—a living up to the Golden Rule, a respect for others, a commitment of mind, heart, soul to one's family, neighborhood, nation—and have also learned that the issue of goodness is not an abstract one, but rather a concrete, expressive one: how to turn the rhetoric of goodness into action, moments that affirm the presence of goodness in a particular lived life.

Another child's testimony—he was thirteen, in middle school, when he told me this: "My dad says a lot of people talk and talk a good line—but their scorecard isn't so good, because talk is cheap. If you just try to remember to be polite, and help someone, if you can; if you try to be friendly to folks, and not be a wise guy, always knocking them down in what you think of them, and what you say, then you're off to a start, because it's on your mind (you see?), it's on your mind that you should be out there doing something about it, what you believe is right, is good, and not just talking it up, the subject [of goodness], and to tell you what I believe: if you do a lot of that [talking it up], you're really talking yourself up, I mean, if you don't match your words with what you end up doing." A silence, a few seconds long, and then a brief, pointed—stunning, even—afterthought: "You know, a guy who's out there, being a good guy, that guy (even him!) could ruin everything; he could keep on calling attention to himself, and all he's doing, all the good, and he comes off as a big ego, someone looking for everyone's applause."

An accomplished righteousness that has turned self-righteous, self-   10
serving is a risk, surely, for many of us, who can be tempted to wag our finger at others, and not so subtly point at ourselves with a good deal of self-satisfaction. In further remarks, that boy worried out loud and at some length about becoming a "goody-goody" person, his cautionary spin on the subject of "goodness," as we were pursuing it. I still remember that moment, that expressed concern, that time of moral alarm: wait a minute, buddy, give this subject another round of consideration, lest you become smug, priggish, all too full of yourself, drunk on your self-congratulatory goodness, even your enacted goodness, all of which can, Sisyphus-like, come tumbling down morally. Yet another of life's ironies that can await any of us around any corner, even an apparently promising one.

Follow-Up Activities   After you've finished reading, use these questions to respond to "The Good Person." You may write out your answers in your own words or prepare them in your mind to discuss in class.

Grab your first impressions.

1. What did you think of the story called "Starry Time"? Why do you think it affected the children so much?

2. What parts of the reading did you like? What parts did you not like? Explain your answer.

Work with new words.

Some words in this reading may be unfamiliar to you. Use the methods of Strategy 3 to explain what the listed words mean.

1. Use context clues.

   a. secular (paragraph 1) _____

      Use the contrast shown between *secular* and *religious,* along with example clues to help you define *secular.*

   b. rhetoric (paragraph 8) _____

      Use logic clues from the paragraph and the heading for the section for paragraphs 5–7.

   c. priggish (paragraph 10) _____

      Use the synonym *smug,* that precedes the word, in addition to the examples of being "all too full of yourself, drunk on your self-congratulatory goodness."

2. Use word parts.

   a. scenario (paragraph 2) _____

      How does this word, meaning "a summary of a possible series of events," relate to its familiar root word, *scene?*

   b. prelude (paragraph 6) _____

   c. speculation (paragraph 7) _____

      Note that this word has the same root as *inspect:* "look" or "see." What special kind of looking is meant by *speculation?*

3. Use the dictionary.

   Choose the correct definition of these words as they are used in the context of this reading.

   a. glean (paragraph 3) _____

   b. ethical (paragraph 7) _____

4. Select additional words you're unsure of from the reading. Use one of these methods to discover their meaning.

Ask and answer questions.

1. What was the message of the story "Starry Time"? How did the children relate that message to their own lives?

2. What does Coles mean by turning "words into action"?

3. What are the two parts that make up Coles's definition of good children in the section called "A Good Person"?

4. In paragraphs 9–10, Coles refers to the discussion of a 13-year-old boy about the challenges we all face in trying to be good. What are these challenges?

Ask and answer your own question.

Write a question of your own. Share your question with others and collaborate on an answer.

Form your final thoughts.

1. What is your definition of a good person? How does yours compare with Coles's definition? How does it compare with that of other students?

2. Describe briefly a story or film that worked for you in the way "Starry Time" did for the children. ■

Chapter 4 Summary

How does Strategy 4 help you *read from the inside out?*

When you **check in,** you take a quick look *inside*—into yourself and the experiences you bring to the subject of the reading. When you **get an overview,** you take a quick look at the *outside*—the information in the pages of the reading. The **overview** tells you what to expect ahead of time, so you become more involved in a dialogue with the writer as you read. Your predictions help you follow the writer's ideas and stimulate you to **respond** to them.

How does the *get an overview* strategy work?

Getting an overview gives you ways to glance over an entire reading in a short time and get a good sense of what the writer will cover. Here are the four steps for Strategy 4.

STRATEGY 4: GET AN OVERVIEW

1 Use the title as a key to finding the subject.

2 Flip through pages to learn more about the subject.

3 Skim paragraphs if you need more information.

4 Predict what the writer will say.

Are you familiar with the meaning of these terms?

overview: a general sense of an entire subject, indicating what will be important in a reading

skimming: high-speed reading just to grasp the broad outlines of a reading

reading cues: parts of the reading, such as the title, headings, introduction, and conclusion, that point to important information

headnotes: notes before a reading about the author and the reading

predicting: using all the elements in the reading to see what to expect

overall point: the writer's most important message that covers—or includes—all the other ideas in the reading

How is the strategy working for you so far?

1. Which parts of the **overview** have you found most helpful in the readings you've practiced with? Which have been least helpful?

2. How successful were you in using skimming to look for information related to the title and subject? What would make skimming a more useful skill for you?

3. Have you tried this strategy for readings in other courses, especially for textbook reading? If so, how well did it work? If not, in what courses could you imagine using this strategy?

4. What did you appreciate about using this strategy? What did you dislike?

For more practice with *getting an overview,* use the Reading Road Trip CD-ROM or Web site.

TIME OUT FOR YOU

How Can You
Read Your Textbooks
from the Inside Out?

Reading from the inside out means involving yourself in what you read—including your textbooks. Authors, editors, and publishers make sure textbooks are chock-full of helpful aids that boost your learning of new material. Knowing how to use these special features will make it easier to apply reading strategies—**checking in, responding, getting an overview, asking questions,** and others—to help you read your textbook from the inside out.

The Front and Back of the Textbook

Don't forget to use the aids found in the front and back of the book. Mark ones you use often with a self-stick removable note, so you'll find them easily. At the beginning of the book, you'll find a *preface* and a *table of contents*.

- *Preface for the student:* In the preface, the textbook author tells you his or her goals for the book. Knowing where the writer is coming from makes it easier for you to **respond.**

- *The table of contents:* This chapter-by-chapter list shows how the whole book is organized, and it often gives you a complete outline of each chapter. It can help you **get an overview.**

Most textbooks have both a *glossary* and *index* at the back of the book.

- *The glossary:* This alphabetical list acts as the book's dictionary for all new terms introduced in the book. It is another aid for **working with new words.**

- *The index:* This alphabetical listing of topics and names is especially helpful for finding specific information you need to review. It can help as you **ask questions** and **find and mark main ideas,** strategies you will learn in the next two chapters.

The Textbook Chapter

Take a look at a chapter from one of your own textbooks. See how the special features in your book match the ones described here. (You may also use the sample textbook chapter on stress, an additional reading in Part III, page 205.)

- *The textbook part (or unit):* Textbooks often group chapters into parts (units), like *Reading from the Inside Out* does. Seeing how your chapter fits in with the part's larger theme or category can help you **get an overview.**

- *Part openings:* These introductions help you get a quick **overview** of all the chapters in that part. In addition, they often have a vivid example to help you **check in** and **respond.**

- *Chapter openings:* These introductions may contain a chapter outline and/or objectives (things to learn from the chapter). Either of these can help you **get an overview** and **ask questions** about the chapter. Dramatic examples in chapter openings also help you **check in** and **respond.**

- *Headings and subheadings:* These subtitles help you see the outline of information in the chapter. Changes in typeface and/or color differentiate between a general subject and a specific topic under that subject. Headings help you **get an overview, ask questions,** and **find and mark main ideas.**

- *Visual features:* You'll find photographs (with captions), and—in many textbooks—drawings or cartoons throughout the chapter. In addition, check for special types of visual information—tables, maps, charts, diagrams, and graphs—that clarify or summarize material. These visual features help you **get an overview, ask questions, respond,** and **find and mark main ideas.**

- *In-chapter boxes or sidebars:* This material is distinguished from the regular text by being placed in a box or on the side of the page; it may also have a special color background. Boxes that list key terms help you **work with new words;** those that add such supplemental material as stories, dramatic examples, or questionnaires can help you **ask questions** and **respond.**

- *Chapter summary:* This condensation of the essentials of the whole chapter can help you **get an overview** and **find and mark main ideas.**

Additional Features Found in Textbooks

What	Where	Why
Study Questions and Activities	Usually at the end of a chapter	For practice in learning essential information
Answer Keys	(When provided) At the end of the chapter or at the end of the book	Allow you to correct your own practice work
Footnotes or Notes (Works Cited or References)	At the bottom of the page (footnotes); at the end of the reading (Notes, Works Cited, or References)	Citations of author, title, and publication information, giving credit for material used and showing where to find these resources
Bibliography and Suggested Readings	End of book	List of sources for information used in book (bibliography); more readings on a subject (suggested readings)
Web site	Within or at the end of a chapter or with the bibliography	Gives valuable sites for accurate information on a subject
Appendix	End of book	Supplemental material

CHAPTER

5

PROBE FOR MEANING:
ASK QUESTIONS

Reading from the inside out involves asking your own questions rather than someone else's—for example, the instructor's or the textbook author's questions. You become more involved in a conversation with the writer when you read to find out how he or she will answer your particular questions. You've already been asking your own questions as you **check in, respond,** and **get an overview.** But Strategy 5, **Ask Questions,** suggests ways to make your questions more effective.

Try the New Strategy: Ask Questions

Asking your own questions works well with any of the reading strategies. But Strategies 4 and 5 work especially well together. You've seen how the **overview** gives you information about what to expect from the reading. **Asking questions** while looking over that information will help you predict important ideas the reading will cover.

STRATEGY 5: ASK QUESTIONS

1 Ask questions about what catches your interest.

2 Ask questions that help you get an overview and predict main ideas.

3 As you read, try to find answers to your questions, and continue to ask more questions.

4 After reading, ask and answer questions, especially about main ideas.

Try this strategy as you prepare to read "How Babies Use Patterns to See" by Laura E. Berk on pages 86–90. **Asking questions** before, during, and after reading will help keep you connected to the reading. Questions will also help guide you as you look for the reading's most important ideas.

Questions for Connecting to the Reading

1 Ask questions about what catches your interest.

During the **check-in,** you focus on yourself and your connection with the subject. The check-in questions you ask all come down to this basic one: *How does the subject relate to me?* For example, a check-in question for the title of this reading could be "How does the way a baby sees compare to the way *I* see?" or "When a baby looks at my face, what is she seeing?" Your own connection with the writer's ideas remains important while you read and after you've finished reading. So continue to ask about any ideas in the reading that interest you, and read to find the answers.

Questions for Predicting the Overall Point and Main Ideas

2 Ask questions that help you get an overview and predict main ideas.

When you **get an overview** you turn your attention to what the writer is saying about the subject. Your questions for an **overview** should help you predict the writer's overall point and main ideas.

The title and the overall point. During an **overview,** you use the title as a key for finding the overall point. Now turn the title into a question. It will become an even more effective key. Use a *why, how, who,* or *what* question. The title of Reading 8 is "How Babies Use Patterns to See." You could easily turn that title into a question:

- How *do* babies use patterns to see?

But you could restate the question in a few different ways:

- What makes patterns important for the way babies see?

- Why are patterns important for the way babies see?

Any of those questions could work as an overall-point question. The *overall-point question* acts as an umbrella question because it covers all the ideas in the reading.

The headings and the main ideas. The ideas that are central to the overall point of a reading are called the *main ideas.* For the writer, they support the overall point. For the reader, they are important for understanding the writer's message. The headings suggest a reading's main ideas. Reading 8's two headings are "Contrast Sensitivity" and "Combining Pattern Elements." Headings like these are easier to understand if you relate them to the title. You can then turn the headings into questions that will help you find the main ideas.

Here is how you could turn these headings into questions:

- Contrast Sensitivity: "What is contrast sensitivity, and how does it help babies use patterns to see?"

- Combining Pattern Elements: "How does combining elements (parts) of patterns help babies learn to see?

By asking questions, your **overview** helps you predict the writer's overall point and main ideas. Questions will also give you things to look for as you read.

Questions That Get Useful Answers

It's not always easy to come up with a good question. Think of the type of question you're asking. Then start off with an appropriate question word:

- *Why, how,* or *what* questions: are the most useful for asking about main ideas and getting a complete answer. (Use *who* to substitute for *what,* if identifying a person.)

- *When* and *where* questions: may be useful for asking about details of time and place, but they don't usually lead to main ideas.

- *Yes-No* questions: stimulate interest and can help you connect to the reading; they don't get at information beyond the one word, *yes* or *no,* so they're usually not helpful in finding main ideas or details.

Answers and New Questions

3 *As you read, try to find answers to your questions, and continue to ask more questions.*

Looking for answers to your questions and asking new questions should be a continuous process as you read.

- *Mark in the margins.* Put check marks by the sentences and paragraphs where you find answers to your questions. Notice especially when ideas or information seem to relate directly to your overall-point question.

- *Ask new questions.* Notice when your reading brings up new questions. Read to answer those new questions. Put a question mark in the margins if you aren't able to find an answer.

- *Use headings, introduction, conclusion, and illustrations.* Continue to use the reading cues to help you answer your questions. Illustrations can be especially helpful for understanding textbook material. For example, use Figure 5.1, on page 87, to get an idea of the way babies see contrast in a checkerboard pattern. Use Figure 5.2, on page 88, to see how babies from birth to 2 months interpret the pattern of a human face.

When you finish reading, see how well your overall-point question worked. Did the main ideas of the reading answer the question you asked? If so, your question worked well to guide your reading. If not, see how you might modify your question to fit the reading more closely.

> 4 *After reading, ask and answer questions, especially about main ideas.*

Look over the reading. See if the parts you noted with a question mark are now clearer after completing the reading. If not, plan to ask other students or your instructor about them.

Finally, take advantage of the questions provided for you in the Follow-Up Activities. You'll find that they all deal with main ideas—the ideas that relate most closely to the overall-point question. For example, for Reading 8 you could use this overall-point question: "How do babies use patterns to see?" You'll see that all the questions in the Follow-Up Activities relate to that overall question.

Your own questions can be about anything that interests you, but for reviewing main ideas, be sure your questions also relate to the overall-point question.

READING 8   HOW BABIES USE PATTERNS TO SEE

LAURA E. BERK

Laura Berk is a professor of psychology at Illinois State University, where she teaches child development courses. This reading comes from the chapter about infant learning in her textbook Child Development *(2000). Earlier in the chapter, Berk tells us that babies aren't born seeing the world as adults do. At birth, the other senses—touch, hearing, and so on— are more highly developed than the sense of sight. It takes babies about a year to fully develop the complex eye-brain system of vision. In this excerpt from the chapter, you'll find out how babies develop one important element of vision—the ability to find meaningful patterns in what they see.*

Be sure to make good use of the visual features in this reading (Figures 5.1–5.4). They will help you understand the somewhat technical explanations about babies' vision. Textbooks frequently use visual features like these (the illustrations, tables, diagrams, and so on, referred to in the table in Chapter 4). This visual information gives you a clearer picture of the written material. It can be as important as the text itself. As you read this excerpt, look at each figure referred to, read the caption, and connect what you see in the picture to the explanation given in the text.

STRATEGY 1: CHECK IN
- What would it be like to see without understanding what you're seeing?
- Based on your own experience or on pictures, TV, or movies, what have you noticed about the way young babies look at faces or objects?
- Do you have any negative feelings about this subject? If so, can you put them aside?

STRATEGY 4: GET AN OVERVIEW
Use the visual features to help you predict ideas.

STRATEGY 2: RESPOND

STRATEGY 3: WORK WITH NEW WORDS

Are young babies sensitive to the pattern, or form, of things they see,   1
and do they prefer some patterns to others? Early research revealed that

stimuli: plural of *stimulus* (something that causes a reaction).

even newborns prefer to look at patterned rather than plain stimuli°—for example, a drawing of the human face or one with scrambled facial features to a black-and-white oval (Fantz, 1961).

Since then, many studies have shown that as infants get older, they prefer more complex patterns. For example, when shown black-and-white checkerboards, 3-week-old infants look longest at ones with a few large squares, whereas 8- and 14-week-olds prefer those with many squares (Brennan, Ames, & Moore, 1966). Infant preferences for many other patterned stimuli have been tested—curved versus straight lines, connected versus disconnected elements, and whether the pattern is organized around a central focus (as in a bull's eye), to name just a few.

2

CONTRAST SENSITIVITY

For many years, investigators did not understand why babies of different ages find certain patterns more attractive than others. Then a general principle was discovered that accounts for early pattern preferences: *contrast sensitivity*° (Banks & Ginsburg, 1985). *Contrast* refers to the difference in the amount of light between adjacent° regions in a pattern. If babies *are sensitive to* (can detect) the contrast in two or more patterns, they prefer the one with more contrast.

3

contrast sensitivity: ability to see contrast between light and dark areas.

adjacent: next to or bordering.

To understand this idea, look at the two checkerboards in the top row of Figure 5.1. To the mature viewer, the one with many small squares has more contrasting elements. Now look at the bottom row, which shows how these checkerboards appear to infants in the first few weeks of life. Because of their poor vision, very young babies cannot resolve° the small features in more complex patterns. To them, the large, bold checkerboard has more contrast, so they prefer to look at it. By 2 months of age, detection of fine-grained detail has improved considerably. As a result, infants become sensitive to the contrast in complex patterns and start to spend much more time looking at them (Dodwell, Humphrey, & Muir, 1987).

4

resolve: distinguish between.

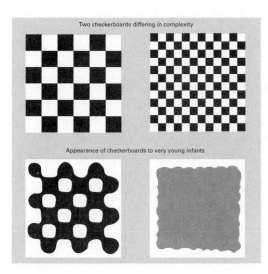

Figure 5.1 The way two checkerboards differing in complexity look to infants in the first few weeks of life. Because of their poor vision, very young infants cannot resolve the fine detail in the more complex checkerboard. It appears blurred, like a gray field. The large, bold checkerboard appears to have more contrast, so babies prefer to look at it.

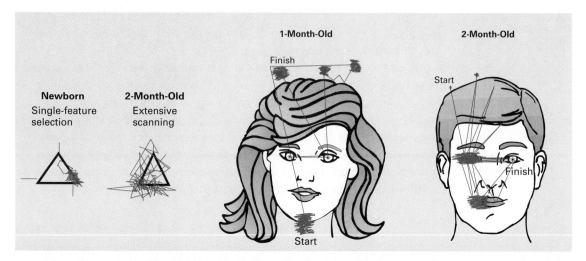

Figure 5.2   Visual scanning of simple and complex patterns by young infants. When scanning a simple triangle, newborns focus only on a single feature, whereas 2-month-olds scan the entire border. When patterns are complex, such as a human face, 1-month-olds limit their scanning to single features on the outskirts of the stimulus, whereas 2-month-olds examine internal features.

COMBINING PATTERN ELEMENTS

In the early weeks of life, infants respond to the separate parts of a pattern. For example, when shown a triangle or a drawing of the human face, very young babies look at the outskirts of the stimulus and stare at single high-contrast features—one corner of the triangle or the hairline and chin of the face (see Figure 5.2). At about 2 months, when scanning ability and contrast sensitivity have improved, infants inspect the entire border of a geometric shape. And they explore the internal features of complex stimuli like the human face, pausing briefly to look at each salient part (Bronson, 1991).

Once babies can take in all aspects of a pattern, at 2 to 3 months they start to combine pattern elements, integrating them into a unified whole. By 4 months, they are so good at detecting pattern organization that they even perceive subjective boundaries that are not really present. For example, look at Figure 5.3. Four-month-olds perceive a square in the center of this pattern, just as you do (Ghim, 1990).

Figure 5.3   Subjective boundaries in a visual pattern. Do you perceive a square in the middle of this figure? By 4 months of age, infants do, too.

subjective form: shape or structure constructed in the mind.

Older infants carry this responsiveness to subjective form° even further. Nine-month-olds can detect the organized, meaningful pattern in a series of moving lights that resemble a person walking, in that they look much longer at this display than they do at upside-down or disorganized versions. Although 3- to 5-month-olds can tell the difference between these patterns, they do not show a preference for one with both an upright orientation° and a humanlike movement pattern (Bertenthal et al., 1985; Bertenthal et al., 1987).   7

upright orientation: right-side-up direction.

By the end of the first year, infants extract meaningful patterns on the basis of very little information. For example, 12-month-olds can figure out an object's shape from a succession of partial views as it passes behind a small opening (Arterberry, 1993). They can also recognize a shape by watching a moving light trace its outline. . . . Finally, 12-month-olds can even detect objects represented by incomplete figures—ones missing as much as two-thirds of their contour (see Figure 5.4; Rose, Jankowski, & Senior, 1997). These findings suggest that by 1 year of age, a global representation° is sufficient for babies to perceive the similarity between two forms.   8

global representation: overall image.

Figure 5.4 Contour-deleted versions of a figure of a motorcycle, used to test whether infants can extract meaningful patterns on the basis of very little visual information. After 12-month-olds habituated to 33 percent (a), 50 percent (b), or 66 percent (c) contour deletions, the intact figure (d) was paired with a novel figure. Infants recognized the corresponding intact figure, since they dishabituated to (looked longer at) the novel form.

(a) 33% Contour Deletion

(b) 50% Contour Deletion

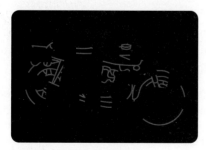

(c) 66% Contour Deletion

(d) Intact Figure

References

Arterberry, M. E. (1993). Development of spatial temporal integration in infancy. *Infant Behavior and Development, 16,* 343–364.

Banks, M. S., & Ginsberg, A. P. (1985). Early visual preferences: A review and new theoretical treatment. In H. W. Reese (Ed.), *Advances in childhood development and behavior* (Vol. 19, pp. 207–246). New York: Academic Press.

Bertenthal, B. I., Profitt, D. R., Kramer, S. J., & Spetner, N. B. (1987). Infants' encoding of kinetic displays varying in relative coherence. *Developmental Psychology, 23,* 171–178.

Bertenthal, B. I., Profitt, D. R., Spetner, N. B., & Thomas, M. A. (1985). The development of infant sensitivity to biomechanical motions. *Child Development, 56,* 531–543.

Brennan, W. M., Ames, E. W., & Moore, R. W. (1966). Age differences in infants' attention to patterns of different complexities. *Science, 151,* 354–356.

Bronson, G. W. (1991). Infant differences in rate of visual encoding. *Child Development, 62,* 44–54.

Dodwell, P. C., Humphrey, G. K., & Muir, D. W. (1987). Shape and pattern perception. In P. Salapated & L. Cohen (Eds.), *Handbook of Infant Perception* (vol. 2, pp. 1–77). Orlando, FL: Academic Press, 1987.

Fantz, R. L. (1961). The origin of form perception. *Scientific American, 204,* 66–72.

Ghim, H. R. (1990). Evidence for perceptual organization in infants: Perception of subjective contours by young infants. *Infant Behavior and Development, 13,* 221–248.

Rose, S. A., Jankowski, J. J., & Senior, G. J. (1997). Infants' recognition of contour-deleted figures. *Journal of Experimental Psychology: Human Perception and Performance, 23,* 1206–1216.

Follow-Up Activities   After you've finished reading, use these questions to respond to "How Babies Use Patterns to See." You may write your answers or prepare them in your mind to discuss in class.

Grab your first impressions.

1. What parts of the reading did you find most interesting? Were there parts that were confusing? If so, did you put question marks in the margin so you can clear up the confusion later?

2. Which of the figures (illustrations) and captions were most interesting to you? Which ones were most helpful in explaining information in the text?

Work with new words.

Some words in this reading may be unfamiliar to you. Use the methods of Strategy 3 to explain what the listed words mean.

1. Use context clues.

   a. detection (paragraph 4) _____

b. subjective boundaries (paragraph 6) _____

c. contour (paragraph 8) _____

d. intact (caption for Figure 5.4) _____

2. Use word parts.

a. outskirts (paragraph 5) _____

b. extract (paragraph 8) _____

c. habituate/dishabituate (caption for Figure 5.4) _____
   Note the word *habit* in these words.

3. Use the dictionary.

   Choose the correct definition of these words as they are used in the context of this reading.

a. scanning (paragraph 5) _____

b. salient (paragraph 5) _____

c. succession (paragraph 8) _____

d. novel (caption for Figure 5.4) _____

4. Select additional words you're unsure of from the reading. Use one of these methods to discover their meaning.

Ask and answer questions.

1. How does Figure 5.1 help you to understand why very young infants prefer to look at black-and-white checkerboards that have a few large squares instead of the checkerboard with many small squares? What does this preference demonstrate about the idea of *contrast sensitivity?*

2. What does Figure 5.2 tell you about the way a brand-new baby looks at a pattern, such as a geometric shape or a human face? What does it tell you about how a 2-month-old looks at a geometric shape or a human face?

3. What have babies learned by about 4 months that enables them to perceive the square in the middle of Figure 5.3, "just as you do"? How does this ability demonstrate the baby's ability to combine pattern elements?

4. What is one example of how infants at the end of their first year can see meaningful patterns even when given very little information?

 ### *Ask and answer your own questions.*

Write three questions of your own.

1. A question that leads to a main idea (a *why, how,* or *what* question)

2. A question that gives an important detail about time (a *when* question)

3. A personal question (using any question word; if using a *yes-no* question, follow up answer with more explanation)

Answer the overall-point question.

Now that you've answered important questions about the reading, try to sum up the main ideas as an answer to the overall-point question: "How do babies use patterns to see?" Collaborate with others on your answer.

Form your final thoughts.

1. How were you able to connect to the information in this reading? For example, did you find out a little about how your own visual perception works? Or were you more interested in the babies' learning? Discuss your responses with others.

2. How were you able to understand the somewhat technical information in this reading? Did the illustrations clarify the ideas for you? What other strategies did you use? Discuss with others what worked best. ■

Apply the New Strategy: Ask Questions

> 1 Ask questions about what catches your interest.
>
> 2 Ask questions that help you get an overview and predict main ideas.
>
> 3 As you read, try to find answers to your questions, and continue to ask more questions.
>
> 4 After reading, ask and answer questions, especially about main ideas.

Now that you understand Strategy 5, put it into practice with Reading 9, "talking back" (or with one of the Additional Readings at the end of Part II, selected by your instructor).

Before beginning to read, **check in**. Then practice **getting an overview** and **asking questions**. Take special note of these elements for this reading. Think of a question for each of the cues you find here.

■ *Headnote*. The headnote tells you that this reading comes from the writer's book *talking back*, subtitled *thinking feminist, thinking black*. You can assume the writer is a black feminist. Sample question: How might being a black feminist relate to ideas about talking back?

■ *Introduction*. The author grew up in a southern black community where children weren't supposed to have their own opinions. Sample question: What was it like for her to grow up that way?

■ *Conclusion*. The very last sentence of the reading is complicated, but see how it relates to the title. What is your question?

■ *Skim a few paragraphs*. Here are sample main ideas you can get from the first sentences of paragraphs.

Paragraph 2: Speaking out was an act of risk and daring.

Paragraph 8: Madness was the punishment for a female who talked too much.

Finally, you may have already noticed that the author doesn't use capital letters for her name or for the title of the reading. Why? Ask a question about this unusual style. What might this suggest? See if you find the answer as you read "talking back."

READING 9   talking back

bell hooks

bell hooks is a writer and professor at Stanford University. This reading is a chapter titled "talking back" from her 1988 book, also titled talking back, *subtitled* thinking feminist, thinking black. *In this reading, the author tells what "talking back" means to her and why it is so important.*

STRATEGY 1: CHECK IN
- Ask and answer a question of your own about what the title, "talking back," means to you.
- How does this title relate to the kind of responding you've been doing with the readings in this book?
- What feelings do you have about "talking back"?

STRATEGY 2: RESPOND

STRATEGY 4: GET AN OVERVIEW

STRATEGY 3: WORK WITH NEW WORDS

In the world of the southern black community I grew up in, "back talk" and "talking back" meant speaking as an equal to an authority figure. It meant daring to disagree and sometimes it just meant having an opinion. In the "old school," children were meant to be seen and not heard. My great-grandparents, grandparents, and parents were all from the old school. To make yourself heard if you were a child was to invite punishment, the back-hand lick, the slap across the face that would catch you unaware, or the feel of switches stinging your arms and legs.

To speak then when one was not spoken to was a courageous act—an act of risk and daring. And yet it was hard not to speak in warm rooms where heated discussion began at the crack of dawn, women's voices filling the air, giving orders, making threats, fussing. Black men may have excelled in the art of poetic preaching in the male-dominated church, but in the church of the home, where the everyday rules of how to live and how to act were established, it was black women who preached. There, black women spoke in a language so rich, so poetic, that it felt to me like being shut off from life, smothered to death if one were not allowed to participate.

It was in that world of woman talk (the men were often silent, often absent) that was born in me the craving to speak, to have a voice, and not just any voice but one that could be identified as belonging to me. To make my voice, I had to speak, to hear myself talk—and talk I did—darting in and out of grown folks' conversations and dialogues, answering questions that were not directed at me, endlessly asking questions, making speeches. Needless to say, the punishments for these acts of speech seemed endless.

They were intended to silence me—the child—and more particularly the girl child. Had I been a boy, they might have encouraged me to speak believing that I might someday be called to preach. There was no "calling" for talking girls, no legitimized rewarded speech. The punishments I received for "talking back" were intended to suppress all possibility that I would create my own speech. That speech was to be suppressed so that the "right speech of womanhood" would emerge.

Within feminist circles, silence is often seen as the sexist "right speech   4
of womanhood"—the sign of woman's submission to patriarchal authority. This emphasis on woman's silence may be an accurate remembering of what has taken place in the households of women from WASP backgrounds in the United States, but in black communities (and diverse ethnic communities), women have not been silent. Their voices can be heard. Certainly for black women, our struggle has not been to emerge from silence into speech but to change the nature and direction of our speech, to make a speech that compels listeners, one that is heard.

Our speech, "the right speech of womanhood," was often the solil-   5
oquy, the talking into thin air, the talking to ears that do not hear you—the talk that is simply not listened to. Unlike the black male preacher whose speech was to be heard, who was to be listened to, whose words were to be remembered, the voices of black women—giving orders, making threats, fussing—could be tuned out, could become a kind of background music, audible but not acknowledged as significant speech. Dialogue—the sharing of speech and recognition—took place not between mother and child or mother and male authority figure but among black women. I can remember watching fascinated as our mother talked with her mother, sisters, and women friends. The intimacy and intensity of their speech—the satisfaction they received from talking to one another, the pleasure, the joy. It was in this world of woman speech, loud talk, angry words, women with tongues quick and sharp, tender sweet tongues, touching our world with their words, that I made speech my birthright—and the right to voice, to authorship, a privilege I would not be denied. It was in that world and because of it that I came to dream of writing, to write.

Writing was a way to capture speech, to hold onto it, keep it close. And   6
so I wrote down bits and pieces of conversations, confessing in cheap diaries that soon fell apart from too much handling, expressing the intensity of my sorrow, the anguish of speech—for I was always saying the wrong thing, asking the wrong questions. I could not confine my speech to the necessary corners and concerns of life. I hid these writings under my bed, in pillow stuffings, among faded underwear. When my sisters found and read them, they ridiculed and mocked me—poking fun. I felt violated,

ashamed, as if the secret parts of my self had been exposed, brought into the open, and hung like newly clean laundry, out in the air for everyone to see. The fear of exposure, the fear that one's deepest emotions and innermost thoughts will be dismissed as mere nonsense, felt by so many young girls keeping diaries, holding and hiding speech, seems to me now one of the barriers that women have always needed and still need to destroy so that we are no longer pushed into secrecy or silence.

Despite my feelings of violation, of exposure, I continued to speak and write, choosing my hiding places well, learning to destroy work when no safe place could be found. I was never taught absolute silence. I was taught that it was important to speak but to talk a talk that was in itself a silence. Taught to speak and yet beware of the betrayal of too much heard speech, I experienced intense confusion and deep anxiety in my efforts to speak and write. Reciting poems at Sunday afternoon church service might be rewarded. Writing a poem (when one's time could be "better" spent sweeping, ironing, learning to cook) was luxurious activity, indulged in at the expense of others. Questioning authority, raising issues that were not deemed appropriate subjects brought pain, punishments—like telling mama I wanted to die before her because I could not live without her—that was crazy talk, crazy speech, the kind that would lead you to end up in a mental institution. "Little girl," I would be told, "if you don't stop all this crazy talk and crazy acting you are going to end up right out there at Western State." 7

Madness, not just physical abuse, was the punishment for too much talk if you were female. Yet even as this fear of madness haunted me, hanging over my writing like a monstrous shadow, I could not stop the words, making thought, writing speech. For this terrible madness which I feared, which I was sure was the destiny of daring women born to intense speech (after all, the authorities emphasized this point daily), was not as threatening as imposed silence, as suppressed speech. 8

Safety and sanity were to be sacrificed if I was to experience defiant speech. Though I risked them both, deep-seated fears and anxieties characterized my childhood days. I would speak but I would not ride a bike, play hardball, or hold the gray kitten. Writing about the ways we are traumatized in our growing-up years, psychoanalyst Alice Miller makes the point in *For Your Own Good* that it is not clear why childhood wounds become for some folk an opportunity to grow, to move forward rather than backward in the process of self-realization. Certainly, when I reflect on the trials of my growing-up years, the many punishments, I can see now that in resistance I learned to be vigilant in the nourishment of my spirit, to be tough, to courageously protect that spirit from forces that would break it. 9

While punishing me, my parents often spoke about the necessity of   10
breaking my spirit. Now when I ponder the silences, the voices that are not
heard, the voices of those wounded and/or oppressed individuals who do
not speak or write, I contemplate the acts of persecution, torture—the ter-
rorism that breaks spirits, that makes creativity impossible. I write these
words to bear witness to the primacy of resistance struggle in any situation
of domination (even within family life); to the strength and power that
emerges from sustained resistance and the profound conviction that these
forces can be healing, can protect us from dehumanization and despair.

These early trials, wherein I learned to stand my ground, to keep my   11
spirit intact, came vividly to mind after I published *Ain't I A Woman* and the
book was sharply and harshly criticized. While I had expected a climate of
critical dialogue, I was not expecting a critical avalanche that had the power
in its intensity to crush the spirit, to push one into silence. Since that time,
I have heard stories about black women, about women of color, who write
and publish (even when the work is quite successful) having nervous break-
downs, being made mad because they cannot bear the harsh responses of
family, friends, and unknown critics, or becoming silent, unproductive.
Surely, the absence of a humane critical response has tremendous impact
on the writer from any oppressed, colonized group who endeavors to
speak. For us, true speaking is not solely an expression of creative power;
it is an act of resistance, a political gesture that challenges politics of domination that would render us nameless and voiceless. As such, it is a courageous act—as such, it represents a threat. To those who wield oppressive
power, that which is threatening must necessarily be wiped out, annihilated, silenced.

Recently, efforts by black women writers to call attention to our work   12
serve to highlight both our presence and absence. Whenever I peruse
women's bookstores, I am struck not by the rapidly growing body of feminist writing by black women, but by the paucity of available published
material. Those of us who write and are published remain few in number.
The context of silence is varied and multi-dimensional. Most obvious are
the ways racism, sexism, and class exploitation act to suppress and silence.
Less obvious are the inner struggles, the efforts made to gain the necessary
confidence to write, to re-write, to fully develop craft and skill—and the
extent to which such efforts fail.

Although I have wanted writing to be my life-work since childhood, it   13
has been difficult for me to claim "writer" as part of that which identifies
and shapes my everyday reality. Even after publishing books, I would often
speak of wanting to be a writer as though these works did not exist. And
though I would be told, "you are a writer," I was not yet ready to fully affirm

this truth. Part of myself was still held captive by domineering forces of history, of familial life that had charted a map of silence, of right speech. I had not completely let go of the fear of saying the wrong thing, of being punished. Somewhere in the deep recesses of my mind, I believed I could avoid both responsibility and punishment if I did not declare myself a writer.

One of the many reasons I chose to write using the pseudonym bell   14
hooks, a family name (mother to Sarah Oldham, grandmother to Rosa Bell Oldham, great-grandmother to me), was to construct a writer-identity that would challenge and subdue all impulses leading me away from speech into silence. I was a young girl buying bubble gum at the corner store when I first really heard the full name bell hooks. I had just "talked back" to a grown person. Even now I can recall the surprised look, the mocking tones that informed me I must be kin to bell hooks—a sharp-tongued woman, a woman who spoke her mind, a woman who was not afraid to talk back. I claimed this legacy of defiance, of will, of courage, affirming my link to female ancestors who were bold and daring in their speech. Unlike my bold and daring mother and grandmother, who were not supportive of talking back, even though they were assertive and powerful in their speech, bell hooks as I discovered, claimed, and invented her was my ally, my support.

That initial act of talking back outside the home was empowering. It   15
was the first of many acts of defiant speech that would make it possible for me to emerge as an independent thinker and writer. In retrospect, "talking back" became for me a rite of initiation, testing my courage, strengthening my commitment, preparing me for the days ahead—the days when writing, rejection notices, periods of silence, publication, ongoing development seem impossible but necessary.

Moving from silence into speech is for the oppressed, the colonized,   16
the exploited, and those who stand and struggle side by side a gesture of defiance that heals, that makes new life and new growth possible. It is that act of speech, of "talking back," that is no mere gesture of empty words, that is the expression of our movement from object to subject—the liberated voice.

Follow-Up Activities   After you've finished reading, use these activities to respond to "talking back." You may write your answers or prepare them in your mind to discuss in class.

Grab your first impressions.

1. What do you think of hooks's explanation of her need to talk back? How does her experience compare with your experience of relating to adults when you were young?

2. Which parts of the reading did you find complex or frustrating? How were you able to deal with those parts?

Work with new words.

Some words in this reading may be unfamiliar to you. Use the methods of Strategy 3 to explain what the listed words mean.

1. Use context clues.

   a. soliloquy (paragraph 5) _____
      Use example clues from the sentence that contains the word.

   b. paucity (paragraph 12)_____
      Note the contrast clues: "not by the rapidly growing body of . . . writing . . . but by the *paucity*."

2. Use word parts.

   a. primacy (paragraph 10) _____

   b. dehumanization (paragraph 10) _____
      Starting with the root *human*, what new word do the prefix *de* and two suffixes *-ize* and *–tion* create?

   c. pseudonym (paragraph 14) _____

   d. retrospect (paragraph 15) _____

3. Use the dictionary.

   Choose the correct definition of these words as they are used in the context of this reading.

   a. vigilant (paragraph 9)_____

   b. annihilated (paragraph 11) _____

   c. defiant (paragraph 9); defiance (paragraph 14) _____

   d. legacy (paragraph14) _____

4. Select additional words you're unsure of from the reading. Use one of these methods to discover their meaning.

Ask and answer questions.

1. What were the different roles for boys and men, as opposed to girls and women, in hooks's world?

2. In paragraph 5, hooks talks about the kind of speech she grew up with and loved. What was that talking like? What made hooks love it so much?

3. What were some of the specific threats and punishments imposed on hooks to keep her from talking back?

4. The author's parents felt "the necessity of breaking [her] spirit." Why would they feel that need? Remember that their world has to be seen within the context of the white mainstream society of the South of the 1950s.

 Ask and answer your own question.

Write a question of your own. Share your question with others and collaborate on an answer.

 Answer the overall-point question.

One version of this question is "Why did the writer's experience of growing up in a southern black community convince her that she had to talk back?" Now that you've answered important questions about the reading, try to sum up the main ideas as an answer to this overall-point question. Collaborate with others on your answer.

 Form your final thoughts.

1. The author explains why she chose her great-grandmother's name to give herself a "writer's identity." But we never learn why she doesn't use capitals for her name or for the title of her book. Based on what she's written here, what can you guess about why she avoids capital letters? Discuss your ideas as a group.

2. Do you agree or disagree with hooks about the importance of talking back? Discuss your response with other students.   ■

Chapter 5 Summary

How does Strategy 5 help you *read from the inside out?*

Asking questions starts a dialogue between you and the writer, in which you read actively to find answers. Any questions you ask can be good for stimulating your interest. But Strategy 5 shows you how to ask questions that keep both the *inside*—your interests and ideas on a subject—and the *outside*—the writer's ideas—in mind.

How does the *asking questions* strategy work?

Asking questions reminds you to ask about what interests you. But for getting the overall point and main ideas, it suggests turning the title, headings, and other cues from the reading into questions. By using *why, how, who,* or *what* with these cues, you create your own questions and read to find the answers. Here are the four steps for Strategy 5.

STRATEGY 5: ASK QUESTIONS

1 Ask questions about what catches your interest.

2 Ask questions that help you get an overview and predict main ideas.

3 As you read, try to find answers to your questions, and continue to ask more questions.

4 After reading, ask and answer questions, especially about main ideas.

Are you familiar with the meaning of these terms?

main ideas: ideas in a reading that are central to the overall point

overall-point question: the question that asks about the writer's overall point; it is an umbrella question because it covers all the ideas in the reading

How is the strategy working for you so far?

1. At what stage does asking questions work best for you (before, during, or after reading)? At what stage does it not work as well? Can you explain why?

2. Are you aware now of reading to answer your own questions? If so, how has this awareness helped your understanding of what you read? If not, why not?

3. Have you tried this strategy for readings in other courses, especially for textbook reading? If so, how well did it work? If not, in what courses could you imagine using this strategy?

4. What did you appreciate about using this strategy? What did you dislike?

For more practice with *asking good questions,* use the Reading Road Trip CD-ROM or Web site.

PART II

ADDITIONAL READINGS ON CHILDHOOD AND FAMILY

The readings that follow will give you further practice in using the first five strategies with a variety of subjects having to do with childhood and family.

READING II-A THINK BIG

BEN CARSON, M.D., WITH CECIL MURPHEY

Ben Carson is a neurosurgeon at Johns Hopkins University Hospital in Baltimore. This reading is an excerpt from his book Think Big *(1992), in which he describes how he was able to meet the challenge of poverty and early academic failure and climb to the top of his profession.*

STRATEGY 1: CHECK IN
- What kind of memories do you have of bringing home report cards to your parents?
- Who helped you believe in your own abilities when you were a child? How did they help you?
- What feelings does this subject bring up for you?

STRATEGY 4: GET AN OVERVIEW

STRATEGY 5: ASK QUESTIONS

"Benjamin, is this your report card?" my mother asked as she picked up the folded white card from the table. 1

"Uh, yeah," I said, trying to sound casual. Too ashamed to hand it to her, I had dropped it on the table, hoping that she wouldn't notice until after I went to bed. 2

It was the first report card I had received from Higgins Elementary School since we had moved back from Boston to Detroit, only a few months earlier. 3

I had been in the fifth grade not even two weeks before everyone considered me the dumbest kid in the class and frequently made jokes about me. Before long I too began to feel as though I really was the most stupid kid in the fifth grade. Despite Mother's frequently saying, "You're smart, Bennie. You can do anything you want to do," I did not believe her. 4

No one else in school thought I was smart, either. 5

Now, as Mother examined my report card, she asked, "What's this grade in reading?" (Her tone of voice told me that I was in trouble.) Although I was embarrassed, I did not think too much about it. Mother knew that I wasn't doing well in math, but she did not know I was doing so poorly in every subject. 6

While she slowly read my report card, reading everything one word at a time, I hurried into my room and started to get ready for bed. A few minutes later, Mother came into my bedroom. 7

"Benjamin," she said, "are these your grades?" She held the card in front of me as if I hadn't seen it before. 8

"Oh, yeah, but you know, it doesn't mean much." 9

"No, that's not true, Bennie. It means a lot."   10

"Just a report card."   11

"But it's more that that."   12

Knowing I was in for it now, I prepared to listen, yet I was not all that   13
interested. I did not like school very much and there was no reason why I
should. Inasmuch as I was the dumbest kid in the class, what did I have to
look forward to? The others laughed at me and made jokes about me
every day.

"Education is the only way you're ever going to escape poverty," she   14
said. "It's the only way you're ever going to get ahead in life and be successful. Do you understand that?"

"Yes, Mother," I mumbled.   15

"If you keep on getting these kinds of grades you're going to spend the   16
rest of your life on skid row, or at best sweeping floors in a factory. That's
not the kind of life that I want for you. That's not the kind of life that God
wants for you."

I hung my head, genuinely ashamed. My mother had been raising me   17
and my older brother, Curtis, by herself. Having only a third-grade education herself, she knew the value of what she did not have. Daily she
drummed into Curtis and me that we had to do our best in school.

"You're just not living up to your potential," she said. "I've got two   18
mighty smart boys and I know they can do better."

I had done my best—at least I had when I first started at Higgins   19
Elementary School. How could I do much when I did not understand anything going on in our class?

In Boston we had attended a parochial school, but I hadn't learned   20
much because of a teacher who seemed more interested in talking to
another female teacher than in teaching us. Possibly, this teacher was not
solely to blame—perhaps I wasn't emotionally able to learn much. My parents had separated just before we went to Boston, when I was eight years
old. I loved both my mother and father and went through considerable
trauma over their separating. For months afterward, I kept thinking that my
parents would get back together, that my daddy would come home again
the way he used to, and that we could be the same old family again—but
he never came back. Consequently, we moved to Boston and lived with
Aunt Jean and Uncle William Avery in a tenement building for two years
until Mother had saved enough money to bring us back to Detroit.

Mother kept shaking the report card at me as she sat on the side of my   21
bed. "You have to work harder. You have to use that good brain that God
gave you, Bennie. Do you understand that?"

"Yes, Mother." Each time she paused, I would dutifully say those words.   22

"I work among rich people, people who are educated," she said. "I 23 watch how they act, and I know they can do anything they want to do. And so can you." She put her arm on my shoulder. "Bennie, you can do anything they can do—only you can do it better!"

Mother had said those words before. Often. At the time, they did not 24 mean much to me. Why should they? I really believed that I was the dumbest kid in fifth grade, but of course, I never told her that.

"I just don't know what to do about you boys," she said. "I'm going to 25 talk to God about you and Curtis." She paused, stared into space, then said (more to herself than to me), "I need the Lord's guidance on what to do. You just can't bring in any more report cards like this."

As far as I was concerned, the report card matter was over. 26

The next day was like the previous ones—just another bad day in 27 school, another day of being laughed at because I did not get a single problem right in arithmetic and couldn't get any words right on the spelling test. As soon as I came home from school, I changed into play clothes and ran outside. Most of the boys my age played softball, or the game I liked best, "Tip the Top."

We played Tip the Top by placing a bottle cap on one of the sidewalk 28 cracks. Then taking a ball—any kind that bounced—we'd stand on a line and take turns throwing the ball at the bottle top, trying to flip it over. Whoever succeeded got two points. If anyone actually moved the cap more than a few inches, he won five points. Ten points came if he flipped it into the air and it landed on the other side.

When it grew dark or we got tired, Curtis and I would finally go inside 29 and watch TV. The set stayed on until we went to bed. Because Mother worked long hours, she was never home until just before we went to bed. Sometimes I would awaken when I heard her unlocking the door.

Two evenings after the incident with the report card, Mother cam home 30 about an hour before our bedtime. Curtis and I were sprawled out, watching TV. She walked across the room, snapped off the set, and faced both of us. "Boys," she said, "you're wasting too much of your time in front of that television. You don't get an education from staring at television all the time."

Before either of us could make a protest, she told us that she had been 31 praying for wisdom. "The Lord's told me what to do," she said. "So from now on, you will not watch television, except for two preselected programs each week."

"Just *two* programs?" I could hardly believe she would say such a terrible thing. "That's not—" 32

"And *only* after you've done your homework. Furthermore, you don't 33 play outside after school, either, until you've done all your homework."

"Everybody else plays outside right after school," I said, unable to   34
think of anything except how bad it would be if I couldn't play with my
friends. "I won't have any friends if I stay in the house all the time—"

"That may be," Mother said, "but everybody else is not going to be as   35
successful as you are—"

"But, Mother—"   36

"This is what we're going to do. I asked God for wisdom, and this is the   37
answer I got."

I tried to offer several other arguments, but Mother was firm. I glanced   38
at Curtis, expecting him to speak up, but he did not say anything. He lay on
the floor, staring at his feet.

"Don't worry about everybody else. The whole world is full of 'every-   39
body else,' you know that? But only a few make a significant achievement."

The loss of TV and play time was bad enough. I got up off the floor,   40
feeling as if everything was against me. Mother wasn't going to let me play
with my friends, and there would be no more television—almost none,
anyway. She was stopping me from having any fun in life.

"And that isn't all," she said. "Come back, Bennie."   41

I turned around, wondering what else there could be.   42

"In addition," she said, "to doing your homework, you have to read   43
two books from the library each week. Every single week."

"Two books? Two?" Even though I was in fifth grade, I had never read   44
a whole book in my life.

"Yes, two. When you finish reading them, you must write me a book   45
report just like you do at school. You're not living up to your potential, so
I'm going to see that you do."

Usually Curtis, who was two years older, was the more rebellious. But   46
this time he seemed to grasp the wisdom of what Mother said. He did not
say a word.

She stared at Curtis. "You understand?"   47

He nodded.   48

"Bennie, is it clear?"   49

"Yes, Mother." I agreed to do what Mother told me—it wouldn't have   50
occurred to me not to obey—but I did not like it. Mother was being unfair
and demanding more of us than other parents did.

The following day was Thursday. After school, Curtis and I walked to   51
the local branch of the library. I did not like it much, but then I had not spent
that much time in any library.

We both wandered around a little in the children's section, not having   52
any idea about how to select books or which books we wanted to check out.

The librarian came over to us and asked if she could help. We explained   53
that both of us wanted to check out two books.

"What kind of books would you like to read?" the librarian asked.   54

"Animals," I said after thinking about it. "Something about animals."   55

"I'm sure we have several that you'd like." She led me over to a sec-   56
tion of books. She left me and guided Curtis to another section of the room.
I flipped through the row of books until I found two that looked easy
enough for me to read. One of them, *Chip, the Dam Builder*—about a
beaver—was the first one I had ever checked out. As soon as I got home, I
started to read it. It was the first book I ever read all the way through even
though it took me two nights. Reluctantly I admitted afterward to Mother
that I really had liked reading about Chip.

Within a month I could find my way around the children's section like   57
someone who had gone there all his life. By then the library staff knew
Curtis and me and the kind of books we chose. They often made suggestions. "Here's a delightful book about a squirrel," I remember one of them
telling me.

As she told me part of the story, I tried to appear indifferent, but as   58
soon as she handed it to me, I opened the book and started to read.

Best of all, we became favorites of the librarians. When new books   59
came in that they thought either of us would enjoy, they held them for us.
Soon I became fascinated as I realized that the library had so many books—
and about so many different subjects.

After the book about the beaver, I chose others about animals—all   60
types of animals. I read every animal story I could get my hands on. I read
books about wolves, wild dogs, several about squirrels, and a variety of
animals that lived in other countries. Once I had gone through the animal
books, I started reading about plants, then minerals, and finally rocks.

My reading books about rocks was the first time the information ever   61
became practical to me. We lived near the railroad tracks, and when Curtis
and I took the route to school that crossed by the tracks, I began paying
attention to the crushed rock that I noticed between the ties.

As I continued to read more about rocks, I would walk along the tracks,   62
searching for different kinds of stones, and then see if I could identify them.

Often I would take a book with me to make sure that I had labeled each   63
stone correctly.

"Agate," I said as I threw the stone. Curtis got tired of my picking up   64
stones and identifying them, but I did not care because I kept finding new
stones all the time. Soon it became my favorite game to walk along the
tracks and identify the varieties of stones. Although I did not realize it, within
a very short period of time, I was actually becoming an expert on rocks.

Two things happened in the second half of fifth grade that convinced   65
me of the importance of reading books.

First, our teacher, Mrs. Williamson, had a spelling bee every Friday   66
afternoon. We'd go through all the words we'd had so far that year.
Sometimes she also called out words that we were supposed to have
learned in fourth grade. Without fail, I always went down on the first word.

One Friday, though, Bobby Farmer, whom everyone acknowledged as   67
the smartest kid in our class, had to spell "agriculture" as his final word. As
soon as the teacher pronounced his word, I thought, I can spell that word.
Just the day before, I had learned it from reading one of my library books.
I spelled it under my breath, and it was just the way Bobby spelled it.

If I can spell "agriculture," I'll bet I can learn to spell any other word in   68
the world. I'll bet I can learn to spell better than Bobby Farmer.

Just that single word, "agriculture," was enough to give me hope.   69

The following week, a second thing happened that forever changed my   70
life. When Mr. Jaeck, the science teacher, was teaching us about volcanoes,
he held up an object that looked like a piece of black, glass-like rock. "Does
anybody know what this is? What does it have to do with volcanoes?"

Immediately, because of my reading, I recognized the stone. I waited,   71
but none of my classmates raised their hands. I thought, *This is strange.*
Not even the smart kids are raising their hands. I raised my hand.

"Yes, Benjamin," he said.   72

I heard snickers around me. The other kids probably thought it was a   73
joke, or that I was going to say something stupid.

"Obsidian," I said.   74

"That's right!" He tried not to look startled, but it was obvious he   75
hadn't expected me to give the correct answer.

"That's obsidian," I said, "and it's formed by the supercooling of lava   76
when it hits the water." Once I had their attention and realized I knew information no other student had learned, I began to tell them everything I knew
about the subject of obsidian, lava, lava flow, super-cooling, and com-
pacting of the elements.

When I finally paused, a voice behind me whispered, "Is that Bennie   77
Carson?"

"You're absolutely correct," Mr. Jaeck said and he smiled at me. If he   78
had announced that I'd won a million-dollar lottery, I couldn't have been
more pleased and excited.

"Benjamin, that's absolutely, absolutely right," he repeated with enthu-   79
siasm in his voice. He turned to the others and said, "That is wonderful!
Class, this is a tremendous piece of information Benjamin has just given us.
I'm very proud to hear him say this."

For a few moments, I tasted the thrill of achievement. I recall thinking,   80
Wow, look at them. They're all looking at me with admiration. Me, the dummy! The one everybody thinks is stupid. They're looking at me to see if this is really me speaking.

Maybe, though, it was I who was the most astonished one in the class.   81
Although I had been reading two books a week because Mother told me to, I had not realized how much knowledge I was accumulating. True, I had learned to enjoy reading, but until then I hadn't realized how it connected with my schoolwork. That day—for the first time—I realized that Mother had been right. Reading is the way out of ignorance, and the road to achievement. I did not have to be the class dummy anymore.

For the next few days, I felt like a hero at school. The jokes about me   82
stopped. The kids started to listen to me. *I'm starting to have fun with this stuff.*

As my grades improved in every subject, I asked myself, "Ben, is there   83
any reason you can't be the smartest kid in the class? If you can learn about obsidian, you can learn about social studies and geography and math and science and everything."

That single moment of triumph pushed me to want to read more. From   84
then on, it was as though I could not read enough books. Whenever anyone looked for me after school, they could usually find me in my bedroom— curled up, reading a library book—for a long time, the only thing I wanted to do. I had stopped caring about the TV programs I was missing; I no longer cared about playing Tip the Top or baseball anymore. I just wanted to read.

In a year and a half—by the middle of sixth grade—I had moved to the   85
top of the class.

Follow-Up Activities   After you've finished reading, use these questions to respond to "Think Big" You may write your answers or prepare them in your mind to discuss in class.

Grab your first impressions.

1. How would you have responded as a child to the plan Carson's mother imposed on her sons? As an adult, what do you think of her methods?

2. What parts of the reading did you like? What did you dislike? Explain your answer.

Work with new words.

Some words in this reading may be unfamiliar to you. Use the methods of Strategy 3 to explain what the listed words mean.

1. Use context clues.

   trauma (paragraph 20)_____

   Use logic clues to find the meaning of this word.

2. Use word parts.

   a. indifferent (paragraph 58) _____

      The prefix *in*, meaning "not," makes this look like "not different," but check the context and the dictionary to find its real meaning.

   b. acknowledged (paragraph 67) _____

      How does this word, meaning "recognize the truth of," relate to *knowledge*, the word you already know?

3. Use the dictionary.

   Choose the correct definition of this word as is used in the context of this reading.

   skid row (paragraph 16) _____

4. Select additional words you're unsure of from the reading. Use one of these methods to discover their meaning.

Ask and answer questions.

1. Why had Carson gotten off to such a bad start in his fifth-grade class? How did his self-image as "dumbest kid in class" affect his schoolwork?

2. What do the words and actions of Carson's mother show about her character? How was she able to get her boys to follow her strict plan to improve their school performance?

3. When did Carson begin to realize that his reading could be of practical use as well as being entertaining?

4. Carson tells us that his success in explaining *obsidian* in class "forever changed his life." How could that single event have had such a profound effect on him?

 Ask and answer your own question.

   Write a question based on any part of this reading. Share your question with others and collaborate on an answer.

 Answer the overall-point question.

   Now that you've answered important questions about the reading, sum up the main ideas as answers to the overall-point question. Collaborate with others on your answer.

Form your final thoughts.

1. Reading played a key role in turning Carson's life around. Did reading or some other important activity have a big effect on your development?

2. Do you believe you can "do anything you want to," as Mrs. Carson says to her son? What does a person need in order to accomplish his or her goals? Share your responses to this idea with others. ■

READING II-B   DOES MEDIA VIOLENCE DESENSITIZE CHILDREN TO VIOLENCE?

MADELINE LEVINE

Madeline Levine is a clinical psychologist and former instructor in child development. This reading is from See No Evil: A Guide to Protecting Our Children from Media Violence *(1998), a discussion of recent research about the effects of media violence on children.*

STRATEGY 1: CHECK IN
- What do you think of the movie and TV violence you grew up seeing? What kind of effect do you think it had on you and other children?
- Do you notice important changes in the amount and type of violence children are exposed to now as opposed to when you were growing up?
- What is your current attitude toward seeing violence in the media?

STRATEGY 4: GET AN OVERVIEW

STRATEGY 5: ASK QUESTIONS

Perhaps the greatest concern that parents have about media violence   1
is that their children seem increasingly desensitized to violence. Given the large amounts of violence witnessed under the guise of entertainment, it seems reasonable to ask whether children's feelings as well as their behaviors are affected by the thousands of acts of violence they have seen. Parents, educators, and therapists are appalled that so many children seem to take even the most horrifyingly graphic depictions of violence in stride. As we have seen . . . there is no question that media violence encourages real-life violence among some children. The question of desensitization to violence is equally compelling and more complex, and it probably affects larger numbers of children.

A mother consulted me after taking her two sons, ages eleven and thir-   2
teen, to see the popular action movie *Demolition Man.* She accompanied her sons because she wanted to see "what all the fuss is about." In a particularly gruesome scene, Simon Phoenix, played by Wesley Snipes, holds up a bloody eye that he has just gouged out of another man's head. The mother reflexively let out a scream and covered her eyes with her hands. Both sons turned to her in disgust and embarrassment and told her, "Be quiet! It's just a movie." Neither son seemed the least bit upset by what he had just seen. The mother wanted to know whether this was a "normal" reaction or whether her sons had become desensitized to media violence. She was worried that their lack of concern about violence on the screen would translate into a general lack of concern about people and a reluctance to be helpful to others.

This mother, along with the many stricken parents who find that their   3
children seem strangely unaffected by even the most sickeningly graphic

scenes, has good reason to be concerned. Two decades of research on the question of whether media violence can desensitize people have consistently shown that repeated exposure to violence blunts emotional reactions and makes people less likely to intervene or seek help for victims.

University researchers find that their experiments dealing with aggression are being delayed because their student assistants are unable to identify aggressive acts. Graduate students hired to help code aggression on television do not always record pushing, shoving, hitting, and in some instances using a gun as acts of aggression. Research assistants need to be educated that physical assault of one person by another is by definition an act of aggression. Depictions of violence in the media have become so routine that normal people no longer recognize it.

What exactly is desensitization? It is a type of learning that makes us increasingly less likely to react to something. When we are first exposed to a new situation, whether to a violent movie, an upsetting argument, or an attractive member of the opposite sex, our bodies respond automatically. Scientists who study arousal and its opposite, desensitization, use physiological measures, such as heart rate, and psychological measures, such as attitude checklists, to determine level of arousal.

The relationship between desensitization and learning is easy to see. If we are sitting at home working on a project and it begins to rain heavily, it may startle us at first, but we quickly become accustomed to the sound and are able to go on with our work. If the rain continued to demand our attention, raised our heart rate, and made us anxious, we would accomplish very little. By itself, desensitization is neither good nor bad but simply a type of learning.

Very young children are aroused by aggressive scenes on television. Research studies have shown that preschoolers show higher levels of emotion when watching aggressive television programs as compared to more neutral programs.[1] Much like the preadolescent who finds himself hacking and choking after his first cigarette drag, young children are initially distressed by threatening and violent images. This arousal diminishes with repeated exposure as the child becomes desensitized to the violence.

Numerous studies have shown that the more people watch media violence, the less sensitive they become to it.[2] This explains why children seem increasingly capable of tolerating more and more explicit scenes of violence in the media. Over and over, in gruelingly graphic movies such as *Natural Born Killers, Seven,* or *Interview with the Vampire,* it is inevitably adults who walk out in distress or disgust. The large numbers of teenagers in the audience stay put. This is partly because one of the rites of passage of adolescence is to remain unfazed by horror movies. However, it also reflects a lessening of the impact of violence on those who have been

The superscript numbers, like [1], refer to notes at the end of the reading listing source.

4

5

6

7

8

exposed to a steady diet of visual abuse from the time they could talk. The more we watch violence, and the less distressed we are by it, the more we risk becoming tolerant of real-life violence.

ARE DESENSITIZED CHILDREN MORE LIKELY TO BEHAVE VIOLENTLY?

The phenomenon of desensitization has been studied for many years. Public outrage over several well-publicized events in the 1960s and 1970s accelerated scientific study in this area. In 1964 Kitty Genovese was raped and murdered outside her New York apartment building. Although more than forty people were aware of her distress, no one came to her aid. The My Lai trials in 1971 revealed that during the Vietnam War, American soldiers witnessed and participated in the killing of unarmed civilians and children with a shocking level of unconcern. Researchers became increasingly interested in the question of whether people who have been exposed to a great deal of prior violence, either directly or vicariously through the media, might eventually exhibit a kind of psychological and physiological tuning out of the normal emotional responses to violent events.

9

In an early study of desensitization, a team of researchers exposed their subjects to films of a tribal ritual involving painful and bloody genital mutilation.[3] Though initially very distressed, the subjects became less emotionally responsive with repeated viewing of the film. Repeatedly exposing a person to a frightening stimulus in order to lessen anxiety is called systematic desensitization, and it is frequently used to treat individuals with phobias. It is a process all parents are familiar with as they try to coax a frightened child into approaching a feared situation or object. Many a mother, with a fearful child attached to her leg, has slowly approached a neighborhood dog while reassuring her child, "You don't have to touch the doggy, just watch Mommy touch her. See, that wasn't so bad." Over time, the parent's patience and reassurance, as well as the child's repeated exposure to the animal, help the child to be less fearful. Desensitization then can help children engage in activities that were previously anxiety-provoking.

10

Unlike the beneficial effects of desensitization described, desensitization to violence works against healthy development. One particular study can serve as a model for the many done on this subject.[4] This study was designed to determine whether children who watched a lot of television were less likely to be aroused by violence than children who watched little television. Researchers divided the children into two groups: heavy viewers and light viewers. The children watched several neutral films and a brutal boxing scene from the Kirk Douglas movie *Champion*. The choice of a boxing scene is important because scenes of violence alternated with

11

nonviolent scenes as each round came to an end and the boxers returned to their corners.

Heavy and light viewers showed no differences in arousal to the neu- 12
tral films. However, when both groups were exposed to the filmed violence, the low-viewing group became more emotionally aroused than the high-viewing group. Interestingly, even during the nonviolent segments of the boxing movie, children who watched little television tended to be some-what more aroused than the frequent viewers. It seems that it was harder for them to recover from having witnessed violence. The scientific litera-ture as well as common sense tells us that it's easier to participate in an activity that doesn't make us anxious than in one that does.[5] It may be exactly this decreased anxiety about aggression that encourages aggres-sive behavior after watching violent media. Kids who no longer feel anx-ious about violence are more likely to participate in it.

DOES DESENSITIZATION DIMINISH THE CAPACITY TO SHOW CARE AND CONCERN FOR OTHERS?

Studies by psychologists Ronald Drabman and Margaret Thomas show 13
that children who have been exposed to more violent programming are less likely to help younger children who are in trouble.[6] In a study with third- and fourth-graders, children were randomly divided into two groups; one group watched a violent television program and the other did not. The children were then led to believe that they were responsible for monitoring the behavior of a group of younger children whom they could observe on a videotape monitor. The children on the videotape played quietly at first and then became progressively more angry and destructive with each other. Whereas 58 percent of the children who had not seen a violent pro-gram sought adult help before the angry children began physically fighting with each other, only 17 percent of the children who had seen a violent film sought adult help before actual physical fighting broke out. The researchers concluded that children who are exposed to media violence may be more likely to consider fighting a normal way to resolve conflict or may be more desensitized to and less aroused by violence.

Arousal is highly correlated with swift intervention in an emergency 14
situation.[7] An experiment that examined how bystanders respond to emer-gencies found that an increased heart rate and the speed of intervention in a staged emergency situation were substantially correlated. More aroused people came to the aid of others in trouble more quickly than those who were less aroused. As we have seen, repeated viewing of media violence lowers arousal level.[8]

In a world in which genocide still comes to us on our nightly news, 15
where random violence has become the most common form of murder in

this country, and where handguns are the leading cause of death of large segments or our population, desensitization is perhaps the greatest threat of all. We are losing our awareness of what it means to be human as we become less responsive to human suffering. Although we may never engage in violent acts or endorse violence ourselves, we may not dislike it nearly as much as we should.

SUMMARIZED RESEARCH FINDINGS

True or false?

- Media violence encourages children to act more aggressively.
- Media violence encourages attitudes that are distorted, fearful, and pessimistic.
- Media violence desensitizes children to real-life violence.
- Desensitized children are more likely to be aggressive than children who are not desensitized.
- Desensitization interferes with a child's capacity for empathy.

ALL OF THESE STATEMENTS ARE TRUE!

Notes

1. D. K. Osborn and R. C. Endsley, "Emotional Reactions of Young Children to TV Violence," *Child Development,* 1971, *42,* 321–331.
2. R. E. Goranson, "Media Violence and Aggressive Behavior: A Review of Experimental Research," in L. Berkowitz (ed.), *Advances in Experimental Social Psychology*, Vol. 5 (Orlando, Fla.: Academic Press, 1970).
3. R. Lazarus, J. Speisman, A. Mordkoff, and L. Davison, "A Laboratory Study of Psychological Stress Produced by a Motion Picture Film," *Psychological Monographs,* 1962, *76.*
4. V. B. Cline, R. G. Croft, and S. Courrier, "Desensitization of Children to Television Violence," *Journal of Personality and Social Psychology,* 1973, *27,* 360–365.
5. A. Bandura, E. B. Blanchard, and B. Ritter, "The Relative Efficacy of Desensitization and Modeling Approaches for Inducing Behavioral, Affective, and Attitudinal Changes," *Journal of Personality and Social Psychology,* 1969, *13,* 173–199.
6. R. S. Drabman and M. H. Thomas, "Does Media Violence Increase Children's Toleration of Real-Life Aggression?" *Developmental Psychology,* 1974, *10,* 418–421.
7. S. L. Gaertner and J. F. Dovidio, "The Subtlety of White Racism, Arousal, and Helping Behavior," *Journal of Personality and Social Psychology,* 1977, *35,* 691–707.
8. M. H. Thomas, R. Horton, E. Lippincott, and R. S. Drabman, "Desensitization to Portrayals of Real-Life Aggression as a Function of Exposure to TV Violence," *Journal of Personality and Social Psychology,* 1977, *35.*

Follow-Up Activities After you've finished reading, use these questions to respond to "Does Media Violence Desensitize Children to Violence?" You may write your answers or prepare them in your mind to discuss in class.

Grab your first impressions.

1. What new information about the effects of media violence did you find in the essay?

2. Do you find yourself mainly agreeing or disagreeing with the author?

Work with new words.

Some words in this reading may be unfamiliar to you. Use the methods of Strategy 3 to explain what the listed words mean.

1. Use context clues.

   a. arousal (paragraph 5)_____
      Use logic clues, and note the contrast signaled by "its opposite, desensitization. . . ."

   b. vicariously (paragraph 9) _____
      Use logic clues, and note the contrast signaled by "either directly or. . . ."

2. Use word parts.

   a. desensitize (title) _____
      How do *de-* and *–ize* make a word related to *sensitive*?

   b. stricken (paragraph 3) _____
      Relate this word to *struck*, since it comes originally from the verb *to strike*.

   c. phobia (paragraph 10) _____

   d. genocide (paragraph 15)_____
      See the roots list for *–cide*; *gen* comes from *genus*, meaning "race" or "kind."

3. Use the dictionary.

   Choose the correct definition of each word as is used in the context of this reading.

   a. guise (paragraph 1)_____

   b. gruelingly (paragraph 8) _____

   c. correlated (paragraph 14) _____

4. Select additional words you're unsure of from the reading. Use one of these methods to discover their meaning.

Ask and answer questions.

See how the following questions relate to Madeline Levine's title question, "Does media violence desensitize children to violence?" In addition, find the questions that relate specifically to her two headings.

1. Why do university researchers have a hard time finding graduate students who can identify aggressive acts? What do research assistants need to be taught?

2. How does desensitization work in combating phobias?

3. In the study described in paragraphs 11 and 12, two groups of children watched television violence. What were the differences in reactions between the light viewers and the heavy viewers? What does Levine conclude from this study?

4. What significant difference in children's behavior does Levine point to in support of her answer that desensitization [to violence] *does* diminish the capacity "to show care and concern for others" (the second heading)?

Ask and answer your own question.

Write a question based on any part of this reading. Share your question with others and collaborate on an answer.

Answer the overall-point question.

Now that you've answered important questions about the reading, sum up the main ideas as answers to the overall-point question. Collaborate with others on your answer.

Form your final thoughts.

1. How do you feel about your own reactions to media violence? Would Levine find you too desensitized? If so, how would you respond to her?

2. What parts of the reading seemed most convincing to you? Are there parts where you would need more information to be convinced? Share your responses to this reading with others. ■

Reading II-C

This reading is different from any you've encountered so far. It is a short story, a work of fiction. Your purpose for reading stories is different from your purpose for reading nonfiction. Short stories give you an experience rather than factual information. They focus on one or two characters in a limited time and place and often have a single point of view. That means events are shown through only one character's eyes. The plot, or action, moves events along until the climax—the point where you know how things will end.

The same strategies you've been practicing for nonfiction work for fiction, too.

1. **Check in** to see what you can bring to the story from your own experience.

2. **Get an overview** but not too much overview. You don't want to spoil any surprises the author has in store for you! Look at these elements.

   ■ *Headnotes.* They may tell you something about the writer or the story.

   ■ *Visual clues.* Watch for extra spaces. They show you how the story is broken up.

   ■ *The first paragraph or so.* The opening will help you see what the characters and situation will be like.

The other strategies you have learned—**respond, work with new words,** and **ask questions**—will work well with short stories.

READING II-C   **POWDER**

TOBIAS WOLFF

STRATEGY 1: CHECK IN
- How do you think this father compares with yours?
- How does the relationship between the father and mother relate to your parents' relationship?
- Note any other experiences or feelings at the beginning of the story.

Thelonious Monk (1917–1982): jazz pianist and composer.

Tobias Wolff is a novelist and short story writer. "Powder" comes from a collection of his short stories called The Night in Question *(1996). The story shows the way a child can feel two things at once: excited and fearful, full of happiness and full of dread.*

Just before Christmas my father took me skiing at Mount Baker. He'd had to fight for the privilege of my company, because my mother was still angry with him for sneaking me into a nightclub during his last visit, to see Thelonious Monk.   1

He wouldn't give up. He promised, hand on heart, to take good care of me and have me home for dinner on Christmas Eve, and she relented. But as we were checking out of the lodge that morning it began to snow, and in this snow he observed some rare quality that made it necessary for us to get in one last run. We got in several last runs. He was indifferent to my fretting. Snow whirled around us in bitter, blinding squalls, hissing like sand, and still we skied. As the lift bore us to the peak yet again, my father looked at his watch and said, "Criminy. This'll have to be a fast one."   2

By now I couldn't see the trail. There was no point in trying. I stuck to him like white on rice and did what he did and somehow made it to the bottom without sailing off a cliff. We returned our skis and my father put   3

Austin-Healey: *sports car.*

chains on the Austin-Healey° while I swayed from foot to foot, clapping my mittens and wishing I was home. I could see everything. The green table-cloth, the plates with the holly pattern, the red candles waiting to be lit.

We passed a diner on our way out. "You want some soup?" my father   4
asked. I shook my head. "Buck up," he said. "I'll get you there. Right, doctor?"

I was supposed to say, "Right, doctor," but I didn't say anything.   5

A state trooper waved us down outside the resort. A pair of sawhorses   6
were blocking the road. The trooper came up to our car and bent down to my father's window. His face was bleached by the cold. Snowflakes clung to his eyebrows and to the fur trim of his jacket and cap.

"Don't tell me," my father said.   7

The trooper told him. The road was closed. It might get cleared, it   8
might not. Storm took everyone by surprise. So much, so fast. Hard to get people moving. Christmas Eve. What can you do.

My father said, "Look. We're talking about five, six inches. I've taken   9
this car through worse than that."

The trooper straightened up. His face was out of sight but I could hear   10
him. "The road is closed."

My father sat with both hands on the wheel, rubbing the wood with his   11
thumbs. He looked at the barricade for a long time. He seemed to be trying to master the idea of it. Then he thanked the trooper, and with a weird, old-maidy show of caution turned the car around. "Your mother will never for-give me for this," he said.

"We should have left before," I said. "Doctor."   12

He didn't speak to me again until we were in a booth at the diner,   13
waiting for our burgers. "She won't forgive me," he said. "Do you under-stand? Never."

"I guess," I said, but no guesswork was required; she wouldn't forgive   14
him.

"I can't let that happen." He bent toward me. "I'll tell you what I want.   15
I want us all to be together again. Is that what you want?"

"Yes, sir."   16

He bumped my chin with his knuckles. "That's all I needed to hear."   17

When we finished eating he went to the pay phone in the back of the   18
diner, then joined me in the booth again. I figured he'd called my mother, but he didn't give a report. He sipped at his coffee and stared out the window at the empty road. "Come on, come on," he said, though not to me. A little while later he said it again. When the trooper's car went past, lights flashing, he got up and dropped some money on the check. "Okay. Vamanos."

The wind had died. The snow was falling straight down, less of it now 19 and lighter. We drove away from the resort, right up to the barricade. "Move it," my father told me. When I looked at him he said, "What are you waiting for?" I got out and dragged one of the sawhorses aside, then put it back after he drove through. He pushed the door open for me. "Now you're an accomplice," he said. "We go down together." He put the car into gear and gave me a look. "Joke, son."

Down the first long stretch I watched the road behind us, to see if the 20 trooper was on our tail. The barricade vanished. Then there was nothing but snow: snow on the road, snow kicking up from the chains, snow on the trees, snow in the sky; and our trail in the snow. Then I faced forward and had a shock. The lay of the road behind us had been marked by our own tracks, but there were no tracks ahead of us. My father was breaking virgin snow between a line of tall trees. He was humming "Stars Fell on Alabama." I felt snow brush along the floorboards under my feet. To keep my hands from shaking I clamped them between my knees.

My father grunted in a thoughtful way and said, "Don't ever try this 21 yourself."

"I won't." 22

"That's what you say now, but someday you'll get your license and 23 then you'll think you can do anything. Only you won't be able to do this. You need, I don't know—a certain instinct."

"Maybe I have it." 24

"You don't. You have your strong points, but not this. I only mention it 25 because I don't want you to get the idea this is something just anybody can do. I'm a great driver. That's not a virtue, okay? It's just a fact, and one you should be aware of. Of course you have to give the old heap some credit, too. There aren't many cars I'd try this with. Listen!"

I did listen. I heard the slap of the chains, the stiff, jerky rasp of the 26 wipers, the purr of the engine. It really did purr. The old heap was almost new. My father couldn't afford it, and kept promising to sell it, but here it was.

I said, "Where do you think that policeman went to?" 27

"Are you warm enough?" He reached over and cranked up the blower. 28 Then he turned off the wipers. We didn't need them. The clouds had brightened. A few sparse, feathery flakes drifted into our slipstream and were swept away. We left the trees and entered a broad field of snow that ran level for a while and then tilted sharply downward. Orange stakes had been planted at intervals in two parallel lines and my father steered a course between them, though they were far enough apart to leave considerable doubt in my mind as to exactly where the road lay. He was humming again, doing little scat riffs° around the melody.

scat riffs: jazz singing with nonsense syllables.

"Okay then. What are my strong points?"   29

"Don't get me started," he said. "It'd take all day."   30

"Oh, right. Name one."   31

"Easy. You always think ahead."   32

True. I always thought ahead. I was a boy who kept his clothes on num-   33
bered hangers to insure proper rotation. I bothered my teachers for homework assignments far ahead of their due dates so I could draw up
schedules. I thought ahead, and that was why I knew that there would be
other troopers waiting for us at the end of our ride, if we even got there.
What I did not know was that my father would wheedle and plead his way
past them—he didn't sing "O Tannenbaum°," but just about—and get me
home for dinner, buying a little more time before my mother decided to
make the split final. I knew we'd get caught; I was resigned to it. And maybe
for this reason I stopped moping and began to enjoy myself.

O Tannenbaum: a Christmas carol.

Why not? This was one for the books. Like being in a speedboat, only   34
better. You can't go downhill in a boat. And it was all ours. And it kept
coming, the laden trees, the unbroken surface of snow, the sudden white
vistas. Here and there I saw hints of the road, ditches, fences, stakes, but
not so many that I could have found my way. But then I didn't have to. My
father was driving. My father in his forty-eighth year, rumpled, kind, bankrupt of honor, flushed with certainty. He was a great driver. All persuasion,
no coercion. Such subtlety at the wheel, such tactful pedalwork. I actually
trusted him. And the best was yet to come—switchbacks and hairpins
impossible to describe. Except maybe to say this: if you haven't driven
fresh powder, you haven't driven.

Follow-Up Activities   After you've finished reading, use these questions to
respond to "Powder." You may write your answers or prepare them in your
mind to discuss in class.

Work with new words.

Some words in this reading may be unfamiliar to you. Use the methods
of Strategy 3 to explain what the listed words mean.

1. Use context clues.

   a. relented (paragraph 2) _____

   b. accomplice (paragraph 19) _____

   c. wheedle (paragraph 33)_____

   d. bankrupt of honor (paragraph 34) _____
      How can someone be "bankrupt" of a quality like honor?

2. Use the dictionary.

Choose the correct definition of these words as they are used in the context of this reading.

a. fretting (paragraph 2) _____

b. squalls (paragraph 2) _____

c. coercion (paragraph 34)_____
   Before using the dictionary, note the contrast clue: *persuasion* in contrast to *coercion*.

3. Select additional words you're unsure of from the reading. Use one of these methods to discover their meaning.

Grab your first impressions.

1. Did you have any experience in childhood that this story reminded you of? How was it similar? How different?

2. What parts did you particularly like or dislike in this story? Were there any parts that puzzled you? Explain your answers.

Ask and answer questions.

1. What does the first half of the story tell you about the father? Give some details that show his strengths and his weaknesses as a father and a husband.

2. After the son moves the barricade, his father says to him, "Now, you're an accomplice . . . we go down together." Why does he say that? What does his following remark, "Joke, son," show about what he meant and about the way the son had reacted to being called an "accomplice"?

3. What is the son like? How does his character contrast with his father's?

4. What more do you learn about the father's strengths and weaknesses in the last paragraph of the story?

 ## *Ask and answer your own question.*

Write a question of your own. Share your question with others and collaborate on an answer.

 ## *Ask and answer the overall-point question.*

In stories, writers don't tell us their overall point. Instead, they suggest an overall point through what the characters do and say. What might be the overall-point question for "Powder"? How might the characters' actions and words answer that question?

Form your final thoughts.

1. What does the last paragraph of the story tell you about the way the son now looks back on that experience?

2. This story is told from the son's point of view, but what can you tell about how the father sees things? What would the story be like told from his point of view? What would the mother's point of view be? Share your ideas with other students. ■

PART II REVIEW
PREDICTING AND QUESTIONING

Now that you've completed Part II, think over the various ideas you've read about childhood and family. Then review the two strategies introduced in this part, and see how they work throughout the reading process.

Linking Ideas on the Theme: Childhood and Family

Respond to the readings in Part II by linking ideas on the theme of "Childhood and Family." Answer these questions in writing or in discussion with others.

1. "How Babies Use Patterns to See" tells about what babies normally like to look at in the first few months of life. "What Deprived Children Tell Us about Human Nature" gives a picture of childhoods that are not normal. Together, what do these readings say is important for a new baby?

2. Compare two readings that describe the relationship between the parent and older child. What are the different purposes of each writer? What are the important differences in the situations they describe?

3. Compare two writers' ideas of what children need in order to develop the best qualities of human beings. Look closely at the similarities and differences in what they say about child development.

4. "Does Media Violence Desensitize Children to Violence?" discusses the harmful effects of TV and movies on children. What other writer talks about harmful influences on children? Look closely at the similarities and differences in what these writers say.

5. You may think of yet another way of linking two readings on this theme. Say what the two readings have in common as well as how they are different.

6. Compare the ideas about childhood in any of these readings to ideas in other sources—other books or a movie or TV program.

7. Write a letter to one of your classmates, saying which reading is your favorite from Part II. Give reasons for your choice. When you get the same kind of letter, read the other student's reasons for his or her choice. Then answer the letter, saying how you reacted to what the student had to say. Discuss these letters in class to get a feeling for the variety in people's tastes in reading.

Using Strategies Throughout the Reading Process

Strategy 4: **Get an Overview**

Strategy 5: **Ask Questions**

The new strategies give you additional ways of moving more easily through each stage of the reading process. You get started by first **checking in**—making personal connections—and then **getting an overview**—seeing what the writer will say about the subject. **Asking questions** makes your overview easier and prepares you for the next stage, when you read. As you read, you **respond,** you find answers to your questions, and ask and answer new ones. You **work with new words** as you need to. After you read, you follow up by **asking and answering more questions** to be sure you've understood the writer. You then **respond** with your own thoughts.

Use the chart as a reminder of how a strategy helps you at each of the three stages: Get Started, Read, Follow Up. The new strategies are highlighted.

STRATEGIES THROUGH PART II

1. Check in
2. Respond
3. Work with new words
4. Get an overview
5. Ask questions

GET STARTED   Begin with strategies that help you think about the subject and find out about what the writer will say.

- Check in
- **Get an overview**
- **Ask questions**

READ   Use strategies that help you read with greater understanding, interpret the language, and respond with your own questions and ideas.

- Respond
- Work with new words
- **Ask questions**

FOLLOW UP   End with strategies that help you look more closely at the language and ideas in the reading, assess your understanding, and respond in a thoughtful way.

- Work with new words
- Respond
- **Ask questions**

How Are the Strategies Working for You?

You now have five strategies to work with. Take some time to evaluate how well they're working so far. First, look back at what you wrote about the first three strategies at the end of Part I. What differences would there be in your answers to those questions now?

Next answer the following questions to help you evaluate Strategies 4 and 5. Then compare your answers with other students, and ask your instructor for ideas on how to get more out of the strategies.

1. Strategies 4 and 5 work together as you **get started**. How much difference have they made so far in helping you concentrate, understand, and/or enjoy what you read?

   _____

   _____

   _____

2. How much time are the **getting started** strategies taking? How much time are you taking for the strategies in the other stages?

   _____

   _____

   _____

3. For which readings did Strategies 4 and 5 work best? Why? For which did they seem least helpful? Why?

   _____

   _____

   _____

4. What can you do to make the strategies work better for you?

   _____

   _____

   _____

PART III

COMPREHENDING MAIN IDEAS

WITH READINGS ON
LEARNING FOR YOURSELF

Compared to what we ought to be, we are only half awake. We are making use of only a small part of our physical and mental resources. The human individual possesses power of various sorts which he habitually fails to use.

—William James

How much of your potential do you feel you are using? What "physical and mental resources" do you think you could make greater use of? A century after William James set up the first psychology laboratory in America for studying the human mind, his comments still strike a chord with most of us. As individuals, we want to learn more about using the resources we have.

All the readings in Part III will give you practice in reading from the inside out as you connect what you have learned about yourself in the past to new ideas and information about understanding yourself and developing your potential.

Here are some questions to help you think about this theme.

■ How would you describe yourself to someone who didn't know you? What are some of the qualities that define who you are?

■ What circumstances and/or people have helped you learn what you want to know about—in or out of school?

■ What causes stress in your life? How do you deal with stress?

■ How do your feelings—either positive or negative—affect your ability to perform the tasks you've set for yourself?

The strategies in Part III, "Comprehending Main Ideas," bring you a clearer picture of the *reading outside*: the writer's ideas. To comprehend an idea means to understand it or grasp it as your own. Comprehending the writer's ideas, then, allows you to bring them *inside* and decide what you think. Strategy 6, **Find and Mark Main Ideas,** shows you how to use the information from your overview to guide you to the writer's most important ideas. A "Time Out for You" feature gives you suggestions for marking those ideas as your own record of them. Strategy 7, **Look for Patterns of Thought,** gives you more help in following the writer's main ideas. Finally, Strategy 8, **Make Inferences,** extends your understanding by showing you how to find ideas that are implied rather than stated outright.

CHAPTER

6

INCREASE YOUR UNDERSTANDING: FIND AND MARK MAIN IDEAS

Strategy 4, **Get an Overview,** and Strategy 5, **Ask Questions,** give you predictions and questions that prepare you to connect with what the writer has to say. Strategy 6, **Find and Mark Main Ideas,** uses this preparation to help you find the writer's main ideas while you read and after you have finished reading. These main ideas are essential to your comprehension of the reading. You need to recognize and grasp the writer's main ideas to understand the reading's overall point.

Try the New Strategy: Find and Mark Main Ideas

Strategy 6, **Find and Mark Main Ideas,** gives you a way to understand the reading outside—the writer's main ideas. As you read, you keep in mind your overall-point question from your **overview.** You can then **find main ideas** to answer that overall question. The strategy also helps you find the supporting ideas that explain each of the main ideas. Marking main ideas with a pen or pencil helps you keep your focus as you read. It also gives you a clear record of ideas that you can come back to when you need to study them.

STRATEGY 6: FIND AND MARK MAIN IDEAS

1 Read with a pen or pencil in your hand.

2 Find the overall point and the main topics.

3 Find the main idea about each topic.

4 Look for supporting ideas.

5 Adjust your marking.

Before reading "How the Self-Concept Develops," **check in, get an overview,** and **ask questions.** The title of this reading is already close to being a question. We can frame the overall-point question in this way: "How *does* the self-concept develop?" As you read, try finding and underlining main ideas that answer this question. Look for supporting ideas that explain each main idea.

READING 10   ## HOW THE SELF-CONCEPT DEVELOPS

STEVEN A. BEEBE, SUSAN J. BEEBE, AND DIANA K. IVY

STRATEGY 1: CHECK IN

STRATEGY 4: GET AN OVERVIEW

STRATEGY 5: ASK QUESTIONS
Be sure to see the "Recap" (summary) at the end of this reading.

Steven and Susan Beebe teach communication courses at Southwest Texas University; Diana Ivy teaches communication at Texas A & M University— Corpus Christi. This reading comes from the chapter called "Self-Awareness and Communication," from their textbook Communication: Principles for a Lifetime *(2001). In this section from the chapter, the authors discuss how each of us develops a sense of our own identity.*

Some psychologists and sociologists have advanced theories that sug-   1
gest we learn who we are through four basic means: (1) our communication with other individuals, (2) our association with groups, (3) roles we assume, and (4) our self-labels.

COMMUNICATION WITH OTHERS

A valued colleague of ours often says, when he teaches communica-   2
tion courses, that every time you lose a relationship you lose an opportunity to see yourself. What he means is that we don't come to know and understand ourselves in a vacuum. We learn who we are by communicating with others, receiving their feedback, making sense out of it, and internalizing or rejecting all or part of it, such that we are altered by the experience. For example, probably someone in your life has told you that you have a good sense of humor. But think about it for a moment: How would you know if you're funny if it were not for others laughing at humorous things you say or do? Sure, you can crack yourself up, but the real test of a sense of humor is how it manifests itself with others.

In 1902, scholar Charles Horton Cooley first advanced the notion that we   3
form our self-concepts by seeing ourselves in a figurative looking glass: We learn who we are by interacting with others, much as we look into a mirror and see our reflection.[1] Like Cooley, George Herbert Mead, author of the important work *Mind, Self, and Society,* also believed that our sense of who we are is a consequence of our relationship with others.[2] So when we form new relationships and sustain the old ones, we gain opportunities to know ourselves better.

The self-concept we develop through communication with our family stays with us throughout our life.

Self-concept development begins at birth. Names and nicknames reveal how we are viewed by important others; thus they are some of our earliest indicators of identity. During the early years of our lives, our parents and siblings are the key individuals who reflect who we are. Sometimes it seems like, as much as we try or might like to, we cannot escape those early messages we received from our families—messages that shaped our view of self more than any other influence. As we become less dependent on family members, friends become highly influential in shaping our attitudes, beliefs, and values. Your earliest peer groups have had a pronounced effect on who you have become. Friends, teachers, and later, co-workers provide feedback on how well we perform certain tasks. This, in turn, helps us shape our sense of identity as adults. The media also has an effect on our view of self, although this indirect effect has less impact than the people in our lives. 4

Haven't you met people whom you just wished you could hand a decent self-concept? They're nice people, but they seem to suffer from a self-concept formed out of years of criticism from important others. We recall the story of one colleague who was quite an accomplished dancer as an undergraduate. She'd known an upbringing of never being quite good enough, never being able to please her demanding mother, hard as she tried. She remembered one particular dance recital, where she felt she had danced the performance of her life. She just knew her mother would be proud, but when her mother joined her backstage after the performance, amidst the accolades of her friends, her mother had only one thing to say: She pointed out one moment in the dance when the woman's arm should have been straight up instead of out to the side. That's all the feedback she got from her mother—stinging criticism about one brief moment in a brilliant evening's worth of performance. 5

Sometimes it's upsetting, as teachers, to meet students who seem to have taken such an emotional pummeling from their parents in their early years that they seem beaten down by life at a very early age. We can recover from such early warping of our self-concepts, but it is quite an undertaking. Fortunately, we see many more students who have well-balanced, fully 6 developed self-concepts. You can tell that they were raised in a supportive, loving environment.

ASSOCIATION WITH GROUPS

I'm a native New Yorker, I'm a soccer player. I'm a rabbi. I'm a real estate agent. I'm a member of the Young Democrats. Each of these self-descriptive statements answers the "Who am I" question by providing identification with a group or organization. Our awareness of who we are is often linked to who we associate with. How many of these kinds of group-associated terms could you use to describe yourself? Religious groups, political groups, ethnic groups, social groups, study groups, and occupational and professional groups play important roles in shaping your self-concept. Some of these groups we are born into; others we choose on our own. Either way, group associations are significant parts of our identities.

7

As we alluded to earlier, peer pressure is a powerful force in shaping attitudes and behavior, and adolescents are particularly susceptible to it. But adolescents are not alone in allowing the attitudes, beliefs, and values of others to shape their expectations and behaviors. Most adults, to varying degrees, ask themselves, "What will the neighbors think? What will my family think?" when they are making choices.

8

ASSUMED ROLES

A large part of most people's answers to the "Who am I" question reflects roles they assume in their lives. Mother, aunt, brother, uncle, manager, salesperson, teacher, spouse, and student are labels that imply certain expectations for behavior, and they are important in shaping self-concept.

9

Gender asserts a powerful influence on the self-concept from birth on. As soon as parents know the sex of their child, many begin associating their children into a gender group by adhering to cultural rules. They give children sex-stereotypical toys, such as catcher's mitts, train sets, or guns for boys, and dolls, tea sets, and "dress-up" kits for girls. These cultural conventions and expectations play a major role in shaping our self-concept and our behavior.[3] Research indicates that up until the age of three, children are not acutely aware of sex roles. Between the ages of three and five, however, masculine and feminine roles begin to emerge (as encouraged by parents), and they are usually solidified between the ages of five and seven.[4] Research shows that by the time we reach adulthood, our self-concepts are quite distinguishable by gender, with men describing themselves more in terms of giftedness, power, and invulnerability, and women viewing themselves in terms of likeability and morality.[5]

10

SELF-LABELS

Although our self-concept is deeply affected by others, we are not   11
blank slates for them to write on. The labels we use to describe our own
attitudes, beliefs, values, and actions also play a role in shaping our self-
concept. From where do we acquire our labels? We interpret what we experience; we are self-reflexive. *Self-reflexiveness* is the human ability to think
about what we're doing while we're doing it. We talk to ourselves about
ourselves. We are both participants and observers in all that we do. This
dual role encourages us to use labels to describe who we are.

When you were younger, perhaps you dreamed of becoming a rocker   12
or a movie star. People along the way may have told you that you were a
great musician or a terrific actor, but as you matured, you probably began
observing yourself more critically. You struck out with a couple of bands;
you didn't get the starring role in a local stage production. So you self-
reflexively decided that you were not, deep down, a rocker or an actor, even
though others may have labeled you as "talented." Sometimes, through
this self-observation, we discover strengths that encourage us to assume
new labels. One woman we know never thought of herself as a "maverick"
until she realized that she was the first woman to successfully complete an
engineering degree at a male-dominated institution.

RECAP
How the Self-Concept Develops

Communication with Others	The self-concept develops as we communicate with others, receive their feedback, make sense out of it, and internalize or reject all or part of it.
Association with Groups	We develop our self-concept partly because of and through our identification with groups or organizations.
Assumed Roles	The self-concept is affected by roles we assume, such as son or daughter, employee, parent, spouse, student.
Self-Labels	The terms we use to describe our attitudes, beliefs, values, and actions play a role in shaping the self-concept.

Notes

1. C. H. Cooley, *Human Nature and the Social Order* (New York: Scribner's, 1912).
2. G. H. Mead, *Mind, Self, and Society* (Chicago: University of Chicago Press, 1934).
3. D. K. Ivy and P. Backlund, *Exploring GenderSpeak: Personal Effectiveness in Gender Communications,* 2nd ed. (New York: McGraw-Hill, 2000).
4. J. C. Pearson, L. Turner, and W. T. Mancillas, *Gender and Communications,* 3rd ed. (Dubuque, Ia.: William C. Brown, 1995).

5. J. E. Stake, "Gender Differences and Similarities in Self-Concept Within Everyday Life Contexts," *Psychology of Women Quarterly* 6 (1992): 349–363.

Follow-Up Activities   After you've finished reading, use these activities to respond to "How the Self-Concept Develops." You may write your answers or prepare them in your mind to discuss in class.

Grab your first impressions.

1. How closely did this reading match your own understanding about how you developed a sense of "who you are"?

2. Did you learn new things about yourself from this reading? Explain your answer.

Work with new words.

Some words in this reading may be unfamiliar to you. Use the methods of Strategy 3 to explain what the listed words mean.

1. Use context clues.

   a. accolades (paragraph 5) _____
      There are *two* context clues that help define this word.

   b. pummeling (paragraph 6) _____
      In "such an emotional pummeling," the word *such* is an example clue.

2. Use word parts.
   adhering (paragraph 10) _____
   The word *adhere* is related to the word *adhesive* (sticking to).

3. Use the dictionary.
   Choose the correct definition of each word as it is used in the context of this reading.

   a. alluded to (paragraph 8) _____

   b. assume (paragraph 9) _____

   c. maverick (paragraph 12) _____

4. Select additional words you're unsure of from the reading. Use one of these methods to discover their meaning.

Ask and answer questions.

1. How do our early experiences with family influence our self-concept? Give some examples the authors use.

2. How do the kinds of groups we associate with contribute to our awareness of who we are?

3. What is the effect of gender on the roles we assume?

4. What is meant by self-reflexiveness? How does it help shape our self-concept?

 Ask and answer your own question.

Write a question of your own. Share your question with others and collaborate on an answer.

 Answer the overall-point question.

Now that you've answered important questions about the reading, try to sum up the main ideas as an answer to this overall-point question: "How *does* the self-concept develop?" Collaborate with others on your answer.

 Form your final thoughts.

1. What group association terms could you come up with to help identify yourself? What roles do you play in your life that help identify you?

2. What are the most important things you learned about yourself from this reading? Discuss with others the kinds of information each of you gained.

Get a Close-Up of the New Strategy: Find and Mark Main Ideas

Marking Ideas

1 *Read with a pen or pencil in your hand.*
2 *Find the overall point and the main topics.*
3 *Find the main idea about each topic.*
4 *Look for supporting ideas.*
5 *Adjust your marking.*

You've already begun reading with a pen or pencil in your hand. You check a part of the reading that answers one of your questions; you add a new question mark next to a puzzling part; you mark unfamiliar words; you briefly note your response to an idea. Now you'll see how marking in your book helps you stay focused on **finding main ideas.** This textbook has wide left margins for marking.

The next steps in this strategy will help you zero in on the main ideas. When you're sure about these ideas, you can use your own system for marking them. The "Time Out for You" at the end of this chapter suggests tools and methods to make your marking effective.

Underlining. A good way to begin practicing marking ideas is *underlining*. Using a pencil works for first attempts, but pen makes a clearer record. Until

1 *Read with a pen or pencil in your hand.*

you're sure which ideas to mark, hold off on using a highlighter. Highlighting makes ideas really stand out, so they have to be the right ones.

Annotating. Making notes is called *annotating*. Taking brief margin notes—an occasional word or two next to your underlining—helps you bring the ideas, the reading outside, to the inside, where you can clarify the meaning for yourself. You'll see some margin notes in the sample marking for this reading on page 141.

Reviewing. With practice, your marking and annotation of a reading will make sense on its own. When you have a test to study for, you'll have a record of the ideas that you can *review,* or look back over, so you won't have to reread all the material.

As you follow the next steps for finding main ideas, check the sample marking for this reading on page 141.

Overall Point and Main Topics

2 *Find the overall point and the main topics.*

Your questions and predictions from your **overview** show you what to look for in a reading.

Overall-point question. The overall-point question from your **overview** is an especially important guide. It reminds you to look at how each part of a reading relates to the whole message. For example, the overall-point question for Reading 10—"How *does* the self-concept develop?"—starts you looking for answers about where our sense of ourselves comes from.

Statement of the overall point. In some readings, the overall point stands out immediately as a clear-cut answer to your overall-point question. In this reading, the writers announce their overall point in their introduction (paragraph 1):

> Some psychologists and sociologists have advanced theories that suggest we learn who we are through four basic means: (1) our communication with other individuals, (2) our association with groups, (3) roles we assume, and (4) our self-labels.

This sentence answers the question of how "we learn who we are (our self-concept)," and it covers four different "means," or ways, we have of learning about ourselves. Note on the sample marking that this sentence is identified as the overall point in the margin.

But not all readings state the overall point so obviously. In Reading 11 you'll see how to state the overall point if there is no direct statement of it in the reading.

Main topics. A reading is really a series of topics that relate to the overall point. A *topic* is what one part or section of the reading is about. Like a subject of the reading as a whole, a topic can be stated in a word or phrase. In this reading, the heading "Communication with Others" names the topic of the first section.

Headings and main topics. Headings in a reading usually give a good idea of the main topics. The four headings for Reading 10 announce four main topics:

- Communication with Others

- Association with Groups

- Assumed Roles

- Self-Labels

Each topic refers to one way in which we develop our self-concept.

In a reading without headings, you'll depend even more on the overall-point question to help you find the main topics. You'll practice finding main topics in a reading without headings in Reading 11.

Topic and Main Idea

3 *Find the main idea about each topic.*

Once you find a main topic, look for what the writer says *about* that topic. For example, in Reading 10 the first topic is "Communication with Others," but you don't know what the writers say about communication with others until you read.

As you read, look for a *main idea sentence* (or sentences) that give a general, or overall, idea about the topic. Often that sentence appears near the heading for that section. For example, in this first section the idea about the topic of communicating with others is found in the third sentence (in paragraph 2).

> We learn who we are by *communicating with others,* receiving their feedback, making sense out of it, and internalizing or rejecting all or part of it, such that we are altered by the experience.

The italicized part of the sentence repeats the topic. The first part of the sentence states the idea that links communication to our self-concept. The rest of the sentence tells more precisely how we use this communication. Note on the sample marking that this main idea has been marked with an MI, for *Main Idea.*

Supporting Ideas

4 *Look for supporting ideas.*

You already know that main ideas support the overall point. Now you need to recognize that *supporting ideas* explain and clarify—or support—a main idea.

General and specific. To understand the relationship between these levels of support, it's helpful to use the terms *general* and *specific.*

■ *General* refers to a large category (for example, fruit or vehicles).

■ *Specific* refers to a particular type or part within the larger category (for example, fruit includes bananas, grapes, and apples; vehicles include cars, buses, and planes).

A general idea is one that covers, or includes, many others. The overall point is the general idea about the whole reading. A main idea is more specific than the overall point because it refers to just one part of that point. But, in relationship to a supporting idea, the main idea is more general because it covers, or includes, several supporting ideas.

The chart here shows how the overall point, main ideas, and supporting ideas relate to each other in terms of general and specific.

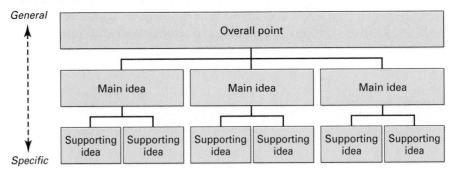

Supporting and main ideas. To find supporting ideas that explain or clarify a main idea, it's useful to turn the main idea into a question. For example, for the first main idea of Reading 10, you could ask the question, "How does communication with others develop our self-concept?" Here are two specific ideas in the section that clearly answer that question.

■ From birth on, the most important communication that influences our self-concept comes from parents and siblings; later we're also influenced by friends, teachers, and co-workers. (paragraph 4)

■ A woman whose sense of herself was damaged by her overly critical mother demonstrates how the influence of others affects our self-concept. (paragraph 5)

These two supporting ideas clearly answer the question of how communication with others affects us. The sample marking on page 142 shows the supporting ideas for this main idea and for the other three main ideas.

Types of supporting ideas. There are many ways to give specific support for a more general idea. Here are some of the kinds of supporting ideas you'll find.

- explanations (such as the explanation you just saw from paragraph 4 about the influence of communication)

- examples (such as the example you just saw from paragraph 5 about the effect of the overly critical mother)

- details about people, places, things

- facts

- statistics

- quotations

Ideas in paragraphs. You don't usually read a paragraph in isolation. Instead, you see how ideas in a reading move logically from one paragraph to the next. Reading with the overall point and main ideas in mind helps you understand each paragraph.

However, sometimes you run into a challenging paragraph. In that case, use the same steps for finding the main idea and supporting ideas in the paragraph that you've used at the more general level of the reading.

1. Find the topic of the paragraph.

2. Look for the main idea about the topic.

3. See how the specific ideas support the main idea.

   Try these steps with paragraph 10 in Reading 10.

1. The topic is *gender,* since every sentence in the paragraph points to gender or sex differences.

2. The main idea about gender can be found in the first sentence. You could turn that idea into a question: "How does gender influence our self-concept from birth on?"

3. The specific supporting ideas answer the question about this influence. From the beginning, parents put children into gender groups. By ages 3 to 5, children, encouraged by parents, begin to understand their gender roles. By adulthood, our self-concept is very influenced by our gender.

5 Adjust your marking.   When you've found and marked the overall point, main ideas, and a few supporting ideas, look over your marking. You may need to make some changes once you have a clearer picture of the relationship of ideas in the reading. The overall point you've marked should be general enough to cover all the main ideas in the reading; each main idea should support the overall point.

Practice the New Strategy

Before applying Strategy 6 to the next reading, practice finding main ideas in Reading 10 one more time.

Find main ideas.

Look for a sentence or sentences that give the main idea about each of these main topics from Reading 10. Once you've decided on a main idea, check to see if what you found is the same idea marked in the sample marking. You can also refer to the "Recap" at the end of the reading to see the authors' restatement of main ideas.

1. "Communication with Others"

   We learn who we are by communicating with others, receiving their feedback, making sense out of it, and internalizing or rejecting all or part of it, such that we are altered by the experience.

2. "Association with Groups." Look for the most general idea about the way association with groups helps us develop our self-concept. In this case, note that the section begins with several specific examples of groups that one of the writers is a member of.

   _____

   _____

3. "Assumed Roles"

   _____

   _____

4. "Self-Labels"

   _____

   _____

Find general and specific ideas in a paragraph.

Each of these pairs of sentences has been taken from a paragraph in Reading 10. The sentences have been shortened slightly. Which sentence is the more general statement of the two? Which is the more specific? Write either *general* or *specific* on the line given.

1. First pair:

   a. Most adults, to varying degrees, ask themselves, "What will the neighbors think? What will my family think?" when they are making choices.
   _____

   b. Peer pressure is a powerful force in shaping attitudes and behavior.
   _____

2. Second pair:

   a. People along the way may have told you that you were a great musician or a terrific actor, but . . . you probably began observing yourself more critically. _____

   b. You struck out with a couple of bands; you didn't get the starring role in a local stage production. _____

3. Third pair:

   a. One woman . . . never thought of herself as a maverick until she realized she was the first woman to successfully complete an engineering degree at a male-dominated institution. _____

   b. Sometimes, through this self-observation, we discover strengths that encourage us to assume new labels. _____   ■

An annotated version of Reading 10, "How the Self-Concept Develops," follows. Notice how the underlining and marginal notes help define and summarize the main ideas in the reading.

SAMPLE MARKING   # HOW THE SELF-CONCEPT DEVELOPS

overall point

Some psychologists and sociologists have advanced theories that sug-   1
gest we learn who we are through four basic means: (1) our communication with other individuals, (2) our association with groups, (3) roles we assume, and (4) our self-labels.

COMMUNICATION WITH OTHERS

A valued colleague of ours often says, when he teaches communica-   2
tion courses, that every time you lose a relationship you lose an opportunity to see yourself. What he means is that we don't come to know and understand ourselves in a vacuum. <u>We learn who we are by communicating with others, receiving their feedback, making sense out of it, and internalizing or rejecting all or part of it</u>, such that we are <u>altered by the experience</u>. For example, probably someone in your life has told you that

MI

you have a good sense of humor. But think about it for a moment: <u>How would you know if you're funny if it were not for others laughing at humorous things you say or do?</u> Sure, you can crack yourself up, but the real test of a sense of humor is how it manifests itself with others.

ex. (

In 1902, scholar Charles Horton Cooley first advanced the notion that we form our self-concepts by seeing ourselves in a figurative looking glass: <u>We learn who we are</u> by <u>interacting with others</u>, much as we <u>look into a mirror and see our reflection.</u>[1] Like Cooley, George Herbert Mead, author of the important work *Mind, Self, and Society,* also believed that our sense of who we are is a consequence of our relationship with others.[2] So when we form new relationships and sustain the old ones, we gain opportunities to know ourselves better.   3

early

<u>Self-concept development begins at birth.</u> Names and nicknames reveal how we are viewed by important others; thus they are some of our earliest indicators of identity. During the <u>early years of our lives,</u> our <u>parents and siblings are the key individuals who reflect who we are.</u> Sometimes it seems like, as much as we try or might like to, we cannot escape those early messages we received from our families—messages that shaped our view of self more than any other influence. As we become less dependent on family members, <u>friends become highly influential</u> in shaping our attitudes, beliefs, and values. Your earliest peer groups have had a pronounced effect on who you have become. <u>Friends, teachers, and later, co-workers provide feedback</u> on how well we perform certain tasks. This, in turn, helps us shape our sense of identity as adults. The media also has an effect on our view of self, although this indirect effect has less impact than the people in our lives.   4

later

ex.—
effects of
demanding
mother

Haven't you met people whom you just wished you could hand a decent self-concept? They're nice <u>people,</u> but they seem to <u>suffer from a self-concept formed out of years of criticism</u> from important others. We recall the story of <u>one colleague</u> who was <u>quite an accomplished dancer as an undergraduate.</u> She'd known an <u>upbringing of never being quite good enough, never</u> being able to <u>please her demanding mother,</u> hard as she tried. She remembered one particular dance recital, where she felt she had danced the performance of her life. She just knew her mother would be proud, but when her mother joined her backstage after the performance, amidst the accolades of her friends, her mother had only one thing to say: She pointed out one moment in the dance when the woman's arm should have been straight up instead of out to the side. That's <u>all the feedback she got from her mother—stinging criticism</u> about one brief moment <u>in a brilliant evening's worth of performance.</u>   5

Sometimes it's upsetting, as teachers, to meet students who seem to have taken such an emotional pummeling from their parents in their early   6 years that they seem beaten down by life at a very early age. We can recover from such early warping of our self-concepts, but it is quite an undertaking. Fortunately, we see many more students who have well-balanced, fully developed self-concepts. You can tell that they were raised in a supportive, loving environment.

ASSOCIATION WITH GROUPS

MI

many possible groups

I'm a native New Yorker, I'm a soccer player. I'm a rabbi. I'm a real estate agent. I'm a member of the Young Democrats. Each of these self-descriptive statements answers the "Who am I" question by providing identification with a group or organization. <u>Our awareness of who we are is often linked to who we associate with.</u> How many of these kinds of group-associated terms could you use to describe yourself? Religious groups, political groups, ethnic groups, social groups, study groups, and occupational and professional groups play important roles in shaping your self-concept. Some of these groups we are born into; others we choose on our own. Either way, group associations are significant parts of our identities.

7

As we alluded to earlier, <u>peer pressure is a powerful force in shaping attitudes and behavior,</u> and adolescents are particularly susceptible to it. But adolescents are not alone in allowing the attitudes, beliefs, and values of others to shape their expectations and behaviors. Most adults, to varying degrees, ask themselves, "What will the neighbors think? What will my family think?" when they are making choices.

8

ASSUMED ROLES

MI

roles

parents put child into gender role

diffs. betw. men + women

<u>A large part of most people's answers to the "Who am I" question reflects roles they assume in their lives.</u> Mother, aunt, brother, uncle, manager, salesperson, teacher, spouse, and student are labels that imply certain expectations for behavior, and they are important in shaping self-concept.

9

<u>Gender asserts a powerful influence on the self-concept</u> (from birth on.) As soon as <u>parents</u> know the sex of their child, many <u>begin associating their children into a gender group by adhering to cultural rules.</u> They give children sex-stereotypical toys, such as catcher's mitts, train sets, or guns for boys, and dolls, tea sets, and "dress-up" kits for girls. These cultural conventions and expectations play a major role in shaping our self-concept and our behavior.[3] Research indicates that up until the age of three, children are not acutely aware of sex roles. <u>Between the ages of three and five,</u> however, <u>masculine and feminine roles begin to emerge</u> (as encouraged by parents), and they are usually solidified between the ages of five and seven.[4] Research shows that by the time we reach adulthood, <u>our self-concepts are quite distinguishable</u> by gender, with men describing themselves more in

10

terms of giftedness, power, and invulnerability, and women viewing them-selves in terms of likeability and morality.[5]

SELF-LABELS

MI

Although our self-concept is deeply affected by others, we are not   11
blank slates for them to write on. <u>The labels we use to describe our own attitudes, beliefs, values, and actions also play a role in shaping our self-concept.</u> From where do we acquire our labels? We interpret what we experience; we are self-reflexive. <u>Self-reflexiveness</u> is the <u>human ability to think about what we're doing while we're doing it.</u> We <u>talk to ourselves about ourselves.</u> We are both participants and observers in all that we do. This <u>dual role</u> encourages us to use labels to describe who we are.

talk about self to self

ex.— change in self-label

When you were younger, perhaps you dreamed of becoming a rocker   12
or a movie star. People along the way may have told you that you were a great musician or a terrific actor, but as you matured, you probably began observing yourself more critically. You struck out with a couple of bands; you didn't get the starring role in a local stage production. So you self-reflexively decided that you were not, deep down, a rocker or an actor, even though others may have labeled you as "talented." Sometimes, through this self-observation, we discover strengths that encourage us to assume new labels. One woman we know never thought of herself as a "maverick" until she realized that she was the first woman to successfully complete an engineering degree at a male-dominated institution.

RECAP

How the Self-Concept Develops

Communication with Others	The self-concept develops as we communicate with others, receive their feedback, make sense out of it, and internalize or reject all or part of it.
Association with Groups	We develop our self-concept partly because of and through our identification with groups or organizations.
Assumed Roles	The self-concept is affected by roles we assume, such as son or daughter, employee, parent, spouse, student.
Self-Labels	The terms we use to describe our attitudes, beliefs, values, and actions play a role in shaping the self-concept.

Apply the New Strategy: Find and Mark Main Ideas

Now that you understand Strategy 6, put it into practice with Reading 11, "School Is Bad for Children" (or with one of the Additional Readings in Part III, selected by your instructor).

In your **overview** for "School Is Bad for Children," notice that at first the title suggests this overall-point question: "Why is school bad for children?" But as you skim, you'll notice that the reading falls into two parts: what Holt sees as the problem and his solution. So you need to make a more complete overall-point question that includes the second part of the reading.

Sample: Why is school bad for children and what are solutions to the problem?

This reading has no headings, so you'll need to rely on your overall-point question to guide you.

Try to group paragraphs into main topics. First you might want to note the topic of each paragraph in the margin (in pencil). Mark in pencil where you see a big change in topic. Where does the big change in topic occur, from why school is bad to solutions to the problem?

Now look for the main idea for each of these two topics. You will also need to find several supporting ideas to explain each main idea. Remember to turn the main idea into a question and look for answers to that question.

Unlike Reading 10, Reading 11 does not give you one clear-cut statement of the overall point. Try to come up with your own statement by combining the two main ideas.

After you've read "School Is Bad for Children," complete your marking. Then compare your marking to the sample on page 152.

READING 11   SCHOOL IS BAD FOR CHILDREN

JOHN HOLT

STRATEGY 1: CHECK IN

STRATEGY 4: GET AN OVERVIEW

STRATEGY 5: ASK QUESTIONS

John Holt (1923–1985) was a teacher and commentator on education who believed children should be allowed to discover their own paths to learning. His unusual ideas about school have been the subject of debate ever since "School Is Bad for Children" was first published in 1969 in a popular magazine of that time, The Saturday Evening Post.

Almost every child, on the first day he sets foot in a school building, is   1
smarter, more curious, less afraid of what he doesn't know, better at finding and figuring things out, more confident, resourceful, persistent and independent than he will ever be again in his schooling—or, unless he is very unusual and very lucky, for the rest of his life. Already, by paying close attention to and interacting with the world and people around him, and without any school-type formal instruction, he has done a task far more difficult, complicated and abstract than anything he will be asked to do in school, or than any of his teachers has done for years. He has solved the mystery of language. He has discovered it—babies don't even know that

language exists—and he has found out how it works and learned to use it. He has done it by exploring, by experimenting, by developing his own model of the grammar of language, by trying it out and seeing whether it works, by gradually changing it and refining it until it does work. And while he has been doing this, he has been learning other things as well, including many of the "concepts" that the schools think only they can teach him, and many that are more complicated than the ones they do try to teach him.

In he comes, this curious, patient, determined, energetic, skillful 2 learner. We sit him down at a desk, and what do we teach him? Many things. First, that learning is separate from living. "You come to school to learn," we tell him, as if the child hadn't been learning before, as if living were out there and learning were in here, and there were no connection between the two. Secondly, that he cannot be trusted to learn and is no good at it. Everything we teach about reading, a task far simpler than many that the child has already mastered, says to him, "If we don't make you read, you won't, and if you don't do it exactly the way we tell you, you can't." In short, he comes to feel that learning is a passive process, something that some-one else does *to* you, instead of something you do for yourself.

In a great many other ways he learns that he is worthless, untrust- 3 worthy, fit only to take other people's orders, a blank sheet for other people to write on. Oh, we make a lot of nice noises in school about respect for the child and individual differences, and the like. But our acts, as opposed to our talk, say to the child, "Your experience, your concerns, your curiosities, your needs, what you know, what you want, what you wonder about, what you hope for, what you fear, what you like and dislike, what you are good at or not so good at—all this is of not the slightest importance, it counts for nothing. What counts here, and the only thing that counts, is what we know, what we think is important, what we want you to do, think and be." The child soon learns not to ask questions—the teacher isn't there to satisfy his curiosity. Having learned to hide his curiosity, he later learns to be ashamed of it. Given no chance to find out who he is—and to develop that person, whoever it is—he soon comes to accept the adults' evaluation of him.

He learns many other things. He learns that to be wrong, uncertain, 4 confused, is a crime. Right Answers are what the school wants, and he learns countless strategies for prying these answers out of the teacher, for conning her into thinking he knows what he doesn't know. He learns to dodge, bluff, fake, cheat. He learns to be lazy. Before he came to school, he would work for hours on end, on his own, with no thought of reward, at the business of making sense of the world and gaining competence in it. In school he learns, like every buck private, how to goldbrick, how not to work when the sergeant isn't looking, how to know when he is looking, how to make him think you are working even when he is looking. He learns that in real life you don't do anything unless you are bribed, bullied or conned into doing it, that nothing is worth doing for its own sake, or that if it is, you can't do it in school. He learns to be bored, to work with a small part of his mind, to escape from the reality around him into daydreams and fantasies—but not like the fantasies of his preschool years, in which he played a very active part.

The child comes to school curious about other people, particularly   5
other children, and the school teaches him to be indifferent. The most interesting thing in the classroom—often the only interesting thing in it—is the other children, but he has to act as if these other children, all about him, only a few feet away, are not really there. He cannot interact with them, talk with them, smile at them. In many schools he can't talk to other children in the halls between classes; in more than a few, and some of these in stylish suburbs, he can't even talk to them at lunch. Splendid training for a world in which, when you're not studying the other person to figure out how to do him in, you pay no attention to him.

In fact, he learns how to live without paying attention to anything going   6
on around him. You might say that school is a long lesson in how to turn yourself off, which may be one reason why so many young people, seeking the awareness of the world and responsiveness to it they had when they were little, think they can only find it in drugs. Aside from being boring, the school is almost always ugly, cold, inhuman—even the most stylish, glass-windowed, $20-a-square-foot schools.

And so, in this dull and ugly place, where nobody ever says anything   7
very truthful, where everybody is playing a kind of role, as in a charade, where the teachers are no more free to respond honestly to the students than the students are free to respond to the teachers or each other, where the air practically vibrates with suspicion and anxiety, the child learns to live in a daze, saving his energies for those small parts of his life that are too trivial for the adults to bother with, and thus remain his. It is a rare child who can come through his schooling with much left of his curiosity, his independence or his sense of his own dignity, competence and worth.

So much for criticism. What do we need to do? Many things. Some are   8
easy—we can do them right away. Some are hard, and may take some time. Take a hard one first. We should abolish compulsory school attendance. At the very least we should modify it, perhaps by giving children every year a large number of authorized absences. Our compulsory school-attendance laws once served a humane and useful purpose. They protected children's rights to some schooling, against those adults who would otherwise have denied it to them in order to exploit their labor, in farm, store,

mine or factory. Today the laws help nobody, not the schools, not the teachers, not the children. To keep kids in school who would rather not be there costs the schools an enormous amount of time and trouble—to say nothing of what it costs to repair the damage that these angry and resentful prisoners do every time they get a chance. Every teacher knows that any kid in class who, for whatever reason, would rather not be there not only doesn't learn anything himself but makes it a great deal tougher for anyone else. As for protecting the children from exploitation, the chief and indeed only exploiters of children these days *are* the schools. Kids caught in the college rush more often than not work 70 hours or more a week, most of it on paper busywork. For kids who aren't going to college, school is just a useless time waster, preventing them from earning some money or doing some useful work, or even doing some true learning.

Objections. "If kids didn't have to go to school, they'd all be out in the streets." No, they wouldn't. In the first place, even if schools stayed just the way they are, children would spend at least some time there because that's where they'd be likely to find friends; it's a natural meeting place for children. In the second place, schools wouldn't stay the way they are, they'd get better, because we would have to start making them what they ought to be right now—places where children would *want* to be. In the third place, those children who did not want to go to school could find, particularly if we stirred up our brains and gave them a little help, other things to do—the things many children now do during their summers and holidays.   9

There's something easier we could do. We need to get kids out of the school buildings, give them a chance to learn about the world at first hand. It is a very recent idea, and a crazy one, that the way to teach our young people about the world they live in is to take them out of it and shut them up in brick boxes. Fortunately, educators are beginning to realize this. In Philadelphia and Portland, Oregon, to pick only two places I happen to have heard about, plans are being drawn up for public schools that won't have any school buildings at all, that will take the students out into the city and help them to use it and its people as a learning resource. In other words, students, perhaps in groups, perhaps independently, will got to libraries, museums, exhibits, courtrooms, legislatures, radio and TV stations, meetings, businesses and laboratories to learn about their world and society at first hand. A small private school in Washington is already doing this. It makes sense. We need more of it.   10

As we help children get out into the world, to do their learning there, we can get more of the world into the schools. Aside from their parents, most children never have any close contact with any adults except people whose sole business is children. No wonder they have no idea what adult   11 life or work is like. We need to bring a lot more people who are *not* full-time teachers into the schools, and into contact with the children. In New York City, under the Teachers and Writers Collaborative, real writers, working writers—novelists, poets, playwrights—come into the schools, read their work, and talk to the children about the problems of their craft. The children eat it up. In another school I know of, a practicing attorney from a nearby city comes in every month or so and talks to several classes about the law. Not the law as it is in books but as he sees it and encounters it in his cases, his problems, his work. And the children love it. It is real, grown-up, true, not *My Weekly Reader,* not "social studies," not lies and baloney.

Something easier yet. Let children work together, help each other, learn   12 from each other and each other's mistakes. We now know, from the experience of many schools, both rich-suburban and poor-city, that children are often the best teachers of other children. What is more important, we know that when a fifth- or sixth-grader who has been having trouble with reading starts helping a first-grader, his own reading sharply improves. A number of schools are beginning to use what some call Paired Leaning. This means that you let children form partnerships with other children, do their work, even including their tests, together, and share whatever marks or results this work gets—just like grownups in the real world. It seems to work.

Let the children learn to judge their own work. A child learning to talk   13 does not learn by being corrected all the time—if corrected too much, he will stop talking. *He* compares, a thousand times a day, the difference between language as he uses it and as those around him use it. Bit by bit, he makes the necessary changes to make his language like other people's. In the same way, kids learning to do all the other things they learn without adult teachers—to walk, run, climb, whistle, ride a bike, skate, play games, jump rope—compare their own performance with what more skilled people do, and slowly make the needed changes. But in school we never give a child a chance to detect his mistakes, let alone correct them. We do it all for him. We act as if we thought he would never notice a mistake unless it was pointed out to him, or correct it unless he was made to. Soon he becomes dependent on the expert. We should let him do it himself. Let him figure out, with the help of other children if he wants it, what this word says, what is the answer to that problem, whether this is a good way of saying or doing this or that. If right answers are involved, as in some math or science, give him the answer book, let him correct his own papers. Why should we teachers waste time on such donkey work? Our job should be to help the kid when he tells us that he can't find a way to get the right answer. Let's get rid of all this nonsense of grades, exams, marks. We don't know now, and we never will know, how to measure what another person knows or understands. We certainly can't find out by asking him question. All we find out is what he doesn't know—which is what most tests are for, anyway. Throw it all out, and let the child learn what every educated person must someday learn, how to measure his own understanding, how to know what he knows or does not know.

We could also abolish the fixed, required curriculum. People remember   14
only what is interesting and useful to them, what helps them make sense of the world, or helps them get along in it. All else they quickly forget, if they ever learn it at all. The idea of a "body of knowledge," to be picked up in school and used for the rest of one's life, is nonsense in a world as complicated and rapidly changing as ours. Anyway, the most important questions and problems of our time are not *in* the curriculum, not even in the hotshot universities, let alone the schools.

Children want, more than they want anything else, and even after years   15
of miseducation, to make sense of the world, themselves, and other human beings. Let them get this job, with our help if they ask for it, in the way that makes most sense to them.

Follow-Up Activities   After you've finished reading, use these activities to respond to "School Is Bad for Children." You may write your answers or prepare them in your mind to discuss in class.

Grab your first impressions.

1. If you had to choose sides in a debate on this reading, which side would you be on? Do you mainly agree or disagree with Holt?

2. How does Holt's description of school match your own experience? What parts do you especially agree or disagree with?

Work with new words.

Some words in this reading may be unfamiliar to you. Use the methods of Strategy 3 to explain what the listed words mean.

1. Use context clues.

   goldbrick (paragraph 4)_____
   Use logic clues and watch for synonyms.

2. Use word parts.

   a. compulsory (paragraph 8)_____
      Use the stronger verb form of this word, *compel* (to *force*) to help you remember this adjective.

   b. miseducation (paragraph 15) _____

3. Use the dictionary.

Choose the correct definition of this word as it is used in the context of this reading.

charade (paragraph 7) _____

4. Select additional words you're unsure of from the reading. Use one of these methods to discover their meaning.

Ask and answer questions.

1. According to Holt, what negative lessons does school teach children from the very beginning?

2. Why does he say, in paragraph 6, that "school is a long lesson in how to turn yourself off"?

3. How does Holt answer the objections he knows people would make about abolishing required schooling?

4. What are some of the ways that children could learn without depending so much on adults? What would the advantages be for this kind of learning?

Ask and answer your own question.

Write a question of your own. Share your question with others and collaborate on an answer.

Answer the overall-point question.

Now that you've answered important questions about the reading, try to sum up the main ideas as an answer to the overall-point question: "Why is school bad for children and what are solutions to the problem?" Collaborate with others on your answer.

Put together the overall point from the two main ideas.

First main idea—*the general problem:* _____

_____

Second main idea—*the general solution:* _____

_____

Put these together as an overall-point statement: _____

_____

_____

_____

Look at the following statements. Is this similar to what you wrote?

First main idea—*the general problem:* Children naturally want to learn, but school destroys their confidence in their own ability and turns off their curiosity.

Second main idea—*the general solution:* Find ways to let children learn on their own, giving them help when they need it.

Put these together as an overall-point statement: Children naturally want to learn, but school destroys their confidence in their own ability and turns off their curiosity, so we should find ways to let children learn on their own, giving them help when they need it.

 Form your final thoughts.

1. Discuss with other students your final response to this reading. There will almost certainly be disagreements about Holt's ideas, so be sure to listen carefully to what people on each side have to say.

2. Notice that this reading was written in 1969. Include in your discussion of Holt's ideas how much or how little things have changed in over thirty years. ■

An annotated version of Reading 11, "School Is Bad for Children," follows. Notice how the underlining and marginal notes help define and summarize the main ideas in the reading.

SAMPLE MARKING   ## SCHOOL IS BAD FOR CHILDREN

General Problem

child starting school

Almost every <u>child, on the first day he sets foot in a school</u> building, is   1
<u>smarter, more curious, less afraid of what he doesn't know, better at finding
and figuring things out, more confident, resourceful, persistent and independent than he will ever be again in his schooling</u>—or, unless he is very
unusual and very lucky, for the rest of his life. Already, by paying close
attention to and interacting with the world and people around him, and
without any school-type formal instruction, he <u>has done a task far more difficult, complicated</u> and abstract than anything he will be asked to do in
school, or than any of his teachers has done for years. He has <u>solved the</u>

already knows

<u>mystery of language.</u> He has discovered it—babies don't even know that
language exists—and he has found out how it works and learned to use it.
He has done it by exploring, by experimenting, by developing his own
model of the grammar of language, by trying it out and seeing whether it
works, by gradually changing it and refining it until it does work. And while

he has been doing this, he has been <u>learning other things as well</u>, including many of the <u>"concepts" that the schools think only they can teach him</u>, and many that are <u>more complicated</u> than the ones they do try to teach him.

In he comes, this curious, patient, determined, energetic, skillful   2
learner. We sit him down at a desk, and what do we teach him? Many things. (First,) that <u>learning is separate from living</u>. "You come to school to learn," we tell him, as if the child hadn't been learning before, as if living were out there and learning were in here, and there were no connection between the two. (Secondly,) that he <u>cannot be trusted to learn and is no good at it</u>. Everything we teach about reading, a task far simpler than many that the child has already mastered, says to him, "If we don't make you read, you won't, and if you don't do it exactly the way we tell you, you can't." In short, he comes to feel that <u>learning is a passive process, something that some-one else does *to* you</u>, instead of something you do for yourself.

@ school child learns (1) (2)

In a great many other ways he learns that he is worthless, untrust-   3
worthy, fit only to take other people's orders, a blank sheet for other people to write on. Oh, we make a lot of nice noises in school about respect for the child and individual differences, and the like. But our <u>acts, as opposed to our talk</u>, say to the child, "<u>Your experience, your concerns, your curiosities, your needs, what you know, what you want, what you wonder about, what you hope for, what you fear, what you like and dislike, what you are good at or not so good at—all this is of not the slightest importance, it counts for nothing</u>. What counts here, and the only thing that counts, is what we know, what we think is important, what we want you to do, think and be." The child <u>soon learns not to ask questions</u>—the teacher isn't there to satisfy his curiosity. Having learned to hide his curiosity, he later learns to be ashamed of it. Given no chance to find out who he is—and to develop that person, whoever it is—he soon comes to accept the adults' evaluation of him.

his exp. etc. not imp.

distrust self

He learns many other things. He learns that to be wrong, uncertain,   4
confused, is a crime. (Right Answers) are what the school wants, and he learns countless strategies for prying these answers out of the teacher, for conning her into thinking he knows what he doesn't know. <u>He learns to dodge, bluff, fake, cheat</u>. He learns to <u>be lazy</u>. Before he came to school, he would work for hours on end, on his own, with no thought of reward, at the business of making sense of the world and gaining competence in it. In school he learns, like every buck private, how to goldbrick, how not to work when the sergeant isn't looking, how to know when he is looking, how to make him think you are working even when he is looking. He learns that in real life you don't do anything unless you are bribed, bullied or conned into doing it, that nothing is worth doing for its own sake, or that if it is, you can't do it in school. He learns to be bored, to work with a small part of his mind, to escape from the reality around him into daydreams and fantasies—but

learns more:

only do what have to

not like the fantasies of his preschool years, in which he played a very active part.

The child comes to school curious about other people, particularly 5 other children, and the school teaches him to be indifferent. The <u>most interesting thing in the classroom</u>—often the only interesting thing in it—is the <u>other children, but he has to act as if these other children</u>, all about him, only a few feet away, <u>are not really there.</u> He cannot interact with them, talk with them, smile at them. In many schools he can't talk to other children in the halls between classes; in more than a few, and some of these in stylish suburbs, he can't even talk to them at lunch. Splendid training for a world in which, when you're not studying the other person to figure out how to do him in, you pay no attention to him.

he's cut off from other kids

In fact, he learns how to live without paying attention to anything going 6 on around him. You might say that school is a long lesson in how to turn yourself off, which may be one reason why so many young people, seeking the awareness of the world and responsiveness to it they had when they were little, think they can only find it in drugs. Aside from being boring, the school is almost always ugly, cold, inhuman—even the most stylish, glass-windowed, $20-a-square-foot schools.

And so, in this dull and ugly place, where nobody ever says anything 7 very truthful, where everybody is playing a kind of role, as in a charade, where the <u>teachers are no more free to respond honestly to the students</u> <u>than the students are free to respond to the teachers or each other</u>, where the air practically vibrates with suspicion and anxiety, the child learns to live in a daze, saving his energies for those small parts of his life that are too trivial for the adults to bother with, and thus remain his. It is a rare child who can come through his schooling with much left of his curiosity, his independence or his sense of his own dignity, competence and worth.

school-boring, ugly, distrusting atmosph.

solutions (8–15)

So much for criticism. What do we need to do? Many things. Some are 8 easy—we can do them right away. Some are hard, and may take some time. Take a hard one first. (We should abolish compulsory school attendance.) At the very least we should modify it, perhaps by giving children every year a large number of authorized absences. Our compulsory school-attendance laws <u>once served a humane and useful purpose</u>. They protected children's rights to some schooling, against those adults who would otherwise have denied it to them in order to exploit their labor, in farm, store, mine or factory. <u>Today the laws help nobody</u>, not the schools, not the teachers, not the children. To keep kids in school who would rather not be there costs the schools an enormous amount of time and trouble—to say nothing of what it costs to repair the damage that these angry and resentful prisoners do every time they get a chance. Every teacher knows that any

End compuls. school

outgrew purpose

school useless/costly if not wanted or needed

kid in class who, for whatever reason, would rather not be there not only doesn't learn anything himself but makes it a great deal tougher for anyone else. As for protecting the children from exploitation, the chief and indeed only exploiters of children these days *are* the schools. Kids caught in the college rush more often than not work 70 hours or more a week, most of it on paper busywork. For kids who aren't going to college, school is just a useless time waster, preventing them from earning some money or doing some useful work, or even doing some true learning.

how work?

① ② ③

Objections. "If kids didn't have to go to school, they'd all be out in the streets." No, they wouldn't. In the first place, even if schools stayed just the way they are, children would spend at least some time there because that's where they'd be likely to find friends; it's a natural meeting place for children. In the second place, schools wouldn't stay the way they are, they'd get better, because we would have to start making them what they ought to be right now—places where children would *want* to be. In the third place, those children who did not want to go to school could find, particularly if we stirred up our brains and gave them a little help, other things to do—the things many children now do during their summers and holidays.

9

Get kids into community.

There's something easier we could do. We need to get kids out of the school buildings, give them a chance to learn about the world at first hand. It is a very recent idea, and a crazy one, that the way to teach our young people about the world they live in is to take them out of it and shut them up in brick boxes. Fortunately, educators are beginning to realize this. In Philadelphia and Portland, Oregon, to pick only two places I happen to have heard about, plans are being drawn up for public schools that won't have any school buildings at all, that will take the students out into the city and help them to use it and its people as a learning resource. In other words, students, perhaps in groups, perhaps independently, will got to libraries, museums, exhibits, courtrooms, legislatures, radio and TV stations, meetings, businesses and laboratories to learn about their world and society at first hand. A small private school in Washington is already doing this. It makes sense. We need more of it.

10

resources

bring working adults into classrm.

As we help children get out into the world, to do their learning there, we can get more of the world into the schools. Aside from their parents, most children never have any close contact with any adults except people whose sole business is children. No wonder they have no idea what adult life or work is like. We need to bring a lot more people who are *not* full-time teachers into the schools, and into contact with the children. In New York City, under the Teachers and Writers Collaborative, real writers, working writers—novelists, poets, playwrights—come into the schools, read their work, and talk to the children about the problems of their craft. The children

11

eat it up. In another school I know of, a practicing attorney from a nearby city comes in every month or so and talks to several classes about the law. Not the law as it is in books but as he sees it and encounters it in his cases, his problems, his work. And the children love it. It is real, grown-up, true, not *My Weekly Reader,* not "social studies," not lies and baloney.

Something easier yet. Let children work together, help each other, learn   12 from each other and each other's mistakes. We now know, from the experience of many schools, both rich-suburban and poor-city, that children are often the best teachers of other children. What is more important, we know that when a fifth- or sixth-grader who has been having trouble with reading starts helping a first-grader, his own reading sharply improves. A number of schools are beginning to use what some call Paired Leaning. This means that you let children form partnerships with other children, do their work, even including their tests, together, and share whatever marks or results this work gets—just like grownups in the real world. It seems to work.

Let the children learn to judge their own work. A child learning to talk   13 does not learn by being corrected all the time—if corrected too much, he will stop talking. *He* compares, a thousand times a day, the difference between language as he uses it and as those around him use it. Bit by bit, he makes the necessary changes to make his language like other people's.

child corrects self in learning lang. etc. In the same way, kids learning to do all the other things they learn without adult teachers—to walk, run, climb, whistle, ride a bike, skate, play games, jump rope—compare their own performance with what more skilled people do, and slowly make the needed changes. But in school we never give a child a chance to detect his mistakes, let alone correct them. We do it all for him. We act as if we thought he would never notice a mistake unless it was pointed out to him, or correct it unless he was made to. Soon he becomes dependent on the expert. We should let him do it himself. Let him figure out, with the help of other children if he wants it, what this word says, what is the answer to that problem, whether this is a good way of saying or doing this or that. If right answers are involved, as in some math or science, give him the answer book, let him correct his own papers. Why should we teachers waste time on such donkey work? Our job should be to help the *let child* kid when he tells us that he can't find a way to get the right answer. Let's *evaluate self* get rid of all this nonsense of grades, exams, marks. We don't know now, and we never will know, how to measure what another person knows or understands. We certainly can't find out by asking him question. All we find out is what he doesn't know—which is what most tests are for, anyway. Throw it all out, and let the child learn what every educated person must someday learn, how to measure his own understanding, how to know what he knows or does not know.

*learn what
needs + wants*

We could also (abolish the fixed, required curriculum.) People remember 14
only what is interesting and useful to them, what helps them make sense
of the world, or helps them get along in it. All else they quickly forget, if
they ever learn it at all. The idea of a "body of knowledge," to be picked up
in school and used for the rest of one's life, is nonsense in a world as complicated and rapidly changing as ours. Anyway, the most important questions and problems of our time are not *in* the curriculum, not even in the
hotshot universities, let alone the schools.

*General
solution*

Children want, more than they want anything else, and even after years 15
of miseducation, to make sense of the world, themselves, and other human
beings. Let them get this job, with our help if they ask for it, in the way that
makes most sense to them.

Chapter 6 Summary

How does Strategy 6 help you *read from the inside out?*

When you **find main ideas,** you improve your comprehension of the
reading outside—the writer's ideas. The strategy helps you see the writer's
overall point and recognize the ideas that support it. **Marking** those ideas
brings them back inside to use for your own purposes.

How does the *find and mark main ideas* strategy work?

You use your overall-point question from your **overview** to guide you in
finding main ideas. As you read, you look for the overall point and main ideas
as answers to your question. Often you find the main ideas by identifying a
series of main topics. You also look for supporting ideas that explain each
main idea. You mark these ideas according to a system that works for you.
Here are the five steps for Strategy 6.

STRATEGY 6: FIND AND MARK MAIN IDEAS

1 Read with a pen or pencil in your hand.

2 Find the overall point and the main topics.

3 Find the main idea about each topic.

4 Look for supporting ideas.

5 Adjust your marking.

Are you familiar with the meaning of these terms?

annotating: writing notes in the margin to supplement underlining

review: go over again to study and remember

support: the information used to explain or clarify the overall point or a main idea

topic: what a main part of a reading is about

main idea: general idea about a topic; it supports the overall point

supporting idea: more specific idea that supports a main idea

general: refers to a large category that includes several items (for example, fruit)

specific: refers to a particular type or part within the larger category (for example, type of fruit, including bananas, grapes, apples)

How is the strategy working for you so far?

1. How successful have you been in dividing a reading into main topics that relate to the writer's overall point?

2. Are you able to find the main idea for a topic? Can you find supporting ideas for a main idea? If not, what more do you need to know to make these steps work better for you?

3. How well has marking ideas worked for you? Does your marking make sense on its own? If not, what can you do to make it work better?

4. Have you tried this strategy for readings in other courses, especially for textbook reading? If so, how well did it work? If not, in what courses could you imagine using it?

5. What did you appreciate about using this strategy? What did you dislike?

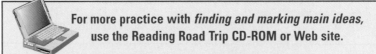

For more practice with *finding and marking main ideas*, use the Reading Road Trip CD-ROM or Web site.

TIME OUT FOR YOU

WHAT WAYS OF MARKING TEXTBOOKS WORK BEST FOR YOU?

Have you ever bought a used textbook that's all marked up? Did the marking help or hinder your own reading and study of it? If you haven't developed your own system, take some time now to do so. Here are some suggestions.

- *Underline ideas with pencil or pen.* Either a pencil or pen can be a good all-round tool for underlining and annotating, writing brief notes in the margins. Pencil is good for first attempts, but pen makes a clearer record.

- *Highlight ideas.* A highlighter gives a clear record of ideas, but use a soft shade so you can read the words, and *think* before you highlight. Once the ideas are in yellow or pink, they'll stand out whether you want them to or not.

- *Use symbols, color, and numbers.*
  1. *Circle* a word or phrase to make it stand out from other underlining.
  2. Use *arrows* to show the relationship between ideas.
  3. Use an *asterisk* (*) beside the overall point of a reading.
  4. Use a different *colored highlighter* or *pen* to indicate the overall point or other special information.
  5. *Number* details to remind you how many there are and to help you remember them.

- *Use abbreviations for your annotations.* Abbreviations can save time and space. Use some common ones, listed in the margin, or make up your own.

Find your favorite tools and systems and use them sensibly. Don't get so involved in marking that you forget to read!

Keep in mind that your marking and annotating should make sense on its own. Don't overmark. Select just enough information so you can use it later without rereading the material.

Some Commonly Used Abbreviations

ex = example
reas = reasons
def = definition
intro = introduction
diffs = differences
amt = amount
et al. = Latin for "and others"
info = information
co = company
vs = versus
# = number
< less than
> more than
= equals

Mark the overall point of the reading and the main ideas, along with some supporting ideas. You may want to mark headings, but because they're already marked (that is, highlighted), you can leave them as is. It's often clearer to mark key phrases rather than whole sentences. The marking then becomes like good notes, leaving out unnecessary words. Also consider the type of writing and your purpose in reading. You will certainly need to mark more details in a biology textbook than in a short story.

CHAPTER

7

SHARPEN YOUR FOCUS: LOOK FOR PATTERNS OF THOUGHT

Get an overview and ask questions work along with Strategy 6, Find and Mark Main Ideas, to help you become involved with the reading and to find and comprehend the writer's main ideas. Strategy 7, Look for Patterns of Thought, will make these strategies even easier to use. You can then respond to the ideas more fully.

Try the New Strategy: Look for Patterns of Thought

Patterns of thought are structures our minds use all the time. All of our thinking and communicating depend on such patterns as *reasons* ("I was late because my car broke down") or *comparisons* ("I had the same problems with my last car!"). Recognizing these familiar patterns as you read helps you comprehend the writer's overall point and the purpose of the main ideas.

STRATEGY 7: LOOK FOR PATTERNS OF THOUGHT

1 Be alert to common patterns of thought.

2 Connect these patterns to the overall point and main ideas.

3 Watch for signal words and phrases.

Before reading "Optimism: The Great Motivator," Reading 12, learn to recognize common patterns of thought in passages from readings in Part III.

Five Common Patterns

1 *Be alert to common patterns of thought.*

You have already seen how the patterns of *examples, contrast,* and *definition* help you get the meaning of a word from the context. They can also help you understand the writer's meaning in a reading as a whole. Two other common patterns of thought are *cause-and-effect reasoning* and *sequence*.

Signal words and phrases for examples

for example, e.g., to illustrate, for instance, to be specific, that is to say, namely

Examples. Examples show specific cases or instances of a general idea. The pattern of examples makes a general idea easier to understand by connecting it to specifics. See how it is used in this passage from Reading 10, "How the Self-Concept Develops."

> We learn who we are by communicating with others, receiving their feedback, making sense out of it, and internalizing or rejecting all or part of it, such that we are altered by the experience. For example, probably someone in your life has told you that you have a good sense of humor. But think about it for a moment: How would you know if you're funny if it were not for others laughing at humorous things you say or do?

Even without the signal phrase "for example," you can pick out the examples pattern here. The first sentence gives the general idea about the influence of others' views on our self-concept. The second sentence shows you just one specific case to demonstrate that general idea.

Try picking out the examples in the following passage from "How Conscious Is Thought?" (Reading 13).

> The mindless processing of information has benefits: If we stopped to think twice about everything we did, we would get nothing done ("I'm reaching for my toothbrush; now I'm putting toothpaste on it; now I'm brushing my upper-right molars"). But mindlessness can also lead to errors and mishaps, ranging from the trivial (putting the butter in the dishwasher or locking yourself out of your apartment) to the serious (driving carelessly while on "automatic pilot").

In this case, the examples, all located within the parentheses, show specific instances of mindlessness.

Often a single, longer example—sometimes called an *illustration*—is used to demonstrate a general statement. Look for the extended example in this passage from Reading 10, "How the Self-Concept Develops." State it in your own words.

> Haven't you met people whom you just wished you could hand a decent self-concept? They're nice people, but they seem to suffer from a self-concept formed out of years of criticism from important others. We recall the story of one colleague who was quite an accomplished dancer as an undergraduate. She'd known an upbringing of never being quite good enough, never being able to please her demanding mother, hard as

she tried. She remembered one particular dance recital, where she felt she had danced the performance of her life. She just knew her mother would be proud, but when her mother joined her backstage after the performance, amidst the accolades of her friends, her mother had only one thing to say: She pointed out the moment in the dance when the woman's arm should have been straight up instead of out to the side. That's all the feedback she got from her mother—stinging criticism about one brief moment in a brilliant evening's worth of performance.

Signal words and phrases for comparison/contrast

For comparison: as, like, similarly, in a similar way, in like manner

For contrast: but, yet, however, nevertheless, nonetheless, while, whereas, on the other hand, in contrast to, contrary to, although

Comparison/contrast. *To compare* (to give similarities) and *to contrast* (to give differences) may be seen as separate patterns. But they often work together.

In "Why Men Don't Last: Self-Destruction as a Way of Life" (Reading 15), Natalie Angier finds a striking *contrast* in the ways that men and women deal with depression and suicidal thoughts.

By standard measures, men have less than half the rate of depression seen in women. When men do feel depressed, they tend to seek distraction in an activity, which, many psychologists say, can be a more effective technique for dispelling the mood than is a depressed woman's tendency to turn inward and ruminate. In the United States and many other industrialized nations, women are about three times more likely than men to express suicidal thoughts or to attempt to kill themselves.

Mark the supporting details in this paragraph that show the contrast between men's and women's ways of dealing with depression.

Now read the paragraph that follows:

And yet . . . men don't last. They die off in greater numbers than women do at every stage of life, and thus their average life span is seven years shorter. Women may attempt suicide relatively more often, but in the United States, four times more men than women die from the act each year.

Mark the supporting details in this paragraph. Did you take note of all these details?

Men	Women
less than half the rate of depression reported in women	more than half the rate of depression reported in men
when depressed seek *distraction in activity*	when depressed turn *inward and think;* more likely to feel suicidal and attempt suicide
life span seven years shorter	life span seven years longer
four times more likely to succeed in killing themselves	attempt suicide more often, but less likely to succeed

Definition and classification. Definition explains the meaning of a word or idea. Writers give a longer, more detailed definition of a word when they want to introduce a new term or to reexamine the meaning of a word. Definition often includes *classification,* a pattern that shows how a word or idea belongs as one type within a larger category. In the following passage, for example, the definition includes classifying *optimism* as one type within the category of *attitudes.* Extended definitions also use comparison/contrast, examples, and further explanation.

Paragraph 3 of "Optimism: The Great Motivator," Reading 12, is an extended definition of optimism.

> Optimism, like hope, means having a strong expectation that, in general, things will turn out all right in life, despite setbacks and frustrations. From the standpoint of emotional intelligence, optimism is an attitude that buffers people against falling into apathy, hopelessness, or depression in the face of tough going. And, as with hope, its near cousin, optimism pays dividends in life (providing, of course, it is a realistic optimism; a too-naive optimism can be disastrous).

This definition says what the word means (in the first sentence). After classifying the word, the definition gives the word's special characteristics (what kind of attitude it is). Finally, optimism is compared to hope, "its near cousin."

Cause-and-effect reasoning. Cause-and-effect reasoning gives logical reasons that answer why or how. A *cause* is the reason for something happening; an *effect* is the result or outcome.

You can see how this pattern works in paragraph 8 from "Optimism: The Great Motivator."

> Just why optimism makes such a difference in sales success speaks to the sense in which it is an emotionally intelligent attitude. Each no a salesman gets is a small defeat. The emotional reaction to that defeat is crucial to the ability to marshal enough motivation to continue. As the noes mount up, morale can deteriorate, making it harder and harder to pick up the phone for the next call. Such rejection is especially hard to take for a pessimist, who interprets it as meaning, "I'm a failure at this; I'll never make a sale"—an interpretation that is sure to trigger apathy and defeatism, if not depression.

The paragraph answers the question *why* optimism makes such a difference in sales success. It begins by showing the cause of emotional difficulty, the rejection that is an inevitable part of sales work.

Mark the phrases that show the general effects of rejection. Then mark the phrases that show the specific effects of rejection on a pessimist.

Now take a look at the rest of the paragraph:

> Optimists, on the other hand, tell themselves, "I'm using the wrong approach," or "That last person was just in a bad mood." By seeing not

themselves but something in the situation as the reason for their failure, they can change their approach in the next call. While the pessimist's mental set leads to despair, the optimist's spawns hope.

Mark the phrases that show the specific effects of rejection on an optimist. Note the way the pattern of comparison/contrast is used in this passage, along with cause-and-effect reasoning.

See the summary of the passage below.

Cause	Effect on optimists	Effect on pessimists	Main idea (results)
Rejection	Look at specific situation as reason for failure	Look at themselves as failures	Optimists have much more success in making sales
	Reevaluate their approach	Become defeated, depressed	

Sequence. The *sequence* pattern is used to give details in a certain order. The sequence or order of details matters when telling stories, giving the history of events, explaining how something works (how plants turn sunlight into food, for example), or giving instructions where one step must be completed before beginning the next.

Look at these instructions from Reading III-A, "Stress Management and Wellness," for doing progressive relaxation:

> With *progressive relaxation,* you first tense a muscle group for 10 seconds, all the while paying attention to the sensations that are created. Then relax that muscle, paying attention to that sensation.

Notice that the sequence is important: you first tense the muscle group, then pay attention to the sensations created, and then relax it, and again pay attention to the sensation.

Frequently items in a sequence are numbered. If not, you might add your own numbers to make the items easier to remember.

Patterns and the Overall Point

As you **get an overview**, see if the title, headings, or other cues from skimming suggest patterns that can help you understand the writer's overall point. Then, as you read, look again for patterns that add to your understanding of the overall point.

Titles. The title of Reading 11, "School Is Bad for Children," tells you to expect cause-and-effect reasoning about the bad effects of school on children. The title of Reading 7, "The Good Person," in contrast, suggests the writer will define what it is to be a good person or give you an example of someone who is good.

Headings. What can you learn from the first two headings of Reading III-A, "Stress Management and Wellness": (1) "Stress-Related Concepts" and (2) "A Model of Stress"? Both headings suggest a pattern of definition—the first defining what these concepts are, the second adding to the definition by using a model.

Skimming. The title of Reading 15, "Why Men Don't Last," suggests the pattern of cause-and-effect reasoning (why don't they last?). Skimming confirms that overall pattern, but shows a second major pattern—the contrast between men and women—as part of the writer's overall point about men.

Patterns and Main Ideas

Patterns can often help you **find and mark main ideas.** Be especially watchful for patterns during some of the steps from Strategy 6.

Grouping the reading into topics. Look for patterns as you divide the reading into topics that relate to the overall point. The title of Reading 10, "How the Self-Concept Develops," gives us our overall-point question: "How *does* it develop?" The question implies the cause-and-effect reasoning pattern. And each of the four topics (revealed in the headings) refers to one cause for our self-concept developing in a certain way.

Finding main ideas about the topic. Look for patterns as you **find and mark main ideas** about the topic. For example, the first topic of the same reading continues the pattern: it shows the *effect* on us of communicating with others. The main idea sentence (sentence 3) gives a general statement of these effects.

Finding supporting ideas about a main idea. Look for patterns as you mark important supporting ideas related to a main idea. The main idea of the last topic, "Self-Labels," is one more in the pattern of cause and effect: the effect of our own attitudes, beliefs, values, and actions. However, definition is another helpful pattern in pointing out the new term, *self-reflexiveness.*

Do look for patterns when you're stuck on a difficult paragraph. The pattern of examples is especially helpful for clarifying a hard topic. But don't apply the strategy rigidly. Not all readings, not even all paragraphs, fall neatly into one pattern. Instead, you'll often find combinations of patterns.

Signal Words and Phrases

3 *Watch for signal words and phrases.*

Signals for patterns. Signal words and phrases are listed with each pattern in the margins. Get used to picking up these signals.

Signal Words and Phrases for Transitions

For clarification: clearly, in fact, certainly, obviously, without a doubt, of course

For addition of more information: in addition, also, as well as, finally, furthermore, moreover, besides, what's more

For summary: in brief, in short, in conclusion, to sum up, to summarize, on the whole

For location (order of things in space): above, below, next to, opposite, within, elsewhere, beyond, close by, adjacent to

Signals for transitions. Writers often signal a change in topic with a *transition* word or phrase that serves as a link or bridge from one thought to the next. Sometimes these are the same words and phrases that signal the five common patterns. Or they may signal *clarification, additional* information, *summary,* or *location* (the order of things in space).

When you read "Optimism: The Great Motivator," you will find several examples of signal words and phrases. Try to identify as many examples as you can, and notice how they're used.

Try looking for patterns of thought as you determine the overall point and find main ideas. You've already seen the pattern of definition and cause-and-effect reasoning in passages from this reading. See if the title suggests an overall pattern. Then skim the reading to see what other patterns you recognize. Let these patterns help you identify the topics of the reading.

READING 12   OPTIMISM: THE GREAT MOTIVATOR

DANIEL GOLEMAN

STRATEGY 1: CHECK IN

STRATEGY 4: GET AN OVERVIEW

STRATEGY 5: ASK QUESTIONS

STRATEGY 6: FIND AND MARK MAIN IDEAS
Use patterns to help you mark main ideas.

Daniel Goleman is a professor of psychology at Harvard University. This reading comes from his book Emotional Intelligence: Why It Can Matter More Than IQ *(1995). Emotional intelligence, according to Goleman, means our ability to respond emotionally in appropriate, productive ways to life's challenges.*

Americans who follow swimming had high hopes for Matt Biondi, a member of the U.S. Olympic Team in 1988. Some sportswriters were touting Biondi as likely to match Mark Spitz's 1972 feat of taking seven gold medals. But Biondi finished a heartbreaking third in his first event, the 200-meter freestyle. In his next event, the 100-meter butterfly, Biondi was inched out for the gold by another swimmer who made a greater effort in the last meter.   1

Sportscasters speculated that the defeats would dispirit Biondi in his successive events. But Biondi rebounded from defeat and took a gold medal in his next five events. One viewer who was not surprised by Biondi's comeback was Martin Seligman, a psychologist at the University of Pennsylvania, who had tested Biondi for optimism earlier that year. In an experiment done with Seligman, the swimming coach told Biondi during a special event meant to showcase Biondi's best performance that he had a worse time than was actually the case. Despite the downbeat feedback, when Biondi was asked to rest and try again, his performance—actually already very good—was even better. But when other team members who were given a false bad time—and whose test scores showed they were pessimistic—tried again, they did even worse the second time.[1]   2

Optimism, like hope, means having a strong expectation that, in general, things will turn out all right in life, despite setbacks and frustrations. From the standpoint of emotional intelligence, optimism is an attitude that   3 buffers people against falling into apathy, hopelessness, or depression in the face of tough going. And, as with hope, its near cousin, optimism pays dividends in life (providing, of course, it is a realistic optimism; a too-naïve optimism can be disastrous).[2]

Seligman defines optimism in terms of how people explain to them- 4 selves their successes and failures. People who are optimistic see a failure as due to something that can be changed so that they can succeed next time around, while pessimists take the blame for failure, ascribing it to some lasting characteristic they are helpless to change. These differing explanations have profound implications for how people respond to life. For example, in reaction to a disappointment such as being turned down for a job, optimists tend to respond actively and hopefully, by formulating a plan of action, say, or seeking out help and advice; they see the setback as something that can be remedied. Pessimists, by contrast, react to such setbacks by assuming there is nothing they can do to make things go better the next time, and so do nothing about the problem; they see the setback as due to some personal deficit that will always plague them.

As with hope, optimism predicts academic success. In a study of five 5 hundred members of the incoming freshman class of 1984 at the University of Pennsylvania, the students' scores on a test of optimism were a better predictor of their actual grades freshman year than were their SAT scores or their high-school grades. Said Seligman, who studied them, "College entrance exams measure talent, while explanatory style° tells you who gives up. It is the combination of reasonable talent and the ability to keep going in the face of defeat that leads to success. What's missing in tests of ability is motivation. What you need to know about someone is whether they will keep going when things get frustrating. My hunch is that for a given level of intelligence, your actual achievement is a function not just of talent, but also of the capacity to stand defeat."[3]

explanatory style: way of explaining successes or failures.

One of the most telling demonstrations of the power of optimism to 6 motivate people is a study Seligman did of insurance salesmen with the MetLife company. Being able to take a rejection with grace is essential in sales of all kinds, especially with a product like insurance, where the ratio of noes to yeses can be so discouragingly high. For this reason, about three quarters of insurance salesmen quit in their first three years. Seligman found that new salesmen who were by nature optimists sold 37 percent more insurance in their first two years on the job than did pessimists. And during the first year the pessimists quit at twice the rate of the optimists.

What's more, Seligman persuaded MetLife to hire a special group of 7 applicants who scored high on a test for optimism but failed the normal screening tests (which compared a range of their attitudes to a standard profile based on answers from agents who have been successful). This special group outsold the pessimists by 21 percent in their first year, and 57 percent in the second.

Just why optimism makes such a difference in sales success speaks to the sense in which it is an emotionally intelligent attitude. Each no a salesperson gets is a small defeat. The emotional reaction to that defeat is crucial to the ability to marshal enough motivation to continue. As the noes mount up, morale can deteriorate, making it harder and harder to pick up the phone for the next call. Such rejection is especially hard to take for a pessimist, who interprets it as meaning, "I'm a failure at this; I'll never make a sale"—an interpretation that is sure to trigger apathy and defeatism, if not depression. Optimists, on the other hand, tell themselves, "I'm using the wrong approach," or "That last person was just in a bad mood." By seeing not themselves but something in the situation as the reason for their failure, they can change their approach in the next call. While the pessimist's mental set leads to despair, the optimist's spawns hope.   8

One source of a positive or negative outlook may well be inborn temperament; some people by nature tend one way or the other. But . . . temperament can be tempered by experience. Optimism and hope—like helplessness and despair—can be learned. Underlying both is an outlook psychologists call *self-efficacy,* the belief that one has mastery over the events of one's life and can meet challenges as they come up. Developing a competency of any kind strengthens the sense of self-efficacy, making a person more willing to take risks and seek out more demanding challenges. And surmounting those challenges in turn increases the sense of self-efficacy. This attitude makes people more likely to make the best use of whatever skills they may have—or to do what it takes to develop them.   9

Albert Bandura, a Stanford psychologist who has done much of the research on self-efficacy, sums it up well: "People's beliefs about their abilities have a profound effect on those abilities. Ability is not a fixed property; there is a huge variability in how you perform. People who have a sense of self-efficacy bounce back from failures; they approach things in terms of how to handle them rather than worrying about what can go wrong."[4]   10

Notes

1. Optimistic swimmers: Martin Seligman, *Learned Optimism* (New York: Knopf, 1991).
2. A realistic vs. naive optimism: see, for example, Carol Whalen et al., "Optimism in Children's Judgments of Health and Environmental Risks," *Health Psychology* 13 (1994).
3. I interviewed Martin Seligman about optimism in *The New York Times* (Feb. 3, 1987).
4. I interviewed Albert Bandura about self-efficacy in *The New York Times* (May 8, 1988).

Follow-Up Activities   After you've finished reading, use these questions to respond to "Optimism: The Great Motivator." You may write your answers or prepare them in your mind to discuss in class.

Grab your first impressions.

1. What did you find most surprising in this reading? Why?

2. From your reading so far, has the author convinced you of the value of optimism? Explain your answer.

Work with new words.

Some words in this reading may be unfamiliar to you. Use the methods of Strategy 3 to explain what the listed words mean.

1. Use context clues.

    a. formulating (paragraph 4) _____

    b. surmounting (paragraph 9) _____

2. Use word parts.

    a. dispirit (paragraph 2) _____

    b. apathy (paragraph 3) _____

    c. defeatism (paragraph 8) _____

3. Use the dictionary.
   Choose the correct definition of each word as it is used in the context of this reading.

    a. naïve (paragraph 3) _____

    b. marshal (paragraph 8) _____

    c. tempered (paragraph 9) _____
       (Be sure to get the right part of speech.)

    d. property (paragraph 10) _____

4. Select additional words you're unsure of from the reading. Use one of these methods to discover their meaning.

Ask and answer questions.

1. Why did Biondi rebound from the bad news about his performance, whereas his teammates did not?

2. What did Martin Seligman's study of incoming freshmen at the University of Pennsylvania show about the effects of optimism?

3. What is the meaning of self-efficacy? Why does becoming more competent at anything you do strengthen your self-efficacy?

4. If optimism has such beneficial effects, why would a "too-naïve optimism" be "disastrous"?

 Ask and answer your own question.

Write a question of your own. Share your question with others and collaborate on an answer.

Look for patterns of thought.

Find the sentence or sentences that demonstrate the specific pattern listed for each of these paragraphs. Explain briefly how the pattern is used.

1. Paragraphs 1 and 2 (the introduction): *examples* and *contrast*

_____

2. Paragraph 5: *cause-and-effect reasoning*

_____

3. Paragraph 6: *cause-and-effect reasoning*

_____

4. Paragraph 9: *definition*

_____

Find and mark main ideas.

Use patterns to help you mark main ideas. Compare your marking to the sample on page 172.

 Form your final thoughts.

1. How would you classify your explanatory style? Is it basically optimistic or pessimistic? Discuss with other students what they think about their explanatory style.

2. Goleman says that people's temperament can be modified (paragraph 9). Do you agree or disagree? How much change could you see taking place in your basic sense of optimism or pessimism? ■

An annotated version of Reading 12, "Optimism: The Great Motivator," follows. Notice how patterns are used to help define the main ideas in the reading.

SAMPLE MARKING   **OPTIMISM: THE GREAT MOTIVATOR**

Intro —
Ex: optimism's
effects

Americans who follow swimming had high hopes for Matt Biondi, a   1
member of the U.S. Olympic Team in 1988. Some sportswriters were touting
Biondi as likely to match Mark Spitz's 1972 feat of taking seven gold medals.
But Biondi finished a heartbreaking third in his first event, the 200-meter
freestyle. In his next event, the 100-meter butterfly, Biondi was inched out
for the gold by another swimmer who made a greater effort in the last meter.

Sportscasters speculated that the defeats would dispirit Biondi in his   2
successive events. But Biondi rebounded from defeat and took a gold
medal in his next five events. One viewer who was not surprised by
Biondi's comeback was Martin Seligman, a psychologist at the University
of Pennsylvania, who had tested Biondi for optimism earlier that year. In an
experiment done with Seligman, the swimming coach told Biondi during a
special event meant to showcase Biondi's best performance that he had a
worse time than was actually the case. Despite the downbeat feedback,
when Biondi was asked to rest and try again, his performance—actually
already very good—was even better. (But) when other team members who
were given a false bad time—and whose test scores showed they were
pessimistic—tried again, they did even worse the second time.[1]

Def.

Optimism, like hope, means having a strong expectation that, in gen-   3
eral, things will turn out all right in life, despite setbacks and frustrations.
From the standpoint of emotional intelligence, optimism is an attitude that
buffers people against falling into apathy, hopelessness, or depression in
the face of tough going. And, as with hope, its near cousin, optimism pays
dividends in life (providing, of course, it is a realistic optimism; a too-naïve
optimism can be disastrous).[2]

optimists
vs.
pessimists

Seligman defines optimism in terms of how people explain to them-   4
selves their successes and failures. People who are optimistic see a failure
as due to something that can be changed so that they can succeed next
time around, (while) pessimists take the blame for failure, ascribing it to
some lasting characteristic they are helpless to change. These differing
explanations have profound implications for how people respond to life.

Ex. of contrast
& effects

For example, in reaction to a disappointment such as being turned down
for a job, optimists tend to respond actively and hopefully, by formulating
a plan of action, say, or seeking out help and advice; they see the setback
as something that can be remedied. Pessimists, by contrast, react to such
setbacks by assuming there is nothing they can do to make things go better
the next time, and so do nothing about the problem; they see the setback
as due to some personal deficit that will always plague them.

As with hope, optimism predicts academic success. In a study of five   5
hundred members of the incoming freshman class of 1984 at the University

acad. success = reas. talent + "keep going" after defeat

of Pennsylvania, the students' <u>scores on a test of optimism</u> were a <u>better predictor</u> of their actual grades freshman year <u>than were their SAT scores</u> or their <u>high-school grades</u>. Said Seligman, who studied them, "College entrance exams measure talent, while explanatory style tells you who gives up. It is the <u>combination of reasonable talent</u> and the <u>ability to keep going in the face of defeat</u> that <u>leads to success</u>. What's missing in tests of ability is ⬭motivation⬭ What you need to know about someone is whether they will keep going when things get frustrating. My hunch is that for a given level of intelligence, your actual achievement is a function not just of talent, but also of the capacity to stand defeat."[3]

Ex: optimism's effects

One of the most telling demonstrations of the power of optimism to motivate people is a study <u>Seligman did of insurance salesmen</u> with the MetLife company. Being <u>able to take a rejection</u> with grace is <u>essential in sales</u> of all kinds, especially with a product like insurance, where the ratio of noes to yeses can be so discouragingly high. For this reason, about three quarters of insurance salesmen quit in their first three years. Seligman found that new salesmen who were by nature <u>optimists sold 37 percent more insurance</u> in their first two years on the job than did pessimists. And during the first year the <u>pessimists quit at twice the rate of the optimists</u>.   6

success even w. failed test

What's more, Seligman persuaded MetLife to hire a <u>special group of applicants</u> who scored <u>high on a test for optimism</u> but <u>failed the normal screening tests</u> (which compared a range of their attitudes to a standard profile based on answers from agents who have been successful). This <u>special group outsold the pessimists</u> by 21 percent in their first year, and 57 percent in the second.   7

why?

Just <u>why optimism makes such a difference in sales success speaks to the sense</u> in which it is <u>an emotionally intelligent attitude</u>. Each no a sales-person gets is a small defeat. The emotional reaction to that defeat is cru-cial to the ability to marshal enough motivation to continue. As the <u>noes mount up, morale can deteriorate</u>, making it harder and harder to pick up the phone for the next call. Such rejection is especially hard to take for a   8

rejection: pessimists ⟶

optimists ⤵

pessimist, who interprets it as meaning, "I'm a <u>failure at this; I'll never make a sale</u>"—an interpretation that is sure to trigger <u>apathy and defeatism, if not depression</u>. Optimists, on the other hand, tell themselves, "I'm using the wrong approach," or "That last person was just in a bad mood." <u>By seeing</u> ⬭not⬭<u>themselves but something in the situation</u> as the <u>reason for their failure</u>, they can ⬭change their approach⬭ in the next call. While the pessimist's mental set leads to despair, the optimist's spawns hope.

One source of a positive or negative outlook may well be inborn tem-perament; some people by nature tend one way or the other. But . . . tem-perament can be tempered by experience. ⬭Optimism⬭ and hope—like helplessness and despair—<u>can be learned</u>. Underlying both is an outlook   9

*overall point
Def. (+ effects)
based on belief
you have control &
can bounce back

psychologists call *self-efficacy,* the belief that one has mastery over the events of one's life and <u>can meet challenges as they come up</u>. Developing a competency of any kind strengthens the sense of self-efficacy, making a person more willing to take risks and seek out more demanding challenges. And surmounting those challenges in turn increases the sense of self-efficacy. This attitude makes people more likely to make the best use of whatever skills they may have—or to do what it takes to develop them.

Albert Bandura, a Stanford psychologist who has done much of the   10
research on self-efficacy, sums it up well: "People's <u>beliefs about their abilities</u> have a <u>profound effect</u> on those abilities. <u>Ability is not a fixed property</u>; there is a <u>huge variability</u> in how you perform. People who have a sense of self-efficacy bounce back from failures; they approach things in terms of how to handle them rather than worrying about what can go wrong."[4]

Apply the New Strategy: Look for Patterns of Thought

Now that you understand Strategy 7, put it into practice with Reading 13, "How Conscious Is Thought?" (or with one of the Additional Readings in Part III, selected by your instructor). Try using patterns along with all the appropriate strategies for getting started. Then, as you read, use patterns for finding main ideas.

| READING 13 | ## HOW CONSCIOUS IS THOUGHT? |

CAROLE WADE AND CAROL TAVRIS

STRATEGY 1: CHECK IN

STRATEGY 4: GET AN
OVERVIEW

STRATEGY 5: ASK
QUESTIONS

STRATEGY 6: FIND AND
MARK MAIN IDEAS

Carole Wade is a professor of psychology at Dominican College in California. Carol Tavris is author of The Mismeasure of Woman *and has co-authored several books with Carole Wade, including* Psychology *(2000), the textbook from which this reading comes. In this excerpt from their chapter on thinking and intelligence, the authors discuss how our minds work even when we are not actually aware of thinking.*

When we think about thinking, we usually have in mind those mental   1
activities, such as solving problems or making decisions, that are carried out in a deliberate way with a conscious goal in mind. However, a great deal of mental processing occurs without conscious awareness.

SUBCONSCIOUS AND NONCONSCIOUS THINKING

Subconscious processes lie outside of awareness but can be brought   2
into consciousness when necessary. These processes allow us to handle

Some well-learned tasks do not require much conscious thought, so this mother is able to do several things at once. There's even a word for this now: "multi-tasking."

more information and to perform more complex tasks than if we depended entirely on conscious thought, and they enable us to perform more than one task simultaneously (Kahneman & Treisman, 1984). Consider all the automatic routines performed "without thinking," though they might once have required careful, conscious attention: knitting, typing, driving a car, decoding the letters in a word in order to read it. Because of the capacity for automatic processing, people can, with proper training, even learn to perform simultaneously such complex tasks as reading and taking dictation (Hirst, Neisser, & Spelke, 1978).

Nonconscious processes, in contrast, remain outside of awareness. For example, you have no doubt had the odd experience of having a solution to a problem "pop into mind" after you have given up trying to find one. With sudden insight, you see how to solve an equation, assemble a cabinet, or finish a puzzle, without quite knowing how you managed to find the solution. Similarly, people will often say they rely on "intuition"—hunches and gut feelings—rather than conscious reasoning to make decisions.   3

Insight and intuition probably involve two stages of mental processing (Bowers et al., 1990). In the first stage, clues in the problem automatically activate certain memories or knowledge, and you begin to see a pattern or structure in the problem, although you cannot yet say what it is. This non-conscious process guides you toward a hunch or a hypothesis. Then, in the second stage, your thinking becomes conscious, and you become aware of a possible solution. This stage may feel like a sudden revelation ("Aha, I've got it!"), but considerable nonconscious mental work has already occurred.   4

Imagine that you are given four decks of cards and are told that you   5
will win or lose money depending on which cards you turn over. Unbe-
knownst to you, two of the decks are stacked so that they will produce pay-
offs at first but will make you lose in the long run, whereas the other two
pay less at first but cause you to win in the long run. Every so often,
someone stops you and asks whether you have figured out the best
strategy for winning. Most people, when presented with this problem, start
to show physiological signs of anxiety before picking cards from the losing
decks and begin avoiding those decks *before* they consciously realize
which decks are riskier. And some learn to make good choices without *ever*
consciously discovering the rules for winning. Interestingly, people with
damage in part of the prefrontal cortex° have trouble learning that two of
the decks are stacked against them; they seem to lack the sort of intuition
that most people take for granted (Bechara et al., 1997).

prefrontal cortex: location
of subconscious thinking
in the brain.

MINDLESSNESS

Usually, of course, much of our thinking is conscious, but we may not   6
be thinking very *hard. . . .* We may act, speak, and make decisions out of
habit, without stopping to analyze what we are doing or why we are doing
it. This sort of mental inertia, which Ellen Langer (1989) has called *mindlessness,* keeps people from recognizing when a change in context requires
a change in behavior.

In one study by Langer and her associates, a researcher approached   7
people as they were about to use a photocopier and made one of three
requests: "Excuse me, may I use the Xerox machine?" "Excuse me, may I
use the Xerox machine, because I have to make copies?" or "Excuse me,
may I use the Xerox machine, because I'm in a rush?" Normally, people will
let someone go before them only if the person has a legitimate reason, as
in the third request. In this study, however, people also complied when the
reason sounded like an authentic explanation but was actually meaningless
("because I have to make copies"). They heard the form of the request, but
not its content, and they mindlessly stepped aside (Langer, Blank, &
Chanowitz, 1978).

The mindless processing of information has benefits: If we stopped to   8
think twice about everything we did, we would get nothing done ("I'm
reaching for my toothbrush; now I'm putting toothpaste on it; now I'm
brushing my upper-right molars"). But mindlessness can also lead to errors
and mishaps, ranging from the trivial (putting the butter in the dishwasher
or locking yourself out of your apartment) to the serious (driving carelessly
while on "automatic pilot").

Jerome Kagan (1989) has argued that fully conscious awareness is   9
needed only when we must make a deliberate choice, when events happen
that cannot be handled automatically, and when unexpected moods and
feelings arise. "Consciousness," he says, "can be likened to the staff of a fire
department. Most of the time, it is quietly playing pinochle° in the back
room; it performs [only] when the alarm sounds." That may be so, but most
of us would probably benefit if our mental firefighters paid a little more
attention to their jobs. Cognitive psychologists have, therefore, devoted a
great deal of study to mindful, conscious thought and the capacity to reason.

pinochle: a card game.

References

Bechara, A., et al. (1997). Deciding advantageously before knowing the
    advantageous strategy. *Science, 275,* 1293–1294.

Bowers, K. S., et al. (1990). Intuition in the context of discovery. *Cognitive
    Psychology, 22,* 72–110.

Hirst, W., Nesser, U., & Spelke, E. (1978, January). Divided attention. *Human
    Nature, 1,* 54–61.

Kagan, J. (1989). *The nature of the child.* New York: Basic Books.

Kahneman, D., & Treisman, A. (1984). Changing views of attention and auto-
    maticity. In R. Parasuraman, D. R. Davies, and J. Beatty (eds.), *Varieties
    of attention.* New York: Academic Books.

Langer, E. J. (1989). *Mindfulness.* Reading, MA: Addison Wesley.

Langer, E. J., Blank, A., & Chanowitz, B. (1978). The mindfulness of osten-
    sibly thoughtful action: The role of placebic information in interpersonal
    interaction. *Journal of Personality and Social Psychology, 36,* 635–642.

Follow-Up Activities   After you've finished reading, use these questions to
respond to "How Conscious Is Thought?" You may write your answers or prepare them in your mind to discuss in class.

Grab your first impressions.

1. What parts of this reading did you like? What parts did you dislike?

2. What are some of the activities you do that have become automatic routines? When do you become aware that you are doing them?

Work with new words.

Some words in this reading may be unfamiliar to you. Use the methods
of Strategy 3 to explain what the listed words mean.

1. Use context clues.

   a. intuition (paragraph 3) _____

   b. inertia (paragraph 6) _____

2. Use word parts.

   a. multi-tasking (caption on page 175) _____

   b. hypothesis (paragraph 4) _____
      If *thesis* means "theory or proposition," how does the prefix *hypo* modify that meaning? Note that this is *hypo,* not *hyper.*

   c. revelation (paragraph 4) _____
      Use the familiar verb form of this word—*reveal*—to remember it.

3. Use the dictionary.

   cognitive (paragraph 9) _____
   Based on the context, what is the correct definition of this word?

4. Select additional words you're unsure of from the reading. Use one of these methods to discover their meaning.

Ask and answer questions.

1. What is the basic difference between subconscious and nonconscious processes?

2. What is multi-tasking? Why is the concept introduced in this section on subconscious thought?

3. What stages does the mind go through when we have an insight or an intuition? Describe each stage in your own words.

4. What problems are caused by the "mental inertia" that Ellen Langer calls *mindlessness?*

 Ask and answer your own question.

Write a question of your own. Share your question with others and collaborate on an answer.

 Form your final thoughts.

1. In which of your courses are you most apt to use insight or intuition? How might your knowledge of the two-stage mental process help you study better?

2. What activities do you do "mindlessly" that you might need to become more aware of? What activities would you like to do more automatically? Discuss with others what you would need to make these modifications.

■

Chapter 7 Summary

How does Strategy 7 help you *read from the inside out*?

When you **look for patterns of thought** in a reading, you use your own familiar way of thinking to understand the *outside*—the writer's ideas. Recognizing these common patterns sharpens your focus, so you can more easily find and understand these ideas (see the "Summary Table of Patterns of Thought" on p. 180). You can then bring them *inside*—to think about and examine for your own purposes.

These are the five common patterns of thought.

1. *examples:* show specific cases or instances of a general idea

2. *comparison and contrast:* gives similarities and/or differences

3. *definition and classification:* explains the meaning of a word and shows the category it belongs in

4. *cause-and-effect reasoning:* explains why or how one event brings about another

5. *sequence:* gives events or items in a particular order

How does the *look for patterns of thought* strategy work?

For this strategy you are reminded to look for common patterns of thought. You look for these patterns that help you use other strategies, especially **get an overview** and **find main ideas.** Here are the three steps for Strategy 7.

STRATEGY 7: LOOK FOR PATTERNS OF THOUGHT

1 Be alert to common patterns of thought.

2 Connect these patterns to the overall point and main ideas.

3 Watch for signal words and phrases.

Are you familiar with the meaning of these terms?

patterns of thought: structures we use to think, such as reasons or examples

transition: a word or phrase that serves as a bridge from one thought to another

Summary Table of Patterns of Thought

Note: Numbers in parentheses refer to pages in this chapter where the pattern is discussed.

Pattern	Description	Signal Words
Generalization with examples	Shows specific instances of a general idea. (162)	for example, e.g., to illustrate, for instance, to be specific, that is to say, namely
Comparison	Gives similarities between two or more things. (163)	as, like, similarly, in a similar way, compared with, in like manner
Contrast	Gives differences between two or more things. (163)	but, yet, however, nevertheless, nonetheless, while, whereas, on the other hand, contrary to, although
Definition	Explains the meaning of a word or an idea. (164)	that is, to define this, means Punctuation clues: parentheses, brackets, dashes
Classification	Shows how a word or idea belongs as one type within a larger category. (164)	category, elements of, characteristics, features, types, kinds, parts
Cause-and-effect reasoning	Explains why or how one event brings about another. (164–165)	for this reason, because, to explain, as a result, consequently, hence, therefore, thus, then
Sequence (for time order)	Gives events in the order they took place in time. (165)	first, before, after, afterward, at last, during, now, at that time, since, until, while
Sequence (for listing in a process)	Gives items in the order in which they should be done (165)	first, second, third, next, the next step, further, then, before, after that, finally, last
Location/spatial order	Shows the place where items are found. (167)	above, below, next to, opposite, within, elsewhere, beyond, close by, adjacent to
Statement and clarification	Makes a statement clearer by saying it in other words or discussing it further. (167)	clearly, in fact, certainly, obviously, without a doubt, of course
Addition	Provides more information. (167)	in addition, also, as well as, finally, furthermore, moreover, besides, what's more
Summary	Brief, condensed statement of the previous ideas. (167)	in brief, in short, in conclusion, to sum up, to summarize, on the whole

How is the strategy working for you so far?

1. Which patterns have you found most common and/or easiest to recognize? How helpful were they in finding main ideas or important details?

2. Which patterns have been more difficult to recognize and/or less common? How helpful were they when you did recognize them?

3. At what stage did this strategy work best for you? Before, during, or after reading? Why?

4. What did you appreciate about using this strategy? What did you dislike?

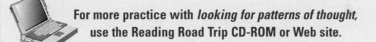

For more practice with *looking for patterns of thought*, use the Reading Road Trip CD-ROM or Web site.

CHAPTER

8

LOOK FOR IMPLIED MEANING:
MAKE INFERENCES

The first two strategies for Part III—**Find and Mark Main Ideas** and **Look for Patterns of Thought**—work together to help you understand the writer's main ideas. But you need more ways of understanding when writers *imply ideas*, that is, suggest meaning rather than stating ideas outright. For example, some titles and headings spell out the main ideas to be covered; others are used to start you thinking on your own. The title of Reading 10, "How the Self-Concept Develops," indicates the overall point, but Reading 9's title, "talking back," implies ideas to let you bring your own associations to the subject. Strategy 8, **Make Inferences**, increases your understanding of a reading by helping you recognize implied ideas.

Try the New Strategy: Make Inferences

In our everyday life we make many well-informed guesses. We see pieces of evidence and put the pieces together. Then we **make an inference,** meaning that we make connections and draw logical conclusions based on evidence. For example, if you saw a young woman on campus wearing paint-stained jeans and carrying a large canvas and paintbrushes, you would probably **make an inference**—or *infer*—that she is on her way to or from an art class. Strategy 8 shows you how to make similar kinds of logical connections as you read.

STRATEGY 8: MAKE INFERENCES

1 Look for what is implied as well as what is stated outright.

2 Use the logic of "putting two and two together."

3 Notice the details.

4 Notice the word choice.

5 Examine your assumptions.

Before reading "A Letter to My Teacher," Reading 14, learn to **make inferences** by looking closely at passages from that reading. In these passages, watch for unstated as well as stated ideas. Take special note of the details a writer selects to get across an idea without putting it into words.

Inferences and Implied Ideas

1 *Look for what is implied as well as what is stated outright.*

Read this sentence: "When their friend crashed his car into a tree, nearly killing himself and his passengers, the students made a pact that they would always have a designated driver when they went to a party."

To get the full meaning from that sentence, your mind goes beyond the stated message. You don't have to be told the friend had been drinking or that the students expected there would be drinking at other parties. You get that information by putting together the idea of the friend crashing the car and the students' decision to have a designated driver at the next party. The writer *implies*—or suggests—the meaning beyond the words. You, the reader, *infer* it—or **make inferences** about it. When reading, we sometimes use the phrase "reading between the lines" to mean we're inferring the writer's meaning.

Logical Connections

2 *Use the logic of "putting two and two together."*

A common expression for inferring is that we "put two and two together." In other words, we use logic to connect separate pieces of information. In the sample sentence, we made the connection between the friend crashing the car and the drinking that often goes on at parties.

A cartoon is a good way to remind you of the kinds of connections you need to make in order to understand implied ideas. Cartoons are only funny if you make the expected connections. You use logic like this whenever you read the funny pages. To get what's funny, often you need to make a connection between the visual image and what the characters say. For example, to understand the cartoon here, you need to remember that students have always given excuses for not having their homework ready. The most well-known excuse—although it may never actually have been used—is "My dog ate my homework."

"He appears to have eaten some homework."

What inference does the cartoonist expect you to make?

What's unexpected about this diary entry?

Or you make a connection between what is shown and what you already know.

In the above cartoon, what connection can you make between the caption, "Low self-esteem," the diary entry, and the way the writer looks?

Read the following introductory passage from "A Letter to My Teacher." Try "putting two and two together" by seeing how the separate pieces of information add up.

> I didn't belong in college. I should have told you that. My father dropped out of school after third grade. My mother went through twelfth grade, but her family thought she was a little uppity for doing so. Like my mother, I finished high school, and immediately got married and started having babies. A decade and a half later, I was a divorced single parent, working as a babysitter during the day and clerking part-time nights in a food store. My income fell far below the poverty level, where I'd lived for much of my life. Statisticians said I didn't belong in college. Who was I to argue?

Find stated and implied ideas.

In this introductory paragraph the author gives a lot of information about herself. Which of these sentences from that paragraph are stated ideas and which are implied? Put *S* for a stated idea and *I* for an implied idea. If an idea is implied, what clues did you use to determine the information?

_____   1. Her father dropped out of school after third grade.

_____   2. She wants to be honest as she explains her background and her experience of college to this professor.

_____ 3. Her mother's family had a low opinion of education past the earlier grades.

_____ 4. Her mother was a role model for her as she grew up.

_____ 5. She got married right after high school.

_____ 6. She had more than one child by the time she was in her early 20s.

_____ 7. She was a divorced single parent.

_____ 8. She had no child support from her ex-husband.

_____ 9. She spent the majority of her time working and taking care of her children.

_____ 10. For much of her life her income was below the poverty level.

_____ 11. Statisticians studying poverty and single parenthood find that very few poor single mothers make it to college.

_____ 12. At the time she describes, she didn't have confidence in her ability to succeed in college.   ■

Details

3 Notice the details.

Pay careful attention to what details the writer includes, as well as what details you might expect but are left out.

What details are included? Ask yourself why a certain piece of information is included. For example, in the introduction to "A Letter to My Teacher," why does the writer tell you about her parents' education? Why are the details about her life immediately following high school included? What do the details about her two jobs imply about what her life is like?

Here is another paragraph from this reading. What do the details that are included imply?

> My stomach began to churn relentlessly at the thought of speaking in front of the class. "How was school today, honey?" my youngest daughter greeted me when I got home, doing a creditable imitation of my usual after-school question to her. But I was already halfway down the hall to the bathroom where I promptly lost my lunch.

Just thinking about an oral presentation made the writer throw up. That detail shows her anxiety was quite serious.

What expected details are left out? Sometimes a detail that might be expected and is *not* included can suggest meaning. For example, notice that the writer does not mention her ex-husband, so we can infer he is not helping raise the children. And we get an added sense of her independence, her sense of responsibility to her kids, as well as her lack of financial resources.

As you read the rest of "A Letter to My Teacher," you will notice other details you might expect that are not there: the writer never mentions difficulties in understanding material or doing assignments. These omissions suggest she had the ability to do well in college. She was meant to go to college after all.

Word Choice

4 Notice the word choice.

Writers choose their words carefully because so many words have special *connotations*, or implied meanings, in addition to their obvious meaning, their *denotation*.

Denotation. A word's explicit, or literal meaning, is called *denotation*, or denotative meaning. Consider the word *drinking*, for example. The first meaning you'd find in the dictionary for that word—its literal definition— would say something about "the act of swallowing liquids." However, when that word is used in other contexts, it has a very different *connotation*. In referring to the friend who had been drinking on page 183, we recognize the connotation of *drinking alcohol*.

Connotation. The cluster of suggestions, implications, or emotional responses that a word carries with it is called *connotation*, or connotative meaning. These connotations may be positive, negative, or specialized in some way. The connotation extends the meaning of the word beyond its denotative meaning.

Some words always carry with them a special connotation. The verb *walk* is purely neutral; its denotative meaning is "to make a forward movement by taking steps." But other words with this same denotative meaning (forward movement) can never be used in a neutral way. Each one of these verb connotes a different kind of walk: *stride, saunter, stroll, meander, glide, lumber, plod, stagger,* and *march*.

Think of the differences in connotation between the following pairs of words, each with the same denotative meaning. Which word in each pair is neutral, and which has a special, usually negative, connotation?

macho	masculine	cheap	economical
frantic	concerned	serious	grim
childish	childlike	snicker	laugh
fragile	flimsy	eat	devour
pushy	aggressive	stubborn	determined

Your Own Assumptions

5 *Examine your assumptions.*

When you make an inference, you are using information you already have to make connections. It usually serves us well to make use of our assumptions as we put clues together. *Assumptions* are ideas we hold based on our previous beliefs and experience; they are ideas we take for granted, that we no longer question. But we need to be careful, since sometimes these assumptions may be proven wrong or not relevant for the present circumstances. For example, the young woman who appeared to be an art student at your college might instead be a young art teacher. Perhaps you assumed too easily that all young people are students.

As you read "A Letter to My Teacher," think about your own assumptions—about poverty, about single mothers. See which of your assumptions were matched by the reading and which, if any, you need to reexamine.

You've already looked for implied ideas in several passages from this reading. As you skim through the reading to predict what the writer's overall point will be, keep in mind the beginning of her letter: she didn't belong in college. Put that idea together with the end of her letter where she writes to say "thanks" and to say she is teaching at a university. What will your overall-point question be?

READING 14   A LETTER TO MY TEACHER

KATE BOYES

Strategy 1: Check In

Kate Boyes lives in Smithfield, Utah. She is the author of a monthly magazine column on living simply, as well as poems and essays. She is also a writer-in-residence in public schools. This reading comes from an anthology called Fortitude: True Stories of True Grit, *published in 2000.*

Strategy 4: Get an Overview

Strategy 5: Ask Questions

Dear Professor,

I didn't belong in college. I should have told you that. My father dropped   1
out of school after third grade. My mother went through twelfth grade, but her family thought she was a little uppity for doing so. Like my mother, I finished high school, and immediately got married and started having babies. A decade and a half later, I was a divorced single parent, working as a babysitter during the day and clerking part-time nights in a food store. My income fell far below the poverty level, where I'd lived for much of my life. Statisticians said I didn't belong in college. Who was I to argue?

Strategy 6: Find and Mark Main Ideas

Strategy 7: Look for Patterns of Thought

But one night when I was emptying the trash at the end of my shift, I   2
noticed a brightly colored catalog in the dumpster behind the store. I fished it out and wiped the ketchup drips off the cover. Flipping through the catalog later, I discovered it listed all the courses available at the local college.

And I discovered something else: Taking only one course would make   3
me eligible for student health insurance. Neither of my jobs included benefits, and every time my kids came down with a cold, I worried about what
would happen to us if we were really sick. I did some careful calculations.
If I took one college course each semester for a year, the cost of tuition,
books and fees would be far lower than even six months of private insurance. My two kids would be covered, too. What a deal!

Becoming a student was a great scheme. But I knew, when I took my   4
first course from you, that I was an imposter.

The very first day of that sociology class, you made an announcement   5
that threatened to expose me. "At the end of the semester, each student
will be required to make an oral presentation," you told us.

My stomach began to churn relentlessly at the thought of speaking in   6
front of the class. "How was school today, honey?" my youngest daughter
greeted me when I got home, doing a creditable imitation of my usual after-
school question to her. But I was already halfway down the hall to the bathroom where I promptly lost my lunch.

Weeks passed before I could sit through class without nausea. I talked   7
myself into going to class each day by telling myself, over and over, that I
was doing this for my kids. I went early to claim the only safe seat—back
row, aisle. Close to the door. Just in case. Back with the whisperers and the
snoozers, behind the tall man who always read the student newspaper
during class, I chewed the fingernails on one hand while I took notes with
the other.

I needed three credits. I didn't need the agony of a presentation. I con-   8
sidered dropping your course and signing up for something else. Anything
else. But I stayed, although I didn't know why. You were new to teaching,
and your lectures certainly weren't polished. You gripped the lectern like a
shield and sometimes your voice died out in the middle of a sentence. But
your enthusiasm for your subject left me longing to know more. I looked
forward to a few quiet hours each week—those rare times when the store
was empty or my little ones were napping—that I spent reading, writing,
and thinking about what I'd heard in your class.

One day while I was thinking, I recalled a fascinating lecture you had   9
given on the importance of defining terms. And I noticed that your syllabus
hadn't defined "oral presentation." Perhaps I had discovered a way out of
the ordeal I dreaded. When the time came for my presentation at the end
of the semester, I carried a tape recorder to the front of the room, pushed
"play," and returned to my seat, where I listened with the other students to
the oral presentation I'd taped the night before.

When I signed up for the next course you taught, a course on women   10
who had shaped American culture and history, I expected you would

require another oral presentation. But I figured a little agony while I started a tape recorder wouldn't be so bad.

In this second course, you came out from behind the lectern and moved up and down the aisles as you spoke. You often stood at the back of the room when you made an important point. Whispering and sleeping ceased when you did that; all heads turned in your direction. You spoke confidently and smoothly, and you called on us by name. 11

I was so caught up in the class that a few weeks passed before I read the syllabus carefully. Then I found your long and precise definition of "oral presentation," a definition that excluded the use of tape recorders. To be sure I understood, you stopped by my desk one day and said, "This time, I want it *live!*" 12

College was sharpening my critical thinking skills, and I put those skills to work when choosing the subject for my presentation. I would speak about Lucretia Mott, a Quaker feminist. When my turn dawned, I came to class dressed like Lucretia, in a long skirt and shawl, a black bonnet covering most of my face. Standing before the other students, I spoke in the first person. Acting a part, I felt as if someone else were giving that presentation. 13

By the time we met again in the classroom, I had had to admit to myself that I was in college for more than my health. I'd scraped together enough credits to be one quarter away from graduation. I had a lean program of study that allowed no frills, just the courses essential for my degree. Your course didn't fit my program, but I decided to take it anyway, and I skipped lunch for weeks to pay for the extra credits. 14

When you handed back our first exam, mine had a note scribbled alongside the grade. You said you wanted me to give my presentation for this course. Not a tape recorder. Not a persona. My body tensed and my breathing grew shallow as I felt the same panic that had gripped me during my first course with you. My only comfort came from knowing that by the time I recovered from fainting during my presentation, the quarter would be over and I would have my degree. 15

You didn't lecture in this course. You pushed the lectern into a corner and arranged our chairs in a circle. You sat with us, your voice one among many. You gave direction to discussions that we carried on long after class periods officially ended. I came early, not to claim an escape seat but to share ideas with other students. I stayed late to be part of the continuing conversation. 16

Three can be a magic number. One day, toward the end of that third course, you turned to me and said, "Kate, would you share with the class what you've learned about the dangers of moving elderly folks from one 17 living place to another?" This was the subject I'd been researching for my presentation, and I knew it cold. I rose and moved to the chalkboard to draw a graph of my findings. Then I stood in front of the class, speaking in my own voice, just as I had spoken during our discussion circles. I was five minutes into my talk when it hit me: I was giving a presentation. My heartbeat accelerated, but I kept my attention on the interested faces before me, and the moment of panic passed. I remember thinking, as I walked back to my seat, that I wasn't an imposter in the classroom any more. I belonged in that room as much as anyone.

I was happy when you stopped to speak with me after class. I thought 18 you might congratulate me on surviving the presentation or on finishing the coursework for my bachelor's degree. Instead, you asked where I planned to go to graduate school.

You were doing it again! Every time I crept over the line between the 19 familiar and the unknown, you pushed the line a little farther forward. I steamed out of the classroom. *She has already forced me to talk in front of people*, I thought resentfully—or at least, partly so. *I'm getting the first college degree in my family. And now she wants more?*

Weeks later—after graduation, after I'd read all the mindless magazines 20 on the rack at work, after I'd thought about life without the stimulation of classes—I cooled down. And applied to graduate school.

I wonder if you knew that the only way I could finance my graduate 21 degree would be by teaching classes as a graduate assistant, a challenge that initially cost me many a sleepless night. The first time my voice gave out in the middle of a lecture, I remembered you. I realized then that you had felt as nervous while teaching as I had felt being taught. I looked over the lectern at a room full of people, many of whom probably felt as I once had: nervous, unsure, but anxious to learn. And I stopped the lecture and arranged the chairs in a circle.

So I write this letter to say thanks. Thanks for opening the circle and 22 thanks for opening my mind. And thanks for giving me a push when I needed it.

By the way, my graduate degree opened up a great job for me. Yes, you 23 guessed it—I'm teaching at a university. With health insurance.

Gratefully,
Kate Boyes

Follow-Up Activities After you've finished reading, use these activities to respond to "A Letter to My Teacher." You may write your answers or prepare them in your mind to discuss in class.

Grab your first impressions.

1. How did your experience of your first college class compare with the author's? What anxieties did you have? How were they similar to or different from hers?

2. What parts of the reading did you like? What parts did you dislike? Explain your answer.

Work with new words and word connotations.

Most of the words in this reading are probably familiar to you. Take this time to check your understanding of the connotation of words.

1. The following phrases or sentences from the reading contain words with special connotations. For each italicized word, explain what that connotation is and say what meaning the writer implies by that word choice.

   a. "[H]er family thought she was a little *uppity* for doing so." (paragraph 1)

   _____

   b. "Becoming a student was a great *scheme*. But I knew, when I took my first course from you, that I was an *impostor.*" (paragraph 4)

   _____

   c. "But I was already halfway down the hall to the bathroom where I promptly *lost my lunch.*" (paragraph 6)

   _____

   d. "I didn't need the *agony* of a presentation." (paragraph 8)

   _____

   e. "You *gripped* the lectern like a *shield.* . . ." (paragraph 8)

   _____

   f. "I'd *scraped together* enough credits. . . ." (paragraph 14)

   _____

   g. "I had a *lean* program of study that allowed no frills. . . ." (paragraph 14)

   _____

   h. "This was the subject I'd been researching . . . , and I knew it *cold.*" (paragraph 17)

   _____

   i. "I *steamed* out of the classroom." (paragraph 19)

   _____

j. "... [A]fter I'd thought about life without the stimulation of classes—
I *cooled down*." (paragraph 20)

_____

2. Select any words you're unsure of from the reading. Use one of the methods from Strategy 3 to discover their meaning.

Ask and answer questions.

1. What led Boyes to decide to take her first college course?

2. Why did she stay in that first class, even though she was terrified of giving the required oral presentation? What were her teacher's strengths and weaknesses?

3. You read earlier that Boyes gave her second oral presentation by playing the role of Lucretia Mott. How did she handle giving her first oral presentation? What did her teacher demand of her for her last oral presentation?

4. What improvements do we see in the way the teacher taught class throughout the three courses Boyes took with her?

Use questions to find main ideas.

1. This reading has no headings, so you have to do your own grouping of ideas into main topics. Look for a few major topics. Because the reading is the story of the writer's college life, the pattern of *sequence* will be helpful in dividing the reading into main topics.

2. At what paragraphs do the main changes in topic come?

3. What are the main ideas for these topics?

4. What are the most important supporting ideas for each of those main ideas?

5. Is there a statement of the overall point? If so, where? If not, write your own.

Use inference to answer questions.

1. Why does Boyes begin her letter by saying she didn't belong in college and she should have told her teacher that?

2. Boyes never explains why she had such an extreme fear of public speaking. Can you make an educated guess based on what she tells us about herself?

3. What can you infer about Boyes from the way she handled the first two oral presentations?

4. What kind of relationship can you infer developed between Boyes and her teacher over the three courses? Give evidence for your answer. For example, why was she so angry at the teacher for asking her about graduate school?

Ask and answer your own question.

Write a question of your own. Share your question with others and collaborate on an answer.

Find and mark main ideas.

When you've done a complete marking, compare yours to those of other students.

Form your final thoughts.

1. Boyes had to overcome several obstacles to be a successful student. What are some of your own obstacles? What are some of your ways of overcoming them? Discuss ideas for succeeding in college with other students.

2. Have you had a teacher in the past who had the kind of positive influence that Boyes's teacher had on her? If so, describe this teacher. If not, what kind of teacher can you imagine would help you in that way? Share your ideas about good teachers with other students. ■

Apply the New Strategy: Make Inferences

Now that you understand Strategy 8, put it into practice with Reading 15, "Why Men Don't Last: Self-Destruction as a Way of Life" (or with one of the Additional Readings in Part III, selected by your instructor).

The title of Reading 15 suggests the pattern of cause-and-effect reasoning—"*Why* Men Don't Last." Look for some main topics that give reasons or causes.

READING 15 WHY MEN DON'T LAST: SELF-DESTRUCTION AS A WAY OF LIFE

NATALIE ANGIER

STRATEGY 1: CHECK IN

Natalie Angier is a Pulitzer Prize–winning science writer. Her latest book is Woman: An Intimate Geography. *In this reading, published first in the* New York Times *in 1999, the author examines what leads so many men into self-destructive behavior.*

ficus trees: indoor tree-like plants often used to decorate gyms.

My father had great habits. Long before ficus trees° met weight   1
machines, he was a dogged exerciser. He did push-ups and isometrics. He climbed rocks. He went for long, vigorous walks. He ate sparingly and

STRATEGY 4: GET AN
OVERVIEW

STRATEGY 5: ASK
QUESTIONS

STRATEGY 6: FIND AND
MARK MAIN IDEAS

STRATEGY 7: LOOK FOR
PATTERNS OF THOUGHT

osteoporosis: disorder causing
brittle bones.

avoided sweets and grease. He took such good care of his teeth that they
looked fake.

My father had terrible habits. He was chronically angry. He threw   2
things around the house and broke them. He didn't drink often, but when
he did, he turned more violent than usual. He didn't go to doctors, even
when we begged him to. He let a big, ugly mole on his back grow bigger
and bigger, and so he died of malignant melanoma, a curable cancer, at 51.

My father was a real man—so good and so bad. He was also Everyman.   3

Men by some measures take better care of themselves than women do   4
and are in better health. They are less likely to be fat, for example; they
exercise more, and suffer from fewer chronic diseases like diabetes, osteo-
porosis° and arthritis.

By standard measures, men have less than half the rate of depression   5
seen in women. When men do feel depressed, they tend to seek distraction
in an activity, which, many psychologists say, can be a more effective technique for dispelling the mood than is a depressed woman's tendency to
turn inward and ruminate. In the United States and many other industrialized nations, women are about three times more likely than men to express
suicidal thoughts or to attempt to kill themselves.

And yet . . . men don't last. They die off in greater numbers than   6
women do at every stage of life, and thus their average life span is seven
years shorter. Women may attempt suicide relatively more often, but in
the United States, four times more men than women die from the act
each year.

Men are also far more likely than women to die behind the wheel or to   7
kill others as a result of their driving. From 1977 to 1995, three and a half
times more male drivers than female drivers were involved in fatal car
crashes. Death by homicide also favors men; among those under 30, the
male-to-female ratio is 8 to 1.

Yes, men can be impressive in their tendency to self-destruct, explo-   8
sively or gradually. They are at least twice as likely as women to be alco-
holics and three times more likely to be drug addicts. They have an eightfold
greater chance than women do of ending up in prison. Boys are much more
likely than girls to be thrown out of school for a conduct or antisocial personality disorder, or to drop out on their own surly initiative. Men gamble
themselves into a devastating economic and emotional pit two to three
times more often than women do.

"Between boys' suicide rates, dropout rates and homicide rates, and   9
men's self-destructive behaviors generally, we have a real crisis in America,"
said William S. Pollack, a psychologist at Harvard Medical School and co-
director of the Center for Men at McLean Hospital in Belmont, Mass. "Until
recently, the crisis has gone unheralded."

It is one thing to herald a presumed crisis, though, and to cite a ream   10
of gloomy statistics. It is quite another to understand the crisis, or to figure
out where it comes from or what to do about it. As those who study the various forms of men's self-destructive behaviors realize, there is not a single,
glib, overarching explanation for the sex-specific patterns they see.

crude evolutionary hypothesis: overly simple evolution-based theory.

A crude evolutionary hypothesis° would have it that men are natural   11
risk-takers, given to showy displays of bravado, aggression and daring all
for the sake of attracting a harem of mates. By this premise, most of men's
self-destructive, violent tendencies are a manifestation of their need to take
big chances for the sake of passing their genes into the river of tomorrow.

Some of the data on men's bad habits fit the risk-taker model. For   12
example, those who study compulsive gambling have observed that men
and women tend to display very different methods and preferences for
throwing away big sums of money.

"Men get enamored of the action in gambling," said Linda Chamberlain,   13
a psychologist at Regis University in Denver who specializes in treating gambling disorders. "They describe an overwhelming rush of feelings and
excitement associated with the process of gambling. They like the feeling of
being a player, and taking on a struggle with the house to show that they can
overcome the odds and beat the system. They tend to prefer the table
games, where they can feel powerful and omnipotent while everybody
watches them."

Dr. Chamberlain noted that many male gamblers engage in other risk-   14
taking behaviors, like auto racing, or hang gliding. By contrast, she said,
"Women tend to use gambling more as a sedative, to numb themselves
and escape from daily responsibilities, or feelings of depression or alienation. Women tend to prefer the solitary forms of gambling, the slot
machines or video poker, where there isn't as much social scrutiny."

anodynes: pain relievers.

Yet the risk-taking theory does not account for why men outnumber   15
women in the consumption of licit and illicit anodynes.° Alcohol, heroin and
marijuana can be at least as numbing and sedating as repetitively pulling
the arm of a slot machine. And some studies have found that men use
drugs and alcohol for the same reasons that women often overeat: as an
attempt to self-medicate when they are feeling anxious or in despair.

oncology: study of cancer.

"We can speculate all we want, but we really don't know why men   16
drink more than women," said Enoch Gordis, the head of the National
Institute on Alcohol Abuse and Alcoholism. Nor does men's comparatively
higher rate of suicide appear linked to the risk-taking profile. To the contrary, Paul Duberstein, an assistant professor of psychiatry and oncology°
at the University of Rochester School of Medicine, has found that people
who complete a suicidal act are often low in a personality trait referred to
as "openness to experience," tending to be rigid and inflexible in their

behaviors. By comparison, those who express suicidal thoughts tend to score relatively high on the openness-to-experience scale.

Given that men commit suicide more often than women, and women 17 talk about it more, his research suggests that, in a sense, women are the greater risk-takers and novelty seekers, while the men are likelier to feel trapped and helpless in the face of changing circumstances.

Silvia Cara Canetto, an associate professor of psychology at Colorado 18 State University in Fort Collins, has extensively studied the role of gender in suicidal behaviors. Dr. Canetto has found that cultural narratives may determine why women attempt suicide more often while men kill themselves more often. She proposes that in Western countries, to talk about suicide or to survive a suicidal act is often considered "feminine," hysterical, irrational and weak. To actually die by one's own hand may be viewed as "masculine," decisive, strong. Even the language conveys the polarized, weak-strong imagery: a "failed" suicide attempt as opposed to a "successful" one.

"There is indirect evidence that there is negative stigma toward men 19 who survive suicide," Dr. Canetto said. "Men don't want to 'fail,' even though failing in this case means surviving." If the "suicidal script" that identifies completing the act as "rational, courageous and masculine" can be "undermined and torn to pieces," she said, we might have a new approach to prevention.

Dr. Pollack of the Center for Men also blames many of men's self- 20 destructive ways on the persistent image of the dispassionate, resilient, action-oriented male—the Marlboro Man who never even gasps for breath. For all the talk of the sensitive "new man," he argues, men have yet to catch up with women in expanding their range of acceptable emotions and behaviors. Men in our culture, Dr. Pollack says, are pretty much limited to a menu of three strong feelings: rage, triumph, lust. "Anything else and you risk being seen as a sissy," he said.

In a number of books, most recently "Real Boys: Rescuing Our Sons 21 From the Myths of Boyhood," he proposes that boys "lose their voice, a whole half of their emotional selves," beginning at age 4 or 5. "Their vulnerable, sad feelings and sense of need are suppressed or shamed out of them," he said—by their peers, parents, the great wide televised fist in their face.

He added: "If you keep hammering it into a kid that he has to look 22 tough and stop being a crybaby and a mama's boy, the boy will start creating a mask of bravado."

That boys and young men continue to feel confused over the proper 23 harmonics° of modern masculinity was revealed in a study that Dr. Pollack conducted of 200 eighth-grade boys. Through questionnaires, he determined their scores on two scales, one measuring their "egalitarianism"—

harmonics: (as used here) characteristics.

the degree to which they think men and women are equal, that men should change a baby's diapers, that mothers should work and the like—and the other gauging their "traditionalism" as determined by their responses to conventional notions, like the premise that men must "stand on their own two feet" and must "always be willing to have sex if someone asks."

On average, the boys scored high on both scales. "They are split on what it means to be a man," said Dr. Pollack.   24

siren song in baritone: very attractive idea related to masculinity.

The cult of masculinity can beckon like a siren song in baritone.° Dr. Franklin L. Nelson, a clinical psychologist at the Fairbanks Community Mental Health Center in Alaska, sees many men who get into trouble by adhering to sentimental notions of manhood. "A lot of men come up here hoping to get away from a wimpy world and live like pioneers by old-fashioned masculine principles of individualism, strength and rugged-ness," he said. They learn that nothing is simple; even Alaska is part of a wider, interdependent world and they really do need friends, warmth and electricity.   25

"Right now, it's 35 degrees below zero outside," he said during a January interview. "If you're not prepared, it doesn't take long at that temperature to freeze to death."   26

Follow-Up Activities   After you've finished reading, use these questions to respond to "Why Men Don't Last: Self-Destruction as a Way of Life." You may write your answers or prepare them in your mind to discuss in class.

Grab your first impressions.

1. What did you find most surprising in this reading? Why?

2. Does your experience match the information the author gives about the differences between men's and women's approaches to problems? Explain your answer.

3. What parts of the reading did you find frustrating? Why? How did you deal with your frustration?

Work with new words.

Some words in this reading may be unfamiliar to you. Use the methods of Strategy 3 to explain what the listed words mean.

1. Use context clues.
   a. bravado (paragraph 11) _____
   b. enamored (paragraph 13) _____
   c. polarized (paragraph 18) _____
      Note the example clues for this word.

2. Use word parts.

   a. dogged (paragraph 1) _____

   b. dispelling (paragraph 5) _____

   c. bravado (paragraph 11) _____

   d. omnipotent (paragraph 13) _____

3. Use the dictionary.
   Choose the correct definition of each word as it is used in the context of this reading.

   a. ruminate (paragraph 5) _____

   b. glib (paragraph 10) _____

   c. premise (paragraph 11) _____

4. Select additional words you're unsure of from the reading. Use one of these methods to discover their meaning.

Ask and answer questions.

1. In what ways do men take better care of themselves than women do?

2. What evidence does the author use to show men's tendency to "self-destruct"?

3. What does the author say is wrong with the first risk-taking theory that she refers to in paragraphs 11 through 14?

4. Why does Dr. William S. Pollock blame "the persistent image of the dispassionate, resilient, action-oriented male—the Marlboro Man" for many of men's self-destructive tendencies?

Use questions to find main ideas.

Answer these questions to help you notice when a new main topic is introduced. Indicate the paragraph number where you find the answer, and give the topic for that and following paragraphs.

1. Where is the question (or problem) from the title repeated?

2. Where is the first theory (or hypothesis) about the causes of self-destructive behavior introduced?

3. Where is this theory rejected as an inadequate explanation?

4. Where is the beginning of the final explanation relating men's self-destructive ways to images of tough masculinity?

Inference Questions

5. Why would "displays of bravado, aggression, and daring" attract a harem of mates?

6. In paragraph 17, the author says that "in a sense, women are the greater risk-takers and novelty seekers." In what sense would she describe women that way?

7. What does Dr. Pollock imply would be the advantages for boys and men if they could express a wider range of emotions?

 Ask and answer your own question.

Write a question of your own. Share your question with others and collaborate on an answer.

 Form your final thoughts.

1. Do you agree with those in the reading who blame many of men's self-destructive tendencies on having too rigid an idea of what it means to be a man? Compare your response with other students.

2. Discuss this reading with male and female students. What parts of the reading seemed to have most personal relevance for each student? Do men and women have different reactions to the reading?

Chapter 8 Summary

How does Strategy 8 help you *read from the inside out?*

Like using **patterns of thought** (Strategy 7), **making inferences** is a familiar way we have of understanding what others are doing and saying. **Making inferences** gives you a more complete understanding of a reading because you grasp ideas that are implied as well as those that are stated outright. This understanding of the reading *outside* allows you to **respond** more fully from the *inside*—with your own ideas.

How does the *make inferences* strategy work?

This strategy helps you understand ideas in a reading that are implied rather than stated directly. You see pieces of evidence—often certain details or words—and put these pieces together in your mind. You then **make an inference**, that is, you make logical connections and conclusions based on that evidence. Here are the five steps for Strategy 8.

STRATEGY 8: MAKE INFERENCES

1 Look for what is implied as well as what is stated outright.

2 Use the logic of "putting two and two together."

3 Notice the details.

4 Notice the word choice.

5 Examine your assumptions.

Are you familiar with the meaning of these terms?

infer (make inferences): make connections and draw logical conclusions based on evidence

imply: suggest meaning by using certain words, details, or other evidence

denotation (denotative meaning): the literal meaning of a word

connotation (connotative meaning): the cluster of specialized associations that accompany a word

assumptions: ideas we take for granted, based on our previous beliefs and experience

How is the strategy working for you so far?

1. How successful have you been at using the logic of "putting two and two together"?

2. What specific pieces of evidence—choice of words or details—have been the most useful for finding implied ideas? Which ones have been less useful? Explain.

3. How did your own assumptions affect your ability to infer ideas accurately? Did they help or did they get in the way? Or did that depend on the subject matter?

4. What did you appreciate about using this strategy? What did you dislike?

For more practice with *making inferences*, use the Reading Road Trip CD-ROM or Web site.

TIME OUT FOR YOU

WHAT WAYS OF TAKING NOTES WORK BEST FOR YOU?

Taking notes on what you read is sometimes the best way to help you learn information, especially if you need to remember a lot of detail for a test. Taking notes as you read makes you stop and talk to yourself about each new idea, restating it in your own words. And then the act of writing on a separate sheet of paper helps imprint information in your mind. Use separate sheets of paper to give you more room to write information than you can put in margin notes. If you aren't in the habit of taking notes on assigned readings, take some time now to learn about note-taking systems and see how they can help you learn new information. They can also help you take good notes during a lecture.

Note Taking for Reading

Use three-hole, 8½ x 11 lined notebook paper for taking notes on assigned readings so you can keep your notes together in your course notebook and reorganize them as you need. Date and label notes, so you'll be able to find what you're looking for later.

There are two basic types of notes you can take on readings.

- *Brief notes*. Writing out the main ideas and supporting ideas of a reading reinforces what you've already understood and marked in the text. (These notes can be turned into an outline, map, or summary, as you'll see in Chapters 9 and 10.)

- *Detailed notes*. Writing out more specific information helps you understand difficult or complicated material by expressing ideas in your own words. Depending on how much detail you need to learn, you might take detailed notes on anything from one paragraph to every paragraph in a reading.

Both types of note taking require you to restate the ideas so you can be sure you understand them. You *paraphrase*—that is, translate the writer's ideas into your own words. (For more about paraphrasing, see page 264 in

Chapter 10.) For brief notes, you also *condense*—reduce or shorten—the wording, generally using only essential words and phrases instead of sentences. For detailed notes, you may want to use complete sentences, if you are trying to understand difficult material.

SSSA. You can be quite flexible and still have organized, readable notes if you keep four essentials in mind—three *S's* and an *A*: space, structure, signals, and abbreviations.

- *Space.* Leave enough room so your words aren't too crowded and you can add something later—a definition, example, or other information.

- *Structure for self-testing.* Distinguish *key words*—words that identify important topics covered in the information—so you can come back to them for self-testing.

- *Signals.* Use graphic signals such as arrows, equals signs, question marks, brackets, or stars to help you get a quick overview when you come back to your notes to study.

- *Abbreviations.* Use standard abbreviations and your own personal ones consistently, so they become second nature. They can save you time. (See the abbreviations list on page 159.)

The Cornell Method. Countless college students have used the Cornell method of note taking successfully. One reason it works so well is that it builds in a structure for self-testing. Consider using or modifying the method to suit your own needs.

1. Draw a line with a ruler 2.5 inches from the left margin on your three-hole notebook paper (see the example here). Your campus bookstore may sell paper with that line already drawn.

2. On the right side, write summaries of the information you need to know. Use complete sentences, clearly stated phrases, or abbreviations.

3. Then reread your notes, looking for key words.

4. On the left side, write each key word next to the related notes. You can then study the notes by covering up the right side and using the key words on the left to question yourself about the topics.

Here's an example from a biology textbook. The passage explains the relationship between the body's nerves and its *hormones*, chemicals produced in one part of the body and carried through the bloodstream to influence another part of the body. Read the passage. Then look at the sample notes on the passage.

The Relationship of Hormones and Nerves

First [hormones and nerves] are *structurally* related. A number of endocrine glands are formed from nervous tissue. For example, the posterior pituitary forms from an extension of the brain, whereas the anterior pituitary is formed from the embryonic mouth.

Second, the two systems are *functionally* related. For example, when the nervous system detects an emergency, the adrenal medulla may release epinephrine (adrenaline) into the system, enabling the individual to react with astonishing vigor. (The story of a little old lady lifting a car off her trapped husband appears periodically.)

Third, the two systems are *chemically* related. A number of chemicals are used to send messages between nerve cells and to act as hormones. Again, we can refer to epinephrine. The same chemical released by the adrenal medulla is used as a signal between certain kinds of nerve cells.

(Wallace, *Biology: The World of Life*)

The Relationship of Hormones + Nerves

Key Words	Summary
1. Structurally related	Hormones and nerves are <u>structurally related</u>: Many endocrine [hormone-producing] glands are formed from nervous tissue Ex. (?)
2. Functionally related Ex. release of epinephrine reaction	They're <u>functionally related</u> Ex: when <u>nervous system senses emergency</u>— adrenal medulla [inner part of adrenal glands] may <u>release epinephrine</u> (adrenaline) into system, <u>so person can react</u> with incredible energy.
3. Chemically related— send messages	They're <u>chemically related</u>: Many <u>chemicals send messages</u> between nerve cells and act as hormones.
Ex. epinephrine signal	Ex: <u>epinephrine</u> is used as <u>signal</u> between certain kinds of nerve cells.

Modify the method to suit you. A circled question mark can be a signal for "being lost," along with a space to fill in definitions or explanations later. Allow space for a diagram, a cluster map of a paragraph, or a sketch. Try using only one side of the paper for notes, so you always have room for visuals and added information you get from a new reading or lecture.

Note Taking for Lectures

You can use the same method for taking notes for lectures that you use for notes on your reading, with two additions: preparation and practice.

Prepare. The more prepared you are with knowledge about the subject of a lecture, the more able you are to listen and take good notes. Ideally, you'll have come to a class having read and understood the assignment, reviewed the notes from the previous class, and thought of some specific questions you hope the lecture will answer. But even minimal preparation will help you follow a lecture. Strategies 4 and 5, **Getting an Overview** and **Asking Questions,** will give you a general sense of the subject and help you pick out major topics as you listen. In addition, be prepared with the tools you need for note taking: the right notebook, paper, pen, and any other tools you need.

Practice. It takes practice to zero in on the important points in a lecture and get them down on paper. And instructors don't always give a formal lecture. They may talk more informally about the subject or combine lecture and class discussion. Instead of trying to make picture-perfect notes, keep to the four essentials: space, structure, signals, and abbreviations. Save time by using abbreviations, but even more important, save time by condensing—summarizing what you hear. If you're still learning to take lecture notes, try to get down some notes for each class, even if you start off with just a few words. Day by day, class by class, you'll get better at writing down important information.

PART III

ADDITIONAL READINGS ON
LEARNING FOR YOURSELF

The readings that follow will give you further practice in using the first eight reading strategies with other readings on the theme of "Learning for Yourself."

READING III-A STRESS MANAGEMENT AND WELLNESS

JERROLD S. GREENBERG AND GEORGE B. DINTIMAN

STRATEGY 1: CHECK IN

STRATEGY 6: FIND AND
MARK MAIN IDEAS

STRATEGY 7: LOOK FOR
PATTERNS OF THOUGHT

STRATEGY 8: MAKE
INFERENCES

Jerrold S. Greenberg is a professor in the Department of Health Education at the University of Maryland. George B. Dintiman is a professor of health and physical education at Virginia Commonwealth University. This chapter comes from their personal health and fitness textbook, Wellness: Creating a Life of Health and Fitness. *The reading gives you ways to manage stress in your own life. It also introduces many features that textbooks use to help students learn new material, such as margin boxes for defining key terms, tables, questionnaires, and chapter objectives and summaries. You may want to refer to the "Time Out for You" on page 80, following Chapter 4, to learn more about using these and other features to read and study your textbooks.*

CHAPTER OBJECTIVES

By the end of this chapter, you should be able to:

1. Define stress, stressor, and stress reactivity.

2. List sources of stress and differentiate between distress and eustress.

3. Describe the bodily changes that occur when a person experiences stress.

4. Manage stress by using coping mechanisms at various levels of the stress response.

5. Use time management techniques to free up time for wellness activities.

6. Detail the role of exercise in the management of stress.

Emilio's wife died last year, and he grieved long and hard for her. He   1
felt that her death was unfair (she was such a kind person), and a sense of helplessness crept over him. Loneliness became part of his days, and tears became the companions of his late evening hours. There were those who were not even surprised at Emilio's own death just one year after his wife's. They officially called it a heart attack, but his friends know he died of a broken heart.

You probably know some Emilio's—people who have died or become 2
ill from severe stress with seemingly little physically wrong with them. That
is what stress can do. You will soon learn how stress can actually change
your body to make you susceptible to illness and disease or other negative
influences. Contrary to what some people might tell you, it is not all in your
mind. You will learn how you can prevent these negative consequences
from occurring and how exercise plays a role in that process.

STRESS-RELATED CONCEPTS

Even the experts do not agree on the definition of *stress*. Some define 3
it as the stimulus that causes a physical reaction (such as being afraid to
take a test), while others view it as the reaction itself (for example,
increases in blood pressure, heart rate, and perspiration). For our purposes
in this text, we define stress as a combination of the cause (*stressor*) and
the physical reaction (*stress reactivity*). The significance of these definitions
is not merely academic. It is important to consider a stressor as having the
potential to result in stress reactivity but not necessarily to do so.

Common Stressors

There are biological stressors (toxins, heat, cold), sociological stressors 4
(unemployment), philosophical stressors (deciding on a purpose in life),
and psychological stressors (threats to self-esteem, depression). Each has
the potential to result in a stress reaction.

We all encounter stressors in our daily lives. You may have stressors 5
associated with school (getting good grades, taking exams, or having
teachers think well of you); with work (too much to do in a given amount of
time, not really understanding what is expected of you, or fear of a company reorganization); with family (still being treated as a child when you
are an adult, arguing often, lack of trust); or with your social life (making
friends, telephoning for dates). Even scheduling exercise into your already
busy day may be a stressor.

Stress Reactivity

When a stressor leads to a stress response, several changes occur in 6
the body. The heart beats faster, muscles tense, breathing becomes rapid
and shallow, perspiration appears under the arms and on the forehead, and

---

Stress   The combination of a stressor and stress reactivity.

Stressor   A stimulus that has the potential to elicit stress reactivity.

Stress reactivity   The physical reaction to a stressor that results in increased muscle tension,
heart rate, blood pressure, and so forth.

A demanding, fast-paced job can cause a great deal of stress if you let it.

blood pressure increases. These and other changes prepare the body to respond to the threat (stressor) by either fighting it off or running away. That is why stress reactivity is sometimes called the *fight-or-flight response*. Although many people consider the fight-or-flight response harmful, it is only bad for you if it is inappropriate to fight or run away, that is, when it is inappropriate to do something physical.

For instance, if you are required to present a speech in front of your class, you cannot run from the assignment (you will fail the class if you do so) and you cannot strike out at the professor or your classmates. It is in these situations, when you do not or cannot use your body's preparedness to do something physical, that the stress reaction is unhealthy. Your blood pressure remains elevated, more cholesterol roams about your blood, your heart works harder than normal, and your muscles remain tense. That, in turn, can lead to various illnesses, such as coronary heart disease, stroke, hypertension, and headaches. At this point, pay attention to your body, particularly to your muscle tension. If you think you can drop your shoulders, that means your muscles are unnecessarily raising them. If your forearm muscles can be relaxed, you are unnecessarily tensing them. This wasted muscle tension—since you are not about to do anything physical—is the result of stress and can cause tension headaches, backache, or neck and shoulder pain. . . .

Psychosomatic Disease

When built-up stress products (for example, increased heart rate and blood pressure) are chronic, go unabated, or occur frequently, they can cause illness and disease. These are called *psychosomatic*, from the Greek words *psyche* (the mind) and *soma* (the body). That does not mean these

---

Fight-or-flight response   A physiological reaction to a threatening stressor; another name for stress reactivity.

Psychosomatic   Illnesses or diseases that are either worsened or develop in the first place because of the body changes resulting from an interpretation of thoughts.

conditions are all in the mind; instead it means that there is a mind-body connection causing the illness. An example is the effect of stress on allergies. Stress results in fewer white blood cells in the immunological system which, in turn, can lead to an allergic reaction (teary eyes, stuffy nose, itchy throat). That is because it is the white blood cells that fight off *allergens* (the substances to which people are allergic): fewer of them will make a person more susceptible to an allergic reaction.

To determine to what degree you experience physical symptoms of stress complete Table 1. If your score indicates excessive physical stress symptoms, pay particular attention to the stress management techniques described later in this chapter.   9

A MODEL OF STRESS

Stress can be better understood by considering the model depicted in Figure I (page 210). The model begins with a *life situation* occurring that is *perceived as distressing*. Once it is perceived this way, *emotional arousal*   10

Exercise is particularly useful as a means of managing stress.

(anxiety, nervousness, anger) occurs that, in turn, results in *physiological arousal* (increased heart rate, blood pressure, perspiration). That can lead to negative *consequences* such as psychosomatic illness, low grades at school, or arguments with family and friends.

Now let us see how the model operates in a stressful situation. Imagine you are a college senior and that all you need to graduate this semester is to pass a physical fitness class. Imagine further that you fail this class (life situation). You might say to yourself, "This is terrible. I will not be able to start work. I must be a real dummy. What will all my friends and relatives think?" In other words, you view the situation as distressing (perceived as distressing). That can result in fear and insecurity about the future, anger at the physical-fitness instructor, or worry about how friends and family members will react (emotional arousal). These emotions can lead to increased heart rate, muscle tension, and the other components of the stress response (physiological arousal). As a result, you can develop a tension headache or an upset stomach (consequences).   11

Table 1   Physical Stress Symptoms Scale

Indicate how often each of the following effects happens to you either while you are experiencing stress or after exposure to a significant stressor. Respond to each item with a number between 0 and 5, using the scale that follows:

0 = Never	2 = Every few months	4 = Once or more each week
1 = Once or twice a year	3 = Every few weeks	5 = Daily

Cardiovascular Symptoms

_____ Heart pounding   _____ Heart racing or beating erratically

_____ Cold, sweaty hands   _____ Headaches (throbbing pain)   Subtotal _____

Respiratory Symptoms

_____ Rapid, erratic, or shallow breathing   _____ Shortness of breath

_____ Asthma attack   _____ Difficulty in speaking because of
                                             poor breathing control   Subtotal _____

Gastrointestinal Symptoms

_____ Upset stomach, nausea, or vomiting   _____ Constipation

_____ Diarrhea   _____ Sharp abdominal pains   Subtotal _____

Muscular Symptoms

_____ Headaches (steady pain)   _____ Back or shoulder pains

_____ Muscle tremors or hands shaking _____ Arthritis   Subtotal _____

Skin Symptoms

_____ Acne   _____ Dandruff

_____ Perspiration   _____ Excessive dryness of skin or hair Subtotal _____

Immunity Symptoms

_____ Allergy flare-up   _____ Common cold

_____ Influenza   _____ Skin rash   Subtotal _____

Metabolic Symptoms

_____ Increased appetite   _____ Increased craving for tobacco or sweets

_____ Thoughts racing or difficulty sleeping   _____ Feelings of anxiety or nervousness   Subtotal _____

Overall Symptomatic Total (add all seven subtotals) _____

What Does Your Score Mean?

0 to 35   **Moderate physical stress symptoms**
           A score in this range indicates a low level of physical stress manifestations, hence minimal overall proba-
           bility of encounter with psychosomatic disease in the near future.

36 to 75   **Average physical stress symptoms**
           Most people experience physical stress symptoms within this range. It is representative of an increased
           predisposition to psychosomatic disease but not an immediate threat to physical health.

76 to 140 **Excessive physical stress symptoms**
           If your score falls in this range, you are experiencing a serious number and frequency of stress symptoms.
           It is a clear indication that you may be headed toward one or more psychosomatic diseases sometime in the
           future. You should take deliberate action to reduce your level of stress.

Source: From _Investigations in Stress Control_ (pp. 101–105), by R. J. Allen and D. Hyde, 1980, Minneapolis: Burgess.

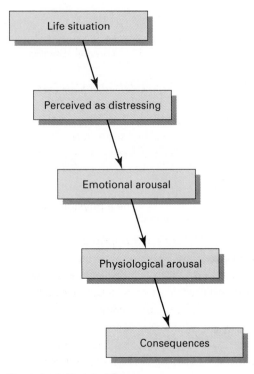

Figure I   A Model of Stress

It is as though a road winds its way through the towns of Life Situation, Perceived as Stressful, Emotional Arousal, Physiological Arousal, and Consequences. And that means that, as with any road, a roadblock can be set up that interferes with travel. Remember, a stressor only has the potential to lead to stress. A roadblock can prevent that stressor from proceeding to the next "town." That is the very essence of stress management; that is, setting up roadblocks on the stress model to interfere with travel to the next level.   12

Using the example of failing a physical-fitness class again, imagine that your reaction was, "It's not good that I failed this course, but I still have my health and people who love me. They'll help me get through this." In this case, the life situation is not perceived as distressing. Consider this change in perception a roadblock preventing emotional arousal. Without emotional arousal, there will be no physiological arousal and no negative consequences. In fact, there might even be positive consequences. Maybe failing the course will result in your studying extra hard the next time with the benefit of learning much more about physical fitness and becoming more fit than you would have been otherwise. In that instance, rather than experience distress you have experienced *eustress*. That is stress that results in personal growth and positive outcomes.   13

EXERCISE'S UNIQUE CONTRIBUTION TO STRESS MANAGEMENT

Exercise is a unique stress-management intervention since it can be plugged in at many levels on the stress model. It is a life situation intervention when you give up stressful habits (for example, cigarette smoking) because they interfere with your exercising. When you make friends through participating in a training program, you may also be using exercise as a life situation intervention since loneliness and social isolation may be remedied.   14

Eustress   Stress that results in personal growth or development and, therefore, the person experiencing it is better for having been stressed.

neurotransmitters: chemicals naturally produced by the brain.

analgesic: pain relieving.

Exercise can be a perception intervention as well. The brain produces neurotransmitters° (endorphins) during exercise, and their euphoric, analgesic° effect serves to relax the brain and the rest of the body. That relaxed state helps us perceive stressors as less stressful.   15

Exercise is also an emotional arousal intervention. During exercise, we focus on what we are doing and away from our problems and stressors. It can therefore be relaxing to engage in physical activity. Furthermore, numerous research studies have found that exercise enhances well-being. It reduces feelings of depression and anxiety while increasing the sense of physical competence. The result is a higher level of self-esteem. And exercise can use up the built-up stress by-products and the body's preparedness to do something physical. Consequently, it can also be a physiological arousal intervention.   16

It is because of its unique ability to be plugged into all the different levels of the stress model that exercise is particularly useful as a means of managing stress. Be careful, however, to exercise in ways recommended in this book rather than inappropriately. Whereas exercise is an excellent stress-management coping mechanism, if it is done incorrectly, it can result in injury or discomfort. In that case, it will be a stressor rather than a stress reliever. And if exercise in itself is not your cup of tea but you participate anyway because you know it is good for you, you can still make it more pleasant. Exercise with a friend. Listen to music while you are exercising. Engage in physical activity outdoors in a pleasant setting, listening to the bird's chirp and the wind rustling through the leaves. These and other accommodations can make your exercise more pleasing and, therefore, make you more likely to maintain your program.   17

MANAGING STRESS

To manage stress you need to set up roadblocks at each level of the stress model.   18

The Life Situation Level

At the life situation level, you can make a list of all your stressors, routine ones that occur regularly and unusual ones that are often unanticipated. Then go through the list trying to eliminate as many of them as you can. For example, if you jog every day but find jogging stressful, try a different aerobic exercise or vary exercises from day to day. If you commute on a crowded highway and often become distressed about the traffic and construction slowdowns, try taking a different route. If you often argue with a friend and the associated stress interferes with your work, see the friend   19 less often or not al all. By habit, you probably tolerate many stressors that can be eliminated, thereby decreasing the stress in your life.

The Perception Level

You can perceive or interpret stressors that cannot be eliminated as less distressing. One way to do that is called *selective awareness*. In every situation there is some good and some bad. Choosing to focus on the good, while not denying the bad, will result in a more satisfying and less distressing life. For example, rather than focusing on the displeasure of standing in line at the checkout counter, you choose to focus on the pleasure of being able to do nothing when your day is usually so hectic.   20

Consider the story about a female college student who wrote her parents that she was in a hospital after having fallen out of her third-floor dormitory window. Luckily, she landed in some shrubs and was only temporarily paralyzed on her right side (that explained why her handwriting was so unclear). In the hospital, she met a janitor, fell in love with him, and now they are planning to elope. The reason for eloping is that he is of a different religion, culture, and ethic background and she suspected her family might object to the marriage. She is confident, though, that the marriage will work since her lover learned from his first marriage not to abuse his spouse and the jail term he served reinforced that lesson. She went on to say in the letter, "Mom and Dad, I really am not in a hospital, have not fallen out of any window, and have not met someone with whom I am planning on eloping. However, I did fail chemistry and wanted you to be able to put that in its proper perspective." Now that is selective awareness.   21

The Emotional Arousal Level

An excellent way to control your emotional responses to stress is to engage regularly in some form of relaxation. Some of the more effective ways of relaxing are described in this section.   22

No research allows us to diagnose which relaxation technique is best for you. The only way to determine that is to try several and evaluate their ability to make you feel relaxed. . . .   23

Progressive Relaxation   With *progressive relaxation,* you first tense a muscle group for 10 seconds, all the while paying attention to the sensations that are created. Then relax that muscle, paying attention to that sen-   24

Selective awareness   A means of managing stress by consciously focusing on the positive aspects of a situation or person.

Progressive relaxation   A relaxation technique in which you contract, then relax, muscle groups throughout the body.

sation. The idea is to learn what muscular tension feels like so you will be more likely to recognize it when you are experiencing it and to be familiar with muscular relaxation so that, when you are tense, you can relax those muscles. It is called *progressive* because you progress from one muscle group to another throughout the body.

Autogenic Training   The relaxation technique called *autogenic training* 25 involves imagining your arms and legs are heavy, warm, and tingly. When you are able to imagine that, you are increasing the blood flow to those areas. This precipitates the relaxation response. After the body is relaxed, think of relaxing images (a day at the beach, a park full of trees and green lawn, a calm lake on a sunny day) to relax the mind.

Body Scanning   Even when you are tense, some part of your body is 26 relaxed. It may be your thigh or your chest or your hand. The relaxation technique called *body scanning* requires you to search for a relaxed body part and transport that feeling to the tenser parts of your body. That can be done by imagining the relaxed part as a fiery, hot ball that you roll to the tenser parts of your body. The more you practice this technique, the more effective you will become with it. This is true with all relaxation techniques.

Biofeedback   This technique involves the use of an instrument to mirror 27 what is going on in the body and to report the results back to the individual. Biofeedback instrumentation can measure and *feed back* to the person numerous physiological parameters: temperature, blood pressure, heart rate, perspiration, breathing rate, muscle tension, brain waves, and many others. One interesting aspect of biofeedback is that individuals can control these previously thought-to-be involuntary responses once the measure has been reported back to them. The physiological parameters already enumerated in this paragraph can be increased or decreased with biofeedback training. Since the body and the mind are connected, changes in either can effect changes in the other. Consequently, when a person is taught to decrease heart rate and muscle tension, for example, the psychological states of anxiety and nervousness may also be decreased. . . .

The Physiological Arousal Level

To manage stress once your body is prepared to do something phys- 28 ical requires engaging in some physical activity, which can range from the

---

Autogenic training   A relaxation technique in which you imagine your arms and legs are heavy, warm, and tingly.

Body scanning   A relaxation technique in which you identify a part of your body that feels relaxed and transport that feeling to another part of your body.

obvious to the obscure. Running around the block as fast as you can will use the stress by-products and do wonders for your disposition. Dribbling a basketball up and down the court mimicking several fast breaks, serving 30 tennis balls as hard as you can, biking as fast as you can, or swimming several laps at breakneck speed, as well as other tiring exercises, can also relieve stress. Still, you need not engage in formal sports activities to relieve stress as this level on the model. You can simply punch your mattress or pillow as hard and as long as you can. You will not hurt them or yourself, but you will feel better.

TYPES A AND B BEHAVIOR PATTERNS AND THE EXERCISER

Researchers have discovered a *behavior pattern* (*Type A*) related to the subsequent development of coronary heart disease. Type A people are aggressive and competitive, never seem to have enough time, do two or more things at once (this is called being *polyphasic*), are impatient, and become angry easily. *Type B behavior pattern* seems to be protective of the development of coronary heart disease. Type B people exhibit no free-floating hostility, always seem to have enough time to get things done and if they do not do so they are not worried, are more cooperative than competitive, and are concerned with quality rather than quantity (it is not how fast they run but whether they enjoy their run). 29

Recent research has clarified the relationship between Type A and coronary heart disease. It appears that the hostility is the trait of major concern. People who tend to become angry easily are more apt to develop coronary heart disease than are others. 30

Our friend Jorge, mentioned in an earlier chapter, characterizes the Type A exerciser. If you remember, on a sunny windless day, Jorge was playing tennis when he hit one too many backhands that went awry. Losing control, he threw his racket over the fence, over several trees, and into the creek alongside the court. As the racket floated downstream never to be seen again, Jorge was at a loss about what to berate more severely, his tennis skills or his temper. This aggressiveness and hostility are classical characteristics of Type A behavior. 31

Type A exercisers are aggressive (they may smack their golf clubs into the ground when they hit a shot off target), hostile (they may accuse their 32

Type A behavior pattern   A constellation of behaviors that makes individuals susceptible to coronary heart disease.

Type B behavior pattern   A combination of behaviors that seem to protect people from contracting coronary heart disease, i.e., lack of hostility, anger, aggression; cooperativeness; focusing on one task at a time.

opponents of cheating), competitive (losing may be more than they can bear); and they evaluate themselves by numbers (how many matches they won rather than whether they played well or had fun participating). If you see yourself as a Type A, think about a change. Use the behavioral change techniques and strategies presented in chapter 3 to become more Type B. You may be healthier, and you will probably be happier.

TIME MANAGEMENT: FREEING UP TIME FOR WELLNESS

To manage stress, you need to set aside time. To exercise regularly and engage in other health-promoting activities, you also need to set aside time. Since stress can capture your attention, energy, and time, it can interfere with your wellness regimen. After all, stress can be a threat to your physical self or to your self-concept. Who can blame you for postponing or canceling wellness activities such as exercise to manage that threat? This section shows you how to organize your time better so you have plenty of time for exercise, managing stress, and the myriad of other wellness activities you need, and choose, to do.   33

To be serious about using time-management strategies you need to realize that: 34

1. Time is one of your most precious possessions.

2. Time spent is gone forever.

3. You cannot save time. Time moves continually and it is used, one way or another. If you waste time, there is no bank where you can withdraw the time you previously saved to replace the time wasted.

4. To come to terms with your mortality is to realize that your time is limited. None of us will live forever, and none of us will be able to do everything we would like to do.

You can *invest* time to free up (not to save) more time than you originally invested. Then you will have sufficient time to use the stress-management techniques presented in this chapter and plenty of time to participate in a regular wellness program. The techniques we will now describe will help you to do that. As you read the following suggestions for better managing your limited time, try to apply these techniques directly to your situation. Most of these techniques you will want to incorporate into your lifestyle; others you will decide are not worth the effort or the time.   35

Assessing How You Spend Time

As a first step, analyze how you spend your time now. To do this, divide your day into 15-minute segments. Record what you are doing every 15 minutes. Review this time diary and total the time spent on each activity   36

❖ ———— *Myth and Fact Sheet* ———— ❖

Myth	Fact
1. Stressful events of necessity cause stress and a stress reaction.	1. Stressful events only have the potential to cause a stress reaction. They need not do so if they are interpreted as nonstressful.
2. There is really nothing that can be done about stress. It is just a normal part of living.	2. There are many ways to manage stress so it does not make you ill or interfere with the satisfaction you derive from living.
3. Exercise is stressful because of the toll it takes physically.	3. Exercise is an excellent way of managing stress since it responds to every level of the stress model.
4. You should try to eliminate all stress from your life.	4. There is an optimal level of stress that results in joy and stimulation and encourages your best performance. Therefore, you need some stress to make life worth living.

throughout the day. For example, you might find you spent 3 hours social-izing, 4 hours eating meals, 3 hours watching television, 1 hour doing homework, 2 hours shopping, 2 hours listening to music, 6 hours sleeping, and 3 hours on the telephone as shown on the example in Table 2. Evaluate your use of time as shown in Table 2 and note in the *adjustment* column that, even though study time is increased by an hour, the other adjustments would free up 6.5 hours a day. That would leave plenty of time to exercise.

A good way to actually make the changes you desire is to draw up a contract with yourself that includes a reward for being successful. . . .   37

Prioritizing

One important technique for managing time is to prioritize your activi-ties. Not all of them are of equal importance. You need to focus on those activities of major importance to you. And only devote time to other activi-ties after the major ones are completed. One of the major activities for which you should prioritize your time is exercise.   38

To prioritize your activities, develop A, B, C lists. On the A list . . . place those activities that *must* get done, that are so important not to do them would be very undesirable. For example, if a term paper is due tomorrow and you have not typed it yet, that gets on your A list.   39

On the B list . . . are those activities you would like to do today and need to get done. If they don't get done today, however, it would not be too terrible. For example, if you have not spoken to a close friend and have been meaning to telephone, you might put that on your B list. Your intent   40

Table 2 Summary of Daily Activities

Activity Needed	Total Time Spent on Activity	Adjustment
Socializing	3 hours	1 hour less
Eating meals	4	1 hour less
Watching television	3	1.5 hours less
Doing homework	1	1 hour more
Shopping	2	1 hour less
Listening to music	2	1 hour less
Sleeping	6	None
On telephone	3	2 hours less

is to call today, but if you don't get around to it, you can always call tomorrow or the next day.

On the C list . . . are those activities you would like to do if you get all 41 the A- and B-list activities done. If the C-list activities never get done, that is no problem. For example, if a department store has a sale and you would like to go browse, put that on your C list. If you do all of the As and Bs, you can go browse.

In addition, make a list of things not to do. For example, if you tend to 42 waste your time watching television, you might want to include that on your not-to-do list. . . . In that way, you will have a reminder not to watch television today. Other time wasters should be placed on this list as well.

Other Ways to Free Up Time for Wellness

There are numerous other time-management strategies you can use to 43 make time for wellness activities.

Say No   Because of guilt, concern for what others might think, or a real 44 desire to engage in an activity, we often have a hard time saying no. A, B, C lists and prioritizing your activities will help identify how much time remains for other activities and make saying no easier.

Delegate to Others   When possible, get others to do things that need to be 45 done but that do not need your personal attention. Conversely, avoid taking on chores that others try to delegate to you. This does not mean that you use other people to do work you should be doing or that you do not help out others when they ask. What it means is that you should be more discriminating regarding delegation of activities. Another way of stating this is not to hesitate to seek help when you are short on time and overloaded. Help others when they really need it and when you have the time available to do so.

❖ ──── *Behavioral Change and Motivational Strategies* ──── ❖

Many things might interfere with your ability to manage stress. Here are some barriers (roadblocks) and strategies for overcoming them.

Roadblock	Behavioral Change Strategy
You may have a lot to do with little time to get it all done. Term papers are due, midterm or final exams are approaching, you are invited to a party, you are expected to attend a dinner celebrating your sister's birthday, your team is scheduled for an intramural game, and your professor is holding a study session.	When responsibilities are lumped together, they often seem overwhelming. Use the behavioral change strategy of *divide and conquer*. Buy a large calendar, and schedule the semester's activities by writing on the calendar when you will perform them, when you will do library research for term papers, when you will begin studying for exams, and when you will read which chapters in which textbooks. Do not forget to include nonacademic activities as well. For example, write your intramural team's schedule and times of parties or dinners to attend on the calendar. You will soon realize that you have plenty of time. You just need to get organized. That realization will go a long way in relieving unnecessary stress.
You are not accomplishing your fitness objectives and because of that you feel distressed. You are not running as fast as you would like to run, nor are you lifting the amount of weight you would like to lift, doing the number of repetitions you would like to do, losing the amount of weight you would like to lose, or participating in aerobic dance classes.	Use *goal-setting* strategies. . . . Set realistic fitness goals, give yourself enough time to achieve them, and make your workout fun. If you are distressed because your goals seem elusive, perhaps they are. Maybe they are too difficult to achieve or too difficult to achieve in the amount of time you have allotted. If you are injuring yourself regularly, perhaps your fitness program is too difficult or too intense. Use *gradual programming* and *tailoring* to devise a program specific to you and to the level of fitness you presently possess.
You try to relax but you cannot. Your thoughts seem nonstop. Your body becomes fidgety. You are anxious to move on to do something that needs doing. Finding the time to engage in a relaxation technique is impossible. You are just too busy.	Use *material reinforcement* to encourage the regular practice of relaxation. Every time you set aside time to relax, reward yourself with something tangible. You might put aside a certain amount of money to buy a healthy snack. Another behavior change technique that could help is *boasting.* Be proud of taking time to relax and share that feeling of pride with friends. That will make you feel good and more likely to engage in that relaxation technique again. You will also need to assess periodically your relaxation method. . . . You will find that some relaxation techniques are more effective for you than others, so you will learn which ones to use regularly.
List roadblocks interfering with your ability to manage stress.	Cite behavioral-change strategies that can help you overcome the roadblocks you just listed. . . .
1. _____	1. _____
2. _____	2. _____
3. _____	3. _____

❖———— *Improving Your Community* ————❖

Reducing Stress

College students taking a health course most frequently learn about how to eliminate stressors from their lives and how to manage the stress they cannot completely eliminate. What they don't usually learn, however, is how they can control the stressful effects they themselves may have on other people. Without realizing it, you too may be a stressor to many of the people in your life. Perhaps you are causing another student to sleep less soundly by leaving your stereo on late at night. Maybe you compete too aggressively on an intramural volleyball team that was established more for fun and exercise than for competition. It's possible that you are pressuring someone you are dating to have sex with you. Whatever the situation, you should be aware that the stress you make for these people is just as likely to make them ill as any other form of stress.

   If you could figure out when and how you create stress for other people, you can adjust your behavior to eliminate much stress. Imagine the effect on our society if we all change our behavior to eliminate much of our stress. Imagine the total effect on our society if we all changed our behavior in such a way as to get rid of the stress we were causing others!

Here's how you can make a start at this:

1. Ask people you interact with on a regular basis to list the ways that you make them feel stressed. You could start with friends, classmates, professors, and family.

2. Next ask these people to rank the ways that you "stress them out" according to severity; that is, which of your behaviors creates the most stress, the next most stress, and so on.

3. Then brainstorm at least three ways you can change your behavior to diminish or eliminate the stress for the first two items in each list.

4. Now choose the behavior change you think would most reduce the stress you create for the people around you. Try these behavior changes. If it works, treat yourself to a small gift! If it doesn't, try the other changes you brainstormed until you find ones that work.

Congratulate yourself for your social consciousness. Your interest in decreasing the stress in society by diminishing the stress you create for other people is to be applauded.

Give Tasks the Once-Over   Many of us will open our mail, read through it, and set it aside to act on it later. This is a waste of time. If we pick it up later, we have to familiarize ourselves with it once again. As much as possible, look things over only once.   46

Use the Circular File   How many times do you receive obvious junk mail and, in spite of knowing what is enclosed in the envelope and that you will eventually throw it all out anyhow, still take the time to open it and read the junk inside? You would be better off bypassing the opening and reading part, and going directly to the throwing out part. That would free up time for more important activities, such as exercise.   47

Limit Interruptions   Throughout the day you will be interrupted. Recognizing this fact, you should actually schedule times for interruptions. That   48 is, don't make your schedule so tight that interruptions will throw you into a tizzy. On the other hand, try to keep these interruptions to a minimum. There are several ways you can accomplish this. You can accept phone calls only between certain hours. You can also arrange to have someone take messages so you can call back later, or you can use an answering machine. Do the same with visitors. Anyone who visits should be asked to return at a more convenient time, or you can schedule a visit with them for later. If you are serious about making better use of your time, you will adopt some of these means of limiting interruptions.

Recognize the Need to Invest Time   The bottom line of time management   49
is that you need to invest time initially in order to free it up later. We often hear people say, "I don't have the time to organize myself the way you suggest. That would put me further in the hole." This is an interesting paradox. If you are so pressed for time that you believe you do not even have sufficient time to get yourself organized, that in itself tells you that you are in need of applying time-management strategies. The investment in time devoted to organizing yourself will pay dividends by allowing you to achieve more of what is really important to you. After all, what is more important than your health and wellness? And what better way is there to achieve health and wellness than freeing up time for regular exercise and other health-promoting activities?

SUMMARY

Stress-Related Concepts

Stress can be defined as a combination of the cause (stressor) and the   50
physical reaction (stress reactivity). A stressor has the potential to result in stress reactivity, but does not necessarily do so. Whether it does depends on how the stressor is perceived or interpreted. Stressors can take a variety of forms: biological (toxins, heat, cold), sociological (unemployment), philosophical (deciding on a purpose in life), or psychological (threats to self-esteem or depression).

When a stressor leads to a stress response, several changes occur in   51
the body. The heart beats faster, muscles tense, breathing becomes rapid and shallow, perspiration appears under the arms and on the forehead, and blood pressure increases. These and other changes make up the fight-or-flight response.

When built-up stress products (for example, increased heart rate and   52
blood pressure) are chronic, go unabated, or occur frequently, they can cause illness and disease. These psychosomatic conditions consist of a

mind-body interaction that causes the illness or makes an existing disease worse.

A Model of Stress

A model to better understand stress and its effects begins with a life sit-   53
uation occurring that is perceived as distressing. Once the situation is perceived this way, emotional arousal occurs (anxiety, nervousness, anger),
which in turn results in physiological arousal (increased heart rate, blood
pressure, muscle tension, perspiration). This can lead to negative consequences such as psychosomatic illness, low grades at school, or arguments
with family and friends. The essence of stress management is to set up
roadblocks on the stress model to interfere with travel to the next level.

The goal, however, is not to eliminate all stress. Certainly, some stress   54
(distress) is harmful. On the other hand, some stress is useful since it
encourages peak performance, or eustress.

Exercise's Unique Contribution to Stress Management

Exercise is a unique stress-management intervention since it can be   55
plugged in at many levels on the stress model. It is a life situation intervention when you give up stressful habits because they interfere with
exercising. It is a perception intervention when your brain produces neurotransmitters during exercise that make you feel relaxed. It is an emotional arousal intervention when you focus on the physical activity and
ignore problems and stressors. And it is a physiological arousal intervention when you use the built-up stress by-products by doing something
physical.

Managing Stress

Managing stress involves interventions at each of the levels of the   56
stress model. At the life situation level, you can assess routine stressors
and eliminate them. At the perception level, you can use selective awareness. At the emotional arousal level, you can do progressive relaxation,
autogenic training, body scanning, biofeedback training, and meditation,
and at the physiological level, you can exercise regularly.

Types A and B Behavior Patterns and the Exerciser

People who are aggressive, competitive, never seem to have enough   57
time, do two or more things at once, are impatient, and become angered
easily exhibit Type A behavior patterns. Type As are prone to coronary
heart disease, with the most harmful characteristic being free-floating hostility. Type B people, who exhibit no free-floating hostility, always seem to

have enough time to get things done, are more cooperative than competitive, and are concerned with quality rather than quantity, seem to be protected from developing coronary heart disease.

Time Management: Freeing Up Time to Exercise

Time cannot be saved, but you can free up time by being more organized. Some effective time-management strategies include assessing how you spend time so you can make sensible adjustments, prioritizing your activities, learning to say no so you do not take on too many responsibilities, delegating tasks to others, looking things over only once, avoiding spending time on junk mail, and limiting interruptions. Time invested in applying time-management strategies will pay off in terms of freeing up time for such important activities as regular exercise.   58

Follow-Up Activities   After you've finished reading, use these questions to respond to "Stress Management and Wellness." You may write your answers or prepare them in your mind to discuss in class.

Grab your first impressions.

1. What did you like in this reading? What did you dislike? Explain your answer.

2. What did you learn from this reading that you can apply to the stressors in your own life?

Work with new words.

Some words in this reading may be unfamiliar to you. Use the methods of Strategy 3 to explain what the listed words mean.

1. Use context clues.

   a. arousal (paragraph 10) _____

   b. enhance (paragraph 16) _____
      Note the example clue here.

2. Use word parts.
   Note that some of these words are key terms, defined for you in boxes near the text where they appear.

   a. hypertension (paragraph 7) _____

   b. psychosomatic (paragraph 8) _____

   c. eustress (paragraph 13) _____

   d. euphoric (paragraph 15) _____

    e. biofeedback (paragraph 27) _____

    f. mortality (paragraph 34) _____

3. Use the dictionary.
   Choose the correct definition of this word as it is used in the context of this reading.

    a. discriminating (paragraph 45) _____

    b. paradox (paragraph 49) _____

4. Select additional words you're unsure of from the reading. Use one of these methods to discover their meaning.

Ask and answer questions.

1. *Stress reactivity* is defined as the physical reaction to a stressor that causes several changes in the body. What are some of these changes?

2. Follow the model on page 210 (Figure 1), using an example of your own. Start with a certain life situation and show how it might lead through all the stages to end in negative consequences.

3. How does exercise act as an intervention for preventing stress reactivity at each stage of the stress model?

4. What is one of the relaxation techniques described in the chapter that you have tried or would like to try? Describe the technique in your own words.

Inference Questions

5. How might a person exercise "inappropriately?" (See paragraph 17.)

6. Why do the writers include the in-chapter box called "Myth and Fact Sheet" on page 216? How can this extra material help you learn about stress?

7. Why do the writers emphasize time management as a way to deal effectively with stress?

Look for patterns of thought.

Identify the primary pattern in the following paragraphs. Explain briefly how the pattern is used. The first one is done for you.

1. Paragraph 1: Example _____

   Emilio is given as an example of how stress can hurt—even kill you. _____

2. Paragraph 3: _____

   _____

3. Paragraph 10 (see also Figure 1): _____

_____

4. Paragraph 30: _____

_____

5. Paragraph 36: _____

_____

Ask and answer your own question.

Write a question of your own. Share your question with others and collaborate on an answer.

Form your final thoughts.

1. Take the Physical Stress Symptoms Scale on page 209. What was your score? Discuss with others how to make good use of this information.

2. What time management methods have you tried from this chapter (including those demonstrated in the in-chapter box on page 218) or from the "Time Out for You: What Matters to You?" on page 50? Share with others methods that have worked well for you.

3. What are some of the ways for lessening the stress you might cause others presented in "Improving Your Community: Reducing Stress," in the in-chapter box on page 219? Discuss with others ways each of you could reduce stress in you own community. ■

READING III-B   LEARNING THE RIVER

MARK TWAIN

STRATEGY 1: CHECK IN

STRATEGY 4: GET AN OVERVIEW

STRATEGY 5: ASK QUESTIONS
Look over the picture and map to get an idea of what the reading will be about.

*Mark Twain (1835–1910) loved writing about the Mississippi River he knew as a child and young man. Born Samuel Clemens, he even derived his pen name from the riverman's term for measuring the water's depth (*mark *meaning measurement and* twain *meaning two). The Mississippi is the setting for Twain's most famous adventures,* Tom Sawyer *and* Huckleberry Finn. *The river takes on even more importance in* Life on the Mississippi, *Twain's memoir of his youthful career as a steamboat pilot.*

This excerpt from Life on the Mississippi *shows Twain's early lessons on how to steer a steamboat—with a load of passengers and 200 tons of cargo—up and down the Mississippi (see Figure 1). The river is full of hazards because silting and rainfall cause constant changes in the depth. A river pilot has to know exactly where the steamboat should go to avoid going aground in the shallows or on a sandbar, but the water everywhere looks the same (see Figure 2, page 227). As the reading begins, Twain mentions the features of the river he's*

STRATEGY 6: FIND AND MARK MAIN IDEAS

STRATEGY 7: LOOK FOR PATTERNS OF THOUGHT

STRATEGY 8: MAKE INFERENCES

lumber: miscellaneous useless articles.

settler: hard question.

protoplasm: liquid substance of cells, used here as an incomprehensible term.

placable: calmed down.

smooth-bore: old-fashioned gun with less firepower than a rifle.

already learned, including its bars (sandbars at or near the surface of the water) and bends (curves in the river). This early stage of learning has given him a feeling of complacency (smug confidence) that Mr. Bixby, his pilot-teacher, will soon "fetch down" (put down), by giving him even harder lessons to learn.

At the end of what seemed a tedious while, I had managed to pack my head full of islands, towns, bars, "points," and bends; and a curiously inanimate mass of lumber° it was, too. However, inasmuch as I could shut my eyes and reel off a good long string of these names without leaving out more than ten miles of river in every fifty, I began to feel that I could take a boat down to New Orleans if I could make her skip those little gaps. But of course my complacency could hardly get start enough to lift my nose a trifle into the air, before Mr. Bixby would think of something to fetch it down again. One day he turned on me suddenly with this settler°:—   1

"What is the shape of Walnut Bend?"   2

He might as well have asked me my grandmother's opinion of protoplasm.° I reflected respectfully, and then said I didn't know it had any particular shape. My gunpowdery chief went off with a bang, of course, and then went on loading and firing until he was out of adjectives.   3

I had learned long ago that he only carried just so many rounds of ammunition, and was sure to subside into a very placable° and even remorseful old smooth-bore° as soon as they were all gone. That word "old" is merely affectionate; he was not more than thirty-four. I waited. By and by he said,—   4

Figure 1   Steamboats on the Mississippi River

"My boy, you've got to know the *shape* of the river perfectly. It is all   5
there is left to steer by on a very dark night. Everything else is blotted out
and gone. But mind you, it hasn't the same shape in the night that it has in
the day-time."

"How on earth am I ever going to learn it, then?"   6

"How do you follow a hall at home in the dark? Because you know the   7
shape of it. You can't see it."

"Do you mean to say that I've got to know all the million trifling varia-   8
tions of shape in the banks of this interminable river as well as I know the
shape of the front hall at home?"

"On my honor, you've got to know them *better* than any man ever did   9
know the shapes of the halls in his own house."

"I wish I was dead!"   10

"Now I don't want to discourage you, but"—   11

"Well, pile it on me; I might as well have it now as another time."   12

I went to work now to learn the shape of the river; and of all the eluding   13
and ungraspable objects that ever I tried to get mind or hands on, that was
the chief. I would fasten my eyes upon a sharp, wooded point that projected far into the river some miles ahead of me, and go to laboriously pho-
tographing its shape upon my brain; and just as I was beginning to succeed
to my satisfaction, we would draw up toward it and the exasperating thing
would begin to melt away and fold back into the bank! If there had been a
conspicuous dead tree standing upon the very point of the cape, I would
find that tree inconspicuously merged into the general forest, and occu-
pying the middle of a straight shore, when I got abreast of it! No prominent
hill would stick to its shape long enough for me to make up my mind what
its form really was, but it was as dissolving and changeful as if it had been
a mountain of butter in the hottest corner of the tropics. Nothing ever had
the same shape when I was coming down-stream that it had borne when I
went up. I mentioned these little difficulties to Mr. Bixby. He said,—

"That's the very main virtue of the thing. If the shapes didn't change   14
every three seconds they wouldn't be of any use. Take this place where we
are now, for instance. As long as that hill over yonder is only one hill, I can
boom right along the way I'm going; but the moment it splits at the top and
forms a V, I know I've got to scratch° to starboard° in a hurry, or I'll bang
this boat's brains out against a rock; and then the moment one of the
prongs of the V swings behind the other, I've got to waltz to larboard°
again, or I'll have a misunderstanding with a snag that would snatch the
keelson° out of this steamboat as neatly as if it were a sliver in your hand.
If that hill didn't change its shape on bad nights there would be an awful
steamboat grave-yard around here inside of a year."

scratch: move quickly.

starboard: right-hand
direction (nautical term).

larboard: left-hand direction
(old-fashioned nautical term).

keelson: structure on the
bottom of a boat.

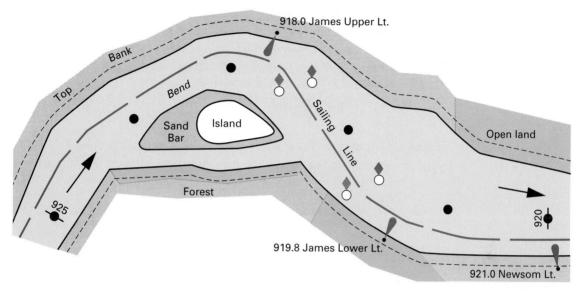

Figure 2   Present-day map of a section of the Mississippi River, showing a bend in the river with a sandbar, and tracing the safe sailing line. (1998 Mississippi Navigation Chart, U.S. Army Corps of Engineers, Mississippi Valley Division)

It was plain that I had got to learn the shape of the river in all the different ways that could be thought of,—upside down, wrong end first, inside out, fore-and-aft, and "thortships°,"—and then know what to do on gray nights when it hadn't any shape at all. So I set about it. In the course of time I began to get the best of this knotty lesson, and my self-complacency moved to the front once more. Mr. Bixby was all fixed, and ready to start it to the rear again. He opened on me after this fashion: 15

"How much water did we have in the middle crossing at Hole-in-the-Wall, trip before last?" 16

I considered this an outrage. I said:— 17

"Every trip, down and up, the leadsmen° are singing through that tangled place for three quarters of an hour on a stretch. How do you reckon I can remember such a mess as that?" 18

"My boy, you've got to remember it. You've got to remember the exact spot and the exact marks the boat lay in when we had the shoalest water, in every one of the five hundred shoal° places between St. Louis and New Orleans; and you mustn't get the shoal soundings and marks of one trip mixed up with the shoal soundings° and marks of another, either, for they're not often twice alike. You must keep them separate." 19

When I came to myself again, I said,— 20

"When I get so that I can do that, I'll be able to raise the dead, and then I won't have to pilot a steamboat to make a living. I want to retire from this 21

"thortships": athwartships, from one side of the ship or boat to the other.

leadsman: sailor who measures depth of water using a heavy line.

shoal: of little depth.

soundings: measurements of water's depth.

roustabout: unskilled laborer.   business. I want a slush-bucket and a brush; I'm only fit for a roustabout.°
I haven't got brains enough to be a pilot; and if I had I wouldn't have
strength enough to carry them around, unless I went on crutches."

   "Now drop that! When I say I'll learn[1] a man the river, I mean it. And   22
you can depend on it. I'll learn him or kill him."

[1]"Teach" is not in the river vocabulary.

Follow-Up Activities   After you've finished reading, use these questions to
respond to "Learning the River." You may write your answers or prepare them
in your mind to discuss in class.

Grab your first impressions.

1. What parts of "Learning the River" did you like? What parts did you dislike? Explain your answer.

2. What parts of this reading most closely matched some of your own experiences of learning something difficult?

Work with new words.

   Some words in this reading may be unfamiliar to you. Use the methods
of Strategy 3 to explain what the listed words mean.

1. Use context clues.

   a. cape (paragraph 13) _____

   b. merged (paragraph 13) _____

   c. abreast (paragraph 13) _____

2. Use word parts.

   a. prominent (paragraph 13) _____
      Use the prefix *pro-* to help you remember this word.

   b. fore-and-aft (paragraph 15) _____

   c. knotty (paragraph 15) _____

3. Use the dictionary.
   Choose the correct definition of these words as they are used in the context of this reading.

   a. subside (paragraph 4) _____

   b. remorseful (paragraph 4) _____

   c. eluding (paragraph 13) _____

   d. conspicuous (paragraph 13) _____

   e. snag (paragraph 14) _____

Ask and answer questions.

1. How does Mr. Bixby react when Twain says he didn't know Walnut Bend had "any particular shape"?

2. What are some examples of the "little difficulties" Twain has in learning the shape of the river?

3. Once Twain learns the shape of the river, he is shocked to find out that Mr. Bixby has yet another type of information that must be memorized. What is this other type of information?

4. What does Twain want to do once he knows he must learn a new set of details about the river?

Inference Questions

Use these questions to infer ideas about the characters and events. Give the details, words, or other evidence you use to make these inferences.

5. What kind of person is Mr. Bixby? What kind of teacher is he? How does Twain feel about him?

6. What does Twain mean by saying in paragraph 15 that Mr. Bixby was "all fixed, and ready to start it [Twain's self-complacency] to the rear again"?

7. Why does Twain say in the second-to-last paragraph that he wouldn't have enough strength to carry around the brains of a pilot?

Look for patterns of thought.

Find the sentence or sentences that demonstrate the specific pattern listed for each of these paragraphs. Explain briefly how the pattern is used. The first one is done for you.

1. Paragraph 5: *cause-and-effect reasoning*

   You'd need to know the shape of the river because it's "all there is to steer by on a very dark night."

2. Paragraphs 8 and 13: *comparison*

3. Paragraph 14: *examples*

4. Paragraph 14: *cause-and-effect reasoning*

Ask and answer your own question.

Write a question of your own. Share your question with others and collaborate on an answer.

 Form your final thoughts.

1. The events in this reading take place in 1857; *Life on the Mississippi* was written and published in the 1880s. Which parts seemed to belong to a distant time in the past? Which parts could you relate to life in the present?

2. What were the advantages of the way Twain learned the river? What were the disadvantages? What could a teacher learn from this reading about how to teach a challenging subject? ■

PART III REVIEW
COMPREHENDING MAIN IDEAS

Now that you've completed Part III, think over what you've read about learning to understand yourself and to make the most of your potential. Then review the three strategies introduced in this part, and see how they work throughout the reading process.

Linking Ideas on the Theme: Learning for Yourself

 Respond to the readings in Part III linking ideas on the theme of "Learning for Yourself." Answer these questions in writing or in discussion with others.

1. Choose two or more writers who discuss the effect of stress and emotions on our lives. What do the writers say are the problems caused by stress and emotions? How do they say we can learn to handle them? Say what these readings have in common as well as how they differ.

2. Self-concept is an obvious topic for both "How the Self-Concept Develops" and "Optimism: The Great Motivator." Say what the ideas in these two readings have in common as well as how they differ. You may also compare one or both of these readings with others in Part III that demonstrate the importance of having a positive self-concept in order to succeed.

3. Choose two or more writers who explore ways that people (children and/or adults) learn—or don't learn. What are the different purposes of each writer? What are the important differences in the situations they describe?

4. "How Conscious Is Thought?" helps us understand the way we think and learn. Compare this reading to another reading that investigates the way we think.

5. You may think of yet another way of linking two readings on this theme. Say what the two readings have in common as well as how they are different.

6. Try linking ideas from one or two of these readings with ideas in something else you've read—including something in an earlier part of this book—or with a movie or TV program you've seen.

7. Write a letter to one of your classmates, saying which reading is your favorite from Part III. Give reasons for your choice. When you get the same kind of letter, read the other student's reasons for his or her choice. Then answer the letter, saying how you reacted to what the student had to say. Discuss these letters in class to get a feeling for the variety in people's tastes in reading.

Using Strategies Throughout the Reading Process

Strategy 6: **Find and Mark Main Ideas**

Strategy 7: **Look for Patterns of Thought**

Strategy 8: **Make Inferences**

The new strategies give you more ways of comprehending what you read. As you get started, **looking for patterns of thought** can help you **get an overview.** Your overview then guides you in **finding and marking main ideas** as you read. After reading, as you follow up, both **looking for patterns of thought** and **making inferences** help you **find main ideas.** By fully comprehending the writer's ideas, you are ready to **respond** with your own thoughts at each stage of the reading process.

Use the chart as a reminder of how a strategy helps you at each of the three stages: Get Started, Read, Follow Up. The new strategies are highlighted.

How Are the Strategies Working for You?

You now have eight strategies to work with. Some of these should already be almost automatic. **Checking in,** for example, should take you only a minute or two in most cases. For other strategies you'll need more practice. It's important once again to evaluate how well the new strategies as well as the earlier ones are working.

First, look back at what you wrote about the strategies at the end of Part II. What differences would there be in your answers to those questions now? Next, answer the following questions to help you evaluate Strategies 6 through 8. Then compare notes with other students, and ask your instructor for ideas on how to get more out of the strategies.

STRATEGIES THROUGH PART III

1. Check in
2. Respond
3. Work with new words
4. Get an overview
5. Ask questions
6. Find and mark main ideas
7. Look for patterns of thought
8. Make inferences

GET STARTED   Begin with strategies that help you think about the subject and find out about what the writer will say.

- Check in
- Get an overview
- Ask questions

READ   Use strategies that help you read with greater understanding, interpret the language, and respond with your own questions and ideas.

- Respond
- Work with new words
- Ask questions
- Find and mark main ideas
- Look for patterns of thought
- Make inferences

FOLLOW UP   End with strategies that help you look more closely at the language and ideas in the reading, assess your understanding, and respond in a thoughtful way.

- Work with new words
- Respond
- Ask questions
- Find and mark main ideas
- Look for patterns of thought
- Make inferences

1. How much time are the **getting started** strategies taking now? How much time are you taking with strategies at other stages?

_____

_____

_____

2. Strategies often work well together. For example, **ask questions** goes along with **get an overview.** What other strategies do you use successfully together?

_____

_____

_____

3. Overall, which strategies would you say have made the biggest difference in your reading so far?

_____

_____

_____

4. Are there specific things you could do to make the strategies more effective? If so, what?

_____

_____

_____

PART IV

SUMMARIZING IN YOUR OWN WORDS

WITH READINGS ON UNDERSTANDING OTHERS

I'm a little boy, 4 years old. We are driving across the country. In North Dakota, I fall out of the car, while it's going slow. I fall to the pavement. Blood everywhere. I'm lying there on the highway thinking, please don't leave me in North Dakota. . . . I was a black kid in a white state, and blood was pouring out of my head. What do you think they were thinking about our family? We went from one town to the next. We . . . were . . . turned . . . away . . . six times. Six times! Nobody would treat me. Finally, a nun at a Catholic hospital took me in. I needed 200 stitches to put my scalp back together. . . . I got to be a King County executive . . . because one person made a decision to treat me.

From Egan, "When to Campaign with Color"

These are the words of Ron Sims, an African American county government executive from King County, Washington. He had been asked to speak to a group of Seattle-area schoolchildren about why the United States celebrates a holiday in honor of Martin Luther King, Jr. After talking about slavery and civil rights, he wonders if he has reached the students. He seems about to take questions, but does not. Instead, he walks closer to the students. "I want to tell you a story about myself," he says.

In Sims's story, one person made a difference. One person broke through the barriers of prejudice. In Part IV we explore these barriers as well as the breakthroughs that allow people to understand and accept one another. The readings on this theme will give you practice in reading from the inside out as you connect your own experiences with what the writers discuss.

Here are some questions to help you think about this theme.

- Have you ever felt like an outsider? If so, was it because you belonged to an excluded group? Have you ever treated someone else like an outsider? Why?

- How do you feel when someone you don't know asks for help? In what situations would you offer to help? In what situations would you not help?

- What has been your experience in getting to know people beyond labels such as *disabled, Asian American, Latino,* or *homeless?*

- How can people of very different backgrounds find common ground?

- What kind of information or activities can help people get along better?

The strategies you've learned so far help you read from the inside out by getting you involved in a reading and increasing your comprehension of the writer's ideas. The strategies in Part IV show you how to bring the writer's ideas *inside* as you take the main ideas and put them into a format that works for you. Strategy 9, **Map Main Ideas,** shows you how to make simple outlines and maps that put main ideas in a visual form. With Strategy 10, **Write a Summary,** you clarify these ideas for yourself as you translate them into a shortened version written in your own words.

As you've seen throughout Parts I, II, and III, new strategies build on old ones. When you learn a new strategy, you incorporate it with parts of strategies you've already learned. You've also seen how to combine strategies, such as **getting an overview** and **asking questions** or **finding and marking main ideas** and **looking for patterns of thought.**

As you learn the new strategies and practice the old ones, you'll begin to choose the ones that are most important for a particular reading. You'll need to use at least some steps from each of Strategies 1 through 6 for almost any reading, because they are essential for becoming involved with and comprehending what you read. In fact, you have probably already found that some of the earlier strategies, especially **check in, respond,** and **work with new words,** have started to be almost automatic. That means you have incorporated them into your own reading process.

Starting with Strategy 7, **Look for Patterns of Thought,** and Strategy 8, **Make Inferences,** begin to make choices: which ones are most useful for a particular reading? After you've learned Strategies 9 and 10, you'll also begin deciding when they are most appropriate to use.

CHAPTER
9

CLARIFY THE INFORMATION:
MAP MAIN IDEAS

In Part III you learned three strategies for comprehending the author's main ideas. With Strategy 9, **Map Main Ideas,** you clarify your understanding by putting main ideas down on paper in a simple format that works for you. Some readers like to sketch outlines, but you may find that a concept map is best for clarifying a reading's overall point and main ideas. This map can then form the basis for a summary (Strategy 10). **Mapping main ideas** gives you one more way of reading from the inside out as you take in the writer's ideas and choose your own way of representing them.

Try the New Strategy: Map Main Ideas

Strategy 9 gives you steps for making a visual map of ideas that is easy to refer back to and to remember. A map of ideas is a skeleton of a reading's organization. You pull out the main ideas from the reading and show on a separate sheet of paper how they relate to each other and to the overall point. Working with the writer's ideas in this way makes them more familiar and meaningful to you.

STRATEGY 9: MAP MAIN IDEAS

1 Place the overall point in a map or outline.

2 Place the main ideas and supporting ideas in relation to the overall point.

Before reading "Why People Don't Help in a Crisis," think about the strategies you'll need to get started and to read. The margin boxes give you reminders, but by this time you are skilled and secure enough in reading to decide which strategies you'll use. In the margin, write down two or three other strategies that you think will help you.

For this reading, as you **get an overview** and **ask questions,** see how the title suggests the cause-and-effect reasoning **pattern of thought.** It will also be important to **find and mark main ideas.** You may find it helpful to collaborate with other students in looking for this reading's main ideas, if your instructor tells you to do so.

READING 16   WHY PEOPLE DON'T HELP IN A CRISIS
_____
                                            JOHN M. DARLEY AND BIBB LATANÉ

John M. Darley is a professor of psychology at Princeton University. He has written frequently about the way adults and children form their moral judgments. Bibb Latané is a professor of psychology at the University of North Carolina at Chapel Hill. He served for several years as director of the Behavioral Sciences Laboratory at Ohio State University. In this reading the authors explore why people may be reluctant to help others in an emergency.

STRATEGY 6: FIND AND MARK MAIN IDEAS

STRATEGY 7: LOOK FOR PATTERNS OF THOUGHT

Kitty Genovese is set upon by a maniac as she returns home from work   1
at 3 A.M. Thirty-eight of her neighbors in Kew Gardens, N.Y., come to their windows when she cries out in terror; not one comes to her assistance, even though her assailant takes half an hour to murder her. No one so much as calls the police. She dies.

Andrew Mormille is stabbed in the head and neck as he rides in a New   2
York City subway train. Eleven other riders flee to another car as the 17-year-old boy bleeds to death; not one comes to his assistance, even though his attackers have left the car. He dies.

Eleanor Bradley trips and breaks her leg while shopping on New York   3
City's Fifth Avenue. Dazed and in shock, she calls for help, but the hurrying stream of people simply parts and flows past. Finally, after 40 minutes, a taxi driver stops and helps her to a doctor.

How can so many people watch another human being in distress and   4
do nothing? Why don't they help?

Since we started research on bystander responses to emergencies, we   5
have heard many explanations for the lack of intervention in such cases. "The megalopolis in which we live makes closeness difficult and leads to the alienation of the individual from the group," says the psychoanalyst. "This sort of disaster," says the sociologist, "shakes the sense of safety and sureness of the individuals involved and causes psychological withdrawal." "Apathy," say others. "Indifference."

All of these analyses share on characteristic: they set the indifferent wit-   6
ness apart from the rest of us. Certainly not one of us who reads about these

incidents in horror is apathetic, alienated, or depersonalized. Certainly these terrifying cases have no personal implications for us. We needn't feel guilty, or re-examine ourselves, or anything like that. Or should we?

If we look closely as the behavior of witnesses to these incidents, the people involved begin to seem a little less inhuman and a lot more like the rest of us. They were not indifferent. The 38 witnesses of Kitty Genovese's murder, for example, did not merely look at the scene once and then ignore it. They continued to stare out of their windows, caught, fascinated, distressed, unwilling to act but unable to turn away.   7

Why, then, didn't they act?   8

There are three things the bystander must do if he is to intervene in an emergency: *notice* that something is happening; *interpret* that event as an emergency; and decide that he has *personal responsibility* for intervention. As we shall show, the presence of other bystanders may at each stage inhibit his action.   9

THE UNSEEING EYE

Suppose that a man has a heart attack. He clutches his chest, staggers to the nearest building, and slumps sitting to the sidewalk. Will a passerby come to his assistance? First, the bystander has to notice that something is happening. He must tear himself away from his private thoughts and pay attention. But Americans consider it bad manners to look closely at other people in public. We are taught to respect the privacy of others, and when among strangers we close our ears and avoid staring. In a crowd, then, each person is less likely to notice a potential emergency than when alone.   10

Experimental evidence corroborates this. We asked college students to an interview about their reactions to urban living. As the students waited to see the interviewer, either by themselves or with two other students, they filled out a questionnaire. Solitary students often glanced idly about while filling out their questionnaires; those in groups kept their eyes on their own papers.   11

As part of the study, we staged an emergency: smoke was released into the waiting room through a vent. Two-thirds of the subjects who were alone noticed the smoke immediately, but only 25 percent of those waiting in groups saw it as quickly. Although eventually all the subjects did become aware of the smoke—when the atmosphere grew so smoky as to make them cough and rub their eyes—this study indicates that the more people present, the slower an individual may be to perceive an emergency and the more likely he is not to see it at all.   12

SEEING IS NOT NECESSARILY BELIEVING

Once an event is noticed, an onlooker must decide if it is truly an emer-   13
gency. Emergencies are not always clearly labeled as such; "smoke"
pouring into a waiting room may be caused by fire, or it may merely indicate a leak in a steam pipe. Screams in the street may signal an assault or
a family quarrel. A man lying in a doorway may be having a coronary—or
he may simply be sleeping off a drunk.

A person trying to interpret a situation often looks at those around him   14
to see how he should react. If everyone else is calm and indifferent, he will
tend to remain so; if everyone else is reacting strongly, he is likely to
become aroused. This tendency is not merely slavish conformity; ordinarily
we derive much valuable information about new situations from how others
around us behave. It's a rare traveler who, in picking a roadside restaurant,
chooses to stop at one where no other cars appear in the parking lot.

But occasionally reactions of others provide false information. The   15
studied nonchalance of patients in a dentist's waiting room is a poor indi-
cation of their inner anxiety. It is considered embarrassing to "lose your
cool" in public. In a potentially acute situation, then, everyone present will
appear more unconcerned than he is in fact. A crowd can thus force inaction on its members by implying, through its passivity, that an event is not
an emergency. Any individual in such a crowd fears that he may appear a
fool if he behaves as though it were.

To determine how the presence of other people affects a person's inter-   16
pretation of an emergency, Latané and Judith Rodin set up another experiment. Subjects were paid $2 to participate in a survey of game and puzzle
preferences conducted at Columbia University by the Consumer Testing
Bureau. An attractive young market researcher met them at the door and
took them to the testing room, where they were given questionnaires to fill
out. Before leaving, she told them that she would be working next door in
her office, which was separated from the room by a folding room-divider.
She then entered her office, where she shuffled papers, opened drawers
and made enough noise to remind the subjects of her presence. After four
minutes she turned on a high-fidelity tape recorder.

On it, the subjects heard the researcher climb up on a chair, perhaps   17
to reach for a stack of papers on the bookcase. They heard a loud crash
and a scream as the chair collapsed and she fell, and they heard her moan,
"Oh, my foot . . . I . . . I . . . can't move it. Oh, I . . . can't get this . . . thing
. . . off me." Her cries gradually get more subdued and controlled.

Twenty-six people were alone in the waiting room when the "accident"   18
occurred. Seventy percent of them offered to help the victim. Many pushed
back the divider to offer their assistance; others called out to offer their help.

Among those waiting in pairs, only 20 percent—eight out of forty— 19
offered to help. The other 32 remained unresponsive. In defining the situation as a nonemergency, they explained to themselves why the other
member of the pair did not leave the room; they also removed any reason
for action themselves. Whatever had happened, it was believed to be not
serious. "A mild sprain," some said. "I didn't want to embarrass her." In a
"real" emergency, they assured us, they would be among the first to help.

THE LONELY CROWD

Even if a person defines an event as an emergency, the presence of 20
other bystanders may still make him less likely to intervene. He feels that
his responsibility is diffused and diluted. Thus, if your car breaks down on
a busy highway, hundreds of drivers whiz by without anyone's stopping to
help—but if you are stuck on a nearly deserted country road, whoever
passes you first is likely to stop.

To test this diffusion-of-responsibility theory, we simulated an emer- 21
gency in which people overheard a victim calling for help. Some thought
they were the only person to hear the cries; the rest believed that others
heard them, too. As with the witnesses to Kitty Genovese's murder, the subjects could not see one another or know what others were doing. The kind
of direct group inhibition found in the other two studies could not operate.

For the simulation we recruited 72 students at New York University to 22
participate in what was referred to as a "group discussion" of personal
problems in an urban university. Each student was put in an individual
room equipped with a set of headphones and a microphone. It was
explained that this precaution had been taken because participants might
feel embarrassed about discussing their problems publicly. Also, the experimenter said that he would not listen to the initial discussion, but would
only ask for reactions later. Each person was to talk in turn.

The first to talk reported that he found it difficult to adjust to New York 23
and his studies. Then, hesitantly and with obvious embarrassment, he
mentioned that he was prone to nervous seizures when he was under
stress. Other students then talked about their own problems in turn. The
number of people in the "discussion" varied. But whatever the apparent
size of the group—two, three, or six people—only the subject was actually
present; the others, as well as the instructions and the speeches of the
victim-to-be, were present only on a pre-recorded tape.

When it was the first person's turn to talk again, he launched into the 24
following performance, becoming louder and having increasing speech difficulties: "I can see a lot of er of er how other people's problems are similar
to mine because er I mean er they're not er e-easy to handle sometimes and

er I er um I think I I need er if if could er er somebody er er er give me give me a little er give me a little help here because er I er *uh* I've got a a one of the er seiz-er er things coming *on* and and er uh uh (choking sounds) . . ."

Eighty-five percent of the people who believed themselves to be alone   25
with the victim came out of their room to help. Sixty-two percent of the people who believed there was one other bystander did so. Of those who believed there were four other bystanders, only 31 percent reported the fit. The responsibility-diluting effect of other people was so strong that single individuals were more than twice as likely to report the emergency as those who thought other people also knew about it.

THE LESSON LEARNED

STRATEGY 8: MAKE
INFERENCES
From the various experiments, what can you infer about how people feel if they see a crisis unfolding and don't help?

People who failed to report the emergency showed few signs of the   26
apathy and indifference thought to characterize "unresponsive bystanders." When the experimenter entered the room to end the situation, the subject often asked if the victim was "all right." Many of them showed physical signs of nervousness; they often had trembling hands and seating palms. If anything, they seemed more emotionally aroused than did those who reported the emergency. Their emotional behavior was a sign of their continuing conflict concerning whether to respond or not.

Thus, the stereotype of the unconcerned, depersonalized *homo*   27
urbanus, blandly watching the misfortunes of others, proves inaccurate. Instead, we find that a bystander to an emergency is an anguished individual in genuine doubt, wanting to do the right thing but compelled to make complex decisions under pressure of stress and fear. His reactions are shaped by the actions of others—and all too frequently by their inaction.   28

And we are that bystander. Caught up by the apparent indifference of others, we may pass by an emergency without helping or even realizing that help is needed. Once we are aware of the influence of those around us, however, we can resist it. We can choose to see distress and step forward to relieve it.

Follow-Up Activities   After you've finished reading, use these questions to respond to "Why People Don't Help in a Crisis." You may write your answers or prepare them in your mind to discuss in class.

Grab your first impressions.

You've practiced **responding** in Parts I through III by answering questions to "grab your first impressions." Now respond on your own. Say what you like and dislike; relate your personal experiences to the reading; consider what more you want to know.

Work with new words.

Some words in this reading may be unfamiliar to you. Use the methods of Strategy 3 to explain what the listed words mean.

1. Use context clues.

   a. assailant (paragraph 1) _____

   b. nonchalance (paragraph 15) _____
      Use the contrast clue suggested by "poor indicator of their *inner anxiety.*"

   c. inhibition (paragraph 21) _____
      Use the example clue suggested by the phrase "the kind of" and referring back to the researchers' studies.

2. Use word parts.

   a. megalopolis (paragraph 5) _____
      Look for the meaning of *mega* and *polis* in the dictionary's etymology for this word.

   b. alienated (paragraph 6) _____

   c. intervene (paragraph 9) _____

3. Use the dictionary.
   Choose the correct definition of each word as it is used in the context of this reading.

   a. corroborates (paragraph 11) _____

   b. diffusion (paragraph 21) _____

   c. simulation (paragraph 22) _____

   d. stereotype (paragraph 27) _____

4. Select additional words you're unsure of from the reading. Use one of these methods to discover their meaning.

Ask and answer questions.

1. What were some of the explanations given about why people don't help in a crisis *before* the research done by Darley and Latané?

2. Why are people less likely to even notice there is an emergency if they are in a crowd rather than alone?

3. Why are people apt to appear less concerned about a potential crisis if they are in a crowd than if they are alone? Which of the experiments helped demonstrate this tendency?

4. What useful **patterns of thought** did you find in this reading? For example, what common pattern did you find in the lengthy introduction (paragraphs 1–9)?

Inference Questions

5. What can we infer from the behavior of the minority of people who *did* report an emergency even though they believed there were other bystanders? Why do you think they might have acted differently from the majority?

6. From the description in "The Lesson Learned" of the people who failed to report the emergency, what kinds of thoughts can you imagine were going through their minds as they heard the victim's increasing difficulties?

7. What can we infer from the last paragraph about the purpose of the authors in writing this reading? What effect do they want their research findings to have on readers?

 Ask and answer your own questions.

Write two questions based on any of the other information in this reading. Share your questions with others and collaborate on answers.   ■

Get a Close-Up of the New Strategy: Map Main Ideas

Placing the Overall Point

1 *Place the overall point in a map or outline.*

Mapping main ideas builds on Strategy 6, **Find and Mark Main Ideas.** You transfer the ideas from the reading to inside your mind and then out again onto a clean sheet of paper where there is plenty of space for you to show their relationship.

Formats for mapping. Your map may take any one of a variety of forms. It can be an informal outline, with the overall point at the top and the main ideas listed under it. Or it can be a cluster map, with the overall point in the center and the main ideas branched around it. Or you can try a box map. For this strategy, we show the steps for making a *cluster map,* but for a sample of an informal outline and a box map, see page 248.

Mapping after marking. Your first step in mapping or outlining is to shorten the overall point and transfer it to paper. In "Why People Don't Help in a

Crisis," the overall point is not stated in one sentence. But you can pull out the overall point from the last two paragraphs of the reading. These paragraphs sum up the main ideas—the answers about why people don't help. For a cluster map, write notes about the overall point in the center of the page, and circle them. See the sample cluster map on page 247. For an outline or a box map, place the overall point at the top of the page.

Placing the Main Ideas and Supporting Ideas

2. Place the main ideas and supporting ideas in relation to the overall point.

Next place the main ideas to show how they support the overall point. In a cluster map, the main ideas come out from the central circle like *branches.* Your map may give you enough information with just the overall point and main ideas. But if you need a supporting idea to make one or more of the main ideas clearer to you, put it down as a branch coming out of the main idea it clarifies.

Mapping before marking. Sometimes a reading is especially challenging. Or it may have no headings that show how it is divided into topics. In these cases, you may want to do some preliminary outlining or mapping and then go back to mark main ideas in the reading. You start with the overall question, as you do in **finding and marking main ideas.** Then you sketch possible main topics on paper to see whether they answer the overall-point question. For Reading 16, for example, your overall-point question is easy to form from the title: "Why *don't* people help in a crisis?" And the reading's headings name the topics for you. This preliminary stage of mapping is shown on page 246. There the central circle for the overall point has a question mark in it, and the surrounding circles show the topics that partially answer that question. When you're confident you've selected the main topics, you can mark them in your book and find the main ideas for the topics and/or complete your map.

Condensing and simplifying wording. As you outline or map ideas, shorten the wording to just the essentials, as you do when you make notes.

For example, the first heading of "Why People Don't Help in a Crisis" is "The Unseeing Eye." The main idea for that topic can be found in paragraph 10. The underlining shows the essential parts of the main idea sentence. These are the parts you would put in note form on your map.

> In a <u>crowd</u>, then, each <u>person</u> is <u>less likely to notice a potential emergency than when alone</u>.

See how that condensed main idea has been transferred to the second circle for main ideas on the sample map on page 247.

Keeping the order of ideas. For any format, be sure to place the ideas in the same order in which the reading presents them. In the sample cluster map, the main ideas are branched around the overall point in a counterclockwise order. It is helpful to include the paragraph numbers on your map.

Consider including the introduction and conclusion on your map if they are long and give helpful examples or other information, as is the case with "Why People Don't Help in a Crisis."

You can see the final stage of the cluster map on page 247.

 Form your final thoughts.

1. How might the "Lessons Learned" in this reading affect your own behavior during a crisis? Share your ideas with other classmates.

2. How does this reading relate to the theme of Part IV: *Understanding Others?* ■

**Preliminary Stage for Cluster Map
"Why People Don't Help in a Crisis"**

- Intro (1-9)
- ?
- Lesson learned (26-28)
- Unseeing eye (10-12)
- Seeing not necessarily believing (13-19)
- Lonely crowd (20-25)

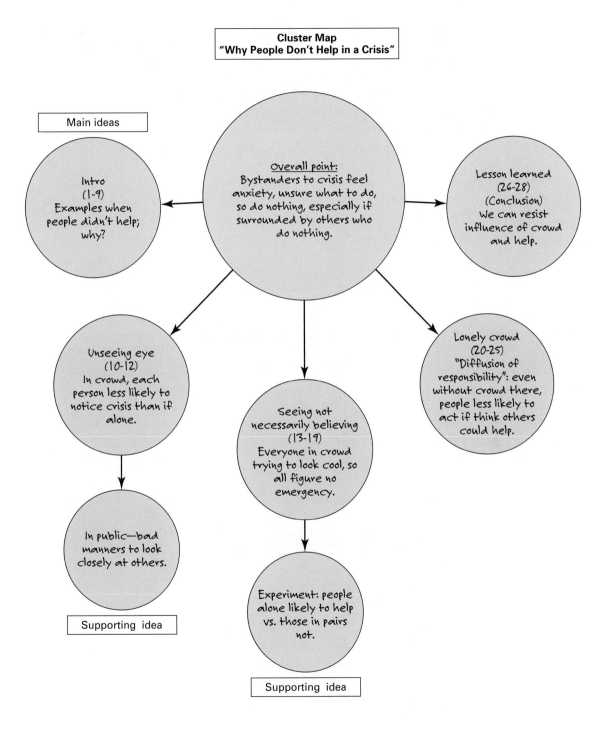

**Cluster Map
"Why People Don't Help in a Crisis"**

Main ideas

Intro
(1-9)
Examples when people didn't help; why?

Overall point:
Bystanders to crisis feel anxiety, unsure what to do, so do nothing, especially if surrounded by others who do nothing.

Lesson learned
(26-28)
(Conclusion)
We can resist influence of crowd and help.

Unseeing eye
(10-12)
In crowd, each person less likely to notice crisis than if alone.

Seeing not necessarily believing
(13-19)
Everyone in crowd trying to look cool, so all figure no emergency.

Lonely crowd
(20-25)
"Diffusion of responsibility": even without crowd there, people less likely to act if think others could help.

In public—bad manners to look closely at others.

Experiment: people alone likely to help vs. those in pairs not.

Supporting idea

Supporting idea

Informal Outline: "Why People Don't Help in a Crisis"

(Overall point) Bystanders to crisis feel anxiety, unsure what to do, so do nothing, especially if surrounded by others who do nothing.

    Intro (1-9): Examples when people didn't help: why?

1. Unseeing Eye (10-12): In crowd, each person less likely to notice crisis than if alone.
    • In public—bad manners to look closely at others.
2. Seeing Not Necessarily Believing (13-19): Everyone in crowd trying to look cool, so all figure no emergency.
    • Experiment showed people alone likely to help vs. those in pairs not.
3. Lonely Crowd (20-25): "Diffusion of responsibility": even without crowd there, people less likely to act if think others could help.
4. Lesson Learned (26-28, Conclusion): We can resist influence of crowd and help.

Box Map: "Why People Don't Help in a Crisis"

Overall Point

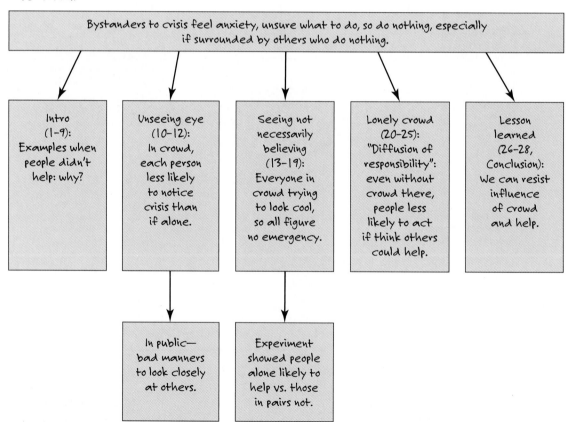

Apply the New Strategy: Map Main Ideas

Now that you understand Strategy 9, put it into practice with Reading 17, "Mother Tongue" (or with one of the Additional Readings in Part IV, selected by your instructor).

Before reading "Mother Tongue," think about the strategies you'll need to get started and to read. The margin boxes give you reminders, but by this time you are skilled and secure enough in reading to decide which strategies you'll use. Write down two or three strategies that you think will help you.

Since this reading has no headings, try mapping the main topics in pencil first, before marking main ideas. You will see from your **overview** that Tan covers both the problems and the benefits of growing up with her mother's "limited" English. Make sure your overall-point question also covers both the problems and the benefits. Then, as you map the main topics, make sure your topics help answer your question. You may find it helpful to collaborate with other students in looking for main ideas in this reading, if your instructor tells you to do so. A sample map of ideas for Reading 17 appears on page 256.

READING 17   MOTHER TONGUE

AMY TAN

STRATEGY 6: FIND AND MARK MAIN IDEAS

STRATEGY 7: LOOK FOR PATTERNS OF THOUGHT

Amy Tan is the daughter of Chinese immigrants who grew up in California. Her first novel, The Joy Luck Club *(1989), was made into a popular film about the difficult relationships between Chinese mothers and their American-born daughters. This reading explores what Tan learned about language from her relationship with her mother.*

I am not a scholar of English or literature. I cannot give you much more than personal opinions on the English language and its variations in this country or others.   1

STRATEGY 8: MAKE INFERENCES
What can you infer about the meaning of the title?

I am a writer. And by that definition, I am someone who has always loved language. I am fascinated by language in daily life. I spend a great deal of my time thinking about the power of language—the way it can evoke an emotion, a visual image, a complex idea, or a simple truth. Language is the tool of my trade. And I use them all—all the Englishes I grew up with.   2

Recently, I was made keenly aware of the different Englishes I do use.   3
I was giving a talk to a large group of people, the same talk I had already given to half a dozen other groups. The nature of the talk was about my writing, my life, and my book, *The Joy Luck Club*. The talk was going along well enough, until I remembered one major difference that made the whole talk sound wrong. My mother was in the room. And it was perhaps the first time she had heard me give a lengthy speech, using the kind of English I

have never used with her. I was saying things like, "The intersection of memory upon imagination" and "There is an aspect of my fiction that relates to thus-and-thus"—a speech filled with carefully wrought grammatical phrases, burdened, it suddenly seemed to me, with nominalized forms,° past perfect tenses, conditional phrases, all the forms of standard English that I had learned in school and through books, the forms of English I did not use at home with my mother.

nominalized form: phrase that functions like a noun.

Just last week, I was walking down the street with my mother, and I again found myself conscious of the English I was using, the English I do use with her. We were talking about the price of new and used furniture and I heard myself saying this: "Not waste money that way." My husband was with us as well, and he didn't notice any switch in my English. And then I realized why. It's because over the twenty years we've been together I've often used that same kind of English with him, and sometimes he even uses it with me. It has become our language of intimacy, a different sort of English that relates to family talk, the language I grew up with.

So you'll have some idea of what this family talk I heard sounds like, I'll quote what my mother said during a recent conversation which I videotaped and then transcribed. During this conversation, my mother was talking about a political gangster in Shanghai who had the same last name as her family's, Du, and how the gangster in his early years wanted to be adopted by her family, which was rich by comparison. Later, the gangster became more powerful, far richer than my mother's family, and one day showed up at my mother's wedding to pay his respects. Here's what she said in part:

"Du Yusong having business like fruit stand. Like off the street kind. He is Du like Du Zong—but not Tsung-ming Island people. The local people call putong, the river east side, he belong to that side local people. That man want to ask Du Zong father take him in like become own family. Du Zong father wasn't look down on him, but didn't take seriously, until that man big like become a mafia. Now important person, very hard to inviting him. Chinese way, came only to show respect, don't stay for dinner. Respect for making big celebration, he shows up. Mean gives lots of respect. Chinese custom. Chinese social life that way. If too important won't have to stay too long. He come to my wedding. I didn't see, I heard it. I gone to boy's side, they have YMCA dinner. Chinese age I was nineteen."

You should know that my mother's expressive command of English belies how much she actually understands. She reads the *Forbes* report, listens to *Wall Street Week,* converses daily with her stockbroker, reads all of Shirley MacLaine's books with ease—all kinds of things I can't begin to understand. Yet some of my friends tell me they understand 50 percent of what my mother says. Some say they understand 80 to 90 percent. Some say they understand none of it, as if she were speaking pure Chinese. But to me, my mother's English is perfectly clear, perfectly natural. It's my mother tongue. Her language, as I hear it, is vivid, direct, full of observation and imagery. That was the language that helped shape the way I saw things, expressed things, made sense of the world.

Lately, I've been giving more thought to the kind of English my mother speaks. Like others, I have described it to people as "broken" or "fractured" English. But I wince when I say that. It has always bothered me that I can think of no way to describe it other than "broken," as if it were damaged and needed to be fixed, as if it lacked a certain wholeness and soundness. I've heard other terms used, "limited English," for example. But they seem just as bad, as if everything is limited, including people's perceptions of the limited English speaker.   8

I know this for a fact, because when I was growing up, my mother's "limited" English limited *my* perception of her. I was ashamed of her English. I believed that her English reflected the quality of what she had to say. That is, because she expressed them imperfectly her thoughts were imperfect. And I had plenty of empirical evidence to support me: the fact that people in department stores, at banks, and at restaurants did not take her seriously, did not give her good service, pretended not to understand her, or even acted as if they did not hear her.   9

My mother has long realized the limitations of her English as well. When I was fifteen, she used to have me call people on the phone to pretend I was she. In this guise, I was forced to ask for information or even to complain and yell at people who had been rude to her. One time it was a call to her stockbroker in New York. She had cashed out her small portfolio and it just so happened we were going to go to New York the next week, our very first trip outside California. I had to get on the phone and say in an adolescent voice that was not very convincing. "This is Mrs. Tan."   10

And my mother was standing in the back whispering loudly, "Why he don't send me check, already two weeks late. So mad he lie to me, losing me money."   11

And then I said in perfect English, "Yes, I'm getting rather concerned. You had agreed to send the check two weeks ago, but it hasn't arrived."   12

Then she began to talk more loudly. "What he want, I come to New York tell him front of his boss, you cheating me?" And I was trying to calm her down, make her be quiet, while telling the stockbroker, "I can't tolerate any more excuses. If I don't receive the check immediately, I am going to have to speak to your manager when I'm in New York next week." And sure enough, the following week there we were in front of this astonished stockbroker, and I was sitting there red-faced and quiet, and my mother, the real Mrs. Tan, was shouting at his boss in her impeccable broken English.   13

We used a similar routine just five days ago, for a situation that was far   14
less humorous. My mother had gone to the hospital for an appointment, to
find out about a benign tumor a CAT scan had revealed a month ago. She
said she had spoken very good English, her best English, no mistakes. Still,
she said, the hospital did not apologize when they said they had lost the CAT
scan and she had come for nothing. She said they did not seem to have any
sympathy when she told them she was anxious to know the exact diagnosis,
since her husband and son had both died of brain tumors. She said they
would not give her any more information until the next time and she would
have to make another appointment for that. So she said she would not leave
until the doctor called her daughter. She wouldn't budge. And when the
doctor finally called her daughter, me, who spoke in perfect English—lo and
behold—we had assurances the CAT scan would be found, promises that a
conference call on Monday would be held, and apologies for any suffering
my mother had gone through for a most regrettable mistake.

I think my mother's English almost had an effect on limiting my possi-   15
bilities in life as well. Sociologists and linguists probably will tell you that a
person's developing language skills are more influenced by peers. But I do
think that the language spoken in the family, especially in immigrant families which are more insular, plays a large role in shaping the language of
the child. And I believe that it affected my results on achievement tests, IQ
tests, and the SAT. While my English skills were never judged as poor, compared to math, English could not be considered my strong suit. In grade
school I did moderately well, getting perhaps B's, sometimes B-pluses, in
English and scoring perhaps in the sixtieth or seventieth percentile on
achievement tests. But those scores were not good enough to override the
opinion that my true abilities lay in math and science, because in those
areas I achieved A's and scored in the ninetieth percentile or higher.

This was understandable. Math is precise; there is only one correct   16
answer. Whereas, for me at least, the answers on English tests were always
a judgment call, a matter of opinion and personal experience. Those tests
were constructed around items like fill-in-the-blank sentence completion,
such as, "Even though Tom was _____, Mary thought he was _____."
And the correct answer always seemed to be the most bland combinations
of thoughts, for example, "Even though Tom was shy, Mary thought he was
charming," with the grammatical structure "even though" limiting the correct answer to some sort of semantic opposites, so you wouldn't get
answers like, "Even though Tom was foolish, Mary thought he was ridiculous." Well, according to my mother, there were very few limitations as to
what Tom could have been and what Mary might have thought of him. So
I never did well on tests like that.

The same was true with word analogies, pairs of words in which you were supposed to find some sort of logical, semantic relationship—for example, "*Sunset* is to *nightfall* as _____ is to _____." And here you would be presented with a list of four possible pairs, one of which showed the same kind of relationship: *red* is to *stoplight, bus* is to *arrival, chills* is to *fever, yawn* is to *boring.* Well, I could never think that way. I knew what the tests were asking, but I could not block out of my mind the images already created by the first pair, "*sunset* is to *nightfall*"—and I would see a burst of colors against a darkening sky, the moon rising, the lowering of a curtain of stars. And all the other pairs of words—red, bus, stoplight, boring—just threw up a mass of confusing images, making it impossible for me to sort out something as logical as saying: "A sunset precedes night-fall" is the same as "a chill precedes a fever." The only way I would have gotten that answer right would have been to imagine an associative situa-tion, for example, my being disobedient and staying out past sunset, catching a chill at night, which turns into feverish pneumonia as punish-ment, which indeed did happen to me.   17

I have been thinking about all this lately, about my mother's English, about achievement tests. Because lately I've been asked, as a writer, why there are not more Asian Americans represented in American literature. Why are there few Asian Americans enrolled in creative writing programs? Why do so many Chinese students go into engineering? Well, these are broad sociological questions I can't begin to answer. But I have noticed in surveys—in fact, just last week—that Asian students, as a whole, always do significantly better on math achievement tests than in English. And this makes me think that there are other Asian-American students whose English spoken in the home might also be described as "broken" or "lim-ited." And perhaps they also have teachers who are steering them away from writing and into math and science, which is what happened to me.   18

Fortunately, I happen to be rebellious in nature and enjoy the challenge of disproving assumptions made about me. I became an English major my first year in college, after being enrolled as pre-med. I started writing non-fiction as a freelancer the week after I was told by my former boss that writing was my worst skill and I should hone my talents toward account management.   19

But it wasn't until 1985 that I finally began to write fiction. And at first I wrote using what I thought to be wittily crafted sentences, sentences that would finally prove I had mastery over the English language. Here's an example from the first draft of a story that later made its way into *The Joy Luck Club,* but without this line: "That was my mental quandary in its nas-cent state." A terrible line, which I can barely pronounce.   20

Fortunately, for reasons I won't get into today, I later decided I should   21
envision a reader for the stories I would write. And the reader I decided
upon was my mother, because these were stories about mothers. So with
this reader in mind—and in fact she did read my early drafts—I began to
write stories using all the Englishes I grew up with: the English I spoke to
my mother, which for lack of a better term might be described as "simple";
the English she used with me, which for lack of a better term might be
described as "broken"; my translation of her Chinese, which could certainly
be described as "watered down"; and what I imagined to be her translation
of her Chinese if she could speak in perfect English, her internal language,
and for that I sought to preserve the essence, but neither an English nor a
Chinese structure. I wanted to capture what language ability tests can never
reveal: her intent, her passion, her imagery, the rhythms of her speech and
the nature of her thoughts.

Apart from what any critic had to say about my writing, I knew I had   22
succeeded where it counted when my mother finished reading my book
and gave me her verdict: "So easy to read."

*STRATEGY 9: MAP
MAIN IDEAS*
1 *Place the overall
point in a map or
outline.*
2 *Place the main
ideas and supporting
ideas in relation to
the overall point.*

Follow-Up Activities   After you've finished reading, use these questions to
respond to "Mother Tongue." You may write your answers or prepare them in
your mind to discuss in class.

Grab your first impressions.

You've practiced **responding** in Parts I through III by answering questions
to "grab your first impressions." Now respond on your own. Say what you
like and dislike; relate your personal experiences to the reading; consider what
more you want to know.

Work with new words.

Some words in this reading may be unfamiliar to you. Use the methods
of Strategy 3 to explain what the listed words mean.

1. Use context clues.

   hone (paragraph 19) _____

2. Use word parts.

   intersection (paragraph 3) _____

3. Use the dictionary.

   a. wrought (paragraph 3) _____

   b. impeccable (paragraph 13) _____

   c. benign (paragraph 14) _____

   d. bland (paragraph 16) _____

4. Select additional words you're unsure of from the reading. Use one of these methods to discover their meaning.

Ask and answer questions.

1. What does Tan mean by the "language of intimacy" she talks about in paragraph 4? What *are* the other "different Englishes" Amy Tan speaks?

2. Why does she see problems with the term *limited English* for the kind of English her mother speaks?

3. What did her experiences translating for her mother teach her about the way people regard speakers of so-called limited English?

Inference Questions

4. Explain the title "Mother Tongue." What is the double meaning in these words?

5. What effect does the fact that Tan is a novelist have on what she has to say? What does she tell us directly and indirectly about her relationship to language?

6. What does Tan show us about her relationship to her mother when she was growing up? What can we infer about how their relationship has changed over the years?

7. What useful **patterns of thought** did you find in this reading? For example, what pattern do you see in paragraphs 18–20 when Tan discusses becoming a writer?

 Ask and answer your own questions.

Write two questions based on any of the other information in this reading. Share your questions with others and collaborate on answers.

Form your final thoughts.

 1. If you have had some of the same difficulties that Tan encountered, write briefly about your experience. Share with other classmates what you would like to about your experience.

 2. If you and your parents are native speakers of English, explain briefly what you learned about the problems for people speaking English as a second language. Compare your experiences with other classmates.

3. All families have their own way of talking among themselves—with inside jokes and special words and phrases. What examples of "family language" can you think of? How is the way you communicate inside your family different from the way you talk outside the family setting? ■

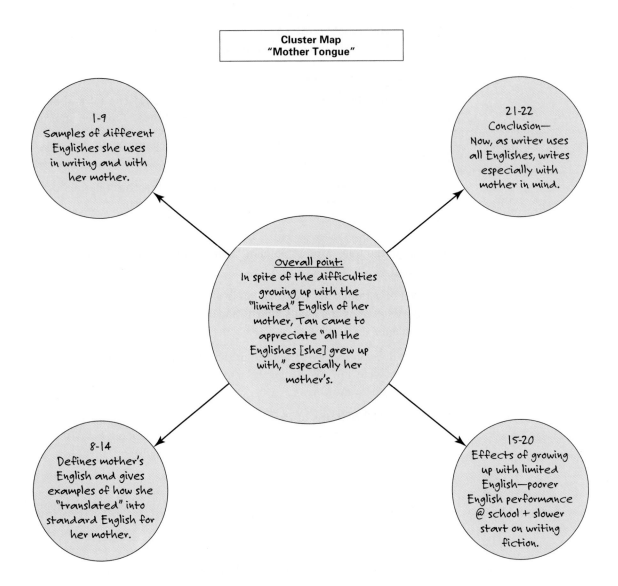

Cluster Map
"Mother Tongue"

1-9
Samples of different
Englishes she uses
in writing and with
her mother.

21-22
Conclusion—
Now, as writer uses
all Englishes, writes
especially with
mother in mind.

Overall point:
In spite of the difficulties
growing up with the
"limited" English of her
mother, Tan came to
appreciate "all the
Englishes [she] grew up
with," especially her
mother's.

8-14
Defines mother's
English and gives
examples of how she
"translated" into
standard English for
her mother.

15-20
Effects of growing
up with limited
English—poorer
English performance
@ school + slower
start on writing
fiction.

Chapter 9 Summary

How does Strategy 9 help you *read from the inside out?*

Mapping main ideas gets you actively involved with the writer's ideas. You work with the reading outside—the writer's ideas—bringing them inside to think about how to put them into a clear format. Your map can later be the basis for your own summary of the reading's ideas. This greater involvement with the writer's ideas helps you **respond** more fully.

How does the *map main ideas* strategy work?

This strategy shows you how to make a simple visual representation of a reading's overall point and main ideas. The suggested version of the map has a central circle for the overall point, with a few surrounding circles for each of the main ideas. However, there are other formats for mapping or outlining you can choose from. Here are the steps for Strategy 9.

STRATEGY 9: MAP MAIN IDEAS

1 Place the overall point in a map or outline.

2 Place the main ideas and supporting ideas in relation to the overall point.

Are you familiar with the meaning of these terms?

outline: vertical listing, with indents, that shows the relationship of ideas—the overall point and main ideas—in a reading

map: cluster or boxed grouping of the overall point and main ideas in a reading

How is the strategy working for you so far?

1. How well did your marking of main ideas translate into a map?

2. In a reading without headings, how well did mapping work to help you break up a reading into main topics *before* marking?

3. Did the sample version of a map on page 247 work for you? If not, what other type of map or simple outline have you tried?

4. What did you appreciate about using this strategy? What did you dislike?

For more practice with *mapping or outlining,* use the Reading Road Trip CD-ROM or Web site.

10

CLARIFY THE INFORMATION: WRITE A SUMMARY

Both **mapping main ideas** and **writing a summary** are important strategies for reading from the inside out. Both require you to do your own thinking about the writer's ideas so you can accurately represent them in a condensed version. Mapping and summarizing express only the writer's ideas—not your own—but they do use your own words. Once you've summarized a reading, you've gained a deeper understanding that prepares you to **respond** more fully, with your own ideas and opinions.

Try the New Strategy: Write a Summary

When you **write a summary,** you increase your comprehension of the writer's ideas. You might start with your map or outline—or even with your marked text. Then restate—in your own words—the writer's overall point, main ideas, and important supporting ideas. Restating in your own words is called *paraphrasing.* When you paraphrase to write a summary, you produce a paragraph that flows logically from one sentence to the next, without distorting what the writer said.

STRATEGY 10: WRITE A SUMMARY

1 Put the writer's ideas in your own words.

2 Base your summary on your marking or mapping.

Before reading "Police and the Community," think about the strategies you'll need to get started and to read. The margin boxes give you reminders, but by this time you are skilled and secure enough in reading to decide which strategies you'll use. In the margin, write down two or three other strategies that you think will help you.

In forming your overall-point question and the overall point for this reading, remember to cover both topics given in the headings: "Policing in a Multicultural Society" and "Community Crime Prevention." Notice also that the first topic is longer than the second, so you'll probably find more supporting ideas for the main idea for that topic.

READING 18   ## POLICE AND THE COMMUNITY

GEORGE F. COLE AND CHRISTOPHER E. SMITH

STRATEGY 6: FIND AND MARK MAIN IDEAS

STRATEGY 7: LOOK FOR PATTERNS OF THOUGHT

STRATEGY 8: MAKE INFERENCES

George F. Cole is a professor of political science at the University of Connecticut. Christopher E. Smith is a professor of criminal justice at Michigan State University. This reading comes from the chapter called "Policing: Issues and Trends" in their textbook Criminal Justice in America. *In this reading the writers discuss ways the police try to work more effectively within a multicultural society.*

The work of a police officer in an American city can be very hard. Hours of boring, routine work can be interrupted by short spurts of dangerous crime fighting. Although police work has always been frustrating and dangerous, officers today must deal with situations ranging from helping the homeless to dealing with domestic violence to confronting shoot-outs at drug deals gone sour. Yet police actions are often mishandled or misinterpreted, with the result that some people are critical of the police.   1

POLICING IN A MULTICULTURAL SOCIETY

Carrying out the complex tasks of policing efficiently and according to the law is a tough assignment even when the police have the support and cooperation of the public. But policing in a multicultural society presents further challenges.   2

In the last quarter-century the racial and ethnic composition of the United States has changed. African Americans have continued to move from the South to northern cities. Hispanic immigrants from Puerto Rico, Cuba, Mexico, and South America have become the fastest growing minority. Immigrants from Eastern Europe, Russia, the Middle East, and Asia have entered the country in greater numbers. Between 1980 and 1990, the U.S. population increased by 23 million. Sixty percent of this increase was made up of nonwhite residents, including Hispanics (6.4 million), African Americans (4.3 million), and Asians and other nonwhites (3.4 million) (Bureau of the Census, 1991. *1990 Census*).   3

Policing requires trust, understanding, and cooperation between officers and the public. People must be willing to call for help and provide   4 information about wrongdoing. But in a multicultural society, relations between the police and minorities are complicated by stereotypes, cultural differences, and language differences.

Officers often attribute undesirable traits to members of minority   5
groups: "Asian Americans are shifty," "Arab Americans are terrorists," "African Americans are lazy," "Polish Americans are stubborn." But minorities may also stereotype the police as "fascist," "dumb," or "pigs." Treating people according to stereotypes, rather than as individuals, creates tensions that harden negative attitudes.

New immigrants often bring with them religious and cultural practices   6
that differ from those of the dominant culture. Many times these practices, while accepted in the home country, are viewed as deviant or are even against the law in this country. The killing of animals by adherents of the Santaría° religion has brought the police to churches in Florida. In Lincoln, Nebraska, arranged marriages of 13- and 14-year-old Iraqi-American sisters to new immigrants twice their ages brought charges of rape. In such cases the police must walk a fine line between upholding American law and respecting the customs of new residents (*New York Times*, December 2, 1996, p. A10).

Santaría: religion practiced originally in Cuba.

Very few officers can speak a language other than English, and only in   7
large urban departments are there officers who speak any of the many languages used by new immigrants. Limited English speakers who report crimes, are arrested, or are victimized may not be understood. Language can be a barrier for the police in responding to calls for help and dealing with organized crime. Language and cultural diversity make if harder for the FBI or local police to infiltrate the Russian, Vietnamese, and Chinese organized crime groups now found in East and West Coast cities.

Public opinion surveys have shown that race and ethnicity are key factors   8
tors shaping attitudes toward the police. Polls show that 25 percent of white Americans say they have a great deal of confidence in the police and 11 percent say they have very little or none. Surprisingly, a greater portion (26 percent) of African Americans say they have a great deal of confidence, yet 21 percent say they have very little or none (BJS, 1997. *Sourcebook:* 119). Even so, most African Americans and Hispanic Americans are similar to most white Americans in their attitudes toward the police. It is young, low-income racial-minority males who have the most negative attitudes toward the police (Walker, Spohn, and DeLone, 1996: 87, 89). . . .

In inner-city neighborhoods—the areas that need and want effective   9
policing—there is much distrust of the police; citizens therefore fail to report crimes and refuse to cooperate with the police. Encounters between officers

and members of these communities are often hostile and sometimes lead to large-scale disorders.

Why do some urban residents resent the police? Studies have shown   10
that this resentment stems from permissive law enforcement and police abuse of power (Dilulio, 1993a:3). In many cities the police have been charged with failure to give protection and services to minority neighborhoods and, as we will see in the next section, with abusing residents physically or verbally.

Almost all studies reveal the prejudices of the police toward the poor   11
and racial minorities. These attitudes lead many officers to see all African Americans or Hispanic Americans as potential criminals, and as a result police tend to exaggerate the extent of minority crime. If both police and citizens view each other with hostility, then their encounters will be strained and the potential for conflict great.

COMMUNITY CRIME PREVENTION

There is a growing awareness that the control of crime and disorder   12
cannot be achieved solely by the police. Social control requires involvement by all members of the community. Community crime prevention can be enhanced if government agencies and neighborhood organizations cooperate.

Community programs to help the police have greatly increased across   13
the country. More than 6 million Americans are members of citizen crimewatch groups, which often have direct ties to police departments. Television and radio stations present the "unsolved crime of the week," and cash rewards are given for information that leads to conviction of the offender.

To what extent can such programs be relied upon to reduce crime and   14
maintain social order? The results are mixed. Research on forty neighborhoods in six cities shows that while crime prevention efforts and voluntary community groups have had some success in more affluent neighborhoods, they are less likely to be found in poor neighborhoods with high levels of disorder. In such areas, "residents typically are deeply suspicious of one another, report only a weak sense of community, perceive they have low levels of personal influence on neighborhood events, and feel that it is their neighbors, not 'outsiders,' whom they must watch with care" (Skogan, 1990:130; McGabey, 1986:230).

However, Kelling and Coles have documented successful community-   15
based crime prevention programs in Baltimore, Boston, New York, San Francisco, and Seattle (Kelling and Coles, 1996). In each city, community-based groups worked with the police and other governmental agencies to

restore order and control crime. Ultimately, the say, the citizens of a community must take responsibility for maintaining civil and safe social conditions. Experience has shown that "while police might be able to *retake* a neighborhood from aggressive drug dealers, police could not *hold* a neighborhood without significant commitment and actual assistance from private citizens" (Kelling and Coles, 1996:248).

Law enforcement agencies need the support and help of the community for effective crime prevention and control. They need support when they take actions designed to maintain order. They need information about wrongdoing and cooperation with investigations.   16

Works Cited

BJS (Bureau of Justice Statistics). 1997. *Sourcebook of Criminal Justice Statistics, 1996.* Washington, D.C.: Government Printing Office.

Bureau of the Census. 1991. *1990 Census.* Washington, D.C.: Government Printing Office.

Dilulio, J. J., Jr. 1993a. "Rethinking the Criminal Justice System: Toward a New Paradigm," *Performance Measures for the Criminal Justice System.* Washington, D.C.: Bureau of Justice Statistics.

Kelling, G. L., and C. M. Coles. 1996. *Fixing Broken Windows: Restoring and Reducing Crime in Our Communities.* New York: Free Press.

McGabey, R. 1986. "Economic Conditions: Neighborhood Organizations and Urban Crime," *Crime and Justice: A Review of Research,* vol. 8, ed. M. Tonry and J. Petersilia. Chicago: University of Chicago Press, 427–478.

New York Times. December 2, 1996, p. A10.

Skogan, W. G. 1990. *Disorder and Decline: Crime and the Spiral of Decay in America.* New York: Free Press.

Walker, S., C. Spohn, and M. DeLone. 1996. *The Color of Justice.* Belmont, Calif.: Wadsworth, 89.

Follow-Up Activities   After you've finished reading, use these questions to respond to "Police and the Community." You may write your answers or prepare them in your mind to discuss in class.

Grab your first impressions.

Respond with your first impressions. Say what you like and dislike; relate your personal experiences to the reading; consider what more you want to know.

Work with new words.

Some words in this reading may be unfamiliar to you. Use the methods of Strategy 3 to explain what the listed words mean.

1. Use context clues.

   a. deviant (paragraph 6) _____

   b. affluent (paragraph 14) _____

2. Use word parts.

   a. infiltrate (paragraph 7) _____

   b. permissive (paragraph 10) _____

3. Use the dictionary.
   Choose the correct definition of each word as it is used in the context of this reading.

   a. dominant (paragraph 6) _____

   b. adherent (paragraph 6) _____

   c. enhanced (paragraph 12) _____

4. Select additional words you're unsure of from the reading. Use one of these methods to discover their meaning.

Ask and answer questions.

1. What are some of the major changes in the last quarter century that have changed the racial and ethnic makeup of the United States?

2. What are some of the examples of stereotypes the police and ethnic minorities have of each other?

3. What are the main challenges in developing effective working relations between new immigrants and the police?

4. What causes people in inner-city neighborhoods to have such strong resentment toward the police?

Inference Questions

5. Why do the writers say that "treating people according to stereotypes, rather than individuals, creates tensions that harden negative attitudes"?

6. What might turn a hostile encounter between police officers and residents of inner-city neighborhoods into a "large-scale disorder"?

7. Why would residents "in poor neighborhoods with high levels of disorder" be so suspicious of their neighbors?

 ## Ask and answer your own questions.

Write two questions based on any of the other information in this reading. Share your questions with others and collaborate on answers.

Get a Close-Up of the New Strategy: Write a Summary

Paraphrasing

1 *Put the writer's ideas in your own words.*

Paraphrasing is a kind of translation of others' words into your own words. Paraphrasing the ideas in a reading helps you check your comprehension. You must thoroughly understand the writer's meaning before you can express that meaning in new words. When you paraphrase for a summary, you can start with the ideas you've already condensed into notes for your map or outline.

Finding your own words. It takes practice to paraphrase accurately. Start off by using language you feel comfortable with—your everyday words. Just be sure those words express the writer's meaning. When you paraphrase, you make two main kinds of changes:

- substitute new words for the writer's words (using synonyms—words that mean the same thing as the original words)

- create a different word order

Examine the sample paraphrase here. Notice the synonyms (such as *badly managed* for *mishandled*) and the changes in word order.

Original sentence (paragraph 1): Yet police actions are often mishandled or misinterpreted, with the result that some people are critical of the police.

Paraphrase: But because what the police do is often badly managed or misunderstood, some people criticize them.

Restating ideas accurately. Be accurate as you restate ideas in your own words. Don't change the meaning by changing or adding ideas. At the same time, try to keep the essential details.

Here are two examples of inaccurate paraphrasing.

Original statement (adapted from the last sentence in paragraph 4): The relations between police and minority groups are complicated by the stereotypes they have of each other and the cultural and language differences that cause misunderstandings.

Inaccurate paraphrase: Police have problems with minority groups because of the stereotypes they have of minorities and misunderstandings of their culture and language.

What's wrong? This paraphrase makes the problem all one sided. It leaves out the *minorities'* stereotypes of the police.

> *Another inaccurate paraphrase:* The relations between police and minority groups are so stereotyped that they have no way of understanding each other, and the immigrants bring strange customs and languages that make policing impossible.

What's wrong? The first part adds a detail that changes the meaning. It says there is "no way of understanding," an exaggeration of what Cole and Smith say. In addition, the second part changes the message by putting all the blame on the immigrants.

Including quotations. You write a summary by paraphrasing the writer's ideas in your own words. But it is sometimes helpful to quote directly. A quotation can call attention to an important term or phrase. For example, in a summary of Reading 17, "Mother Tongue," it would be useful to see Tan's exact words: "all the Englishes I grew up with." That phrase is an unusual and effective way to describe her different ways of speaking English. In Reading 18, Cole and Smith make a clear, general statement in paragraph 2—"policing in a multi-cultural society presents further challenges"—that works well as part of the overall point.

When you do use the author's words, always remember to copy the words exactly and to show you are quoting by using quotation marks.

Setting aside your own ideas. A summary should give a fair representation of the writer's ideas. Don't include what you think until after you've summarized the ideas. Then you'll be ready to **respond** with your own opinions.

Practice paraphrasing.

Try using the guidelines just described to practice paraphrasing these sentences from "Police and the Community."

1. Carrying out the complex tasks of policing efficiently and according to the law is a tough assignment even when the police have the support and cooperation of the public. (paragraph 2)

_____

_____

2. Many times these practices, while accepted in the home country, are viewed as deviant or are even against the law in this country. (paragraph 6)

_____

_____

3. In inner-city neighborhoods—the areas that need and want effective policing—there is much distrust of the police; citizens therefore fail to report crimes and refuse to cooperate with the police. (paragraph 9)

_____

_____

4. These attitudes lead many officers to see all African Americans or Hispanic Americans as potential criminals, and as a result police tend to exaggerate the extent of minority crime. (paragraph 11)

_____

_____

5. Research on forty neighborhoods in six cities shows that while crime prevention efforts and voluntary community groups have had some success in more affluent neighborhoods, they are less likely to be found in poor neighborhoods with high levels of disorder. (paragraph 14)

_____

_____   ■

Summarizing the Overall Point and Main Ideas

2 *Base your summary on your marking or mapping.*

Summarizing begins where **marking** and **mapping**—or outlining—leave off. You have already identified the overall point, main ideas, and important supporting ideas. It is possible to base your summary on a thorough marking of ideas in your book. But when you're still learning to summarize, you're better off starting from a map.

Putting the main ideas into a summary. Here are some guidelines for writing a summary based on the ideas from your marking, map, or informal outline.

- Change any notes into *complete sentences*. A complete sentence has to have a subject and verb. For example, here is a note from the informal outline on page 267:

Immigrants' different languages and cultures = more barriers.

To turn that note into a complete sentence, you need a verb in place of the equals sign:

Immigrants' different languages and different cultures *cause* more barriers.

- Paraphrase the writer's ideas, using your own words; condense the ideas if you haven't already made notes for a map or outline.

- Start with a sentence for the overall point.

- Write a sentence for each main idea and for each supporting idea you include.

- Follow the order of ideas in the reading.

- If you need a more complete summary, add more supporting ideas to each main idea.

Practice the New Strategy

Here is an informal outline in note form for "Police and the Community." Notice that for the first main idea two supporting ideas are given in order to explain the two aspects of police and minority relations.

"Police and the Community"

(Overall point) "Policing in multicultural society presents further challenges," so "community crime prevention" tries to improve police-community relations

1. "Policing in a Multicultural Society": work made harder by stereotypes on both sides & by cultural & language differences. (2-7)

   • Immigrants' different language and culture = more barriers

   • People in inner city—esp., poor, racial-minority males—least confidence in police because of ineffective or abusive policing (8-11)

2. "Community Crime Prevention": Across country, increase in programs that involve community to help police, but results = mixed (12-16)

   • Works better in wealthier areas, but a few big cities have some success.

Write a summary.

Write your own summary of Reading 18, based on this outline.

Is the summary here like the one you wrote? See how the notes from the sample outline have been made into complete sentences. The underlining shows the slight changes and added words that make ideas clearer and more complete.

Sample Summary of "Police and The Community"

"Policing in <u>a</u> multicultural society presents further challenges," so "community crime prevention" <u>programs</u> try to improve community-police relations <u>in order to involve the public in helping the police. The</u> relations between police and minority <u>groups are</u> <u>complicated by</u> <u>the</u> stereotypes <u>they have of each other</u> and the cultural and language differences <u>that cause misunderstandings.</u> Immigrants' different languages and cultures <u>cause</u> more barriers. People in the inner city, <u>especially</u> <u>those who are</u> poor, racial-minority males, <u>have the</u> least confidence in <u>the</u> police <u>because of</u> ineffective or abusive policing. Across <u>the</u> country <u>there has been an</u> increase in <u>"community crime prevention"</u> programs that involve the community to help the police, but <u>the</u> results <u>of these programs have been</u> mixed. <u>They</u> work better in wealthier areas, but a few big cities have <u>had</u> some success <u>in getting the community involved with the police.</u>

Form your final thoughts.

1. How does the information in this reading compare with what you know about policing in your own area—or in areas near you? Are you aware of community crime prevention programs? If so, what kind of success are they having?

2. Discuss with your classmates the stereotypes about both police and minorities that complicate fair and effective policing. What kind of information or activities might improve relations between the two?   ■

Apply the New Strategy: Write a Summary

Now that you understand Strategy 10, put it into practice with Reading 19, "Don't Let Stereotypes Warp Your Judgments" (or with one of the Additional Readings in Part IV, selected by your instructor).

Before reading "Don't Let Stereotypes Warp Your Judgments," think about the strategies you'll need to get started and to read. The margin boxes give you reminders, but by this time you are skilled and secure enough in reading to decide which strategies you'll use. In the margin, write down two or three other strategies that you think will help you.

Since this reading has no headings, try mapping the main topics in pencil first, before marking main ideas. Let Strategy 7, **Look for Patterns of Thought,** help you find topics. The reading talks about *why* we use stereotypes, so cause-and-effect reasoning is an important pattern. But notice the patterns of definition and examples as well. You may find it helpful to collaborate with other students in mapping the main ideas in this reading, if your instructor tells you to do so. A sample map of ideas appears on page 274.

READING 19   DON'T LET STEREOTYPES WARP YOUR JUDGMENTS

ROBERT L. HEILBRONER

Robert L. Heilbroner is a professor emeritus of economics at the New School for Social Research. He is the author of many articles and several books, including The Nature and Logic of Capitalism *in 1985. In this reading, he shows us how our stereotypes get in the way of understanding others. As you* **check in,** *think about how stereotypes limit your own thinking. (See, for example, Figure 10.1).*

STRATEGY 6: FIND AND
MARK MAIN IDEAS

STRATEGY 7: LOOK FOR
PATTERNS OF THOUGHT

STRATEGY 8: MAKE
INFERENCES

1   Is a girl called Gloria apt to be better-looking than one called Bertha? Are criminals more likely to be dark than blond? Can you tell a good deal about someone's personality from hearing his voice briefly over the phone? Can a person's nationality be pretty accurately guessed from his photograph? Does the fact that someone wears glasses imply that he is intelligent?

2   The answer to all these questions is obviously, "No."

3   Yet, from all the evidence at hand, most of us believe these things. Ask any college boy if he'd rather take his chances with a Gloria or a Bertha, or ask a college girl if she'd rather blind-date a Richard or a Cuthbert. In fact, you don't have to ask: college students in questionnaires have revealed that names conjure up the same images in their minds as they do in yours—and for as little reason.

4   Look into the favorite suspects of persons who report "suspicious characters" and you will find a large percentage of them to be "swarthy" or "dark and foreign-looking"—despite the testimony of criminologists that criminals do *not* tend to be dark, foreign or "wild-eyed." Delve into the main asset of a telephone stock swindler and you will find it to be a marvelously confidence-inspiring telephone "personality." And whereas we all think we know what an Italian or a Swede looks like, it is the sad fact that

Figure 10.1   Who has the higher grade point average? Stereotypes can give us the wrong information: the brunette wearing glasses may not be getting better grades than the blonde.

when a group of Nebraska students sought to match faces and nationalities of 15 European countries, they were scored wrong in 93 percent of their identifications. Finally, for all the fact that horn-rimmed glasses have now become the standard television sign of an "intellectual," optometrists know that the main thing that distinguishes people with glasses is just bad eyes.

Stereotypes are a kind of gossip about the world, a gossip that makes   5
us prejudge people before we ever lay eyes on them. Hence it is not surprising that stereotypes have something to do with the dark world of prejudice. Explore most prejudices (note that the word means prejudgment) and you will find a cruel stereotype at the core of each one.

For it is the extraordinary fact that once we have typecast the world, we   6
tend to see people in terms of our standardized pictures. In another demonstration of the power of stereotypes to affect our vision, a number of Columbia and Barnard students were shown 30 photographs of pretty but unidentified girls, and asked to rate each in terms of "general liking," "intelligence," "beauty" and so on. Two months later, the same group were shown the same photographs, this time with fictitious Irish, Italian, Jewish and "American" names attached to the pictures. Right away the ratings changed. Faces which were now seen as representing a national group went down in looks and still farther down in likeability, while the "American" girls suddenly looked decidedly prettier and nicer.

Why is it that we stereotype the world in such irrational and harmful   7
fashion? In part, we begin to type-cast people in our childhood years. Early in life, as every parent whose child has watched a TV Western knows, we learn to spot the Good Guys from the Bad Guys. Some years ago, a social psychologist showed very clearly how powerful these stereotypes of childhood vision are. He secretly asked the most popular youngsters in an elementary school to make errors in their morning gym exercises. Afterwards, he asked the class if anyone had noticed any mistakes during gym period. Oh, yes, said the children. But it was the *unpopular* members of the class—the "bad guys"—they remembered as being out of step.

We not only grow up with standardized pictures forming inside us, but   8
as grown-ups we are constantly having them thrust upon us. Some of them, like the half-joking, half-serious stereotypes of mothers-in-law, or country yokels, or psychiatrists, are dinned into us by the stock jokes we hear and repeat. In fact, without such stereotypes, there would be a lot fewer jokes. Still other stereotypes are perpetuated in the advertisements we read, the movies we see, the books we read.

And finally, we tend to stereotype because it helps us make sense out   9
of a highly confusing world, a world which William James once described as "one great, blooming, buzzing confusion." It is a curious fact that if we

don't *know* what we're looking at, we are often quite literally unable to *see* what we're looking at. People who recover their sight after a lifetime of blindness actually cannot at first tell a triangle from a square. A visitor to a factory sees only noisy chaos where the superintendent sees a perfectly synchronized flow of work. As Walter Lippmann has said, "For the most part we do not first see, and then define; we define first, and then we see."

Stereotypes are one way in which we "define" the world in order to see it. They classify the infinite variety of human beings into a convenient handful of "types" towards whom we learn to act in stereotyped fashion. Life would be a wearing process if we had to start from scratch with each and every human contact. Stereotypes economize on our mental effort by covering up the blooming, buzzing confusion with big recognizable cutouts. They save us the "trouble" of finding out what the world is like— they give it its accustomed look.   10

Thus the trouble is that stereotypes make us mentally lazy. As S. I. Hayakawa, the authority on semantics, has written: "The danger of stereotypes lies not in their existence, but in the fact that they become for all people some of the time, and for some people all the time, *substitutes for observation*." Worse yet, stereotypes get in the way of our judgment, even when we do observe the world. Someone who has formed rigid preconceptions of all Latins as "excitable," or all teenagers as "wild," doesn't alter his point of view when he meets a calm and deliberate Genoese,° or a serious-minded high school student. He brushes them aside as "exceptions that prove the rule." And, of course, if he meets someone true to type, he stands triumphantly vindicated. "They're all like that," he proclaims, having encountered an excited Latin, an ill-behaved adolescent.   11

Genoese: a person from Genoa, Italy.

Hence, quite aside from the injustice which stereotypes do to others, they impoverish ourselves. A person who lumps the world into simple categories, who type-casts all labor leaders as "racketeers," all businessmen as "reactionaries," all Harvard men as "snobs," and all Frenchmen as "sexy," is in danger of becoming a stereotype himself. He loses his capacity to be himself—which is to say, to see the world in his own absolutely unique, inimitable and independent fashion.   12

Instead, he votes for the man who fits his standardized picture of what a candidate "should" look like or sound like, buys the goods that someone in his "situation" in life "should" own, lives the life that others define for him. The mark of the stereotype person is that he never surprises us, that we do indeed have him "typed." And no one fits this straitjacket so perfectly as someone whose opinions about other people are fixed and inflexible.   13

Impoverishing as they are, stereotypes are not easy to get rid of. The world we type-cast may be no better than a Grade B movie, but at least we   14 know what to expect of our stock characters. When we let them act for themselves in the strangely unpredictable way that people do act, who knows but that many of our fondest convictions will be proved wrong?

Nor do we suddenly drop our standardized pictures for a blinding vision of the Truth. Sharp swings of ideas about people often just substitute one stereotype for another. The true process of change is a slow one that adds bits and pieces of reality to the pictures in our heads, until gradually they take on some of the blurriness of life itself. Little by little, we learn not that Jews and Negroes and Catholics and Puerto Ricans are "just like everybody else"—for that, too, is a stereotype—but that each and every one of them is unique, special, different and individual. Often we do not even know that we have let a stereotype lapse until we hear someone saying, "all so-and-so's are like such-and such," and we hear ourselves saying, "Well—maybe."   15

Can we speed the process along? Of course we can.   16

First, we can become aware of the standardized pictures in our heads, in other peoples' heads, in the world around us.   17

Second, we can become suspicious of all judgments that we allow exceptions to "prove." There is no more chastening thought than that in the vast intellectual adventure of science, it takes but one tiny exception to topple a whole edifice of ideas.   18

chary: cautious.

Third, we can learn to be chary° of generalizations about people. As F. Scott Fitzgerald once wrote: "Begin with an individual, and before you know it you have created a type; begin with a type, and you find you have created—nothing."   19

Most of the time, when we type-cast the world, we are not in fact generalizing about people at all. We are only revealing the embarrassing facts about the pictures that hang in the gallery of stereotypes in our own heads.   20

Follow-Up Activities   After you've finished reading, use these questions to respond to "Don't Let Stereotypes Warp Your Judgments." You may write your answers or prepare them in your mind to discuss in class.

Grab your first impressions.

Respond with your first impressions. Say what you like and dislike; relate your personal experiences to the reading; consider what more you want to know.

Work with new words.

Some words in this reading may be unfamiliar to you. Use the methods of Strategy 3 to explain what the listed words mean.

1. Use context clues.

    a. perpetuated (paragraph 8) _____

    b. edifice of ideas (paragraph 18) _____

2. Use word parts.

    a. irrational (paragraph 7) _____

    b. preconception (paragraph 11) _____

    c. inimitable (paragraph 12) _____

3. Use the dictionary.
    Choose the correct definition of each word as it is used in the context of this reading.

    a. semantics (paragraph 11) _____

    b. vindicate (paragraph 11) _____

    c. chastening (paragraph 18) _____

4. Select additional words you're unsure of from the reading. Use one of these methods to discover their meaning.

Ask and answer questions.

1. How did the study done with Columbia and Barnard students demonstrate "the power of stereotypes to affect our vision"?

2. According to Heilbroner, why do stereotypes have such power to influence our thinking?

3. Why does Heilbroner think it harms the person who *does* the stereotyping as well as the person being stereotyped?

4. Heilbroner quotes Walter Lippmann in paragraph 9: "For the most part we do not first see, and then define; we define first, and then we see." Explain how this statement relates to our need for stereotypes.

5. Give one example of each of the following patterns of thought in this reading: definition, examples, cause-and-effect reasoning.

Inference Questions

6. What do people mean when they say something is the "exception that proves the rule"? What does the author think about this response?

7. Explain Heilbroner's sentence in paragraph 15, "Often we do not even know that we have let a stereotype lapse until we hear someone saying, 'all so-and-so's are like such-and-such,' and we hear ourselves saying, 'Well—maybe.'"

Ask and answer your own questions.

Write two questions based on any of the other information in this reading. Share your questions with others and collaborate on answers.

Write a summary.

Base your summary of "Don't Let Stereotypes Warp Your Judgment" on the sample map below.

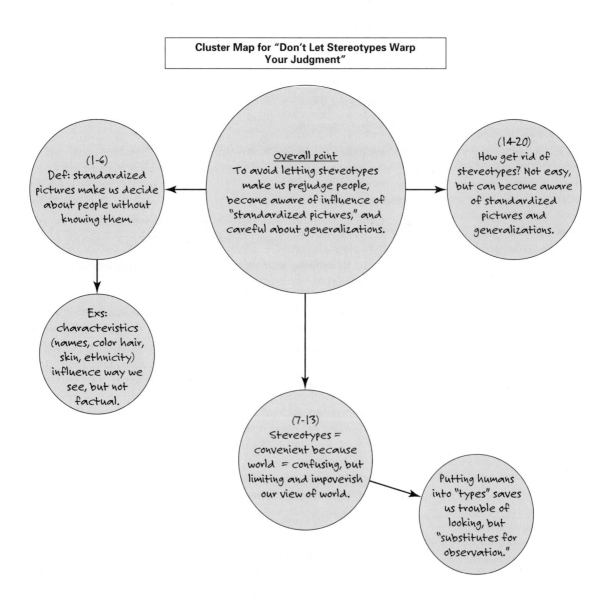

Cluster Map for "Don't Let Stereotypes Warp Your Judgment"

(1-6)
Def: standardized pictures make us decide about people without knowing them.

Overall point
To avoid letting stereotypes make us prejudge people, become aware of influence of "standardized pictures," and careful about generalizations.

(14-20)
How get rid of stereotypes? Not easy, but can become aware of standardized pictures and generalizations.

Exs: characteristics (names, color hair, skin, ethnicity) influence way we see, but not factual.

(7-13)
Stereotypes = convenient because world = confusing, but limiting and impoverish our view of world.

Putting humans into "types" saves us trouble of looking, but "substitutes for observation."

Form your final thoughts.

1. Heilbroner's first recommendation is to "become aware of the standardized pictures in our heads, in other peoples' heads, [and] in the world around us." Try using those three categories to come up with some stereotypes: (a) that you still hold on to; (b) that people you know hold on to; (c) that we see in the world around us—especially in the media.

2. Write briefly about an example in your own life where "bits and pieces of reality" (paragraph 15) slowly changed your ideas about a group you had mainly known through stereotypes.

3. Discuss with others the ways the barriers created by stereotypes can be broken down on your own campus. ■

Chapter 10 Summary

How does Strategy 10 help you *read from the inside out?*

Like **mapping, summarizing** gets you to bring the writer's ideas inside to work with them in your own mind. In a **summary** you get even more involved with these ideas as you translate them into your own words and organize them to flow logically from one sentence to the next. **Summarizing** increases your understanding of a reading and therefore helps you give a fair response to the reading outside—what the writer has said.

How does the *write a summary* strategy work?

The information that goes into a **summary** comes from **marking** or **mapping** or a simple outline. Be sure your summary follows the order of ideas in the reading and represents only what the writer says. Most of the summary is made up of accurate paraphrases of the overall point, main ideas, and a few supporting ideas. Including a few appropriate quotations helps clarify ideas.

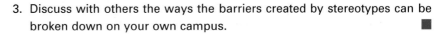

STRATEGY 10: WRITE A SUMMARY

1. Put the writer's ideas in your own words.

2. Base your summary on your marking or mapping.

Are you familiar with the meaning of these terms?

paraphrase: a kind of translation of others' words into your own words

summary: brief—usually one paragraph—restatement of main ideas *complete sentence:* sentence that has a subject and verb and expresses a complete thought

How is the strategy working for you so far?

1. How well have you been able to transform your map into a summary? If you tried basing your summary on marking only, how well did that work?

2. How successful was your paraphrasing into complete sentences? Did you find a way to use appropriate quotations from the reading in your summary?

3. Did you compare your summaries with those of other students? If so, did that help you see where to improve your own? If not, how have you evaluated your summaries?

4. What did you appreciate about using this strategy? What did you dislike?

For more practice with *writing a summary*, use the Reading Road Trip CD-ROM or Web site.

PART IV

ADDITIONAL READINGS ON
UNDERSTANDING OTHERS

The readings that follow will give you further practice in using appropriate strategies with other readings on the theme of "Understanding Others."

READING IV-A TRAVELING

GRACE PALEY

Grace Paley is known as a master of the short story. Her best-known collections of short stories are The Little Disturbances of Man *(1959),* Enormous Changes at the Last Minute *(1974), and* Later the Same Day *(1985). In "Traveling," first published in the* New Yorker *in 1997, Paley tells the true story of travels that had an impact on her entire family.*

Before reading "Traveling," think about the strategies you'll need to get started and to read. The margin boxes give you reminders, but by this time you are skilled and secure enough in reading to decide which strategies to use. It is helpful to note the sequence pattern in this reading; see how the writer moves from one time period to another. You will also find **making inferences** *and* **working with words** *particularly helpful.*

STRATEGY 8: MAKE INFERENCES

What can you infer about the kind of person the writer's mother was? What kind of person is the writer herself?

My mother and sister were traveling South. The year was 1927. They had begun their journey in New York. They were going to visit my brother, who was studying at the Medical College of Virginia, in Richmond. Their bus was an express and had stopped only in Philadelphia, Wilmington, and now Washington. Here the darker people who had got on in Philadelphia or New York rose from their seats, put their bags and boxes together, and moved to the back of the bus. People who boarded in Washington knew where to seat themselves. My mother had heard that something like this would happen. My sister had heard of it, too. They had not lived in it. This reorganization of passengers by color happened in silence. My mother and sister remained in their seats, which were about three-quarters of the way back. 1

When everyone was settled, the bus driver began to collect tickets. My sister saw him coming. She pinched my mother—"Ma! Look!" Of course, my mother saw him, too. What frightened my sister was the quietness. The white people in front, the black people in back—silent. 2

Negroes: term used for African Americans during the time period the writer describes.

The driver sighed, said, "You can't sit here, ma'am. It's for them"— waving over his shoulder at the Negroes,° among whom they were now sitting. "Move, please." 3

My mother said, "No."   4

He said, "You don't understand, ma'am. It's against the law. You have   5
to move to the front."

My mother said, "No."   6

When I first tried to write this scene, I imagined my mother saying,   7
"That's all right, mister. We're comfortable. I can't change my seat every
minute." I read this invention to my sister. She said it was nothing like that.
My mother did not try to be friendly or pretend innocence. While my sister
trembled in the silence, my mother said for the third time—quietly—"No."

Somehow, finally, they were in Richmond. There was my brother, in   8
school among so many American boys. After hugs and my mother's anxious
looks at her young son, my sister said, "Vic, you know what Mama did?"

My brother remembers thinking, What? Oh! She wouldn't move? He   9
had a classmate, a Jewish boy like him, but from Virginia, who had had a
public confrontation with a Negro man. He had punched that man hard,
knocked him down. My brother couldn't believe it. He was stunned. He
couldn't imagine a Jewish boy wanting to knock anyone down. He had
never wanted to. But he thought, looking back, that he had been set down
to work and study in a nearly foreign place, and had had to get used to it.
Then he told me about the Second World War, when the disgrace of black
soldiers forced to sit behind white German P.O.W.s shook him. Shamed him.

About fifteen years later, in 1943, in early summer, I rode the bus for   10
about three days from New York to Miami Beach, where my husband and
hundreds of other boys in sweaty fatigues were trudging up and down the
streets and beaches to prepare themselves for war.

By late afternoon of the second long day, we were well into the South,   11
beyond Richmond, maybe in South Carolina or Georgia. My excitement
about travel in the wide world was damaged a little by a sudden fear that I
might not recognize Jess, or he me. We hadn't seen each other for two
months. I took a photograph out of my pocket; yes, I would know him.

I had been sleeping, waking, reading, writing, dozing, waking. So many   12
hours, the movement of the passengers was like a tide that sometimes
ebbed and now seemed to be noisily rising. I opened my eyes to the sound

colored: term used for African
Americans during the time
period the writer describes.

of people brushing past my aisle seat. And looked up to see a colored°
woman holding a large sleeping baby, who, with the heaviness of sleep, his
arms tight around her neck, seemed to be pulling her head down. I looked
around and noticed that I was in the last white row. The press of new trav-
elers had made it impossible for her to move farther back. She seemed so
tired, and I had been sitting and sitting for a day and a half at least. Not
thinking, or maybe refusing to think, I offered her my seat.

She looked to the right and left as well as she could. Softly, she said, 13
"Oh, no." I became fully awake. A white man was standing right beside her,
but on the other side of the invisible absolute racial border. Of course, she
couldn't accept my seat. Her sleeping child hung mercilessly from her neck.
She shifted a little to balance the burden. She whispered to herself, "Oh, I
just don't know." So I said, "Well, at least give me the baby." First, she
turned, barely looking at the man beside her. He made no move. Then, to
my surprise, but obviously out of sheer exhaustion, she disengaged the
child from her body and placed him on my lap. He was deep in child-sleep.
He stirred, but not enough to bother himself or me. I liked holding him,
aligning him along my twenty-year-old young woman's shape. I thought
ahead to that holding, that breathing together that would happen in my life
if this war would ever end. I was so comfortable under his nice weight. I
closed my eyes for a couple of minutes but suddenly opened them to look
up into the face of a white man talking. In a loud voice, he addressed me:
"Lady, I wouldn't of touched that thing with a meat hook."

I thought, Oh, this world will end in ice.° I could do nothing but look 14
straight into his eyes. I did not look away from him. Then I held that little
boy a little tighter, kissed his curly head, pressed him even closer, so that
he began to squirm. So sleepy, he reshaped himself inside my arms. His
mother tried to narrow herself away from that dangerous border, too frightened at first to move at all. After a couple of minutes, she leaned forward a
little, placed her hand on the baby's head, and held it there until the next
stop. I couldn't look up into her mother face.

> **this world will end in ice:**
> refers to Robert Frost's lines
> about hate in his poem, "Fire
> and Ice."

I write this remembrance more than fifty years later. I look back at that 15
mother and child. I see how young she is. Her hand on his head is quite
small, though she tries by spreading her fingers wide to hide him from
the white man. But the child I'm holding, his little face as he turns toward
me, is the dark-brown face of my *own* grandson, my daughter's boy, the
open mouth of the sleeper, the full lips, the thick little body of a child who
runs wildly from one end of the yard to the other, leaps from dangerous
heights with experienced caution, muscling his body, his mind, for coming
realities.

Of course, when my mother and sister returned from Charlottesville 16
the family at home wanted to know: How was Vic doing in school among
all those Gentiles? Was the long bus ride hard? Was the anti-Semitism
really bad or just normal? What happened on the bus? I was probably
present at that supper, the attentive listener and total forgetter of information that immediately started to form me.

Then, last year, my sister, casting the net of old age (through which   17
recent experience easily slips), brought up that old story. First, I was angry.
How come you never told me about your bus ride with Mama? I mean,
really, so many years ago.

I don't know, she said. Anyway, you were only about four years old   18
and, besides, maybe I did.

I asked my brother why we'd never talked about that day. He said he   19
thought now that it had had a great effect on him: he had tried unraveling
its meaning for years—then life, family, work happened. So I imagined him,
a youngster, really, a kid from the Bronx in Virginia in 1927—why, he was a
stranger there himself.

In the next couple of weeks, we continued to talk about our mother, the   20
way she was principled, adamant, and at the same time so shy. What else
could we remember . . . Well, I said, I have a story about those buses, too.
Then I told them: how it happened on just such a journey, when I was still
quite young, that I first knew my grandson, first held him close but could
protect him for only about twenty minutes fifty years ago.

STRATEGY 9: MAP MAIN IDEAS STRAGEGY 10: WRITE A SUMMARY	**Follow-Up Activities** After you've finished reading, use these questions to respond to "Traveling." You may write your answers or prepare them in your mind to discuss in class. *Grab your first impressions.* **Respond** with your first impressions. Say what you like and dislike; relate your personal experiences to the reading; consider what more you want to know. *Work with new words.* 1. Most of the words in this reading are probably familiar to you. However, the writer uses some words in unexpected ways. Explain the way the italicized words are used. a. "Here *the darker people* who had got on in Philadelphia or New York . . . moved to the back of the bus." (paragraph 1) ———————————————————————————— b. "[T]he movement of the passengers was like a *tide* that sometimes *ebbed* and now seemed to be noisily *rising.*" (paragraph 12) ———————————————————————————— c. "A white man was standing right beside her, *but on the other side of the invisible absolute racial border.*" (paragraph 13) ————————————————————————————

d. "Lady, I wouldn't of *touched that thing with a meat hook."* (paragraph 13)

_____

e. "Oh, this *world will end in ice*" refers to a poem by Robert Frost, "Fire and Ice," that begins, "Some say the world will end in fire/Some say in ice." What makes Paley say the world will end in ice? (paragraph 14)

_____

f. "[M]y sister, *casting the net of old age (through which recent experience easily slips)* brought up that old story." (paragraph 17)

_____

g. "Then I told them: how it happened on just such a journey, when I was still quite young, that I first knew my *grandson."* (paragraph 20)

_____

2. Select additional words you're unsure of from the reading. Use one of the methods from Strategy 3 to discover their meaning.

Ask and answer questions.

1. The first incident in this reading takes place in 1927. What are the other time periods?

2. Why was Paley's mother supposed to change seats once the bus got to Washington? What was the situation in the southern part of the United States during both bus trips that she describes?

3. Where and when was Paley going on her own bus trip? Why was she taking this trip?

4. What happens when Paley tries to help an exhausted black woman by holding the woman's sleeping baby on her lap? How does she feel about the baby?

Inference Questions

5. Why was Virginia in 1927 "a nearly foreign place" for Paley's brother Vic? What were the differences for Jews and blacks between living in New York and living in Virginia at that time?

6. Who is the woman she is looking back at in paragraph 15? Who is the child? Why does this child seem to be her own grandson?

7. What can you tell about the kind of person Paley's mother was? What kind of qualities did Paley get from her mother?

Ask and answer your own questions.

Write two questions based on any of the other information in this reading. Share your questions with others and collaborate on answers.

Form your final thoughts.

1. Now that you have a good understanding of this reading, write about what you liked and didn't like in the way the writer presents her ideas.

2. Discuss with others how this reading relates to the theme for Part IV: *Understanding Others*.

3. Find the short Robert Frost poem "Fire and Ice." See how it adds to your understanding of what Paley says in this reading.   ■

READING IV-B   MANAGING WORKFORCE DIVERSITY

RONALD J. EBERT AND RICKY W. GRIFFIN

Ronald J. Ebert teaches business at the University of Missouri, Columbia, and Ricky W. Griffin teaches business at Texas A & M University. This reading comes from the chapter "Managing Human Resources and Labor Relations" in their textbook Business Essentials *(2000). Here the authors discuss the challenges of managing workers in a multicultural society.*

Before reading "Managing Workforce Diversity," think about the strategies you'll need to get started and to read. The margin boxes give you reminders, but by this time you are skilled and secure enough in reading to decide which strategies to use. In forming your overall-point question and the overall point for this reading, remember to cover both topics given in the headings: "Diversity as a Competitive Advantage" and "Diversity Training." Also, note the comparison/ contrast pattern (differences between past and present) and cause-and-effect reasoning (for example, why is "diversity a competitive advantage"?).

An extremely important set of human resource challenges centers on 1 *workforce diversity*—the range of workers' attitudes, values, beliefs, and behaviors that differ by gender, race, and ethnicity. The diverse workforce is also characterized by individuals of different ages and physical abilities. In the past, organizations tended to work toward *homogenizing* their workforces, getting everyone to think and behave in similar ways. Partly as a result of affirmative action° efforts, however, many U.S. organizations are now creating workforces that are more diverse, thus embracing more women, more ethnic minorities, and more foreign-born employees than ever before.

affirmative action: encouragement of increased representation of women and minorities.

Figures 1 and 2 help put the changing U.S. workforce into perspective. 2 Figure 1 shows changes in the percentages of different groups of workers— white males, white females, blacks, Hispanics, and Asians and others—in

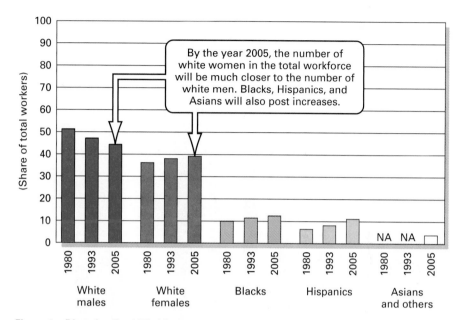

Figure 1   Diversity: Total Workforce
NA = Not Available

the total workforce in the years 1980, 1993, and (as projected) 2005. Figure 2 (page 284) shows changes among managerial and professional workers for blacks and Hispanics between 1983 and 1997. The first picture is one of increasing diversity over the past decade. The second is one of a slower but steady trend toward diversity: By 2005, says the Labor Department, half of all workers entering the labor force will be women and more than one-third will be blacks, Hispanics, Asian Americans, and others.

DIVERSITY AS A COMPETITIVE ADVANTAGE

Today, organizations are recognizing not only that they should treat everyone equitably, but also that they should acknowledge the individuality of each person they employ. They are also recognizing that diversity can be a competitive advantage. For example, by hiring the best people available from every single group rather than hiring from just one or a few groups, a firm can develop a higher-quality labor force. Similarly, a diverse workforce can bring a wider array of information to bear on problems and can provide insights on marketing products to a wider range of consumers. Says the head of workforce diversity at IBM: "We think it is important for our customers to look inside and see people like them. If they can't . . . the prospect of them becoming or staying our customers declines."

3

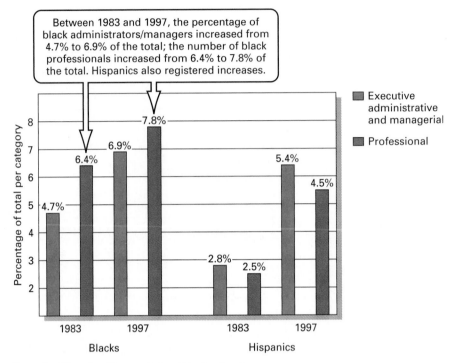

Between 1983 and 1997, the percentage of black administrators/managers increased from 4.7% to 6.9% of the total; the number of black professionals increased from 6.4% to 7.8% of the total. Hispanics also registered increases.

Figure 2   Diversity: Managerial and Professional

Admittedly, not all U.S. companies have worked equally hard to adjust   4
their thinking and diversify their workforces. In fact, experts estimate that
only a handful of U.S. corporations are diversifying with any effect. Even
among those making progress, it has nevertheless been slow.[1] In a recent
survey of executives at 1,405 participating firms, only 5 percent believed that
they were doing a "very good job" of diversifying their human resources.°

human resources:
a company's workforce.

Many others, however, have instituted—and, more importantly, main-
tained—diversity programs. The experience of these companies (including
IBM, Xerox, Avon, AT&T, Burger King, Levi Strauss, and Hoechst Celanese)
has made it possible to draw up some general guidelines for a successful
workforce diversity program:

compensation scales:
amounts and ranges of
salaries and other benefits.

- Make diversity a specific management goal.
- Analyze compensation scales° and be scrupulously fair in tracking indi-
  vidual careers.
- Continue to focus on diversity in the midst of downsizing.
- Contribute to the supply of diverse workers.
- Celebrate diversity.
- Respond to the concerns of white males.

DIVERSITY TRAINING

Another guideline calls for companies to use *diversity training*—programs designed to improve employees' understanding of differences in attitudes and behavior patterns among their coworkers. However, there is no consensus yet on how to *conduct* such programs—on exactly what to teach and how to do it. [5]

Not surprisingly, there are sometimes repercussions to such an approach. Indeed, some recent studies have shown that focusing strictly on such issues as race and gender can arouse deep feelings and be almost as divisive as ignoring negative stereotyping in the first place. Other studies suggest that too many training programs are limited to correcting affirmative action problems: Backlash occurs when participants appear to be either "winners" (say, black women) or "losers" (white men) as a result of the process. [6]

Many companies therefore try to go beyond mere awareness training. Du Pont, for example, offers a course for managers on how to seek and use more diverse input before making decisions. Sears offers what it calls diversity-friendly programs: bus service for workers who must commute from the inner city to the suburbs and leaves of absence for foreign-born employees to visit families still living overseas. Finally, one consultant emphasizes that it is extremely important to integrate training into daily routines: "Diversity training," he says, "is like hearing a good sermon on Sunday. You must practice what you heard during the week." [7]

Notes

1. Mark Adams, "Building a Rainbow, One Stripe at a Time," *HR Magazine* (August 1998), pp. 72–78.

STRATEGY 9: MAP MAIN IDEAS

STRAGEGY 10: WRITE A SUMMARY

Follow-Up Activities After you've finished reading, use these questions to respond to "Managing Workforce Diversity." You may write your answers or prepare them in your mind to discuss in class.

Grab your first impressions.

Respond with your first impressions. Say what you like and dislike; relate your personal experiences to the reading; consider what more you want to know.

Work with new words.

Some words in this reading may be unfamiliar to you. Use the methods of Strategy 3 to explain what the listed words mean.

1. Use context clues.

    a. workforce diversity (paragraph 1 _____

    b. diversity training (paragraph 5)_____

2. Use word parts.

    a. equitably (paragraph 3) _____
       See how part of the word *equal* begins this word.

    b. diversify (paragraph 4)_____

    c. downsizing (paragraph 4) _____

    d. divisive (paragraph 6) _____
       Note how the suffixes for these words modify their meaning.

    e. backlash (paragraph 6)_____

3. Use the dictionary.
   Choose the correct definition of each word as it is used in the context of this reading.

    a. array (paragraph 3)_____

    b. scrupulously (paragraph 4)_____

    c. consensus (paragraph 5)_____

    d. repercussions (paragraph 6)_____

4. Select additional words you're unsure of from the reading. Use one of these methods to discover their meaning.

Read the information in the bar graphs.

1. Look at Figure 1. It shows that in 1980 white males made up just a little over 50% of the workforce. What percentage of the workforce did the other groups make up in 1980? What changes in these percentages took place between 1980 and 1993? What changes are projected to take place by 2005?

2. Look at Figure 2. What percentage of administrators/managers were black in 1983? What percentage of professionals were black in 1983? What were these percentages in 1997? What changes in percentages of administrators/managers and professionals are shown for Hispanics over those same two years?

Ask and answer questions.

1. As part of their definition of workforce diversity, Ebert and Griffin include categories of difference such as gender. What are the four other categories of difference they include in their definition?

2. Why are some organizations recognizing that "diversity can be a competitive advantage"? What are the advantages to an organization of a diverse workforce?

3. How successful have *most* U.S. corporations been in diversifying? What are some companies that have been successful?

4. What is the purpose of diversity training programs?

Inference Questions

5. Why are there repercussions to the diversity programs? What are some of these repercussions?

6. What does the consultant quoted at the end of the reading mean when he says, "Diversity training is like hearing a good sermon on Sunday. You must practice what you heard during the week."

 Ask and answer your own questions.

Write two questions based on any of the other information in this reading. Share your questions with others and collaborate on answers.

 Form your final thoughts.

1. How diverse is the workforce in the job you now have or in jobs you've had in the past or on your campus? How have the managers tried to help employees get along with one another? What suggestions do you have for improving?

2. Were you able to relate this reading to other readings on the theme of "Understanding Others? If so, how did that help to enliven the information and the facts and figures? If not, discuss with others how linking ideas in these readings might help. ■

READING IV-C   PERHAPS THE WORLD ENDS HERE

JOY HARJO

STRATEGY 3: WORK WITH NEW WORDS
Look for unusual uses of words; see stanza 6: how can dreams drink coffee with us?

Joy Harjo is an enrolled member of the Muscogee (Creek) Nation of Oklahoma. She is a poet who has written several award-winning books of poetry, including She Had Some Horses, In Mad Love and War, *and* The Woman Who Fell from the Sky. *This poem comes from the 1997 anthology of poetry edited by Harjo and Gloria Bird,* Reinventing the Enemy's Language.

Before reading "Perhaps the World Ends Here," think about the strategies you'll want to use for reading a poem. You will get a great deal from this poem just by using the first two strategies: **check in** *and* **respond.** *You'll see in the Follow-up Activities that* **making inferences** *and* **working with words** *will also* *be helpful. Ideas in a poem are not presented in a logical, organized form. But there may be a use for steps from another strategy, such as paraphrasing, from* **writing a summary.** *Are there any other steps from strategies you might use?*

The world begins at a kitchen table. No matter what,   1
we must eat to live.

The gifts of earth are brought and prepared, set on the   2
table. So it has been since creation, and it will go on.

We chase chickens or dogs away from it. Babies teethe   3
at the corners. They scrape their knees under it.

It is here that children are given instructions on what   4
it means to be human. We make men at it,
we make women.

At this table we gossip, recall enemies and the ghosts   5
of lovers.

Our dreams drink coffee with us as they put their arms   6
around our children. They laugh with us at our poor
falling-down selves and as we put ourselves back
together once again at the table.

This table has been a house in the rain, an umbrella   7
in the sun.

Wars have begun and ended at this table. It is a place   8
to hide in the shadow of terror. A place to celebrate
the terrible victory.

We have given birth on this table, and have prepared   9
our parents for burial here.

At this table we sing with joy, with sorrow.   10
We pray of suffering and remorse.
We give thanks.

Perhaps the world will end at the kitchen table,   11
while we are laughing and crying,
eating of the last sweet bite.

Follow-Up Activities   After you've finished reading, use these questions to respond to "Perhaps the World Ends Here." You may write your answers or prepare them in your mind to discuss in class.

Grab your first impressions.

Respond with your first impressions. Say what you like and dislike; relate your personal experiences to the reading; consider what more you want to know.

Work with new words.

1. Most of the words in this reading are probably familiar to you. However, the poet uses some words in unexpected ways. Explain the way the italicized words are used.

    a. *The world begins at a kitchen table.* No matter what, we must eat to live. (stanza 1)

    _____

    b. *So it has been since creation, and it will go on.* (stanza 2)

    _____

    c. At this table we gossip, recall enemies and *the ghosts/ of lovers.* (stanza 5)

    _____

    d. *Our dreams drink coffee with us as they put their arms/ around our children.* (stanza 6)

    _____

    e. *They laugh with us at our poor falling-down selves and as we put ourselves back together once again at the table.* (stanza 6)

    _____

    f. *This table has been a house in the rain, an umbrella in the sun.* (stanza 7)

    _____

    g. *Wars have begun and ended at this table.* (stanza 8)

    _____

2. Select additional words you're unsure of from the reading. Use one of the methods from Strategy 3 to discover their meaning.

Use inference to answer questions.

Poems depend on implied meanings, so all of these questions are inference questions.

1. Why is the kitchen table such an important place in Harjo's mind? What happens there that makes her say the world begins there?

2. What instructions are children given at the table about "what it means to be human"? How are men and women "made" at the table?

3. How is the table a place "to hide in the shadow of terror" or "a place to celebrate a terrible victory"?

4. In many cultures, birth and death both take place at home. Do you think Harjo really means the table was used for giving birth and preparing parents for burial? Explain your answer.

5. How do the last lines of the poem connect with all the other images of the kitchen table Harjo gives before these? What does "eating of the last sweet bite" mean to you? Why might the world end at the kitchen table?

 Form your final thoughts.

1. What are your family's traditions about sitting around the table? Do you share mealtimes with one another? If not, what other ways does your family have of coming together and sharing your lives?

2. This poem shows us how people come together around "the kitchen table." What kind of "coming together" does Harjo refer to? Is this just a family? An extended family? Or can it be a larger group? What kind of community might be able to gather together in this way?

3. This poem celebrates the ritual of eating together. What do you think is important about this ritual, and why has it been so important throughout the world and across the centuries? ■

PART IV REVIEW
SUMMARIZING IN YOUR OWN WORDS

Now that you've completed Part IV, think over what you've read about barriers and breakthroughs to understanding. Review the two strategies introduced in this part, and see how they work throughout the reading process.

Linking Ideas on the Theme: Understanding Others

 Respond to the readings in Part IV by linking ideas on the theme of "Understanding Others." Answer these questions in writing or in discussion with others.

1. Some of the readings deal with the barriers put up between people because of hatred and/or prejudice against a certain race, ethnic group, or disability. Find ways of linking two readings that explore these barriers.

2. People are often suspicious about others because they don't see others as individual human beings but as defined only by group membership. Choose two writers who discuss the problems caused by simply grouping people into the category of "other."

3. Choose two writers who discuss creating changes that bring greater understanding between people who wouldn't ordinarily know or trust one another. Say what the two readings have in common as well as how they differ.

4. You may think of yet another way of linking two readings on this theme. Say what the two readings have in common as well as how they are different.

5. Try linking ideas from one or two of these readings with ideas in something else you've read—including something in an earlier part of this book—or with a movie or TV program you've seen.

6. Decide on your favorite reading for Part IV. Find others in the class who chose the same reading. Look up the writer on the Internet to find out more about him or her. If it is possible, send a group or individual e-mail to the author, saying what you liked about his or her piece.

Using Strategies Throughout the Reading Process

Strategy 9: **Map Main Ideas**

Strategy 10: **Write a Summary**

You have seen how the strategies in Part IV incorporate the earlier strategies for predicting and comprehending main ideas. These new strategies help you work with the main ideas so you can put them into your own clear format: a **map of main ideas** or a brief written **summary.**

STRATEGIES THROUGH PART IV

1. Check in
2. Respond
3. Work with new words
4. Get an overview
5. Ask questions
6. Find and mark main ideas
7. Look for patterns of thought
8. Make inferences
9. Map main ideas
10. Write a summary

GET STARTED   Begin with strategies that help you think about the subject and find out about what the writer will say.

- Check in
- Get an overview
- Ask questions

READ   Use strategies that help you read with greater understanding, interpret the language, and respond with your own questions and ideas.

- Respond
- Work with new words
- Ask questions
- Find and mark main ideas
- Look for patterns of thought
- Make inferences

FOLLOW UP   End with strategies that help you look more closely at the language and ideas in the reading, assess your understanding, and respond in a thoughtful way.

- Work with new words
- Respond
- Ask questions
- Find and mark main ideas
- Look for patterns of thought
- Make inferences
- Map main ideas
- Write a summary

Use the chart here as a reminder of how a strategy helps you at each of the three stages of reading: Get Started, Read, Follow Up. The new strategies are highlighted.

How Are the Strategies Working for You?

With the Part IV strategies you have the last in a group of strategies that build your comprehension, first by finding main ideas and important support and then recording the ideas in your own words. Take some time now to evaluate Strategies 9 and 10 along with the other strategies.

First, look back at what you wrote about the strategies at the end of Part III. What differences would there be in your answers to those questions now? Next, answer the following questions to help you evaluate Strategies 9 and 10. Then compare notes with other students, and ask your instructor for ideas on how to get more out of the strategies.

1. Which strategies have become a regular part of your reading? Which ones do you use less often? Why?

   _____

   _____

   _____

2. Which strategies do you combine as you're going through each stage of reading? (For example, *summarizing* works well with *mapping* and/or *marking main ideas.*)

   _____

   _____

   _____

3. How do you decide which strategies to use for a particular reading?

   _____

   _____

   _____

4. Overall, which strategies have made the biggest difference in your reading so far?

   _____

   _____

   _____

5. Are there specific things you could do to make the strategies more effective? If so, what?

_____

_____

_____

PART V

INTERPRETING LANGUAGE AND PURPOSE

WITH READINGS ON NATURE'S ADVENTURES AND CHALLENGES

> The great [Colorado] plateau and its canyon wilderness is a treasure. . . . We would guard and defend and save it as a place for all who wish to rediscover the nearly lost pleasures of adventure, not only in the physical sense but also mental, spiritual, moral, aesthetic and intellectual adventure. A place for the free.
>
> Come on in. The earth, like the sun, like the air, belongs to everyone—and to no one.
>
> —Edward Abbey

Abbey's invitation to "come on in" relates to a specific place. But the writers in Part V have a similar message about the natural world in general. They invite us to enjoy nature, but also to respect it. Some focus on adventures in the wilderness; others on interaction with animals; others on environmental challenges. But underlying their writings is an invitation, like Abbey's, to "come on in" to enjoy the natural world. These readings will give you practice in reading from the inside out as you compare and contrast your own relationship to nature with the ideas and experiences of the writers.

Here are some questions to help you think about this theme.

1. How much interest do you have in being outside in nature? If you live in suburban or urban environments—as most of us do—how do you enjoy some contact with nature?

2. What outdoor activities—if any—do you enjoy? What appeals to you about being outside?

3. How much interest do you have in animals, whether your own pets or other animals? What do you think we humans can learn from animals?

4. How much concern have you had so far about the damage humans have caused to our natural environment? What do you see as some of the greatest dangers we face on a global scale?

The strategies you've learned so far help you read from the inside out by getting you involved in a reading and helping you comprehend and summarize the writer's ideas, so you can **respond** in a thoughtful way to those ideas. The strategies in Part V help you move to a deeper level of understanding and **responding.** Strategy 11, **Find Meaning in Metaphors,** shows you how to figure out words and phrases used in unusual ways to make a vivid impact. When you use Strategy 12, **Determine the Writer's Purpose,** you understand where the writer is coming from. This understanding, in turn, helps you determine what you think about a reading.

By now, you've incorporated more of the earlier strategies, such as **getting an overview** and **finding and marking main ideas,** into your own reading process. In Part V you'll continue combining strategies, incorporating earlier strategies into the new ones. You'll also make more decisions about which of the later strategies (starting with Strategy 7) are most important for a particular reading. After you've learned Strategies 11 and 12, you'll also begin making judgments about when they are most appropriate to use.

CHAPTER 11

DEEPEN YOUR UNDERSTANDING: FIND MEANING IN METAPHORS

Strategy 3, **Work with New Words,** gives you a process for dealing with vocabulary, so unfamiliar words won't get in the way of what the writer is saying. But earlier readings, such as "The Voice You Hear When You Read Silently" and "Traveling," showed you that familiar words may be used in unexpected—sometimes confusing—new ways. Strategy 11, **Find Meaning in Metaphors,** builds on what you already know by explaining how to interpret these imaginative expressions.

Try the New Strategy: Find Meaning in Metaphors

Our everyday language is full of expressions that use words in unexpected ways to create a vivid, often visual, impression. We know what *traffic bottlenecks* are. They are not, literally, the necks of bottles on highways. They are lanes narrowing down—just as a bottle narrows at its neck—with too much traffic trying to squeeze into too narrow a space. Used in this way, *bottleneck* is a *metaphor,* a comparison that uses an object or idea in place of another to suggest a likeness or a picture in our minds. A metaphor is a *figure of speech,* an expression that heightens the effect and meaning of language. Strategy 11 will show you how to recognize and interpret metaphorical expressions that are not part of our ordinary speech.

STRATEGY 11: FIND MEANING IN METAPHORS

1 Recognize metaphors.

2 Analyze the surprising comparison.

Before reading some short passages about nature, learn to recognize and interpret metaphors.

Metaphorical Expressions

1 Recognize
metaphors.

Metaphorical expressions are based on a surprising comparison that highlights a particular image or idea. When words are used metaphorically, you cannot take them literally. That is, these words don't have their ordinary or primary meanings. They are being used as a comparison to something else—a bottleneck to a narrow passage for traffic.

Look at another example of metaphorical expression. How is *rusty* used in the following sentence?

I haven't played the piano in such a long time. I'm really *rusty*.

Look at the visual on page 299 to see how *rusty*, which literally refers to the "reddish, brittle coating on metal left in moist air," can also describe a human being.

We use hundreds of common expressions metaphorically, not literally— "tip of the iceberg," "a ton of work to do," "dying of thirst." You and your classmates can come up with your own examples.

Metaphorical expressions actually come in two types: similes and metaphors. Both are figurative language or figures of speech. They are based on an imaginative comparison. For our purposes in this book, we use *metaphor* in its broader meaning to cover all figurative, or nonliteral, language.

Simile. A *simile* is a clear-cut or explicit comparison because it uses the words *like* or *as*. "The fear was *like* a snake that wound its way through her whole body" is a simile that shows how penetrating fear can be.

Metaphor. A *metaphor* is an implied comparison that does *not* use like or as. See the contrast between the two in the following table.

Comparisons

Type	Definition	Example
simile	explicit comparison, using *like* or *as*	"Fear was *like* a snake that wound its way through her whole body."
metaphor	implied comparison	"Fear was a snake that wound its way through her whole body."

Literal versus metaphorical expressions. We make literal comparisons all the time between things that have obvious similarities. For example, we can better

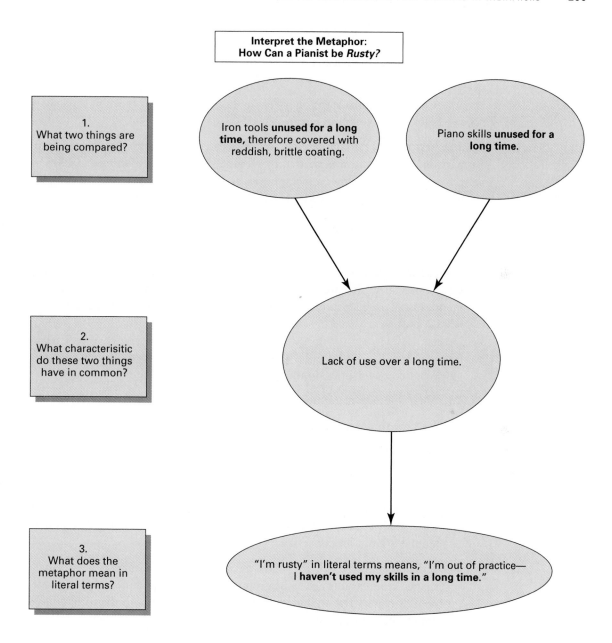

understand what a tiger is like by comparing it to another member of the cat family—our pet tabby cat; we can get an idea about flying a plane by comparing it to driving another vehicle—the family car. We expect to compare two kinds of cats or two kinds of vehicles. You'll recognize a metaphor or simile because it is based on an unexpected, even startling, comparison.

Which one of the following is a simile, and which is a literal comparison?

A Monterey pine leans out over the Pacific . . . and it looks like a wind-swept fir tree.

A Monterey pine leans out over the Pacific . . . and it looks like a shaggy black finger pointing out to sea.

The first is a literal comparison. Why? Because there is no unexpected comparison. The second was written by Diane Ackerman in *A Natural History of the Senses*. It is a simile, a metaphorical comparison. The surprising comparison lets us see the tree overlooking the ocean in a new way.

Interpreting Metaphors

2 Analyze the surprising comparison.

We usually understand everyday expressions like *bottleneck* and *rusty* because we've heard them so often. But you may have to stop and think about what a new metaphor means. Once you recognize that the expression can't be literal, but must be metaphorical, it's helpful to ask three questions to be sure what it means.

1. What two things are being compared?

2. What characteristics do these two things have in common?

3. What does the metaphor mean in literal terms?

See how these questions work to interpret the following metaphor:

There have been tornadoes. They lay their elephant trunks out in the sage until they find houses, then slurp everything up and leave.

(Ehrlich, "The Solace of Open Spaces")

1. The tornadoes are compared to elephants using their trunks to "slurp" water. This is an unexpected comparison because a weather system and an animal are not literally alike.

2. The first characteristic they have in common is the tornado's long funnel-shaped cloud as it touches the ground, which has the same shape as an elephant's trunk. The second characteristic is the way both the tornado and the elephant's trunk suck things up.

3. Wherever a tornado's funnel cloud touches the ground it sucks up everything in its path.

Judging the metaphor. You can tell how effective a metaphor is by seeing what would be lost if the same idea were written in purely literal terms. In this case we would miss the clear picture of the tornado as the elephant's trunk, along with imagining the elephant's slurping action.

Practice the New Strategy

STRATEGY 11: FIND
MEANING IN
METAPHORS

1 Recognize
metaphors.

2 Analyze the
surprising
comparison.

As you read the following short passages on Part V's theme, "Nature's Adventures and Challenges," practice **finding meaning in metaphors**. After reading each passage, first identify the metaphorical expression, saying whether it is a metaphor or a simile. Then, interpret its meaning, using these questions:

1. What two things are being compared?

2. What characteristic do these two things have in common?

3. What does the metaphor mean in literal terms?

Find meanings in metaphors.

Identify the metaphorical expression (a metaphor or a simile) in each passage. Then, interpret its meaning.

bobo: bird found in forests of the Dominican Republic.

1. Looking over his shoulder, Victor spots the red-eyed bobo° flying through the trees as if stitching together the forest with the rise and fall of its wings. If the lady is here to see the park, she should not miss the flight of the bobo.

   (Alvarez, "Víctor")

   _____

   _____

   _____

2. I still keep in mind a certain wonderful sunset which I witnessed when steamboating was new to me. A broad expanse of the river was turned to blood; in the middle distance the red hue brightened into gold, through which a solitary log came floating, black and conspicuous.

   (Twain, *Life on the Mississippi*)

   _____

   _____

   _____

jumar: type of ascender.

ascender: device you clamp on a rope to climb up the rope.

3. If, for some reason, a [mountain] climber lost his top jumar° and his chest roller, he'd fall backward and end up hanging from the ascenders° on his feet. There is almost no way to recover from this calamity. You simply hang there, upside down, until you freeze to death. Popsicle on a rope.

   (Cahill, "Terror Unlimited")

   _____

   _____

   _____

4. On March 24, 1989, a supertanker ran aground and spilled more than 10 million gallons of crude oil into Prince William Sound in Alaska. This ecological disaster was a shocking reminder that our technological tentacles reach far; as we burn gasoline in Los Angeles, Chicago or New York, the impact of our demand for oil is felt thousands of miles away.

(Campbell et al., *Biology*)

_____

_____

_____

banking: tilting (while flying).

5. The valley before me has darkened. I know somewhere out there, too far away to see now, long scarves of geese are riding and banking° against these rising winds, and that they are aware of the snow. In a few weeks Tule Lake will be frozen and they will be gone.

(Lopez, "Reflection on White Geese")

_____

_____

_____

Big Sur: dramatic part of the California coastline.

6. I pause on a wind-ripped slope of Big Sur.° A Monterey pine leans out over the Pacific, making a ledge for the sunset.

(Ackerman, *Natural History of the Senses*)

_____

_____

_____

Grab your first impressions.

1. What did you like about the descriptions of nature in these passages? What did you dislike? Which metaphors did you like best? Why?

2. What is your attitude about metaphorical language? Has your attitude changed after trying Strategy 11? Why or why not?   ■

Apply the New Strategy: Find Meaning in Metaphors

Now that you understand Strategy 11, put it into practice with Reading 20, "Terror Unlimited" (or with one of the Additional Readings in Part V, selected by your instructor).

Choose appropriate strategies for reading "Terror Unlimited." To follow Cahill's ideas, you'll find it especially helpful to **work with new words** and **make inferences** during and after reading. Finally, since this reading has no headings, try mapping main topics in pencil first, before marking main ideas. You may find it helpful to collaborate with other students in mapping the main ideas in this reading, if your instructor tells you to do so.

READING 20 | TERROR UNLIMITED

TIM CAHILL

STRATEGY 11: FIND MEANING IN METAPHORS
1 *Recognize metaphors.*
2 *Analyze the surprising comparison.*

STRATEGY 7: LOOK FOR PATTERN OF SEQUENCE as Cahill moves back and forth in time to tell his story.

Tim Cahill is well known for writing about his adventures from a humorous perspective. He is one of the founding editors of the magazine Outside *and has collected columns from the magazine in his books, such as* Pecked to Death by Ducks *and* Jaguars Ripped My Flesh. *In this reading, taken from* Outside, *he tells about an unexpected kind of terror.*

1 I can't remember the host's name—only that the show was one of a series being taped for a proposed talk show on ABC. It was to be called *Stories.* I was a guest on the program. During each and every commercial break I got up and vomited in a wastebasket set discreetly off camera for this purpose.

2 Worst case of stage fright in television history, probably.

3 The format was rather formal: four guys sitting around a coffee table, complete with little cups of coffee, all of us wearing coats and ties.

4 I have never worn a tie since. It's been over ten years now. The show was filmed at seven in the morning, but we were supposed to look as if we'd just finished dinner and were having a spontaneous discussion. My impression was that some network exec had attended a dinner party in which the conversation had been about something other than television and had thought, "Hey, wow—good television."

5 The host said that one of the best episodes they'd filmed so far had to do with people who had seen or had contact with flying saucers. Those folks told good stories.

6 There were two other guests at the coffee table. One was Hugh Downs, the distinguished ABC broadcaster, a gentleman adventurer who once dove in a cage while great white sharks cruised by outside. The other interviewee was Dick Bass, the businessman-turned-mountaineer who, at the time, was the oldest man to have climbed Mount Everest. We were to tell hair-raising stories of manly courage, or so I gathered. My job was to blather on about various adventures I'd written about in the past—in other words, about my life before a sudden and vividly loathsome awareness of personal extinction

had confined me to my own house for two months with a condition subsequently diagnosed as panic disorder.

Now, the concept of a fearless adventurer suffering panic for no reason   7
at all is High Comedy on the face of it. I knew that. There was a part of me, just observing, that thought, This is actually the funniest story of *Stories*, happening right here on camera: big adventure guy paralyzed by fear, for no apparent reason.

Sometime after the second commercial break, when it became achingly   8
obvious that I was suffering through a bout of intense emotional torment, Hugh Downs, a nice guy who is as calm and reassuring in person as he has always been on the small screen, sought to hearten and comfort me. "You know," he said, "the great Ethel Merman once said, 'Stage fright's a waste of time. What can they do, kill me?'"

I thought, Thank you, Hugh, you blithering simpleton. Ethel Merman is   9
dead. Does that tell you something, anything at all?

A stagehand counted down from ten and the filming started again. The   10
host asked, "What would you say your closest call was? Tim? Dick?" He meant, Tell me a tale about how you came face to face with death and spat in its vile face. I could taste the bile rising in the back of my throat. Steel bands tightened around my chest, and I was possessed by a sense of vertigo so intense I could barely catch my breath. I was going to die, perhaps right then and there—but if not then, sometime, sooner or later. The perception wasn't simply academic. It was visceral. Death was nigh, and despite Samuel Johnson's° smug prediction, it did not concentrate my mind wonderfully.

Samuel Johnson: 18th-century writer who said that being in danger of dying makes one extremely alert.

Panic disorder strikes at least 1.6 percent of the population. It is char-   11
acterized by feelings of intense terror, impending death, a pounding heart, and a shadowy sense of unreality. My own version featured several daily attacks of ten to 30 minutes in which I felt smothered and unable to catch my breath. There were chest pains, flushes and chills, along with a looming sense of imminent insanity. The attacks struck randomly, like lightning out of a clear blue sky. The idea that people might see me in this state of helpless terror was unacceptable. I stayed home, cowering in solitude, unable to read or concentrate or write or even watch television. My overwhelming conviction was that I was going crazy. So when a producer called from ABC and asked me if I wanted to tell hairy-chested stories of virile derring-do, I told her, "You bet." I thought, this terror thing has gone on long enough. I'm going to stroll right over to the abyss and stare directly into it. And I'm going to do it on national TV. Face the fear, boyo.

El Capitan: famous sheer cliff face in Yosemite, California.

The producer had seen a picture of me climbing El Capitan,° in Yosemite,   12
on a single rope. It looked pretty scary. Could I talk about that? No problem.

El Cap, I explained, is shaped rather like the prow of a ship, and my companions had anchored a mile-long rope in half a dozen places up top and tossed it over the precipice so that it fell free for 2,600 feet. A half-mile drop.   13

rappelling: descend (as from a cliff) by sliding down a rope.

The rope-walking and rappelling° techniques we had used are most commonly employed by cavers. Caves generally follow the course of underground rivers, and sometimes these rivers form waterfalls. Over millennia, the rivers sink deeper into the earth, and the bottoms of the waterfalls become mostly dry pits, sometimes hundreds of feet deep. Many cavers like to "yo-yo the pits," which is to say, drop a rope, rappel down, and climb back up solely for the sport of it, never mind the exploration aspect.   14

Calvinists: Protestants who believe that, to earn a reward, they must work hard first.

talus: slope formed by rock debris.

That's what we were doing at Yosemite: We were going to yo-yo El Cap. Because cavers are Calvinists,° we were going to reverse the usual process: We'd climb first in order to "earn" the rappel. I recall standing on the talus° slope at the bottom of the vertical granite wall with my climbing companion, photographer Nick Nichols. We calculated that the climb would take us five to six hours. Aside from the cruel weight of cameras that Nick carried, our backpacks contained some bits of spare climbing gear, a few sandwiches, and only two quarts of water. We intended to hydrate big-time before we started, and each of us choked down a gallon of water as we contemplated the cliff face.   15

Nick wanted me to follow him on the rope, for photographic reasons. His professional sense of the situation told him that the better picture was shooting down, at my terrified face, with the world dropping out forever below. The alternative was six hours of my butt against the sky. And so we strapped on our gear—seat harnesses, Gibbs ascenders on our feet, a chest roller that held us tight to the rope, a top jumar for safety—and proceeded to climb the rope. There was a goodly crowd of people watching us from the road. Some of them had binoculars.   16

About an hour into the climb, Nick called down that he had some bad news. The water we had drunk earlier had gone directly to his bladder. I contemplated the physics of the situation and shouted up, "Can't you hold it?"   17

"Four more hours?" he whined. "No way."   18

"Why didn't you think of this before we started?" I yelled. I sounded like my father discussing the same subject with me as a child on a long road trip.   19

In time, we devised a solution that might keep me dry. I climbed up to Nick, unclipped my top jumar, popped the rope out of my chest roller, and climbed above the ascenders he wore on his feet before clipping back into the rope. In that position—with me directly behind Nick, my chest against his back and my arms wrapped tightly around him—he unzipped and did what he had to do. It took an inordinately long time to void a gallon of water. The rope was spinning ever so slowly, so that, in the fullness of time,   20 we were facing the road, and the crowd, and the people with binoculars. I feared an eventual arrest for public lewdness.

The television producer listened to the story and suggested the spin-   21
ning yellow fountain aspect of the El Cap climb wasn't precisely what a family audience might want to hear. She wondered if there was any time during the ascent in which the choice was life or death.

Well, yes, in fact, a certain lack of foresight on my part presented me   22
with a number of unsatisfactory choices. I explained that, as Nick and I climbed, the wind came up and blew us back in forth in exciting 70-foot pendulum swings. This went on for some hours.

Had we simply dropped the rope off the prow of El Cap, the sharp   23
granite rock would have sawed it in half, snap bang splat, like that. Instead, the rope was draped over a long solid rubber tube about as big around as a basketball. Brackets at each end were bolted to the rock so that the tube was placed within an inch of the cliff wall. The final obstacle on the climb was to muscle up over the tube. This was tricky. I was affixed to the rope. The rope itself weighed several hundred pounds and was impossible to drag up over the tube. Instead, there was another rope, a short one, anchored above and dangled over the tube. It was necessary to unclip from the long rope and clip into the short one in order to make the summit—a maneuver I had neglected to consider when I clipped into the long rope on the talus slope five hours earlier. I had been contemplating the climb, not the summit, and had also been preoccupied with a different danger peculiar to this type of climbing: If, for some reason, a climber lost his top jumar and his chest roller, he'd fall backward and end up hanging from the ascenders on his feet. There is almost no way to recover from this calamity. You simply hang there, upside down, until you freeze to death. Popsicle on a rope.

carabiner: metal ring used as a connector to hold a freely running rope.

With this in mind, I'd run the long rope through the carabiner° that held   24
my seat harness together, reasoning that in a bad upside-down emergency I might still be able to pull myself upright. What this rig meant at the summit, however, was that I was going to have to unclip my seat harness to get off the long rope and onto the short one.

But . . . a seat harness, as every climber knows, is the essential con-   25
trivance that marries one to the rope. Unclipping wasn't certain death, but the probabilities weren't good. I assessed my chances for over an hour. It was getting cold and late. Nick had switched ropes and summited with no problems at all. I, on the other hand, was in deep trouble.

The half-mile drop yawning below was sinking into darkness as the sky   26
above burst into flame. This sunset, I understood, might well be my last, and I followed its progress as I would that of a ripening bruise on my thigh:

At first the sky seemed very vividly wounded, all bright bloody reds that eventually began an ugly healing process involving pastel oranges and pinks that eventually purpled down into blue-black night. The temperature dropped. My sweat-soaked shirt was beginning to freeze to my body. I would have to do something.

Stories never made it on the air. Not the adventure segment nor even   27
the one about flying saucers, which proves that sometimes the most fervent of our prayers are actually answered. Hugh Downs has announced his imminent retirement from ABC, and Dick Bass is no longer the oldest man to have climbed Mount Everest.

And me? I haven't had a panic attack in ten years, knock wood. My   28
doctor recognized the symptoms straightaway and prescribed certain medications that had an almost immediate ameliorative effect. He suggested therapy as well, but a pamphlet he gave me about panic disorder was pretty much all I needed. There were others, I learned, who have had to deal with uncontrolled anxiety. They included scientists such as Charles Darwin and Isaac Newton; actors Laurence Olivier and Kim Basinger; writers Isaac Asimov and Alfred Lord Tennyson. Barbra Streisand and Sigmund Freud (natch) were on the list, along with the Norwegian Expressionist Edvard Munch, whose signature painting, *The Scream*, seems to me to be the perfect depiction of a panic attack.

The idea that I wasn't suffering alone—that the malady had a name—   29
was strangely reassuring. Panic disorder feels like standing on the gallows, the rough rope on your neck, waiting, waiting, waiting for the floor to fall away into the never-ending night. But there is no rope, and no immediate threat. None at all.

Personal extinction is surely something to contemplate, but contem-   30
plating personal extinction doesn't get the grocery shopping done. In my experience, fear of collapsing into a puddle of terror at the Mini Mart—agoraphobia—feels precisely the same as real physical fear in the face of an actual threat. The difference is this: There is almost always something you can do when confronted with an authentic life-or-death situation.

At the summit of El Cap, for instance, my companions rigged up a pair   31
of loops made of webbing, anchored them off, and dropped them over the rubber tube. I placed my feet in the loops and laboriously muscled the heavy long rope up over the roller: a triumph of brute strength over clear thinking. There was no thinking at all, really, not in the ordinary sense of brooding contemplation. Risk sets its own rules, and one reacts to them instinctively, with an empty mind, in a state that some psychologists believe is akin to meditation. And, like those enlightened ones who sit cross-legged

in empty rooms, uttering weenie aphorisms, risk-takers sometimes feel they've caught a glimpse into eternity, into the wisdom of the Universe, and into the curve of blinding light itself. Just a glimpse.

We didn't talk about that on *Stories*. Sitting there sweating, waiting to   32
vomit during the commercials, I was incapable of saying what I felt: that the stories we tell are the way we organize our experiences in order to under-stand our lives. I didn't say that risk is always a story about mortality, and that mortality is the naked and essential human condition. We put these stories together—in poems and essays and novels and after-dinner con-versations—in an effort to crowbar some meaning out of the pure terror of our existence.

The stories are prisms through which we perceive the world. They are   33
like the lenses we look through in the optometrist's office: Put them together incorrectly, and it's all a blur. But drop in the correct stories, turn them this way and that, and—all at once—there is a sudden clarity. Call it enlightenment and admit that none of us ever get all the way there. We only see glimpses of it in a flashbulb moment when certain selected stories fall together just right. That's all. In my own case, I know that fear always feels the same, that it is about perceived mortality, and that while courage continually escapes me, appearing on one silly un-aired television show remains the purest and the bravest thing I've ever done.

STRATEGY 9: MAP MAIN IDEAS

STRAGEGY 10: WRITE A SUMMARY

Follow-Up Activities   After you've finished reading, use these questions to respond to "Terror Unlimited." You may write your answers or prepare them in your mind to discuss in class.

Grab your first impressions.

Respond with your first impressions. Say what you like and dislike; relate your personal experiences to the reading; consider what more you want to know.

Work with new words.

Some words in this reading may be unfamiliar to you. Use the methods of Strategy 3 to explain what the listed words mean.

1. Use context clues.

   a. precipice (paragraph 13) _____

   b. inordinately (paragraph 20) _____

   c. lewdness (paragraph 20) _____

   d. calamity (paragraph 23) _____

2. Use the dictionary.

Choose the correct definition of each word as it is used in the context of this reading.

a. vertigo (paragraph 10) _____

b. visceral (paragraph 10) _____

c. imminent (paragraph 11) _____

d. virile (paragraph 11) _____

e. abyss (paragraph 11) _____

f. prisms (paragraph 33) _____

3. Select additional words you're unsure of from the reading. Use one of these methods to discover their meaning.

Find meaning in metaphors.

Read the following interpretation of a tricky metaphor from paragraph 32. Then use Strategy 11 to identify and interpret three other metaphorical expressions in "Terror Unlimited."

We put these stories together . . . in an effort to crowbar some meaning out of the pure terror of our existence. (paragraph 32)

The startling phrase in the sentence is *crowbar some meaning*. The implied comparison is between the crowbar and storytelling, because both the crowbar and storytelling can be used to pry out something that is difficult to get at. A literal version of the sentence would say that storytelling allows us to get meaning out of our lives. But that would leave out the picture of the crowbar prying something out of the ground, so we would lose the sense of effort and power that Cahill attaches to storytelling.

Now interpret these metaphorical expressions. First identify the expression as a simile or a metaphor. Then analyze the surprising comparison.

1. "The [panic] attacks struck randomly, like lightning out of a clear blue sky." (paragraph 11)

_____

_____

2. ". . . [A] producer . . . asked me if I wanted to tell hairy-chested stories." (paragraph 11)

_____

_____

3. "The stories are prisms through which we perceive the world." (paragraph 33)

_____

_____

Ask and answer questions.

1. What was the idea behind the proposed talk show on ABC, called *Stories?* Why was Cahill asked to be a guest on the particular episode he describes?

2. In paragraph 6, Cahill reveals that he had a "condition subsequently diagnosed as panic disorder." Given the terrible effects of the disorder, what makes him agree to tape the show and put himself through the "worst case of stage fright in television history"?

3. What are the rope-walking and rappelling techniques cavers use that Cahill describes in paragraph 14? What does he mean when he says he and his photographer companion were going to "yo-yo" El Capitan in Yosemite?

4. What was the principal danger Cahill had tried to avoid by running the long rope through the carabiner that held his seat harness together? What new danger did that maneuver cause for him?

5. What did Cahill's friends do to help him make it to the summit?

Inference Questions

6. What does Cahill mean by saying in paragraph 30 that "personal extinction is surely something to contemplate, but contemplating personal extinction doesn't get the grocery shopping done"?

7. Why does Cahill say that when he was working to get up the summit, "There was no thinking at all, really." (paragraph 31). How does facing risk affect a person's mind? How does "risk [set] its own rules"?

8. Cahill ends by saying, "appearing on one silly un-aired television show remains the purest and the bravest thing I've ever done." Why does he think that for him appearing on a TV show took more courage than facing the dangers he describes during his ascent of El Cap?

 ## Ask and answer your own questions.

Write two questions based on any of the other information in this reading. Share your questions with others and collaborate on answers.

Form your final thoughts.

1. Write about a time when you successfully faced a risk of some kind. How did that experience compare to either the psychological or physical risks that Cahill discusses? Share what you would like about this experience with other classmates.

2. How well did Cahill help you feel the different kinds of fears he experienced? How well could you visualize his ascent up the face of El Capitan? What metaphors or other literal descriptions were particularly successful?

■

Chapter 11 Summary

How does Strategy 11 help you *read from the inside out?*

Like **working with new words, finding meaning in metaphors** helps remove language barriers between you and the writer's ideas. By understanding a writer's imaginative uses of familiar words or phrases, you stay in touch with the reading outside—the writer's ideas—so you can **respond** to them with your own thoughts. You might actually find that your response is heightened by the writer's use of metaphorical expressions because they are often visual.

How does the *find meaning in metaphors* strategy work?

Here are the two steps for Strategy 11.

STRATEGY 11: FIND MEANING IN METAPHORS

1 Recognize metaphors.

2 Analyze the surprising comparison.

You first recognize a metaphor when a word or phrase could *not* be taken literally. You see there is some kind of implied comparison (metaphor) or explicit comparison (simile) between two things that are not normally seen as similar. When you're sure the language is metaphorical,

1. Look for the two unlike things that are being compared,

2. Look for the quality or characteristic these two things have in common,

3. Determine what the metaphor would mean in literal terms.

Are you familiar with the meaning of these terms?

metaphorical expression: figure of speech that heightens the effect and meaning of language

figurative expression: nonliteral comparison, often highly visual

literal: ordinary or primary meaning of a word; *rusty nail* uses the literal meaning of *rusty*; *rusty pianist* uses its metaphorical meaning

simile: specific kind of metaphorical expression that uses *like* or *as* to make an explicit comparison

metaphor: implied comparison that does not use *like* or *as*

How is the strategy working for you so far?

1. How successful have you been at recognizing metaphors?

2. How successful have you been at interpreting the meaning of metaphors?

3. What have been your favorite metaphors so far? How did they add to the picture or ideas of the reading they come from?

4. What did you appreciate about using this strategy? What did you dislike?

 For more practice with *understanding metaphors*, use the Reading Road Trip CD-ROM or Web site.

CHAPTER
12

EXPAND YOUR RESPONSE: DETERMINE THE WRITER'S PURPOSE

By using appropriate strategies, you're now better able to comprehend a writer's ideas. Strategy 12, **Determine the Writer's Purpose,** helps you see the writer's reasons for writing. Understanding the writer's purpose will help you anticipate the kind of language and ideas you'll find in the reading. Then you can **respond** more fully by considering how well the writer's purpose was achieved.

Try the New Strategy: Determine the Writer's Purpose

Using steps from Strategy 12 as you **get an overview** helps you get a sense of the writer's purpose before you read. During and after reading, the strategy helps you understand why writers present ideas in a certain way and how they want you to respond to these ideas.

STRATEGY 12: DETERMINE THE WRITER'S PURPOSE

1 Recognize the type of writing.

2 Recognize the intended audience.

3 Identify the writer's perspective.

4 See how the tone reflects the purpose.

To help you learn about **determining the writer's purpose** before reading "A Global Green Deal," Reading 21, work through the strategy steps described here, using sample passages on the theme of "Nature's Adventures and Challenges."

Types of Writing

1 *Recognize the type of writing.*

Writers use different types of writing for different purposes. Each type has a different use and answers a different general question.

Narration. Narration is used to tell a story. It answers this question: "What happened?" Narration is included whenever a writer tells about past events. However, when a writer's main purpose is to narrate events—or tell a story—he or she is usually writing one of the following: a short story (such as Reading II-C, "Powder"), a personal narrative (such as Reading 1, "I Don't Like to Read—Sam-I-Am!"), or historical writing (such as Reading VI-D, "The Formation of Modern American Mass Culture").

Description. Description shows what someone or something is like. It answers this question: "What does it look, sound, feel, smell, or taste like?" Descriptive writing can be found in any reading where the writer appeals to one of our five senses. Description is an important secondary purpose for many of the writers in this book. For example, in Reading 9, "talking back," bell hooks's description of the way women talked in her small town was important for showing why she loved listening to them.

Exposition. Exposition—or expository writing—explains something or instructs. It answers this question: "What is it? Why or how did it happen?" The purpose for college textbook writers is to instruct students about a field of knowledge. You've had several examples of textbook writing in this book, including Reading 8, "How Babies Use Patterns to See," and Reading 13, "How Conscious Is Thought?" Although much of your college reading will be textbook reading, you will also read other writers whose purpose is to explain ideas. Examples of this kind of exposition include "Why People Don't Help in a Crisis" and "Optimism: The Great Motivator."

Argument. An argument is written to persuade you. It answers this question: "Why should you believe something or do something?" You can tell when the writer's main purpose is to persuade the reader, if the reading puts forward a strong position on something that not everyone will agree with. You can tell from the title that Reading 11, "School Is Bad for Children," is an argument.

As you get an overview of a reading, try to determine whether the writer's main purpose is to narrate, describe, explain, or persuade. Think about Tim Cahill's "Terror Unlimited" (Reading 20 in Chapter 11), for example. The title and first sentences of paragraphs in that reading suggest two purposes: to *narrate* what happened and to *explain* about the terror he experienced.

In the next two samples, we have the kind of information we could get in an overview. What could we learn about each writer's purpose just from this small amount of information?

1. "How technology and the population explosion compound our impact on habitats and other species," an excerpt from a textbook, *Biology: Concepts and Connections,* by Campbell et al.

   The fact that this is a textbook excerpt tells us this reading is exposition, meant to explain or instruct. If we connect the writing type to the excerpt's title, we can predict that the reading will explain about human beings' impact on the environment.

2. Reading 21, "A Global Green Deal," an article by Mark Hertsgaard from *Time* magazine.

   The first sentence of this reading is, "So what do we do?" The last paragraph begins with, "None of this will happen without an aroused citizenry" and ends with, "It's time to repeat that history on behalf of a Global Green deal." These sentences alone indicate that this reading is an *argument* to *persuade* us to do something.

The Intended Audience

2 *Recognize the intended audience.*

A writer's purpose depends partly on the people he or she wants to reach—the *intended audience.* For example, writers for an academic journal, such as the *Journal of the American Medical Association,* write mainly to instruct or persuade fellow doctors or people in the medical professions. They use technical language to explain complex information and the formal style expected of serious professional journals. Science writers for magazines like *Time* or *Newsweek,* however, avoid overly technical terms and use a more informal language because the readers of these popular newsmagazines are not specialists in a particular field. They represent the general reader.

Type of vocabulary. Both the biology textbook excerpt we referred to earlier and the *Time* article, "A Global Green Deal," deal with the subject of environmental problems. But look at the difference in vocabulary in their very first sentences.

1. Excerpt from *Biology: Concepts and Connection*s

   "Technology and other cultural advancements have produced many benefits. . . . But they also fuel our population explosion; and feeding, clothing, and housing billions of people even at a minimal level *strains the biosphere."*

2. Excerpt from "A Global Green Deal"

"*So what do we do?* Everyone knows the planet is *in bad shape,* but most people are resigned to passivity."

The italicized words and phrases demonstrate the differences between more technical, formal vocabulary in the textbook and the informal words in a popular magazine.

Writing style. The sentence structures in the two excerpts are also different. Notice the longer, more complex sentences in the textbook and the shorter sentences in the magazine article.

Audience and purpose. When predicting a writer's purpose, take into account who the typical reader of the material would probably be. Later, when deciding what you think about a reading, consider how the writer's approach worked in terms of his or her intended audience. For example, a textbook might not have as much immediate appeal as a magazine article, but its more thorough information may better serve the needs of its student readers.

Perspective

3 *Identify the writer's perspective.*

Your *perspective* on a subject is your way of looking at it, or your position on it, based on your experience and beliefs. For example, you probably have a certain perspective on the effect of sex in the media on children. Your perspective depends partly on your experience. Was your experience of seeing sex in TV programs and movies as a child harmful to you or not? Does your experience talking with today's kids suggest they're getting too many sexual messages from the media or not? Your perspective on this subject may also be affected by your beliefs about appropriate sexual behavior—beliefs you've acquired from your family, your religion, and your peers.

A writer's perspective on a subject affects his or her purpose for writing. We can see how perspective affects purpose by imagining two different authors writing about drilling for oil in the Alaskan wilderness. An oil company executive would have a certain perspective based on experience and beliefs about the U.S. need for access to energy sources. His or her purpose would be to persuade readers of the need to drill in Alaska. An environmentalist would have a different perspective, placing great value on protecting the natural environment as irreplaceable. His or her purpose would be to persuade readers that drilling for oil in the Alaska wilderness should be prohibited.

In this textbook, the headnotes about writers that appear after reading titles give you an idea of a writer's perspective before you begin reading. You'll need to consider the writer's perspective especially carefully when reading an argument such as we might see on either side of the oil drilling debate. By knowing the writer's perspective—where he or she is coming from—you can be more aware of the ideas, information, and reasoning you'll find in the reading. We look more closely at how to analyze and evaluate arguments in Part VI.

Purpose and Tone

4 See how the tone reflects the purpose.

Tone in writing is like the tone of voice people use when talking: both reveal attitude and mood. When we talk, changes in our voice and facial expression tell listeners a lot about the message we're conveying. Try this: say these four words out loud—"I have some news"—first in a happy tone, then in a sad, an indifferent, or an angry tone. As you change your mood, you naturally say these words very differently. You emphasize different words, vary the pitch and loudness of your voice, and use a lot or a little energy.

Inferring tone. There is tone in writing, too, but it's not so obvious as tone of voice. Often you have to use the same kinds of evidence you use for **making inferences**—the logic of putting two and two together, selection of details, and the choice of words. You can infer tone from purpose. If the purpose is to tell a positive story about learning to read, as Rebecca Grabiner does in Reading 1, the tone will be light and lively. If a writer wants to persuade people to drill, or not to drill, in the Alaska wilderness, the tone might be serious, perhaps upset, or it might be enthusiastic about promising solutions.

Identify tone by making inferences.

By making inferences, match each of these tones to the appropriate passage provided.

a. Neutral, instructive tone   c. Emotional, panicky tone

b. Positive, persuasive tone   d. Serious, sad tone

_____ 1. What we need is a Global Green Deal: a program to renovate our civilization environmentally from top to bottom in rich and poor countries alike.

(Hertsgaard, "Global Green Deal," Reading 21)

_____ 2. Even in the most remote wilderness, where the strictest laws forbid the felling of a single tree, the sound of that saw will be clear, and a walk in the woods will be changed—tainted—by its whine.

(McKibbon, *End of Nature*)

_____ 3. I could taste the bile rising in the back of my throat. Steel bands tightened around my chest, and I was possessed by a sense of vertigo so intense I could barely catch my breath.

(Cahill, "Terror Unlimited," Reading 20)

_____ 4. Compounds called chlorofluorocarbons (CFCs), such as freons used as refrigerants and as propellants in aerosol cans, release chlorine when they break down.

(Campbell et al., *Biology*)

(answers: 1. b; 2. d; 3. c; 4. a)   ■

Objective and subjective tone. A person who has a neutral attitude, free from emotional attachment to one or another side, is said to be *objective* about the subject. Being *subjective* is just the opposite: the person has an emotional involvement or a personal *bias*—or leaning—toward one side or the other. The table here demonstrates the usual distinction made between kinds of writing that are expected to be either objective or subjective.

Types of Writing

Objective Writing	Subjective Writing
newspaper reporting	newspaper editorials and opinion pieces
textbook writing	articles or books written from a certain cultural, political, or personal perspective

To demonstrate the difference between an objective and a subjective tone, look at two versions of roommate problems that colleges try to anticipate and solve. An objective approach to the problem might state it in this way:

Colleges can no longer assume that roommates will automatically get along without some complex methods for making a match between them. For example, popular musical tastes among young people now vary far more than they did twenty-five years ago, when choosing what to play was likely to involve two clear-cut types of music: the Rolling Stones and the Bee Gees.

The same information might be presented in a far more subjective way.

Gone, gone are the days when colleges can assume that roommates will be civil to each other. Now colleges have to set up intricate question-naires and procedures to assure that every need of every selfish and fussy young person can be met. For example, the popular musical tastes of this pampered generation have disintegrated into dozens of narrow-interest categories. In the more civil era of the previous generation, there were just two types of music—the Rolling Stones and the Bee Gees—and even those who could not agree on one or the other could get along.

The objective version simply explains the current situation. What can you see about the subjective writer? What tone of voice would she use if she were speaking? How did you pick up on her tone of voice?

Irony. The most familiar kind of irony is its harshest form: sarcasm. You can easily recognize the sarcasm when someone says, "You're a big help!" and clearly means the opposite.

Irony always depends on the opposition between the literal meaning of the words and the intended message. What makes a tone ironic is that the person uses words that apparently say one thing while indicating that the opposite, or at least a totally different message, is intended.

It's important to recognize irony in writing, so you aren't misled into believing the writer meant the words literally. For example, Jean-Dominique Bauby's *The Diving Bell and the Butterfly* is about the limits in his life after the author suffered a paralyzing stroke. He reports being told about his condition, and his response: "Of course the party chiefly concerned is the last to hear the good news." This statement is bitterly ironic, since this news would of course be so terrible to hear. For an example of an entire reading based on irony, see Reading VI-C, "Memo from Coach."

Now read "A Global Green Deal," and try to determine the writer's purpose. What can knowing the writer's purpose help you understand?

STRATEGY 12: DETERMINE THE WRITER'S PURPOSE

1 *Recognize the type of writing.*

2 *Recognize the intended audience.*

3 *Identify the writer's perspective.*

4 *See how the tone reflects the purpose.*

READING 21   A GLOBAL GREEN DEAL

MARK HERTSGAARD

Green Deal: intended to echo President Franklin D. Roosevelt's program, the New Deal.

Mark Hertsgaard is a journalist who has written books and articles on a variety of subjects. He has contributed to the New York Times, *the* New Yorker, Outside, *and numerous other publications. His latest book,* Earth Odyssey: Around the World in Search of Our Environmental Future *(2000), has been praised for its thorough yet readable treatment of a difficult and complicated subject. Hertsgaard wrote this argument for the* Time *Earth Day 2000 issue.*

Earlier in the chapter you saw excerpts from this reading that helped you define Hertsgaard's purpose: to persuade his readers to make changes to help protect the environment. He expects his readers to be general Time *magazine readers, not readers with special expertise or interests. To match his purpose, his tone seems positive and persuasive.*

*To follow Hertsgaard's ideas, you'll find it especially helpful to **find meaning in metaphors**—some of which may already be familiar to you. Since this reading has no headings, try mapping main topics in pencil first, before marking main ideas. You may find it helpful to collaborate with other students in mapping the main ideas in this reading, if your instructor tells you to do so.*

STRATEGY 11: FIND MEANING IN METAPHORS

So what do we do? Everyone knows the planet is in bad shape, but   1
most people are resigned to passivity. Changing course, they reason, would require economic sacrifice and provoke stiff resistance from corporations and consumers alike, so why bother? It's easier to ignore the gathering storm clouds and hope the problem magically takes care of itself.

Such fatalism is not only dangerous but mistaken. For much of the   2
1990s I traveled the world to write a book about our environmental predica-
ment. I returned home sobered by the extent of the damage we are causing
and by the speed at which it is occurring. But there is nothing inevitable
about our self-destructive behavior. Not only could we dramatically reduce
our burden on the air, water and other natural systems, we could make
money doing so. If we're smart, we could make restoring the environment
the biggest economic enterprise of our time, a huge source of jobs, profits
and poverty alleviation.

What we need is a Global Green Deal: a program to renovate our civi-   3
lization environmentally from top to bottom in rich and poor countries
alike. Making use of both market incentives and government leadership, a
21st century Global Green Deal would do for environmental technologies
what government and industry have recently done so well for computer
and Internet technologies: launch their commercial takeoff.

Getting it done will take work, and before we begin we need to under-   4
stand three facts about the reality facing us. First, we have no time to lose.
While we've made progress in certain areas—air pollution is down in the
U.S.—big environmental problems like climate change, water scarcity and
species extinction are getting worse, and faster than ever. Thus we have to
change our ways profoundly—and very soon.

Second, poverty is central to the problem. Four billion of the planet's 6   5
billion people face deprivation inconceivable to the wealthiest 1 billion. To
paraphrase Thomas Jefferson, nothing is more certainly written in the book
of fate than that the bottom two-thirds of humanity will strive to improve
their lot. As they demand adequate heat and food, not to mention cars and
CD players, humanity's environmental footprint will grow. Our challenge is
to accommodate this mass ascent from poverty without wrecking the natural systems that make life possible.

Third, some good news: we have in hand most of the technologies   6
needed to chart a new course. We know how to use oil, wood, water and
other resources much more efficiently than we do now. Increased efficiency—doing more with less—will enable us to use fewer resources and
produce less pollution per capita, buying us the time to bring solar power,

hydrogen fuel cells: electro-
chemical devices that work
much like a battery.

hydrogen fuel cells° and other futuristic technologies on line.

Efficiency may not sound like a rallying cry for environmental revolu-   7
tion, but it packs a financial punch. As Joseph J. Romm reports in his book
Cool Companies, Xerox, Compaq and 3M are among many firms that have
recognized they can cut their greenhouse-gas emissions in half—and enjoy
50% and higher returns on investment—through improved efficiency, better
lighting and insulation and smarter motors and building design. The rest of

us (small businesses, homeowners, city governments, schools) can reap the same benefits.

Super-refrigerators use 87% less electricity than older, standard models while costing the same (assuming mass production) and performing better, as Paul Hawken and Amory and L. Hunter Lovins explain in their book *Natural Capitalism.* In Amsterdam the headquarters of ING Bank, one of Holland's largest banks, uses one-fifth as much energy per square meter as a nearby bank, even though the buildings cost the same to construct. The ING center boasts efficient windows and insulation and a design that enables solar energy to provide much of the building's needs, even in cloudy Northern Europe.   8

Examples like these lead even such mainstream voices as AT&T and Japan's energy planning agency, NEDO, to predict that environmental restoration could be a source of virtually limitless profit. The idea is to retrofit our farms, factories, shops, houses, offices and everything inside them. The economic activity generated would be enormous. Better yet, it would be labor intensive; investments in energy efficiency yield two to 10 times more jobs than investments in fossil fuel and nuclear power. In a world where 1 billion people lack gainful employment, creating jobs is essential to fighting the poverty that retards environmental progress.   9

But this transition will not happen by itself—too many entrenched interests stand in the way. Automakers often talk green but make only token efforts to develop green cars because gas-guzzling sport-utility vehicles are hugely profitable. But every year the U.S. government buys 56,000 new vehicles for official use from Detroit. Under the Global Green Deal, Washington would tell Detroit that from now on the cars have to be hybrid-electric or hydrogen-fuel-cell cars. Detroit might scream and holler, but if Washington stood firm, carmakers soon would be climbing the learning curve and offering the competitively priced green cars that consumers say they want.   10

We know such government pump-priming works; it's why so many of us have computers today. America's computer companies began learning to produce today's affordable systems during the 1960s while benefiting from subsidies and guaranteed markets under contracts with the Pentagon and the space program. And the cyberboom has fueled the biggest economic expansion in history.   11

The Global Green Deal must not be solely an American project, however. China and India, with their gigantic populations and ambitious development plans, could by themselves doom everyone else to severe global warming. Already, China is the world's second largest producer of greenhouse gases° (after the U.S.). But China would use 50% less coal if it simply   12

greenhouse gases: carbon dioxide and other gases that slow the escape of heat from Earth's surface.

installed today's energy-efficient technologies. Under the Global Green Deal, Europe, America and Japan would help China buy these technologies, not only because that would reduce global warming but also because it would create jobs and profits for workers and companies back home.

Governments would not have to spend more money, only shift existing   13
subsidies away from environmentally dead-end technologies like coal and nuclear power. If even half the $500 billion to $900 billion in environmentally destructive subsidies now offered by the world's governments were redirected, the Global Green Deal would be off to a roaring start. Governments need to establish "rules of the road" so that market prices reflect the real social costs of clear-cut forests and other environmental abominations. Again, such a shift could be revenue neutral.° Higher taxes on, say, coal burning would be offset by cuts in payroll and profits taxes, thus encouraging jobs and investment while discouraging pollution. A portion of the revenues should be set aside to assure a just transition for workers and companies now engaged in inherently antienvironmental activities like coal mining.

revenue neutral: resulting in neither profit nor loss for an organization.

All this sounds easy enough on paper, but in the real world it is not so   14
simple. Beneficiaries of the current system—be they U.S. corporate-welfare recipients,° redundant German coal miners or cut-throat Asian logging interests—will resist. Which is why progress in unlikely absent a broader agenda of change, including real democracy: assuring the human rights of environmental activists and neutralizing the power of Big Money through campaign-finance reform.

corporate-welfare recipients: tax breaks or government money to assist corporations.

The Global Green Deal is no silver bullet. It can, however, buy us time   15
to make the more deep-seated changes—in our often excessive appetites, in our curious belief that humans are the center of the universe, in our sheer numbers—that will be necessary to repair our relationship with our environment.

None of this will happen without an aroused citizenry. But a Global   16
Green Deal is in the common interest, and it is a slogan easily grasped by the media and the public. Moreover, it should appeal across political, class and national boundaries, for it would stimulate both jobs and business throughout the world in the name of a universal value: leaving our children a livable planet. The history of environmentalism is largely the story of ordinary people pushing for change while governments, corporations and other established interests reluctantly follow behind. It's time to repeat that history on behalf of a Global Green Deal.

Follow-Up Activities   After you've finished reading, use these questions to respond to "A Global Green Deal." You may write your answers or prepare them in your mind to discuss in class.

Grab your first impressions.

Respond with your first impressions. Say what you like and dislike; relate your personal experiences to the reading; consider what more you want to know.

Work with new words.

Some words in this reading may be unfamiliar to you. Use the methods of Strategy 3 to explain what the listed words mean.

1. Use context clues.

   a. alleviation (paragraph 2) _____

   b. abominations (paragraph 13) _____

2. Use word parts.
   Check the etymology in your dictionary definition to find the meanings of these word parts.

   a. fatalism (paragraph 2) _____
      See how the word *fate* helps you get the meaning of *fatalism*.

   b. retrofit (paragraph 9) _____

   c. entrenched (paragraph 10) _____
      See how the word *trench* helps you get the meaning of *entrenched*.

   d. cyberboom (paragraph 11) _____

3. Use the dictionary.
   Choose the correct definition of each word as it is used in the context of this reading.

   a. subsidies (paragraph 11) _____

   b. inherently (paragraph 13) _____

   c. redundant (paragraph 14) _____

4. Select additional words you're unsure of from the reading. Use one of these methods to discover their meaning.

Find meaning in metaphors.

Use Strategy 11 to interpret these metaphorical expressions.

1. "humanity's environmental footprint will grow" (paragraph 5)

2. "it packs a financial punch" (paragraph 7)

3. "talk green" (paragraph 10)

4. "The Global Green Deal is no silver bullet." (paragraph 15)

Ask and answer questions.

1. What evidence does Hertsgaard give that our environmental problems demand immediate attention?

2. According to Hertsgaard, what effect does world poverty have on our environmental future?

3. What is one example that Hertsgaard gives to show that increased efficiency can both help the environment and be good for business?

4. How could the U.S. government promote increased efficiency in automobiles? What challenges would the government face in making this change?

Inference Questions

5. Hertsgaard calls the Green Deal "revenue neutral." Who does he say would be against the plan? Why?

6. At the end of the article, Hertsgaard emphasizes that this plan is a way to buy time until we can make more fundamental changes. What changes does he refer to?

Questions About Purpose

7. On page 317 we defined the tone of one of Hertsgaard's sentences as positive and persuasive. Was this the tone throughout the article? How does his tone relate to Hertsgaard's purpose?

8. What is Hertsgaard's overall point about his subject? What was his purpose in writing about it?

Ask and answer your own questions.

Write two questions based on any of the other information in this reading. Share your questions with others and collaborate on answers.

Form your final thoughts.

1. Remember that Hertsgaard wrote this argument as a final piece for the *Time* Earth Day 2000 issue. It was preceded by many articles about specific environmental problems. Discuss with others how persuasive you think Hertsgaard's argument would be for the readers of that issue. Was the argument as persuasive for you? Why or why not?

2. Write about an environmental problem that personally concerns you. Compare notes with others about the kinds of environmental problems they are concerned about. Discuss ways you could imagine proceeding to get more information or take some action. ■

Apply the New Strategy: Determine the Writer's Purpose

Now that you understand Strategy 12, put it into practice with Reading 22, "Infernal Paradise" (or with one of the Additional Readings in Part V, selected by your instructor).

Determine the writer's purpose by considering the type of writing, the intended audience, and the writer's perspective. As you read, see how the tone reflects the purpose. In addition, choose additional, appropriate strategies. For reading "Infernal Paradise," you'll find it especially helpful to **make inferences** and **find meaning in metaphors.** Finally, since this reading has no headings, try mapping main topics in pencil first, before marking main ideas. You may find it helpful to collaborate with other students in mapping the main ideas in this reading, if your instructor tells you to do so.

READING 22 | INFERNAL PARADISE

BARBARA KINGSOLVER

> **STRATEGY 7: LOOK FOR PATTERNS OF THOUGHT**
> Note the sequence (her "story") as well as cause-and-effect reasoning.

Barbara Kingsolver is a well-known writer of novels and short stories as well as nonfiction on a wide range of subjects. She came to writing first through her career as a scientific writer and journalist. "Infernal° Paradise" is excerpted from an essay in High Tide at Tucson *(1995), a collection of writings on common themes in her writings: family, community, and concern for the natural world.*

> **infernal:** hellish, fiery.
>
> **Haleakala:** the world's largest inactive volcano, on Maui, Hawaii.
>
> **obsidian:** dark natural glass formed by cooling molten lava.

Entering the crater at dawn seemed unearthly, though Haleakala° is   1
entirely of the earth, and nothing of human artifice. The cliffs absorbed and enclosed us in a mounting horizon of bleak obsidian° crags. A lake of cloud slid over the rim, wave by wave, and fell into the crater's separate atmosphere, dispersing in vapor trails. The sharp perimeter of cliffs contains a volcanic bowl three thousand feet deep and eight miles across as the crow flies (or twice that far as the hiker hikes). The depression would hold Manhattan, though fortunately it doesn't.

We walked and slid down miles of gravelly slope toward the crater   2
floor, where the earth had repeatedly disgorged its contents. Black sworls of bubbling lava had once flowed around red cinder cones, then cooled to a tortured standstill. I stood still myself, allowing my eye a minute to take in the lunatic landscape. In the absence of any human construction or familiar vegetation like, say, trees, it was impossible to judge distances. An irregular dot on the trail ahead might be a person or a house-sized boulder.

> **STRATEGY 11: FIND MEANING IN METAPHORS**

Down below, sections of the trail were sketched across the valley, crossing dark lava flows and green fields, disappearing into a velvet fog that hid the crater's eastern half.

The strange topography of Haleakala Crater makes its own weather. 3
Some areas are parched as the Sahara, while others harbor fern forests
under a permanent veil of cloud. Any part of the high-altitude crater can
scorch in searing sun, or be lashed by freezing rain, or both, on just about
any day of the year. Altogether it is one of the most difficult landscapes
ever to host natural life. It is also one of the few places in Hawaii that looks
as it did two hundred years ago—or for that matter, two thousand.
Haleakala is a tiny, threatened ark.

To learn about the natural history of Hawaii is to understand a story of 4
unceasing invasion. These islands, when they first lifted their heads out of
the waves a million years ago, were naked, defiant rock—the most isolated
archipelago in the world. Life, when it landed here, arrived only through
powerful stamina or spectacular accident: a fern's spore° drifting on the
trade wind, a seed in the craw of a bird, the bird itself. If it survived, that
was an accident all the more spectacular. Natural selection led these sur-
vivors to become new species unique in the world: the silversword, for
example, a plant that lives in lava beds and dies in a giant flowery starburst;
or the nēnē, a crater-dwelling goose that has lost the need for webbed feet
because it shuns the sea, foraging instead in foggy meadows, grown lan-
guid and tame in the absence of predators. Over the course of a million
years, hundreds of creatures like these evolved from the few stray immigrants. Now they are endemic species, living nowhere on earth but here.
For many quiet eons they thrived in their sequestered home.

spore: asexual, usually single-celled reproduction organ, usually in nonflowering plants.

Then humans arrived, also through stamina and spectacular accident. 5
The Polynesians came first, bringing along some thirty plants and animals
they considered indispensable, including bananas, taro, sugar cane, pigs,
dogs, chickens. And also a few stowaways: rats, snails, and lizards. All of
these went forth and multiplied throughout the islands. Each subsequent
wave of human immigration brought fresh invasions. Sugar cane and pineapples filled the valleys, crowding out native herbs. Logging operations
decimated the endemic° rain forests. Pigs, goats, and cattle uprooted and
ate whatever was left. Without a native carnivore to stop them, rats flourished like the Pied Piper's° dream. Mongooses were imported in a harebrained plan to control them, but the mongoose° forages by day and the rat
by night, so these creatures rarely encounter one another. Both, though,
are happy to feast on the eggs of native birds.

endemic: native to a particular place.

Pied Piper: main character of story about ridding a town of rats.

mongoose: cat-sized mammal, known for ability to kill venomous snakes.

More species have now become extinct in Hawaii than in all of North 6
America. At least two hundred of the islands' endemic plant species are gone
from the earth for good, and eight hundred more are endangered. Of the
original cornucopia of native birds, many were never classified, including
fifty species that were all flightless like the dodo°—and now, like the dodo, all
gone. A total of only thirty endemic bird species still survive.

dodo: extinct, heavy, flightless bird.

It's quite possible now to visit the Hawaiian Islands without ever laying eyes on a single animal or plant that is actually Hawaiian—from the Plumeria lei at the airport (this beloved flower is a Southeast Asian import) to the farewell bouquet of ginger (also Asian). African flame trees, Brazilian jacarandas, mangos and banyans from India, coffee from Africa, macadamia nuts from Australia—these are beautiful impostors all, but to enjoy them is to dance on a graveyard. Exotics are costing native Hawaii its life.   7

Haleakala Crater is fortified against invasion, because of its protected status as a national park, and because its landscape is hostile ground for pineapples and orchids. The endemics had millennia to adapt to their difficult niche, but the balance of such a fine-tuned ecosystem is precarious, easily thrown into chaos: the plants fall prey to feral° pigs and rats, and are rendered infertile by insect invaders like Argentine ants and yellow jacket wasps, which destroy native pollinators.   8

feral: wild.

Humans have sated their strange appetites in Haleakala too, and while a pig can hardly be blamed for filling its belly, people, it would seem, might know better. The dazzling silverswords, which grown nowhere else on earth, have been collected for souvenirs, leis, scientific study, Oriental medicine, and—of all things—parade floats. These magical plants once covered the ground so thickly a visitor in 1873 wrote that Haleakala's slopes glowed silvery white "like winter in moonlight." But in 1911 a frustrated collector named Dr. Aiken complained that "wild cattle had eaten most of the plants in places of any access." However, after much hard work he "obtained gunny sacks full." By 1930, it was possible to count the surviving members of this species.   9

The nēnē suffered an even more dire decline, nearly following the dodo. Since it had evolved in the absence of predators, nothing in this gentle little goose's ground-dwelling habits prepared it for egg-eating rodents, or a creature that walked upright and killed whenever it found an easy mark. By 1951, there were thirty-three nēnē geese left living in the world, half of them in zoos.   10

Midway through the century, Hawaiians began to protect their islands' biodiversity. Today, a tourist caught with a gunny-sack of silverswords would find them pricey souvenirs—there's a $10,000 fine. The Park Service and the Nature Conservancy, which owns adjacent land, are trying to exclude wild pigs from the crater and native forests by means of a fence, though in such rugged ground it's a task akin to dividing needles from haystacks. Under this fierce protection, the silverswords are making a gradual comeback. Nēnē geese have been bred in captivity and reintroduced to the crater as well, but their population, numbered at two hundred and declining, is not yet considered saved. Meanwhile, the invasion creeps forward: even within the protected boundaries of a national park, 47 percent of the   11 plant species growing in Haleakala are aliens. The whole ecosystem is endangered. If the silverswords, nēnē geese, and other colorful endemics of Hawaii survive this century, it will be by the skin of their teeth. It will only happen because we decided to notice, and hold on tight.

STRATEGY 9: MAP MAIN IDEAS

STRAGEGY 10: WRITE A SUMMARY

Follow-Up Activities   After you've finished reading, use these questions to respond to "Infernal Paradise." You may write your answers or prepare them in your mind to discuss in class.

Grab your first impressions.

Respond with your first impressions. Say what you like and dislike; relate your personal experiences to the reading; consider what more you want to know.

Work with new words.

Some words in this reading may be unfamiliar to you. Use the methods of Strategy 3 to explain what the listed words mean.

1. Use context clues.

    a. artifice (paragraph 1) _____

    b. sequestered (paragraph 4) _____

    c. carnivore (paragraph 5) _____

    d. adjacent (paragraph 11) _____

2. Use word parts.
   You know some of these word parts. Check the etymology in your dictionary definition for the others.

    a. disgorged (paragraph 2) _____

    b. topography (paragraph 3) _____

    c. ecosystem (paragraph 8) _____

    d. biodiversity (paragraph 11) _____

3. Use the dictionary.
   Choose the correct definition of each word as it is used in the context of this reading.

    a. infernal (title) _____

    b. perimeter (paragraph 1) _____

    c. lunatic (paragraph 2) _____

    d. foraging (paragraph 4) _____

4. Select additional words you're unsure of from the reading. Use one of these methods to discover their meaning.

Ask and answer questions.

1. What made it so hard for Kingsolver to judge distances on her walk down the volcanic crater?

2. Why is Haleakala Crater "one of the most difficult landscapes ever to host natural life"?

3. What kind of "unceasing invasion" does Kingsolver refer to in paragraph 4? What were some of the effects of humans' arrival on the Hawaiian Islands described in paragraph 5?

4. Why does Haleakala Crater still look much as it did two thousand years ago?

Inference Questions

5. How did the rat and mongoose affect the native bird population?

6. Kingsolver says that Haleakala Crater is "hostile ground for pineapples and orchids." What can you infer about the growth of these two plants in the rest of Hawaii?

7. What does Kingsolver mean when she says in paragraph 9, "Humans have sated their strange appetites in Haleakala too, and while a pig can hardly be blamed for filling its belly, people, it would seem, might know better"?

8. What is the creature in paragraph 10 "that walked upright and killed whenever it found an easy mark"?

Ask and answer your own questions.

Write two questions based on any of the other information in this reading. Share your questions with others and collaborate on answers.

Interpret language and purpose using Strategies 11 and 12.

Combine **finding meaning in metaphors** and **determining the writer's purpose** by looking closely at some of Kingsolver's words and phrases. First, look for the tone and metaphors in this sentence from paragraph 7.

> [T]hese [non-native species of plants] are beautiful imposters all, but to enjoy them is to dance on a graveyard.

The first surprising word in the sentence is *imposters.* In this case, the word refers to the fact that the plants are not what they seem: they are not natural to the islands, as they seem to be, but were brought there. But because *imposter* usually refers to a deception (a person pretending to be someone else), that word has a stronger, more negative connotation than simply "non-native." The next even more startling phrase is *dance on a graveyard*. "To dance on someone's grave" means to have fun at someone else's expense. Kingsolver modifies this common expression. In her metaphor, she compares enjoying non-native plants to dancing (having fun) on a whole graveyard (the extinction of all native plants). Thus this metaphor adds to the tone of alarm about the disappearance of Hawaii's native species.

Now interpret the tone and/or metaphors in three other sentences in "Infernal Paradise." Be sure to keep in mind the context for these sentences.

1. Interpret the metaphor and say how it affects the tone.

   Haleakala is a tiny, threatened ark. (paragraph 3)

2. Interpret the metaphor and say how the italicized word affects the tone.

   These islands, when they first lifted their heads out of the waves a million years ago, were naked, *defiant* rock. (paragraph 4)

3. Say how the italicized word affects the tone of this sentence.

   Mongooses were imported in a *harebrained* plan to control them [rats], but the mongoose forages by day and the rat by night, so these creatures rarely encounter one another. (paragraph 5)

 Form your final thoughts.

1. How well did Kingsolver explain the threat to Hawaii's native species? Did her tone and metaphorical language work to reflect her purpose? How were you affected by what she says?

2. How important do you think it is to save endangered species? Discuss your opinion with other classmates. ■

Chapter 12 Summary

How does Strategy 12 help you *read from the inside out?*

By **determining the writer's purpose** you know more about where the writer is coming from. Because you know more what to expect from a reading, you get a broader view of the reading outside—both the writer's ideas and his or her intentions in presenting them. You can then **respond** more fully as you take into account what the writer intended as well as your personal feelings and ideas.

How does the *determine the writer's purpose* strategy work?

You determine the writer's purpose by asking about the type of writing, the intended audience, and the writer's perspective on the subject. You see how the tone of the writing reflects the purpose. Here are the four steps for Strategy 12.

STRATEGY 12: DETERMINE THE WRITER'S PURPOSE

1 Recognize the type of writing.

2 Recognize the intended audience.

3 Identify the writer's perspective.

4 See how the tone reflects the purpose.

Are you familiar with the meaning of these terms?

narration: tells a story

description: shows what someone or something looks like

exposition: explains something or informs

argument: persuades you to believe something or do something

perspective: way of looking at a subject; your position on it

intended audience: the people a writer wants to reach

general reader: someone who has no special background in a subject

purpose: the writer's reasons for writing

tone: shows the writer's attitude or mood

objective: neutral, free from emotional attachment to one side or the other

subjective: having emotional involvement or bias (leaning) to one side or the other

bias: leaning to one or another side of a debatable question; emotional involvement

irony: use of words to convey meaning that is opposite to—or very different from—the literal meaning

sarcasm: ironic use of a term to mean its opposite

How is the strategy working for you so far?

1. What has helped you the most to determine the writer's purpose?

2. How has your awareness of the writer's purpose helped your understanding of a reading? If it hasn't helped, can you say why?

3. How successful have you been in detecting the tone of a reading?

4. What did you appreciate about using this strategy? What did you dislike?

For more practice with *determining the writer's purpose,*
use the Reading Road Trip CD-ROM or Web site.

PART V

ADDITIONAL READINGS ON
NATURE'S ADVENTURES AND CHALLENGES

The readings that follow will give you further practice in using appropriate strategies with other readings on the theme of "Nature's Adventures and Challenges."

READING V-A   IMPRINTING: A FORM OF LEARNING

ROBERT A. WALLACE

STRATEGY 7: LOOK FOR PATTERNS OF THOUGHT
Look for clear examples, and watch how contrast helps clarify cause-and-effect reasoning about song sparrows.

Robert Wallace was a professor of biology at the University of Florida until his death in 1996. He was the author of several biology textbooks and other non-fiction books on science. This reading comes from the chapter on animal behavior in his textbook Biology: The World of Life *(1996). The reading tells about the famous experiment that made a researcher the parent to a group of baby geese.*

*Choose appropriate strategies for reading "Imprinting: A Form of Learning." In addition to **determining the writer's purpose**, you'll find it especially helpful to **look for patterns** as you **find and mark main ideas** in each paragraph.*

STRATEGY 6: FIND AND MARK MAIN IDEAS
Look for the topic and then the main idea for each paragraph.

On your annual visits to the farm, you may have seen young ducklings waddling along after their mother, perhaps on the way to the pond. It's a quaint sight, but you're there to see where milk comes from and so you think no more about it. However, if you had visited a farm in southern Germany some years ago, you might have seen a more unusual sight—a column of young goslings following a white-haired Austrian down to the pond (Figure 1). The man was Konrad Lorenz, a future recipient of the Nobel Prize, and the following behavior of the goslings was the product of an experiment he devised.

What he did was to let them see him moving around and making noises a few hours after they had hatched. If they had seen and heard him after that, they would have treated him like any other human. But Lorenz was the figure they encountered during their *critical period,* a window of time when the young are particularly sensitive to certain aspects of their environment. At this time, the goslings, and the young of many other species as well, learn the traits of whatever is around them. Normally, of course, this would be their mother, but these goslings developed from eggs that were artificially incubated and so the figure that they saw during their

1

2

Figure 1   Konrad Lorenz, in a famous photograph, leading a group of goslings that had imprinted on him.

critical period was Konrad Lorenz, and as a result they learned to regard him as one of their own.

Lorenz called this kind of learning *imprinting,* and he defined it as learning that occurs over a defined, relatively brief period of time in which the animal learns to make a specific response to certain aspects of its environment.

A great deal of research has been done on imprinting in the last few decades and we have learned that it is difficult to draw hard and fast rules about its development. It is regarded, though, as a curious interaction of learned and instinctive patterns. In the case of the goslings, they learned the general characteristics of the stimulus for the innate following response.

Many animals also learn species identification during this critical period; that is, they learn the image of an appropriate mate. As they approach their first breeding season, they seek out an individual with traits generally similar to those of the individual they had followed soon after hatching. If they are raised by parents of another species, they focus on individuals with traits similar to those of their foster parents when it is time to breed. Lorenz once had a tame jackdaw (a European crow) that he had hand-reared, and it would try to "courtship feed" him during mating season. On occasion when Lorenz turned his mouth away, he would receive an earful of worm pulp! . . .

Imprinting is especially important in the development of song in many species. For example, for male white-crowned sparrows to be able to sing the song of their species, they must hear the song at a particular time during a brief critical period early in life. If they are exposed to the song after this period, they will produce abnormal songs, lacking the finer details. At the period during which they must hear the song, they are not yet even able to sing.

White-crowned sparrows are wide ranging, and the species forms subpopulations that tend to breed among themselves and sing their own local dialects of the basic song. If young birds from different populations are isolated at hatching and reared in soundproof chambers, they all begin to sing the same rather basic song. Thus, they are apparently born with the basic pattern; the local embellishments of each population are learned later.

Interestingly, isolated hatchling white-crowned sparrows can learn the   8
recorded dialect of any subpopulation of the species while in their learning periods. But if they are exposed to the song of another species, they will not learn that song and will sing as if they had been reared in a soundproof cage. Finally, if a young white-crowned sparrow is deafened after it has heard the proper song but before it has had a chance to sing, it will sing only garbled passages. It apparently must hear its own song in order to match it to its inborn "template." The development of song in white-crowned sparrows, then, serves as an example of the interaction of learned and innate patterns in producing an adaptive response.

Follow-Up Activities   After you've finished reading, use these questions to respond to "Imprinting: A Form of Learning." You may write your answers or prepare them in your mind to discuss in class.

Grab your first impressions.

Respond with your first impressions. Say what you like and dislike; relate your personal experiences to the reading; consider what more you want to know.

Work with new words.

Some words in this reading may be unfamiliar to you. Use the methods of Strategy 3 to explain what the listed words mean.

1. Use context clues.

    a. traits (paragraph 2) _____

    b. incubated (paragraph 2) _____

    c. embellishments (paragraph 7) _____

2. Use the dictionary.
   Choose the correct definition of each word as it is used in the context of this reading.

    a. species (paragraph 2) _____

    b. stimulus (paragraph 4) _____

    c. innate (paragraph 4) _____

    d. template (paragraph 8) _____

3. Select additional words you're unsure of from the reading. Use one of these methods to discover their meaning.

Ask and answer questions.

1. What is imprinting? What is meant by the term *critical period* in relation to imprinting?

2. What was the experiment Konrad Lorenz devised that demonstrated imprinting? Why did the goslings regard Lorenz as "one of their own"?

3. How would you paraphrase these words from the end of paragraph 4: "They [the goslings] learned the general characteristics of the stimulus for the innate following response"?

4. What is meant by saying that animals learn "species identification"? What happened when Lorenz hand-reared a jackdaw? How did the jackdaw's actions demonstrate learning species identification?

5. What happens if white-crowned sparrows are not exposed to the song of their species during the critical period? How do researchers infer that these birds are born with the basic pattern of their species' song?

6. How do the experiments with white-crowned sparrows demonstrate the concept that imprinting is a "curious interaction of learned and instinctive patterns" (paragraph 4)?

Questions About Purpose

7. Knowing this is a textbook excerpt tells you a lot about the purpose of the reading. However, why do you think the writer began with "your annual visit to the farm"? How does the tone of this and some of the other parts of this reading reflect his purpose?

8. What is Wallace's overall point in this excerpt? How does his purpose relate to his overall point?

 Ask and answer your own questions.

Write two questions based on any of the other information in this reading. Share your questions with others and collaborate on answers.

 Form your final thoughts.

1 How successful was Wallace at using examples and explanations to help you understand the concept of imprinting? Discuss with others which parts of the reading worked well and which less well.

2. Discuss with others how this reading relates to Reading 6: "What Deprived Children Tell Us about Human Nature." Both readings deal with the interrelationship of traits that are inborn and those that are learned from the environment. What are similarities and differences between the ideas in these two readings?

READING V-B   THE GORILLA'S EMBRACE

Barbara Smuts is a professor at the University of Michigan, editor of Primate
Societies, *and author of* Sex and Friendship in Baboons. *This reading was published first in the Summer 1999 issue of* Whole Earth. *In this piece Smuts shows
how her extensive research on animal behavior has given her both a scientific
understanding and a personal, affectionate view of the animals she's studied.*

*Choose appropriate strategies for reading "The Gorilla's Embrace." In addi-
tion to **determining the writer's purpose,** you'll find it especially helpful to **make
inferences** and **look for patterns of thought.** Finally, because this reading has
no headings, try mapping main topics in pencil first, before marking main ideas.*

STRATEGY 12: DETERMINE THE WRITER'S PURPOSE
How does Smuts see the animals she studies? How does this perspective affect her purpose in writing?

STRATEGY 8: MAKE INFERENCES
What can you infer that Smuts means by *person* in this reading?

1   For the heart to truly share another's being, it must be an embodied heart, prepared to encounter directly the embodied heart of another. I have met the "other" in this way, not once or a few times in my life, but over and over during years spent in the company of "persons" like you and me, who happen to be nonhuman.

2   These nonhuman persons included gorillas at home in the perpetually wet, foggy mountaintops of central Africa, chimpanzees carousing in the hot, rugged hills of western Tanzania,° baboons lazily strolling across the golden grass plains of highland Kenya,° and dolphins gliding languorously through the green, clear waters of Shark Bay. In each case, I was lucky to be accepted by the animals as a mildly interesting, harmless companion, permitted to travel amongst them, eligible to be touched by hands and fins—although I refrained, most of the time, from touching in turn.

Tanzania and Kenya: countries in East Africa.

3   I mingled with these animals under the guise of scientific research, and, indeed, most of my activities while "in the field" were designed to gain objective, replicable information about the animals' lives. Doing good science, it turned out, consisted mostly of spending every possible moment with the animals, watching them with the utmost concentration, and documenting myriad aspects of their behavior. In this way, I learned much that I could confidently report as scientific findings. But while one component of my being was engaged in rational inquiry, another part of me, by necessity, was absorbed in the physical challenge of functioning in an unfamiliar landscape devoid of other humans or any human-created objects save what I carried on my back. When I first began working with baboons, my main problem was learning to keep up with them while remaining alert to poisonous snakes, irascible buffalo, aggressive bees, and leg-breaking pig holes. Fortunately, these challenges eased over time, mainly because I was traveling in the company of expert guides—baboons who could spot a predator a mile away and seemed to possess a sixth sense for the proximity of snakes. Abandoning myself to their far superior knowledge, I moved as a humble disciple, learning from masters about being an African anthropoid.°

anthropoid: member of primate group of apes (gorilla, chimpanzee, etc.), monkeys, humans.

Thus I became (or, rather, regained my ancestral right to be) an animal,   4
moving instinctively through a world that felt (because it was) like my
ancient home. Having begun to master this challenge, I faced another one
equally daunting: to comprehend and behave according to a system of
baboon etiquette bizarre and subtle enough to stop Emily Post° in her tracks.
This task was forced on me by the fact that the baboons stubbornly resisted
my feeble but sincere attempts to convince them that I was nothing more
than a detached observer, a neutral object they could ignore. Right from the
start, they knew better, insisting that I was, like them, a social subject vulnerable to the demands and rewards of relationship. Since I was in their
world, they determined the rules of the game, and I was thus compelled to
explore the unknown terrain of human-baboon intersubjectivity. Through
trial and embarrassing error, I gradually mastered at least the rudiments of
baboon propriety. I learned much through observation, but the deepest lessons came when I found myself sharing the being of a baboon because
other baboons were treating me like one. Thus I learned from personal
experience that if I turned my face away but held my ground, a charging
male with canines bared in threat would stop short of attack. I became
familiar with the invisible line defining the personal space of each troop
member, and then I discovered that the space expands and contracts
depending on the circumstances. I developed the knack of sweetly but firmly
turning my back on the playful advances of juveniles, conveying, as did the
older females, that although I found them appealing, I had more important
things to do. After many months of immersion in their society I stopped
thinking so much about what to do and instead simply surrendered to
instinct, not as mindless, reflexive action, but rather as action rooted in an
ancient primate legacy of embodied knowledge.

Living in this way with baboons, I discovered that to be an animal is to   5
be "full of being," full of "joy." Like the rest of us, baboons get grouchy, go
hungry, feel fear and pain and loss. But during my times with them, the
default state seemed to be a lighthearted appreciation of being a baboon
body in baboon-land. Adolescent females concluded formal, grown-up-
style greetings with somber adult males with a somersault flourish.
Distinguished old ladies, unable to get a male's attention, stood on their
heads and gazed up at the guy upside down. Grizzled males approached
balls of wrestling infants and tickled them. Juveniles spent hours perfecting
the technique of swinging from a vine to land precisely on the top of mom's
head. And the voiceless, breathy chuckles of baboon play echoed through
the forest from dawn to dusk.

During the cool, early morning hours, the baboons would work hard   6
to fill their stomachs, but as the temperature rose, they became prone to

Emily Post: author of books
on manners.

Barbara displaying her teeth to the cameraman, not baboons. A facial expression of joy.

taking long breaks in especially attractive locales. In a mossy glade or along the white-sanded beach of an inland lake, they would shamelessly indulge a passion for lying around in the shade on their backs with their feet in the air. Every now and then someone would concur about the agreeableness of the present situation by participating in a chorus of soft grunts that rippled through the troop like a gentle wave. In the early days of my fieldwork, when I was still preoccupied with doing things right, I regarded these siestas as valuable opportunities to gather data on who rested near whom. But later, I began to lie around with them. Later still, I would sometimes lie around without them—that is, among them, but while they were still busy eating. Once I fell asleep surrounded by 100 munching baboons only to awaken half an hour later, alone except for an adolescent male who had chosen to nap by my side (presumably inferring from my deep sleep that I'd found a particularly good resting spot). We blinked at one another in the light of the noonday sun and then casually sauntered several miles back to the rest of the troop, with him leading the way.

There were 140 baboons in the troop, and I came to know every one as   7
a highly distinctive individual. Each one had a particular gait, which allowed me to know who was whom, even from great distances when I couldn't see anyone's face. Every baboon had a characteristic voice and unique things

to say with it; each had a face like no other, favorite foods, favorite friends, favorite bad habits. Dido, when chased by an unwelcome suitor, would dash behind some cover and then dive into a pig hole, carefully peeking out every few moments to see if the male had given up the chase. Lysistrata liked to sneak up on an infant riding on its mother's back, knock it off (gently), and then pretend to be deeply preoccupied with eating some grass when mom turned to see the cause of her infant's distress. Apié, the alpha male, would carefully study the local fishermen from a great distance, wait for just the right moment to rush toward them, take a flying leap over their heads to land on the fish-drying rack, grab the largest fish, and disappear into the forest before anyone knew what was happening.

I also learned about baboon individuality directly, since each one 8 approached his or her relationship with me in a slightly different way. Cicero, the outcast juvenile, often followed me and sat quietly a few feet away, seemingly deriving some small comfort from my proximity. Leda, the easygoing female, would walk so close to me I could feel her fur against my bare legs. Dakar, feisty adolescent male, would catch my eye and then march over to me, stand directly in front of me, and grab my kneecap while staring at my face intently (thanks to Dakar, I've become rather good at appearing calm when my heart is pounding). Clearly, the baboons also knew me as an individual. This knowledge was lasting, as I learned when I paid an unexpected visit to one of my study troops seven years after last being with them. They had been unstudied during the previous five years, so the adults had no recent experience with people coming close to them, and the youngsters had no such experience at all. I was traveling with a fellow scientist whom the baboons had never met, and, as we approached on foot from a distance, I anticipated considerable wariness toward both of us. When we got to within about one hundred yards, all of the youngsters fled, but the adults merely glanced at us and continued foraging. I asked my companion to remain where he was, and slowly I moved closer, expecting the remaining baboons to move away at any moment. To my utter amazement, they ignored me, except for an occasional glance, until I found myself walking among them exactly as I had done many years before. To make sure they were comfortable with me, as opposed to white people in general, I asked my friend to come closer. Immediately, the baboons moved away. It was me they recognized, and after a seven-year interval they clearly trusted me as much as they had on the day I left.

Trust, while an important component of a friendship, does not, in and 9 of itself, define it. Friendship requires some degree of mutuality, some give-and-take. Because it was important, scientifically, for me to minimize my interactions with the baboons, I had few opportunities to explore the possibilities of such give-and-take with them. But occasional events hinted that such relations might be possible, were I encountering the baboons first and foremost as fellow social beings, rather than as subjects of scientific inquiry. For example, one day, as I rested my hand on a large rock, I suddenly felt the gentlest of touches on my fingertips. Turning around slowly, I came face-to-face with one of my favorite juveniles, a slight fellow named Damien. He looked intently into my eyes, as if to make sure that I was not disturbed by his touch, and then he proceeded to use his index finger to examine, in great detail, each one of my fingernails in turn. This exploration was made especially poignant by the fact that Damien was examining my fingers with one that looked very much the same, except that his was smaller and black. After touching each nail, and without removing his finger, Damien glanced up at me for a few seconds. Each time our gaze met, I wondered if he, like me, was contemplating the implication of the realization that our fingers and fingernails were so alike.

I experienced an even greater sense of intimacy when, in 1978, I had   10
the exceptional privilege of spending a week with Dian Fossey° and the mountain gorillas she had been studying for many years. One day, I was out with one of her groups, along with a male colleague unfamiliar to the gorillas and a young male researcher whom they knew well. Digit, one of the young adult males, was strutting about and beating his chest in an early challenge to the leading silverback male. My two male companions were fascinated by this tension, but after a while I had had enough of the macho energy, and I wandered off. About thirty meters away, I came upon a "nursery" group of mothers and infants who had perhaps moved off for the same reasons I had. I sat near them and watched the mothers eating and the babies playing for timeless, peaceful moments. Then my eyes met the warm gaze of an adolescent female, Pandora. I continued to look at her, silently sending friendliness her way. Unexpectedly, she stood and moved closer. Stopping right in front of me, with her face at eye level, she leaned forward and pushed her large, flat, wrinkled nose against mine. I know that she was right up against me, because I distinctly remember how her warm, sweet breath fogged up my glasses, blinding me. I felt no fear and continued to focus on the enormous affection and respect I felt for her. Perhaps she sensed my attitude, because in the next moment I felt her impossibly long ape arms wrap around me, and for precious seconds, she held me in her embrace. Then she released me, gazed once more into my eyes, and returned to munching on leaves.

After returning from Africa, I was very lonely for nonhuman company.   11
This yearning was greatly eased by my dog Safi. Safi and I are equals. This does not mean we are the same; we are, in fact, very different, she with the

Dian Fossey: researcher of gorillas, subject of movie *Gorillas in the Mist.*

blood of wolves, me with the blood of apes. It does mean I regard her as a "person." Relating to other beings as "persons" has nothing to do with whether or not we attribute human characteristics to them. It has to do with recognizing that they are social creatures like us whose idiosyncratic, subjective experience of us plays the same role as our subjective experience of them. When Safi or the baboons relate to us as individuals, and when we relate to them as individuals, it is possible for both to have a personal relationship. If a human being relates to a nonhuman being as an anonymous object, rather than as a being with its own subjectivity, it is the human, and not the other animal, who relinquishes personhood.

The limitations most of us encounter with other animals reflect not   12
their shortcomings, as we too often assume, but our own narrow views. Treating members of other species as persons, as beings with potential far beyond our normal expectations, will bring out the best in them. Each animal's best includes unforeseeable gifts.

Follow-Up Activities   After you've finished reading, use these questions to respond to "The Gorilla's Embrace." You may write your answers or prepare them in your mind to discuss in class.

Grab your first impressions.

Respond with your first impressions. Say what you like and dislike; relate your personal experiences to the reading; consider what more you want to know.

Work with new words.

Some words in this reading may be unfamiliar to you. Use the methods of Strategy 3 to explain what the listed words mean.

1. Use context clues.

   a. predator (paragraph 3) _____

   b. somber (paragraph 5) _____

   c. proximity (paragraph 8) _____

   d. relinquishes (paragraph 11) _____

2. Use word parts.

   a. embodied (paragraph 1) _____

   b. intersubjectivity (paragraph 4) _____

   c. propriety (paragraph 4) _____
      The word *proper* is part of this word.

3. Use the dictionary.

Choose the correct definition of each word as it is used in the context of this reading.

a. replicable (paragraph 3) _____

b. devoid (paragraph 3) _____

c. rudiments (paragraph 4) _____

d. poignant (paragraph 9) _____

4. Select additional words you're unsure of from the reading. Use one of these methods to discover their meaning.

Ask and answer questions.

1. How does Smuts study animals? How is her work defined as "scientific research"? How is it that she "became (or, rather, regained my ancestral right to be) an animal"?

2. What made it hard to retain a completely detached, neutral view of the baboons she was studying? What are some examples Smuts gives of being expected to join in as a part of the animals' social organization?

3. What are some examples she gives of the individual differences she finds among all the different baboons she gets to know?

4. What incident does Smuts tell that shows how well the baboons got to know and trust her as an individual human being?

Inference Questions

5. What did the gorilla's embrace show Smuts? Why did she have few opportunities to have such intimacy with the animals she studied?

6. What is Smuts's definition of *person?* Why do you think she uses that term for animals as well as people?

Questions About Purpose

7. Where do you see an objective tone in this reading? Where a subjective tone? What words would you use to describe some of the emotional tone: serious? joyful? concerned? other? Explain your choice(s).

8. What is Smuts's overall point about her subject? What is her purpose in writing about it?

 ## *Ask and answer your own questions.*

Write two questions based on any of the other information in this reading. Share your questions with others and collaborate on answers.

Form your final thoughts.

1. What has your own contact with animals been like? Does your experience match what Smuts describes in any way? Discuss your answer with other students.

2. How well did Smuts describe her experiences with the baboons and gorillas? How convincing were her ideas about the value of "personal relationships" with animals?

READING V-C   VÍCTOR

JULIA ALVAREZ

STRATEGY 12: DETERMINE THE WRITER'S PURPOSE

What is the writer's perspective—including her attitudes and feelings—about the natural environment she shows in this story?

STRATEGY 8: MAKE INFERENCES

What can you infer about the kind of knowledge Víctor has? How is it different from the kind the visitor has?

Julia Alvarez is a novelist and poet, now teaching at Middlebury College in Vermont. Her writing, such as the novel How the García Girls Lost Their Accents (1992), often deals with the immigrant experience of belonging to two worlds: the United States and her native country, the Dominican Republic, where she now lives part of the year. "Víctor," a story that takes place in the Dominican Republic, first appeared in Off the Beaten Path: Stories of Place (1998).

Before reading "Víctor," think about the strategies you'll want to use for reading a story. You will get a great deal from this story just by using the first two strategies, **check in** and **respond. Making inferences** and **finding meaning in metaphors** will also be helpful. Finally, in **working with new words,** be sure to use the context clues. There are several specialized terms for birds, animals, and plants that you don't need to know in order to enjoy the story. There are also some Spanish words whose meaning is usually clear from the context.

Whenever Don Bernardo comes to the national park, he asks for Víctor's   1
father as his guide. "And tell him to bring Víctor along," he invariably adds.

Today, Don Bernardo has a strange guest with him. Víctor can tell that   2
Don Bernardo is not quite at ease with this lady, as if she were here to report on his work as director of parks. But she seems harmless enough. A skinny lady who is not Americana but looks Americana in her blue pants and T-shirt with letters written across it. She is carrying a notebook, and from a ribbon around her neck dangles a pen where the Virgencita's° medallion should go.

Don Bernardo looks down and notices Víctor. "Ho, there, Víctor! How   3
is the little man?"

As he always does when he doesn't know what to say or where to look,   4
Víctor lifts his unbuttoned shirt over his head. He hides underneath it like the lizard under the frond of the elephant fern.

"Mira, muchacho," his father scolds in a voice that threatens to cuff his   5
ear. After all, Don Bernardo made a point of introducing this lady as an honored visitor who writes books and teaches in an American school. "You can say hello like a person."

Virgencita: Virgin Mary.

"Hello," Víctor says loud and clear, like a person.   6

Don Bernardo laughs. "Víctor is as smart as a pencil," he tells the lady,   7
who smiles at him and says, "Is that so?" Just as she is not americana but
looks americana, she is dominicana but speaks Spanish as if she were worried there might be a little stone in among the words that will crack her
mouthful of white teeth. Each word is carefully spoken and cleanly finished
before the next one starts. "So tell me, Víctor," she says, "what grade are
you in?"

Víctor glances at his father. "In the third grade," he offers.   8

"Did you complete it or are you about to start it this September?"   9

Looking over her shoulder, Víctor spots the red-eyed bobo flying   10
through the trees as if stitching together the forest with the rise and fall of
its wings. If the lady is here to see the park, she should not miss the flight
of the bobo. "Look!" he points. "A bobo!"

She turns around, craning her neck to see what he sees.   11

Víctor keeps pointing, but the lady is not quick enough and the bobo   12
disappears into the dark-green curtain of the rain forest.

"Bo-bo," the lady says the name slowly, writing it down in her little   13
book. "Where were we?" she asks when she looks back up.

"Lead on, Víctor!" Don Bernardo commands.   14

Víctor darts ahead, his shirt flapping behind him like the tail of the   15
bobo when it sits on the branch of the cedar, calling bo-bo, bo-bo, bo-bo,
as if it were trying to talk like a person, expecting an answer.

The lady walks behind him on the trail. "Wow," she says over every   16
little thing.

"Wow-oh." Víctor tries out the words under his breath. "Wow-oh,   17
wow-oh." The words sound like the call of the big-eyed lechuza at night.

"Wow! Look at that flower!" The lady points.   18

"That's a campana," Víctor explains. "Careful when you touch it.   19
Wasps love to build in its leaves."

"It's so so beautiful," the lady says, writing down the name of the   20
flower in her notebook. "Cam-pa-na." She breaks it down into little pieces
as if she were about to feed the word to a baby who cannot chew solid
food. Her voice is clear and measured like a schoolteacher's. "What is
that?" She looks up. Behind her, Don Bernardo stops to listen.

"That little bird singing is a barrancolf," Víctor explains. "And over   21
there is a tinaja," he adds. "You want me to cut one down for you?"

"Cut it down?" A scolding look spreads across the lady's face.   22

"I can cut you an orchid if you prefer." Víctor hesitates. His father has   23

turista: woman tourist.   taught him to figure out what will please a turista° so the tip will be a good

bromeliad: family of tropical plants including pineapple and ornamentals.

one. The ladies, when they come, always like a delicate orchid or tufted bromeliad° to take home to the capital in their jeeps or scouts. The chauffeur, usually along carting the ice chest, carries it back in his free hand.

Don Bernardo catches up and wags his finger. "You know better than to disturb things in the rain forest, Víctor." 24

"You know better," his father agrees. Víctor recognizes the look that says, You have put you foot down beside a wasp nest. Watch out. 25

"I know better." Víctor nods. 26

"Víctor is as smart as a pencil," Don Bernardo repeats. "How old did you say you were, Víctor?" He winks at the lady as if preparing her for a merriment. 27

Víctor looks at his father. "Ten," he says solemnly. 28

"But, Víctor," Don Bernardo says, eyeing him kindly, "you have been ten years old for the last three years I have been coming to the park." 29

"You mean to say he doesn't know how old he is?" the lady asks Don Bernardo. The director of parks glances at his feet. Every time he comes to the park, he teases Víctor and his guests smile along with him. 30

"Don't you know how old you are, Víctor?" the lady persists. 31

Víctor lifts his shirt over his head and looks up at the trail. It winds through the trees and then up the incline toward the collection of white rocks the turistas like to photograph. "Nine," he tries, and then "fourteen," but none of the numbers seem to please the lady, who shakes her head at Don Bernardo. 32

"Something should be done about this," she says, making a note in her book. Don Bernardo nods gravely, his hands in his pockets. Víctor glances at his father, who narrows his eyes at his son as if to say, Stand very still, boy. If you don't make a move, maybe the wasps will go away. 33

They continue down the trail, but the exploration is no fun anymore. 34

"One-two-three-four," the lady makes him slowly count out loud. 35

"What is the first month of the year, Víctor?" 36

"October?" 37

"Víctor! The *first* month? I already told you." 38

He tries a few more before he gets it right. They stop by a bush of bejuco de gato so the lady can write the name down. 39

"Those leaves are good for pain," Víctor explains to her. 40

"How do you spell bejuco anyhow?" she asks Don Bernardo, who spells the word for her. That gets her started on something else. "Can you spell *your* name, Víctor?" 41

Víctor feels silence tingling the inside of his mouth—as if he had taken a bite of bejuco de gato and his tongue had gone numb. He looks down at 42 the lady's pants covered with melao and amor seco, nettles that are hard to take out. "You want me to pick those off?" he offers her.

"V-I-C-T-O-R," she instructs him.   43

He repeats the letters after her.   44

"Well done!" Don Bernardo nods, but he does not add his usual   45
phrase, "Víctor is as smart as a pencil." Perhaps he will no longer ask for Víctor every time he visits the park.

"Onetwothreefourfive!" Víctor pipes up, wanting to impress them   46
both. Sure enough, Don Bernardo is laughing again!

At the fork in the trail, Don Bernardo explains to the lady that one path   47
leads to the river, the other climbs up to the white rocks. The lady decides she wants to see the river, but then she confuses things by saying, "So take a right, Víctor."

"To the river?" he asks her just to make sure.   48

That look comes on her face again. "Which is your left, Víctor, and   49
which is your right?"

"It depends," he says, outsmarting her for once. "Which way do you   50
want to go?"

This time even she laughs, little hiccup laughs that sound like the cal-   51
calf calling to the sun as it rises up in the morning.

At the river, Don Bernardo and the lady sit on the rocks and talk in low,   52
earnest voices about matters that sound important. "Thirty percent offi-cially," Don Bernardo is explaining, "but it depends what you mean by illiteracy."

Víctor looks over at his father, perched on a fallen log, a papagallo stem   53
in his mouth. He wishes he had picked one, too, for the sweet sap tastes so good on a hot day. Víctor can tell his father is calculating how much Don Bernardo will tip them for this tour. The farther the turistas go, the more they tip. But Don Bernardo and his guest had barely gone two kilometers before the lady discovered that Víctor did not know his numbers. The walk slowed as the lady stopped often to draw figures with a stick on the forest floor.

Beyond them, the trail cuts through to the heart of the green preserve.   54
So many things are disappearing that will never be seen again on this earth! Or so Víctor has overheard at the lodge when his father attends the mandatory workshops the forestry service gives for the guides. But Víctor sees no sign of danger: the cocaría, whose flower stains blue and whose seeds if chewed cure toothache, is bursting with blossoms. Beside it, the leaves of cola de caballo bob in the slight breeze of late afternoon. The day is waning and there is still so much to show. The bamboo knock against one another like knuckles rapping on a desk asking for attention.

Bo-bo, bo-bo, calls the bobo.   55

"Bo-bo, bo-bo," Víctor answers back.   56

"Ho, Víctor!" Don Bernardo wakes Víctor from his daydreaming.   57

"Time to head back."   58

A soft light is falling through the canopy of thick branches. The air is   59
cool. The forest is always so much more pleasant than the village school-
house with the sun beating down on its zinc roof.

As they climb back up the stone steps, the lady notices a narrow foot-   60
path that cuts away from the river in the same general direction as the trail.
"Where does this go?" she wants to know.

"That's an old mule track up to the white rocks," Víctor's father   61
explains. "But it's too overgrown to walk."

"It looks fine," the lady says. "It'll give us some new things to look at.   62
Don't you think so, Don Bernardo?" she addresses the director of parks. But
it is clear from her face that her mind is already made up.

"There's a lot of campanas," Víctor begins, seconding his father's   63
hesitation.

But the lady has already sprung forward, thrashing through the under-   64
growth so that all Víctor sees through the bobbing of the fern fronds is the
blue of her pants and the flash of white paper in her little book. The men
exchange a look. Finally, Don Bernardo shrugs and says. "Let's go."

Víctor has almost caught up to her when he hears the cry that comes   65
as no surprise. She has pressed through a narrow avenue of campanas and
the wasps are after her.

Quick, Víctor looks around and snaps off a branch from a nearby   66
guayuyo tree. Beating a way toward her through the buzzing in the air, he
yanks her by the hand back out to the river. Her notebook falls to the
ground as she races beside him, Don Bernardo and his father giving them
a wide berth as they jump into the water.

When she comes to the surface, Víctor can see that one eye is already   67
swollen shut. He searches the bank for the leaves of bejuco de gato to ease
the pain and oreja de burro to keep down the swelling. Meanwhile his
father and Don Bernardo are rubbing guayuyo leaves on their arms and
face to keep away the few wasps who have followed the intruders to the
river. The forest has gone absolutely still. Not even the bold bobo calls to
find out what is going on.

As soon as the lady is soothed with the leaves he has brought her,   68
Víctor rubs guayuyo on his own face and arms, and runs off to retrieve
the little book filled with things he has tried to teach her about the rain
forest.

Follow-Up Activities   After you've finished reading, use these questions to respond to "Víctor." You may write your answers or prepare them in your mind to discuss in class.

Grab your first impressions.

Respond with your first impressions. Say what you like and dislike; relate your personal experiences to the reading; consider what more you want to know.

Work with new words and find meaning in metaphors.

1. Use context clues to understand the special names referred to in this story for birds, animals, or plants native to the rain forest in the Dominican Republic. You can also use context clues for most of the Spanish words.

2. Alvarez uses many metaphors and similes. Use Strategy 11 to identify and interpret these metaphorical expressions.

   a. [S]he speaks Spanish as if she were worried there might be a little stone in among the words that will crack her mouthful of white teeth. (paragraph 7)

      _____

   b. Víctor recognizes the look that says, You have put your foot down beside a wasp nest. Watch out. (paragraph 25)

      _____

   c. Víctor feels silence tingling the inside of his mouth—as if he had taken a bite of the bejuco de gato and his tongue had gone numb. (paragraph 42)

      _____

   d. The bamboo knock against one another like knuckles rapping on a desk asking for attention. (paragraph 54)

      _____

3. Select additional words you're unsure of from the reading. Use one of the methods from Strategy 3 to discover their meaning.

Ask and answer questions, using inferences.

Stories depend a great deal on implied meanings, so most of these questions require making some **inferences**.

1. Who are the characters in this story? Explain briefly the role of Don Bernardo, Víctor, Víctor's father, and the woman visitor.

2. How is this visitor to the national park different from other turistas that Don Bernardo and Víctor have been used to? Explain how you can infer these differences.

3. What does the lady turista keep missing in what Víctor is trying to show her? Why doesn't she see what he is showing her?

4. When is the association between wasps and the campana flower first mentioned? Why is that association important for the ending of the story?

5. What are the different views we get of Víctor? Think about what Alvarez says about him, what the lady thinks of him, and what Don Bernardo thinks. What is your view of him?

6. What can you infer from this story about Alvarez's perspective on threats to the rain forest?

7. Remember, the term *irony* refers to the use of words to convey meaning that is opposite to—or very different from—the literal meaning. What irony can you find in the last sentence of the story, when Víctor runs to get the book of things "he has tried to teach [the lady] about the rain forest"?

Form your final thoughts.

1. What is Alvarez's purpose in telling this story? How well do you think she achieved her purpose? Discuss your opinion of the story with other students.

2. How well do you think Alvarez showed the qualities of her characters? How well did she describe what the tropical forest is like? Discuss your answers with others. ∎

PART V REVIEW
Interpreting Language and Purpose

Now that you've completed Part V, think over what you've read about current interest and concern for the natural world and the place—and role—of human beings in it. Then review the two strategies introduced in this part, and see how they work throughout the reading process.

Linking Ideas on the Theme:
Nature's Adventures and Challenges

 Respond to the readings in Part V by linking ideas on the theme of "Nature's Adventures and Challenges." Answer these questions in writing or in discussion with others.

1. Several writers show what we can learn through contact with nature—perhaps from being in certain places or from having contact with certain animals. Find ways of linking two readings that explore what nature taught these writers.

2. In "Terror Unlimited," Tim Cahill tells about his hair-raising adventure on El Capitan. Other writers describe very different adventures they find in nature. Compare the adventures of another writer with those of Cahill's.

3. "A Global Green Deal" by Mark Hertsgaard is about dealing with threats to the natural environment caused by human beings. What other readings express concern for the environment? Choose one of these readings to compare with Hertsgaard's piece.

4. You may think of yet another way of linking two readings on this theme. Say what the two readings have in common as well as how they are different.

5. Try linking ideas from one or two of these readings with ideas in something else you've read—including something in an earlier part of this book—or with a movie or TV program you've seen.

6. Decide on your favorite reading for Part V. Then look over your favorites from the previous parts. Can you see any pattern in the types of readings you prefer versus the ones you like least? Or are your choices based more

on particular qualities in specific reading? Discuss your choice with others in the class, looking for similarities and differences in the kind of readings people chose.

Using Strategies Throughout the Reading Process

Strategy 11: **Find Meaning in Metaphor**

Strategy 12: **Determine the Writer's Purpose**

You have seen how the strategies in Part V—**find meaning in metaphor** and **determine the writer's purpose**—incorporate the earlier strategies for predicting, comprehending, and summarizing main ideas. These new strategies help you deepen your understanding and expand your response to a reading.

Use the chart on the next page as a reminder of how a strategy helps you at each of the three stages: Get Started, Read, Follow Up. The new strategies are highlighted.

How Are the Strategies Working for You?

You've now learned almost all of the reading strategies. At this point you've incorporated some of these strategies into your reading. You've also practiced choosing the most appropriate strategies, depending on the specific demands of each reading. Take some time, once again, to evaluate the two new strategies along with the previous ones.

First, look back at what you wrote about the strategies at the end of Part IV. What differences would there be in your answers to those questions now?

Next, answer the following questions to help you evaluate Strategies 11 and 12. Finally, compare notes with other students, and ask your instructor for ideas on how to get more out of the strategies.

1. Which of the earlier strategies have become a regular part of your reading? Which ones do you use less often? Why?

   _____

   _____

   _____

2. Which strategies do you now combine as you're going through each stage of reading? (For example, part of **determining the writer's purpose** uses steps from **making inferences**.)

   _____

   _____

   _____

STRATEGIES THROUGH PART V

1. Check in
2. Respond
3. Work with new words
4. Get an overview
5. Ask questions
6. Find and mark main ideas
7. Look for patterns of thought
8. Make inferences
9. Map main ideas
10. Write a summary
11. Find meaning in metaphors
12. Determine the writer's purpose

GET STARTED   Begin with strategies that help you think about the subject and find out about what the writer will say.

- Check in
- Get an overview
- Ask questions
- Determine the writer's purpose

READ   Use strategies that help you read with greater understanding, interpret the language, and respond with your own questions and ideas.

- Respond
- Work with new words
- Find meaning in metaphors
- Ask questions
- Find and mark main ideas
- Look for patterns of thought
- Make inferences
- Determine the writer's purpose

FOLLOW UP   End with strategies that help you look more closely at the language and ideas in the reading, assess your understanding, and respond in a thoughtful way.

- Work with new words
- Respond
- Find meaning in metaphors
- Ask questions
- Find and mark main ideas
- Look for patterns of thought
- Make inferences
- Map main ideas
- Write a summary
- Determine the writer's purpose

3. How do you decide which strategies to use for a particular reading?

_____

_____

_____

4. Overall, which strategies would you say have made the biggest difference in your reading so far?

_____

_____

_____

5. Are there specific things you could do to make the strategies more effective? If so, what?

_____

_____

_____

PART VI

ANALYZING AND EVALUATING

WITH READINGS ON POPULAR CULTURE AND EVERYDAY LIFE

> Movies fed the desires of a mass-consumption economy and set national trends in clothing and hairstyles. They also served as a form of sex education. Rudolph Valentino, best known as the romantic hero of *The Sheik* (1921), epitomized sexual passion on the screen, and the message was not wasted on the nation's youth. "It was directly through the movies that I learned to kiss a girl on her ears, neck, and cheeks, as well as on the mouth," confessed one boy. The sociologist Edward Alsworth Ross concluded that movies made young people more "sex-wise, sex-excited, and sex-absorbed" than they'd been in any previous generation. The impact of the movies on sexual attitudes and morality has remained strong ever since.
>
> —Henretta et al., *America's History*

In this passage from the college textbook *America's History*, the authors discuss how powerful the two-decade-old movie industry had become by the 1920s. Over the last century, the media—movies, radio, music, newspapers, magazines, television, and now the Internet—have continued to influence not only our sexual attitudes but a great deal of what we think and do. Through the power of the media, Americans across the country take part in a popular culture that helps shape our everyday lives.

Popular culture refers to the parts of our culture that are not normally taught in school—from movies to sports, popular music to advertising. Each reading in Part VI gives you a closer look at an aspect of this culture. You're likely to be an expert on a lot of popular culture, without ever having studied it. So you'll be in a good position to see what you think about a writer's ideas on a particular subject.

Here are some questions to help you think about this theme.

- How important is music in your life? What kind of music do you like to listen to?

- What importance do you attach to following the latest trends in fashion, movies, or other aspects of popular culture? Has your attitude changed over the last few years? Why or why not?

- How do you think the visual media affect you? How often do you find yourself wanting to buy something, do something, or look like someone because of media images?

- During any week, which of the following are you most likely to do: go to a movie, watch a video, watch TV, listen to music, listen to the radio (at home or in the car), talk on a cell phone, surf the Net, communicate by e-mail? Which of those things are the most important to you?

The strategies you've learned so far help you read from the inside out by getting you involved in a reading, showing you how to comprehend and summarize main ideas and interpret the writer's language and purpose. With strategies in Part VI you have all the strategies you need to bring the writer's ideas inside, examine them, and decide what you think about them. Strategy 13, **Analyze the Information,** shows you how to look closely at the kind of support given in two types of writing: argument and exposition. Strategy 14, **Make an Evaluation,** helps you put all the previous strategies together so you can make a complete response that is both objective and subjective.

In Part VI you'll continue combining strategies, incorporating earlier strategies into the new ones, and deciding which of the later strategies (starting with Strategy 7) are most important for a particular reading. Strategies 13 and 14 draw on all that you've learned in previous strategies and thus give you more practice in applying appropriate strategies to help you comprehend, evaluate, and enjoy what you read.

CHAPTER

13

TEST THE AUTHOR:
ANALYZE THE INFORMATION

The strategies you've learned so far help you comprehend a writer's ideas and interpret his or her language and purpose. Strategy 13, **Analyze the Information,** builds on these strategies and gives you the steps to test how accurately and thoroughly the author has covered a subject. This strategy is essential for judging the worth of an argument. But it is also important for examining the information found in *exposition*—writing that explains or informs.

Try the New Strategy: Analyze the Information

Strategy 13 builds on Strategy 12, in which you determine the writer's purpose in relation to the overall point in an argument or an explanation. Strategy 13 helps you examine how well the writer supports this overall point. Then, when you **respond** to the argument or explanation, you can expand your response to include your testing of the writer's support.

STRATEGY 13: ANALYZE THE INFORMATION

1 Understand the uses of facts and opinions.

2 Check the reliability of the information.

3 Test the support.

As you get an overview and ask questions about "Hip-Hop Nation," Reading 23, think about which strategies will help you most. Before reading the piece, write down two or three strategies that you think will help you, in addition to Strategy 13, **Analyze the Information.**

READING 23   HIP-HOP NATION

CHRISTOPHER JOHN FARLEY

Christopher John Farley is a staff writer for Time *magazine, writing on national affairs and also serving as the magazine's pop music critic. Articles by Farley have also appeared in the* Boston Globe, Chicago Tribune, *and* Essence. *As a graduate of Harvard (1988), Farley was one of the few African American members of the humor magazine* Harvard Lampoon. *This reading is an excerpt from his longer 1999* Time *article on the influence of hip-hop on all of popular culture, not just music.*

1   Music mixes with memory. As we think back over the 20th century, every decade has a melody, a rhythm, a sound track. The years and the sounds bleed together as we scan through them in our recollections, a car radio searching for a clear station. . . .

2   And how will we remember the last days of the '90s? Most likely, to the rough-hewn beat of rap. Just as F. Scott Fitzgerald lived in the jazz age, just as Dylan and Jimi Hendrix were among the rulers of the age of rock, it could be argued that we are living in the age of hip-hop. "Rock is old," says Russell Simmons, head of the hip-hop label Def Jam, which took in nearly $200 million in 1998. "It's old people's s____. The creative people who are great, who are talking about youth culture in a way that makes sense, happen to be rappers."

3   Consider the numbers. In 1998, for the first time ever, rap outsold what previously had been America's top-selling format, country music. Rap sold more than 81 million CDs, tapes and albums last year, compared with 72 million for country. Rap sales increased a stunning 31% from 1997 to 1998, in contrast to 2% gains for country, 6% for rock and 9% for the music industry overall. Boasts rapper Jay-Z, whose current album, Vol. 2 . . . Hard Knock Life (Def Jam), has sold more than 3 million copies: "Hip-hop is the rebellious voice of the youth. It's what people want to hear."

4   Even if you're not into rap, hip-hop is all around you. It pulses from the films you watch (Seen a Will Smith movie lately?), the books you read (even Tom Wolfe peels off a few raps in his best-selling new novel), the fashion you wear (Tommy Hilfiger, FUBU). Some definitions are in order: rap is a form of rhythmic speaking in rhyme; hip-hop refers to the backing music for rap, which is often composed of a collage of excerpts, or "samples," from other songs; hip-hop also refers to the culture of rap. The two terms are nearly, but not completely, interchangeable. . . .

5   Madison Avenue has taken notice of rap's entrepreneurial spirit. Tommy Hilfiger has positioned his apparel company as the clothier of the hip-hop set, and he now does a billion dollars a year in oversize shirts, loose jeans and so on. "There are no boundaries," says Hilfiger. "Hip-hop

has created a style that is embraced by an array of people from all backgrounds and races." However, fans are wary of profiteers looking to sell them back their own culture. Says Michael Sewell, 23, a white congressional staff member and rap fan: "I've heard rap used in advertising, and I think it's kind of hokey°—kind of a goofy version of the way old white men perceive rap."

hokey: corny, phony.

But the ads are becoming stealthier and streetier. Five years ago, Sprite recast its ads to rely heavily on hip-hop themes. Its newest series features several up-and-coming rap stars (Common, Fat Joe, Goodie Mob) in fast-moving animated clips that are intelligible only to viewers raised on Bone-Thugs-N-Harmony and Playstation. According to Sprite brand manager Pina Sciarra, the rap campaign has quadrupled the number of people who say that Sprite is their favorite soda. . . .   6

The hip-hop world began in the Bronx in 1971. Cindy Campbell needed a little back-to-school money, so she asked her brother Clive to throw a party. Back in Kingston, Jamaica, his hometown, Clive used to watch dance-hall revelers. He loved reggae, Bob Marley and Don Drummond and the Skatalites. He loved the big sound systems the deejays had, the way they'd "toast" in a singsong voice before each song. When he moved to the U.S. at age 13, he used to tear the speakers out of abandoned cars and hook them onto a stereo in his room.   7

The after-school party, held in a rec room of a Bronx high-rise, was a success: Clive and Cindy charged 25 [cents] for girls and 50 [cents] for boys, and it went till 4 A.M. Pretty soon Clive was getting requests to do more parties, and in 1973 he gave his first block party. He was Kool Herc now—that was the graffito tag he used to write on subway cars—and he got respect. At 18 he was the first break-beat deejay, reciting rhymes over the "break," or instrumental, part of the records he was spinning. He had two turntables going and two copies of each record, so he could play the break over and over, on one turntable and then the next. Americans didn't get reggae, he thought, so he tried to capture that feel with U.S. funk songs—James Brown and Mandrill. He had dancers who did their thing in the break—break dancers, or, as he called them, b-boys. As they danced, Herc rapped, "Rocking and jamming/That's all we play/When push comes to shove/The Herculoids won't budge/So rock on, my brother. . . ."   8

Joseph Saddler loved music too. He thought Kool Herc was a god—but he thought he could do better. Saddler figured most songs had only about 10 seconds that were good, that really got the party going, so he wanted to stretch those 10 seconds out, create long nights of mixing and dancing. Holed up in his Bronx bedroom, he figured out a way to listen to one turntable on headphones while the other turntable was revving up the   9 crowd. That way a deejay could keep two records spinning seamlessly, over and over again. Herc was doing it by feel. Saddler wanted the show to be perfect.

So he became Grandmaster Flash. He played his turntables as if he   10
were Jimi Hendrix, cuing records with his elbow, his feet, behind his back. He invented "scratching"—spinning a record back and forth to create a scratchy sound. He tried rapping, but he couldn't do it, so he gathered a crew around him—the Furious Five, rap's first supergroup.

Things happened fast. This is the remix.° There were start-up labels like   11
Sugar Hill and Tommy Boy. Then in 1979 came Rapper's Delight—the first rap song most people remember. Grandmaster Flash warned, "Don't touch me 'cause I'm close to the edge." Then there was Run-D.M.C. rocking the house, and the Beastie Boys hollering, "You gotta fight for your right—to party!" and Public Enemy saying, "Don't believe the hype," and Hammer's harem-style balloon pants. Then gangsta rap: N.W.A. rapping . . .; Snoop drawling "187 on an undercover cop"; and Tupac crying, "Even as a crack fiend, mama/You always was a black queen, mama." Then Mary J. Blige singing hip-hop soul; Guru and Digable Planets mixing rap with bebop; the Fugees "Killing me softly with his song"; Puffy mourning Biggie on CD and MTV.

> We in the '90s
> And finally it's looking good
> Hip-hop took it to billions
> I knew we would.
>
> —Nas, We Will Survive

All major modern musical forms with roots in the black community—   12
jazz, rock, even gospel—faced criticism early on. Langston Hughes, in 1926, defended the blues and jazz from cultural critics. Hardcore rap has triumphed commercially, in part, because rap's aesthetic of sampling connects it closely to what is musically palatable. Some of the songs hard-core rappers sample are surprisingly mainstream. DMX raps about such subjects as having sex with bloody corpses. But one of his songs, I Can Feel It, is based on Phil Collins' easy-listening staple In the Air Tonight. Jay-Z's hit song Hard-Knock Life draws from the musical Annie. Tupac's Changes uses Bruce Hornsby. Silkk the Shocker samples the not-so-shocking Lionel Richie.

The underlying message is this: the violence and misogyny and lustful   13
materialism that characterize some rap songs are as deeply American as the hokey music that rappers appropriate. The fact is, this country was in love with outlaws and crime and violence long before hip-hop—think of Jesse James, and Bonnie and Clyde—and then think of the movie Bonnie and Clyde, as well as Scarface and the Godfather saga. In the movie You've

remix: usually, combining sounds to produce a recording; here a quick review.

Got Mail, Tom Hanks even refers to the Godfather trilogy as the perfect guide to life, the I-Ching for guys. Rappers seem to agree. Snoop Dogg's sophomore album was titled The Doggfather. Silkk the Shocker's new album is called Made Man. On his song Boomerang, Big Pun echoes James Cagney in White Heat, yelling, "Top of the world, Ma! Top of the world!"

Corporate America's infatuation with rap has increased as the genre's political content has withered. Ice Cube's early songs attacked white racism; Ice-T sang about a Cop Killer; Public Enemy challenged listeners to "fight the power." But many newer acts such as DMX and Master P are focused almost entirely on pathologies within the black community. They rap about shooting other blacks but almost never about challenging governmental authority or encouraging social activism. "The stuff today is not revolutionary," says Bob Law, vice president of programming at WWRL, a black talk-radio station in New York City. "It's just, 'Give me a piece of the action.'" 14

Dionysian: related to Dionysus, Greek god of unrestrained emotion, frenzy.

Hip-hop is getting a new push toward activism from an unlikely source— Beastie Boys. The white rap trio began as a Dionysian° semiparody of hip-hop, rapping about parties, girls and beer. Today they are the founders and headliners of the Tibetan Freedom Concert, an annual concert that raises money for and awareness about human-rights issues in Tibet. Last week Beastie Boys, along with the hip-hop-charged hard-rock band Rage Against the Machine and the progressive rap duo Black Star, staged a controversial concert in New Jersey to raise money for the legal fees of Mumia Abu-Jamal, a black inmate on death row for killing a police officer. Says Beastie Boy Adam Yauch: "There's a tremendous amount of evidence that he didn't do it and he was a scapegoat." 15

Yauch says rap's verbal texture makes it an ideal vessel to communicate ideas, whether satirical, personal or political. That isn't always a good thing. "We've put out songs with lyrics in them that we thought people would think were funny, but they ended up having a lot of really negative effects on people. [Performers] need to be aware that when you're creating music it has a tremendous influence on society." 16

Follow-Up Activities   After you've finished reading, use these questions to respond to "Hip-Hop Nation." You may write your answers or prepare them in your mind to discuss in class.

Grab your first impressions.

Respond with your first impressions. Say what you like and dislike; relate your personal experiences to the reading; consider what more you want to know.

Work with new words.

Some words in this reading may be unfamiliar to you. Use the methods of Strategy 3 to explain what the listed words mean.

1. Use context clues.

    a. palatable (paragraph 12) _____

    b. genre (paragraph 14) _____

2. Use word parts.

    a. streetier (paragraph 6) _____
       You won't find this word in your dictionary. Why? Where does it come from?

    b. graffito (paragraph 8) _____
       Connect word part *graph* with the word *graffiti* (plural) and *graffito*.

    c. misogyny (paragraph 13) _____

3. Use the dictionary.
   Choose the correct definition of each word as it is used in the context of this reading.

    a. collage (paragraph 4) _____

    b. entrepreneurial (paragraph 5) _____

    c. stealthy (from *stealthier*) (paragraph 6) _____

    d. revelers (paragraph 7) _____

    e. parody (from *semiparody*) (paragraph 15) _____

4. Select additional words you're unsure of from the reading. Use one of these methods to discover their meaning.

Ask and answer questions.

1. How does Farley define each of these terms: *hip-hop* and *rap?*

2. What role does he say Madison Avenue has played in the rise of hip-hop culture?

3. What innovations did Clive Campbell, later known as Kool Herc, make that gave hip-hop its start?

4. How did Grandmaster Flash improve on what Kool Herc had done?

Inference Questions

5. What does Farley mean when he says in paragraph 5 that fans of hip-hop are "wary of profiteers looking to sell them back their own culture"?

6. What does Bob Law mean in paragraph 14 when he says, "It's just, 'Give me a piece of the action'"?

7. Why does Farley say that the Beastie Boys are an unlikely source for the new push toward activism in hip-hop?

Questions About Metaphorical Language and Tone

8. Explain Farley's metaphorical language in paragraph 1 when he says, "The years and the sounds bleed together as we scan through them in our recollections, a car radio searching for a clear station."

9. Farley uses an informal, neutral tone throughout most of the reading. However, in at least two cases, his tone is slightly different. Say whether the tone in each of the following sentences is (1) informal, neutral; (2) very casual, slangy; or (3) less neutral, somewhat slanted in favor of hip-hop.

    _____ a. The underlying message is this: the violence and misogyny and lustful materialism that characterize some rap songs are as deeply American as the hokey music that rappers appropriate.

    _____ b. He played his turntables as if he were Jimi Hendrix, cuing records with his elbow, his feet, behind his back.

    _____ c. But the ads are becoming stealthier and streetier.

    _____ d. Corporate America's infatuation with rap has increased as the genre's political content has withered.

 Ask and answer your own questions.

Write two questions based on any of the other information in this reading. Share your questions with others and collaborate on answers.   ■

Get a Close-Up of the New Strategy: Analyze the Information

1 *Understand the uses of facts and opinions.*

2 *Check the reliability of the information.*

3 *Test the support.*

A good argument depends on the quality of the information the writer uses to support his or her overall point. This information is often referred to as *evidence*, which furnishes some proof that what the writer argues is true. A good argument also depends on the way the information is presented: evidence must be presented in a sound, logical manner. For example, we wouldn't accept an argument in favor of changing the length of the school year without good support demonstrating how much the change would improve our children's education. And we would only be convinced if the writer presented the evidence in clear, logical steps that led to that overall point.

Expository writing must also use good support and a good presentation of that support in explaining a subject. An explanation of why the school year is shorter in the United States than in other countries should contain accurate and complete information, presented in a clear, logical way, even though the writer is not making an argument for change.

Analyzing a writer's information depends on your understanding of the writer's purpose and overall point for the reading. In "Hip-Hop Nation," Farley's overall point is that hip-hop was the most influential music of the 1990s. His purpose in the reading is to explain hip-hop from an objective—although somewhat favorable—perspective to a general *Time* magazine audience. Use Strategy 13 to **analyze the information** he uses.

Fact and Opinion

1 *Understand the uses of facts and opinions.*

When you read from the inside out, you read with a questioning mind. You don't believe everything you see in print, but instead you talk back to the writer. Strategy 13 helps you question and test what you see in print—the writer's ideas—before accepting what you read. One important part of this testing involves understanding how the writer uses facts and opinions to support his or her overall point. First, be sure you can distinguish a fact from an opinion.

Look at the following statements. Find the two statements that are *not* facts.

1. The United States of America is made up of 50 states.

2. The sun is about 93 million miles from the earth.

3. Rap sold more than 81 million CDs, tapes, and albums in 1998.

4. Hip-hop is the most important youth culture on the planet.

5. Rap, a form of rhythmic speaking in rhyme, has gained far too much influence on America's youth.

Facts. A *fact* can be proven or verified by going to a reliable source. The first three statements are facts, since each one is either widely known to be true (as in the case of the first one) or can be verified. You could go to an encyclopedia or any astronomy text to verify the second statement. The third statement comes from Farley's article (paragraph 3); if we felt the need to verify that information, we could find it in an appropriate music industry publication.

Opinions. The fourth statement is an *opinion*, which cannot be proven or disproven, but is open to debate. That statement was made by Kevin Powell, curator of the fall 2000 Hip-Hop Nation exhibit in the Brooklyn Museum, in an interview conducted by Time.com's Tony Karon. Powell could not prove his statement to be factually true, and other reasonable people might argue strongly against what he says. His opinion is a judgment based on his observations and beliefs.

The fifth statement is a combination of fact and opinion. The first part of the sentence, "Rap is a form of rhythmic speaking in rhyme," is a factual definition. However, the last part of the sentence is an opinion. Most writing includes both facts and opinion, sometimes in the same sentence, as in this last example.

It's important to recognize factual statements, so you can see how well they support the writer's ideas. However, you need to be aware that information presented as factual may be wrong. The writer may present—intentionally or not—facts that are incorrect. Facts also may be so out of date or incomplete as to be misleading.

Opinions, however, are more complicated to analyze. Whereas we reject any false statement that is presented as a fact, we can't simply reject a statement just because it's an opinion. Some opinions are more valuable than others. Opinions that are simply *personal preferences* don't carry much weight. For example, if you prefer country music over hip-hop, your preference alone would not be enough to convince others that country is more important for the culture.

Other opinions to watch out for are unsupported, *sweeping generalizations*—general statements that seem overly inclusive. Because Powell's statement that "hip-hop is the most important youth culture on the planet" covers all of youth on the planet, it seems like a sweeping generalization. However, you might want to look at the interview at Time.com to determine whether he gives enough evidence and reasons to support his opinion.

Analyzing facts and opinions. The value of an opinion depends on how well it is supported. Opinions that are widely held by experts in a field may be as valuable as facts. For example, a writer might use as a fact that someone who lived to be age 90 smoked two packs of cigarettes every day of his adult life. However, this single fact is of little use in countering the opinion, based on years of factual evidence and shared by the entire medical community, that smoking is hazardous to the health of most people. Opinions that the writer supports by his or her observations, reasons, or other evidence may also be valuable. Indeed, a good part of the analysis of information depends on how well the author's opinions are supported.

The table on the next page summarizes how to distinguish valuable from poor support provided by both facts and opinions.

Support

	Facts: Can be proven	Opinions: Can't be proven; open to debate
Valuable Support	Facts you know to be true or you could verify	Opinions supported by observations, reasons, or other evidence Opinions widely held by experts in a field
Poor Support	Incorrect "facts" Incomplete facts that are therefore misleading	Unsupported personal beliefs or preferences Unsupported, sweeping generalizations

Reliable Information

2 *Check the reliability of the information.*

Part of testing the writer's information is to check on its *reliability*. Can you *rely* on—or trust—the information's accuracy and thoroughness?

To answer these questions, consider the following.

1. *Look at the kind of publication.* Remember that a general-interest magazine provides only an introduction to a topic. For more thorough information, you would go to an academic or professional journal or to a book written by an authority in the field. These articles and books usually include notes and a good bibliography.

2. *Look at the date of publication.* Some fields, such as technology or the sciences, require current information; others, such as the humanities, usually don't.

3. *Find out about the author.* What background, past writings, or experience does he or she have in the field? Is the author associated with a publication or a particular institution? If so, what are his or her views or goals? Does the writer have anything to *gain* from presenting certain information?

Check reliability.

Using the questions just cited, consider the reliability of the information in "Hip-Hop Nation."

1. The kind of publication?

2. The date of the article?

3. The author?   ■

Testing the Support

3 *Test the support.*   Writers of both explanations and arguments use many different kinds of information to support an overall point. For example, in his explanation of hip-hop to a general audience, Farley used examples, facts, and opinions to show the origins of hip-hop, what it is like today, and what its influence is. He doesn't take a position for or against the music, so this reading is not a clear-cut argument. If it were, we would want to examine his support even more critically.

Testing the writer's support applies mainly to arguments. Support for an argument should be examined closely, since the writer's purpose is to convince you to believe something or do something. Here are three questions that can help determine how *credible*—believable—an argument is, that is, how well it is supported.

These are the questions to ask to test the credibility of an argument.

1. What type of support is used (such as examples, facts, expert opinions)?

2. How well does the reasoning support the argument?

3. How objective is the support?

Type of support. Credible arguments can be based on many different kinds of support. Writers usually use some combination of facts and opinions as support. In addition, they may use examples—from research, observation, or from personal experience.

Reasoning. Providing good evidence is not enough. The author must also use good reasoning in order to make a convincing argument. A reason given in support of a specific opinion should make sense, and the major supporting reasons should all work together to make the argument convincing.

Objectivity. An argument should be objective. You looked at the difference between being objective and subjective on page 318 under the discussion of tone. As you saw there, authors always write from a certain perspective—their way of looking at, or their position—on a subject. They may even show some feelings about the subject and still write a piece that is objective overall. However, when testing the support for an argument, you need to see if the writer's perspective prevents him or her from being objective—from giving both sides of an argument a fair presentation. A good argument deals with ideas that the *other* side might state. When the writer's perspective seems too narrow-minded or limited, it is often called a *bias*—a leaning toward one side or another, and the argument is said to be too biased, or slanted, in one direction. If you think the argument is too one sided, refer back to the author's biography: does he or she have anything to gain from presenting this argument?

For example, take a look at this statement from a multipage special advertising supplement for Zocor, a cholesterol-lowering drug.

> Like diamonds, statins [cholesterol-lowering drugs] are for life. Once one begins treatment, it continues indefinitely. Most patients find the investment worthwhile. A study published in the medical journal *Circulation* in 1998 showed that statins dramatically lowered the risk of dying from heart disease.
>
> (*New York Times Magazine*, December 9, 2001)

The writer (or writers) of this statement represent Merck, a large drug company. We expect advertising to be one-sided: it's meant to sell us something. So we know the drug company representatives do have something to gain from convincing readers of the value of statins. What they say in this statement—and elsewhere in the long advertisement—may be true. As general readers, we can't easily verify what is said about statins. But in this case, we would want to check out what a more objective medical expert might have to say as well. Although we expect bias in advertising, be aware that it can appear in other writing as well.

Practice the New Strategy

Practice the steps for **analyzing the information** with Reading 23. You will get further practice with the last step—testing the support for an argument—with the more clear-cut argument presented in Reading 24, "Buy This 24-Year-Old and Get All His Friends Absolutely Free."

Analyze information.

1. Look at these statements from Farley's article and try to determine which are facts and which are opinions. Some of these statements may combine both fact and opinion. The first answer is supplied for you.

   a. "Just as F. Scott Fitzgerald lived in the jazz age, just as Dylan and Jimi Hendrix were among the rulers of the age of rock, it could be argued that we are living in the age of hip-hop." *opinion*

   b. "In 1998, for the first time ever, rap outsold what previously had been America's top-selling format, country music." _____

   c. "Boasts rapper Jay-Z, whose current album, Vol. 2 . . . Hard Knock Life (Def Jam), has sold more than 3 million copies: 'Hip-Hop is the rebellious voice of the youth.'" _____

   d. "According to Sprite brand manager Pina Sciarra, the rap campaign has quadrupled the number of people who say that Sprite is their favorite soda." _____

e. "The fact is, this country was in love with outlaws and crime and violence long before hip-hop—think of Jesse James, and Bonnie and Clyde, as well as Scarface and the Godfather saga." _____

2. What evidence does Farley use to support the following opinions? If he does not give specific support, does his opinion depend on widely held beliefs?

a. "Even if you're not into rap, hip-hop is all around you." (paragraph 4)

_____

b. "Hardcore rap has triumphed commercially, in part, because rap's aesthetic of sampling connects it closely to what is musically palatable." (paragraph 12)

_____

c. "The underlying message is this: the violence and misogyny and lustful materialism that characterize some rap songs are as deeply American as the hokey music that rappers appropriate." (paragraph 13)

_____

d. "Corporate America's infatuation with rap has increased as the genre's political content has withered."(paragraph 14)

_____

 Form your final thoughts.

1. How well do you think Farley explained the rise and present power of hip-hop in this excerpt? In your answer, be sure to describe your previous knowledge about and experience with the music (and/or culture). What did Farley add to what you already knew?

2. How do you feel about some of Farley's opinions that you examined on page 368? Explain why you feel as you do.

3. Share your opinions on what Farley had to say. Poll your group about their musical tastes. See if you can come up with a summary response that takes into account the different responses to this piece.   ■

Apply the New Strategy: Analyze the Information

Now that you understand Strategy 13, put it into practice with Reading 24, "Buy This 24-Year-Old and Get All His Friends Absolutely Free" (or with one of the Additional Readings in Part VI, selected by your instructor).

As you **get an overview** and **ask questions,** think about which strategies will help you most in reading "Buy This 24-Year-Old and Get All His Friends Absolutely Free." Write down two or three strategies that you think will help you, in addition to Strategy 13, **Analyze the Information.**

READING 24   BUY THIS 24-YEAR-OLD AND GET
ALL HIS FRIENDS ABSOLUTELY FREE

JEAN KILBOURNE

Jean Kilbourne is recognized internationally for her investigation of alcohol and tobacco advertising and the portrayal of women in advertising. She is best known for her award-winning documentaries, Killing Us Softly, Slim Hopes, *and* Pack of Lies. *She is a frequent lecturer on college campuses and has twice been named Lecturer of the Year by the National Association for Campus Activities. This excerpt comes from the first chapter of her book* Can't Buy My Love: How Advertising Changes the Way We Think and Feel *(1999).*

If you're like most people, you think that advertising has no influence   1
on you. This is what advertisers want you to believe. But, if that were true, why would companies spend over $200 billion a year on advertising?[1] Why would they be willing to spend over $250,000 to produce an average television commercial and another $250,000 to air it?[2] If they want to broadcast their commercial during the Super Bowl, they will gladly spend over a million dollars to produce it and over one and a half million to air it.[3] After all, they might have the kind of success that Victoria's Secret did during the 1999 Super Bowl. When they paraded bra-and-panty-clad models across TV screens for a mere thirty seconds, one million people turned away from the game to log on to the Website promoted in the ad.[4] No influence?

Ad agency Arnold Communications of Boston kicked off an ad cam-   2
paign for a financial services group during the 1999 Super Bowl that represented eleven months of planning and twelve thousand "man-hours" of work.[5] Thirty hours of footage were edited into a thirty-second spot. An employee flew to Los Angeles with the ad in a lead-lined bag, like a diplomat carrying state secrets or a courier with crown jewels. Why? Because the Super Bowl is one of the few sure sources of big audiences[6]— especially male audiences, the most precious commodity for advertisers. Indeed, the Super Bowl is more about advertising than football:[7] The four hours it takes include only about twelve minutes of actually moving the ball.

Three of the four television programs that draw the largest audiences   3
every year are football games. And these games have coattails:[8] twelve prime-time shows that attracted bigger male audiences in 1999 than those in the same time slots the previous year were heavily pushed during foot-

coattails: influence of a popular movement or candidate.

ball games. No wonder the networks can sell this prized Super Bowl audience to advertisers for almost any price they want. The Oscar ceremony, known as the Super Bowl for women, is able to command one million dollars for a thirty-second spot because it can deliver over 60 percent of the nation's women to advertisers.[8] Make no mistake: The primary purpose of the mass media is to sell audiences to advertisers. *We* are the product. Although people are much more sophisticated about advertising now than even a few years ago, most are still shocked to learn this.

Magazines, newspapers, and radio and television programs round us up, rather like cattle, and producers and publishers then sell us to advertisers, usually through ads placed in advertising and industry publications. "The people you want, we've got all wrapped up for you," declares *The Chicago Tribune* in an ad placed in *Advertising Age,* the major publication of the advertising industry, which pictures several people, all neatly boxed according to income level.   4

Although we like to think of advertising as unimportant, it is in fact the most important aspect of the mass media. It *is* the point. Advertising supports more than 60 percent of magazine and newspaper production[9] and almost 100 percent of the electronic media. Over $40 billion a year in ad   5

Magazines and other mass media place ads in advertising and industry publications to sell advertising space, in effect selling audiences to advertisers. Attractive young people are often the subject of these ads, because advertisers increasingly want to target a young audience.

revenue is generated for television and radio and over $30 billion for magazines and newspapers.[10] As one ABC executive said, "The network is paying affiliates to carry network commercials, not programs. What we are is a distribution system for Procter & Gamble."[11] And the CEO of Westinghouse Electric, owner of CBS, said, "We're here to serve advertisers. That's our raison d'être."[12]

raison d'être: reason or justification for being.

6   The media know that television and radio programs are simply fillers for the space between commercials. They know that the programs that succeed are the ones that deliver the highest number of people to the advertisers. But not just any people. Advertisers are interested in people aged eighteen to forty-nine who live in or near a city. *Dr. Quinn, Medicine Woman,* a program that was number one in its time slot and immensely popular with older, more rural viewers, was canceled in 1998 because it couldn't command the higher advertising rates paid for younger, richer audiences.[13] This is not new: the *Daily Herald,* a British newspaper with 47 million readers, double the combined readership of *The Times, The Financial Times, The Guardian,* and *The Telegraph,* folded in the 1960s because its readers were mostly elderly and working class and had little appeal to advertisers.[14] The target audience that appeals to advertisers is becoming more narrow all the time. According to Dean Valentine, the head of the United Paramount Network, most networks have abandoned the middle class and want "very chic shows that talk to affluent, urban, unmarried, huge-disposable-income 18-to-34-year-olds because the theory is, from advertisers, that the earlier you get them, the sooner you imprint the brand name."[15]

7   "Tripod Delivers Gen-X," proclaims a sinister ad for a Website and magazine that features a delivery man carrying a corpselike consumer wrapped from neck to toe in brown paper. Several other such "deliveries" are propped up in the truck. "We've got your customers on our target," says an ad for financial services that portrays the lower halves of two people embedded in a target. "When you've got them by the ears their hearts and minds will follow," says an ad for an entertainment group. And an ad for the newspaper *USA Today* offers the consumer's eye between a knife and a fork and says, "12 Million Served Daily." The ad explains, "Nearly six million influential readers with both eyes ingesting your message. Every day." There is no humanity, no individuality in this ad or others like it—people are simply products sold to advertisers, of value only as potential consumers.

8   Newspapers are more in the business of selling audiences than in the business of giving people news, especially as more and more newspapers are owned by fewer and fewer chains. They exist primarily to support local advertisers, such as car dealers, realtors, and department store owners. A

full-page ad in *The New York Times* says, "A funny thing happens when people put down a newspaper. They start spending money." The ad continues, "Nothing puts people in the mood to buy like newspaper. In fact, most people consider it almost a prerequisite to any spending spree." It concludes, "Newspaper. It's the best way to close a sale." It is especially disconcerting to realize that our newspapers, even the illustrious *New York Times,* are hucksters at heart.

Once we begin to count, we see that magazines are essentially catalogs   9
of goods, with less than half of their pages devoted to editorial content (and much of that in the service of the advertisers). An ad for a custom publishing company in *Advertising Age* promises "The next hot magazine could be the one we create exclusively for your product." And, in fact, there are magazines for everyone from dirt-bike riders to knitters to mercenary soldiers, from *Beer Connoisseur* to *Cigar Aficionado*. There are plenty of magazines for the wealthy, such as *Coastal Living* "for people who live or vacation on the coast." *Barron's* advertises itself as a way to "reach faster cars, bigger houses and longer prenuptial agreements" and promises a readership with an average household net worth of over a million.

The Internet advertisers target the wealthy too, of course. "They give you   10
Dick," says an ad in *Advertising Age* for an Internet news network. "We give you Richard." The ad continues, "That's the Senior V.P. Richard who lives in L.A., drives a BMW and wants to buy a DVD player and a kayak." Not surprisingly there are no magazines or Internet sites or television programs for the poor or for people on welfare. They might not be able to afford the magazines or computers but, more important, they are of no use to advertisers.

This emphasis on the affluent surely has something to do with the   11
invisibility of the poor in our society. Since advertisers have no interest in them, they are not reflected in the media. We know so much about the rich and famous that it becomes a problem for many who seek to emulate them, but we know very little about the lifestyles of the poor and desperate. It is difficult to feel compassion for people we don't know.

· · ·

Through focus groups and depth interviews, psychological researchers   12
can zero in on very specific target audiences—and their leaders. "Buy this 24-year-old and get all his friends absolutely free," proclaims an ad for MTV directed to advertisers. MTV presents itself publicly as a place for rebels and nonconformists. Behind the scenes, however, it tells potential advertisers that its viewers are lemmings who will buy whatever they are told to buy.

The MTV ad gives us a somewhat different perspective on the concept   13
of "peer pressure." Advertisers, especially those who advertise tobacco

and alcohol, are forever claiming that advertising doesn't influence anyone, that kids smoke and drink because of peer pressure. Sure, such pressure exists and is an important influence, but a lot of it is created by advertising. Kids who exert peer pressure don't drop into high school like Martians. They are kids who tend to be leaders, whom other kids follow for good or for bad. And they themselves are mightily influenced by advertising, sometimes very deliberately as in the MTV ad. As an ad for *Seventeen* magazine, picturing a group of attractive young people, says, "Hip doesn't just happen. It starts at the source: *Seventeen*." In the global village, the "peers" are very much the same, regardless of nationality, ethnicity, culture. In the eyes of the media, the youths of the world are becoming a single, seamless, soulless target audience—often cynically labeled "Generation X," or, for the newest wave of teens, "Generation Y." "We're helping a soft drink company reach them, even if their parents can't," says an ad for newspapers featuring a group of young people. The ad continues, "If you think authority figures have a hard time talking to Generation X, you should try being an advertiser," and goes on to suggest placing ads in the television sections of newspapers.

Of course, it's not only young people who are influenced by their peers.   14
Barron's tells its advertisers, "Reach the right bird and the whole flock will follow." The MTV ad promises advertisers that young "opinion leaders" can influence what their friends eat, drink, and wear, whereas *Barron's* sells them leaders "whose simple 'yes' can legitimize a new product, trigger eight-figure purchases, and alter the flow of cash and ideas throughout the economy." Advertisers sometimes criticize my work by saying I imply that consumers are brainwashed, stupid, and easily led. Although I never say this, it often seems that the advertisers themselves describe consumers as sitting ducks.

Notes

1. Coen, 1999, 136.
2. Garfield, 1998, 53.
3. Reidy, 1999, D1.
4. Ryan, 1999, D1.
5. Reidy, 1999, E1, E2.
6. Carter, 1999, BU1.
7. Twitchell, 1996, 71.
8. Johnson, 1999, C5.
9. Twitchell, 1996, 46.
10. Endicott, 1998, S-50.
11. Collins, 1992, 13.

12. Ross, 1997, 14.
13. Bierbaum, 1998, 18.
14. Masterman, 1990, 3.
15. Hirschberg, 1998, 59.

References

Bierbaum, T. (1998, June 8–June 14). Ailing demos bar 'Dr. Quinn.' *Variety,* 18.

Carter, B. (1999, January 30). Where the boys are. *New York Times,* BU1, BU2.

Coen, R. J. (1999). Spending spree. The Advertising Century (*Advertising Age* special issue), 126, 136.

Collins, R. (1992). Dictating content: How advertising pressure can corrupt a free press. Washington, DC: Center for Science in the Public Interest.

Endicott, R. C. (1998, November 9). Top 100 megabrands. *Advertising Age,* S-50, S-58.

Garfield, B. (1998, April 20). Fabian turns Denny's meals into side dish. *Advertising Age,* 53.

Hirschberg, L. (1998, September 20). What's a network to do? *New York Times Magazine,* 59–62.

Johnson, G. (1999, March 21). 'And the winner is . . . advertisers.' *Boston Globe,* C5.

Masterman, L. (1990, Fall). New paradigms for media education. *Telemedium,* 1–4.

Reidy, C. (1999, January 28). Super Bowl ad campaign goes down to wire. *Boston Globe,* D1, D5.

Reidy, C. (1999, January 30). A super bowl berth. *Boston Globe,* E1, E2.

Ross, C. (1997, February 3). Jordan brings the heart of a marketer to CBS-TV. *Advertising Age,* 1, 14.

Ryan, S. C. (1999, February 3). Victoria's Secret success at Super Bowl has ad world abuzz. *Boston Globe,* D1, D7.

Twitchell, J. B. (1996). Adcult USA: The triumph of advertising in American culture. New York: Columbia University Press.

Follow-Up Activities   After you've finished reading, use these questions to respond to "Buy This 24-Year-Old and Get His Friends Absolutely Free." You may write your answers or prepare them in your mind to discuss in class.

Grab your first impressions.

Respond with your first impressions. Say what you like and dislike; relate your personal experiences to the reading; consider what more you want to know.

Work with new words.

Some words in this reading may be unfamiliar to you. Use the methods of Strategy 3 to explain what the listed words mean.

1. Use context clues.

   a. commodity (paragraph 2) _____

   b. affiliates (paragraph 5) _____

2. Use word parts.

   prenuptial (paragraph 9) _____

3. Use the dictionary.
   Choose the correct definition of each word as it is used in the context of this reading.

   a. chic (paragraph 6) _____

   b. sinister (paragraph 7) _____

   c. hucksters (paragraph 8) _____

   d. affluent (paragraph 11) _____

4. Select additional words you're unsure of from the reading. Use one of these methods to discover their meaning.

Ask and answer questions.

1. Why are advertisers willing to spend over a million dollars to advertise during the Super Bowl? Why is the Oscar ceremony known as the Super Bowl for women?

2. In paragraph 3, Kilbourne says, "The primary purpose of the mass media is to sell audiences to advertisers." Where and how do these media producers sell audiences to advertisers?

3. Which television programs succeed, and which ones are likely to be canceled? Why?

4. Describe the target audience that advertisers want. Why are people in this audience so valuable to advertisers?

Inference Questions

5. How are the poor affected by the current advertising practices as Kilbourne describes them?

6. Explain what she means by the title of the chapter from which this excerpt is taken.

Questions Involving Analysis

7. Using the questions from page 366, consider the reliability of the infor-mation in "Buy This 24-Year-Old . . . "

   a. What is the kind of publication? On pages 374–375, consult the notes and the references (sometimes called the bibliography) to see the type of research the author has conducted.

   _____

   b. What is the date of the book this reading comes from?

   _____

   c. What is the author's expertise?

   _____

8. For each of the following statements, say whether the type of support is an example or a reason.

   a. *Dr. Quinn, Medicine Woman* was canceled because it didn't reach the right audience. (paragraph 6) _____

   b. She follows her statement in paragraph 5 that advertising is the most important aspect of the mass media by saying, "Advertising supports more than 60 percent of magazine and newspaper production and almost 100 percent of the electronic media." _____

9. Test Kilbourne's reasoning. Her overall point, as stated in paragraph 3, says, "Make no mistake: The primary purpose of the mass media is to sell audiences to advertisers." Do each of her main ideas support her overall point? Do these reasons build on one another to make her argument con-vincing? Summarize her reasoning in your own words.

   a. The example of the Super Bowl demonstrates how much advertisers will pay for an audience.

   _____

   b. Through ads in advertising/industry publications, the media sell target audiences to advertisers, abandoning programming for those who aren't the urban, young, and affluent.

   _____

   c. Advertising drives the print media and the Internet to concentrate on audiences with money, resulting in the disappearance of poor people from these media.

   _____

d. The examples of MTV and *Barron's* demonstrate how young and/or affluent audiences are targeted.

10. How objective is Kilbourne's support?

a. In general, the support in the excerpt is well reasoned and objective. However, notice how she uses a fact in paragraph 2 to support her idea that the Super Bowl is more about advertising than football. She says in that paragraph, "[T]he four hours it [the Super Bowl] takes include only about twelve minutes of actually moving the ball." What does she imply about how football is played in that sentence? Is that an accurate description of the game?

b. The opposite position from Kilbourne's is that advertising doesn't have much influence on us. Find places in paragraphs 1, 5, and 13 where Kilbourne acknowledges this opposing view. What does she say to argue against it?

 Ask and answer your own questions.

Write two questions based on any of the other information in this reading. Share your questions with others and collaborate on answers.

 Form your final thoughts.

1. Before reading "Buy This 24-Year-Old . . . ," what was your opinion about advertising? Did Kilbourne's argument change your mind about the impact of advertising on our society as a whole? If so, in what ways? If not, why not?

2. Choose a commercial for a program on MTV or other TV program that is aimed directly at teens and young adults. Analyze the ways in which the commercial tries to appeal to that audience. Does your analysis support what Kilbourne says about the influence of advertising or not? Explain.

3. Share your opinions on the reading selection. Remember, this is an excerpt from an entire book. Discuss as a group what other information you might want from Kilbourne's book and/or from her documentaries before judging the credibility of her general argument against advertising. ∎

Chapter 13 Summary

How does Strategy 13 help you *read from the inside out?*

Reading from the inside out reminds you to talk back as you read and to question the writer. When you **analyze the information,** you use your own logical thinking to question and test what the writer has said. You extend your dialogue with the writer to include asking about the fairness and accuracy of the information in the reading. You can then give a fair and complete response to what the writer says.

How does the *analyze the information* strategy work?

Analyzing the information shows you how to examine the reliability, fairness, and accuracy of the support in exposition and argument. It gives guidelines for looking at different types of support—such as facts, well-established opinions, examples, reasons, good, logical reasoning, and objective and complete support. Here are the steps for Strategy 13.

STRATEGY 13: ANALYZE THE INFORMATION

1 Understand the uses of facts and opinions.

2 Check the reliability of the information.

3 Test the support.

Are you familiar with the meaning of these terms?

evidence: piece of information that furnishes some proof that what the writer argues is true

reliable information: information you can rely on or trust to be fair, accurate, and complete

fact: information that can be verified or proven

opinion: information that cannot be proven or disproven, but may be valuable support if well supported

personal preferences: opinions based only on what you like

sweeping generalizations: general statements that seem overly inclusive

credible argument: believable argument in terms of kinds of support and reasoning

How is the strategy working for you so far?

1. What have you looked at to determine the reliability of the information used by a writer?

2. How successful have you been at determining when facts and opinions are used as good support? Explain.

3. How successful have you been at assessing the support for an argument?

4. What did you appreciate about using this strategy? What did you dislike?

For more practice with *analyzing the information*, use the Reading Road Trip CD-ROM or Web site.

CHAPTER

14

DECIDE WHAT YOU THINK: MAKE AN EVALUATION

Throughout this book you've found ways to read from the inside out. Now, with Strategy 14, **Make an Evaluation,** you come back inside to your own thoughts for a final evaluation of the outside—the writer's ideas. This final strategy introduces no new steps. Instead it reminds you to put everything together. Use all the strategies you've learned for comprehending and analyzing to think objectively about the reading. Then come back to your personal response to think subjectively about the reading. Your final thinking—both objective and subjective—becomes your **evaluation** of the writer's ideas.

Try the New Strategy: Make an Evaluation

Strategy 14 depends on your choosing appropriate steps from among the first 11 strategies. Those strategies will give you a thorough comprehension of what the writer says. Once you've understood the reading, you can think more objectively about it, using steps from Strategies 12, **Determine the Writer's Purpose,** and 13, **Analyze the Information.** You can then make an **evaluation** by putting together this objective analysis with your subjective response.

STRATEGY 14: MAKE AN EVALUATION

1 Think objectively.

2 Think subjectively.

As you **get an overview** and **ask questions** about "Don't Further Empower Cliques," Reading 25, think about which strategies will help.

By now you have used the first six strategies enough to see how to apply them to any reading. As you **get an overview,** you can also tell a lot about which of the other seven strategies you'll need for a particular reading. For example, if a reading gives explanations, you might need Strategy 7, **Look for Patterns of Thought,** to watch out for cause-and-effect reasoning; if skimming shows some unusual use of language, you'll want to use Strategy 11, **Find Meaning in Metaphors;** if you want to clarify the main ideas, you might choose either Strategy 9, **Map Main Ideas,** or Strategy 10, **Write a Summary.**

Before reading the piece, write down two or three strategies that you think will help you most.

<hr>

READING 25   DON'T FURTHER EMPOWER CLIQUES

BERNARD LEFKOWITZ

Bernard Lefkowitz, an award-winning author, writes for many U.S. magazines and newspapers, and he has also written books on social issues. This reading first appeared in the Los Angeles Times *shortly after the Columbine High School massacre in 1999. In it he examines the sometimes destructive power of popular high school cliques, using the insights he gained while researching and writing his book* Our Guys: The Glen Ridge Rape and the Secret Life of the Perfect Suburb *(1997).*

While it's difficult to generate sympathy for a couple of teenagers who decide to vent their grievances through the barrel of a gun, the carnage at Columbine High School should not eclipse an important part of this story: the power of high school cliques to make life miserable for many adolescents.   1

When I heard that the two young murderers in Littleton, Colorado, had targeted athletes who, they said, had ridiculed them, it sounded a lot like what young people told me ten years ago when I was researching the rape of a retarded young woman by a group of teenage athletes at Glen Ridge High School.   2

In that attractive upper-middle-class New Jersey suburb, thirteen jocks were present in the basement where the young woman's body was penetrated by a baseball bat and a broomstick. The country was sickened by the inhumanity of a bunch of guys who were among the most admired and envied young men in their community and high school.   3

After the rape, they came to school and openly boasted about what they had done. Weren't they afraid of being punished? Later, many people who knew them concluded that they had come to feel omnipotent after being treated like big-time celebrities for years by their school and by many parents in town.   4

And why shouldn't they feel omnipotent? When you walked into the high school the first thing you saw were halls lined with trophy cases celebrating the exploits of the athletes. The school held two-hour assemblies to   5 honor the jocks. But assemblies to honor the best students rarely lasted more than twenty minutes. The school yearbook displayed ten photographs of the most mediocre football player. But the outstanding scholar was lucky to get one grainy photo.

The message the school sent to its impressionable students was: You don't count unless you're part of this clique or at least pay homage to it. Instead of celebrating the individuality and diversity of all its students, it chose to honor this one type of youngster—aggressive, arrogant, and intensely competitive—above all the others. This left many kids feeling alienated and isolated, and not only during this brief passage into adulthood. Ten years later, I still hear from Glen Ridge graduates who remain enraged, not only by how they were mistreated by the athletes but by the school's unqualified adulation of them.

After my book was published, I received hundreds of letters from people, some in their 70s and 80s, who recalled how excluded they felt when their schools anointed one group of guys as leaders. Educators are reluctant to discourage the formation of cliques because that may be considered interference in the students' "private" lives. They are disinclined to challenge parents who are proud of their child's membership in a popular group. Then, too, some educators tolerate cliques because they think they are just a passing phenomenon.

That's unfortunate because there is much that schools can do to demonstrate that all students, rather than the few members of favored cliques, have value. They can promote activities and projects that bring together students with diverse interests and skills. They can celebrate achievements that are intellectual and artistic as well as athletic. And they can demonstrate that there's a single standard of acceptable conduct that is applied to everyone. In Glen Ridge, as in many other schools, the athletes got away with behavior for which others were punished.

We don't know much about how Columbine High School responded to student cliques. But I do know that schools are not passive entities. Educators make collective judgments about which students are valuable and which aren't. Often, educators are quick to venerate kids who are superficially attractive—who are handsome, who are athletic, who come from wealthy families. And too often they marginalize youngsters who are awkward or unsocial or iconoclastic.

Kids with supportive families and friends may ultimately succeed in life although they were treated like outcasts in school. But even they will not easily recover from the wounds they suffered as adolescents. For youngsters who already feel abandoned, the power granted to cliques by school authorities, and the inevitable abuse of that power, may be potentially devastating.

This doesn't explain the pathological behavior of two kids turned killers   11
at Columbine High School. That will require a calmer and more thoughtful
investigation into how they grew up and their school lives than is possible
in the heat of the moment. But we should take the opportunity that the
catastrophe in Littleton offers to reflect on the damage that cliques can
inflict on youngsters when they are most vulnerable.

Follow-Up Activities   After you've finished reading, use these questions to
respond to "Don't Further Empower Cliques." You may write your answers or
prepare them in your mind to discuss in class.

Grab your first impressions.

Respond with your first impressions. Say what you like and dislike; relate
your personal experiences to the reading; consider what more you want
to know.

Work with new words.

Some words in this reading may be unfamiliar to you. Use the methods
of Strategy 3 to explain what the listed words mean.

1. Use context clues.

   a. grievances (paragraph 1) _____

   b. anointed (paragraph 7) _____

   c. venerate (paragraph 9) _____

2. Use word parts.

   a. omnipotent (paragraph 4) _____

   b. impressionable (paragraph 6) _____

   c. pathological (paragraph 11) _____

3. Use the dictionary.
   Choose the correct definition of each word as it is used in the context of
   this reading.

   a. cliques (paragraph 1) _____

   b. carnage (paragraph 1) _____

   c. adulation (paragraph 6) _____

   d. iconoclastic (paragraph 9) _____

4. Select additional words you're unsure of from the reading. Use one of
   these methods to discover their meaning.

Ask and answer questions.

1. When Lefkowitz interviewed people in the New Jersey suburb, what did many of them say about why the young men boasted at school about raping the young retarded woman?

2. What kind of attention did Glen Ridge High School give to its athletes? How did this attention compare with that given to other types of students?

3. How does Lefkowitz define the type of student schools tend to value most? What kind of message does he say this preference sends to the student body of a school?

4. What are some suggestions Lefkowitz gives that would help make other students—those not in the favored cliques—feel valued?

Inference Questions

5. What types of behavior do you think the athletes at Glen Ridge might have gotten away with—that others would have been punished for?

6. What are some ways "kids with supportive families and friends" can do all right in life even if they feel isolated at school? Why will "youngsters who already feel abandoned" (paragraph 10) be affected so much more?

7. What does Lefkowitz assume Columbine High School was like at the time of the 1999 massacre?

Recognize tone.

The terrible nature of the subject matter Lefkowitz writes about in paragraphs 2 through 4 contributes to the serious, disturbing tone in this reading. In the following phrases and sentences from the reading, underline certain words or details that add to this tone.

1. The country was sickened by the inhumanity of a bunch of guys. . . . (paragraph 3)

2. The school yearbook displayed ten photographs of the most mediocre football player. But the outstanding scholar was lucky to get one grainy photo. (paragraph 5)

3. I still hear from Glen Ridge graduates who remain enraged, not only by how they were mistreated by the athletes, but by the school's unqualified adulation of them. (paragraph 6)

4. Educators make collective judgments about which students are valuable and which aren't. (paragraph 9)

5. [E]ven they will not easily recover from the wounds they suffered as adolescents. (paragraph 10)

6. [T]he power granted to cliques by school authorities . . . may be potentially devastating. (paragraph 10)

 Ask and answer your own questions.

Write two questions based on any of the other information in this reading. Share your questions with others and collaborate on answers.

What strategies did you use?

What strategies did you write down after your overview of Reading 25, "Don't Further Empower Cliques"? Did you find these strategies helpful? What other strategies did you use?   ■

Get a Close-Up of the New Strategy: Make an Evaluation

Thinking Objectively

1 *Think objectively.*

Once you're sure you understand the reading's overall point and main ideas, use strategies to think objectively about the writer's ideas.

For any type of writing, you can use Strategy 12, **Determine the Writer's Purpose,** to think objectively about what you've read. Decide how well the writer accomplished his or her purpose. You may not like every reading. But even in a reading you don't generally like, you can recognize objectively whether the writer has communicated an idea successfully—through a metaphor, for example, or by creating a believable character in a story. Notice in any type of writing if there is a special aspect that is an important part of the reading, such as use of a particular tone or use of metaphorical language. If so, did that aspect help achieve the writer's purpose? Give some examples to support what you say.

For exposition or argument, use Strategy 13, **Analyze the Information.** How reliable and credible is the information used to support the overall point? Give some examples to back up your analysis. Reading 25 is an argument, persuading us to see high school cliques as the source of misery for many adolescents. Thus you can analyze objectively how persuasive Lefkowitz is. An analysis of information has been incorporated into the sample evaluation for this reading on pages 388–389.

Thinking Subjectively

2 *Think subjectively.*

After each reading you've been asked to "grab your first impressions." This instruction has given you a chance to **respond** honestly to what you've just read. Like **checking in,** responding makes sure you connect the reading with your own personal experience as much as possible, so the reading remains lively and interesting for you. You've also been asked to "form your final thoughts," after working with a reading and gaining a better understanding of it.

Thinking subjectively about a reading as part of your evaluation is much more like forming your final thoughts than just grabbing your first impressions. Once you're sure you comprehend the reading and have looked at it objectively, what is your personal opinion about it? Take account of your general reading likes and dislikes. You may generally dislike short stories, for example. In that case, you can recognize that a story is "well done," and you may even like some things in it. But you can also allow for the fact that stories are generally less appealing to you. That general personal opinion can go in as part of your final evaluation.

In addition, take account of your own ideas on the subject *before* reading. For example, you don't have to change your opinion about a subject just because you think the writer did a good job of arguing. You can still have your opinion—although you may find yourself seeing things slightly differently after a good argument.

Much of your subjective thinking in the evaluation can also be based on the way you originally **responded.** You can note difficulties you had with comprehension. You can say what specific parts you especially liked or didn't like, and why.

Make an evaluation.

Read the sample summary (based on Strategy 10) before thinking about how you would evaluate "Don't Further Empower Cliques." That way you will have added assurance you have understood the main ideas. After reading the summary, write notes or prepare in your mind for discussion in class how you would evaluate this reading.

Sample Summary of "Don't Further Empower Cliques"

Bernard Lefkowitz's purpose in "Don't Further Empower Cliques" is to persuade us that high schools should make changes in their treatment of students. His overall point is that high schools give too much power to cliques, especially cliques of student athletes, and those cliques make life miserable for many other students. He begins by referring to the then recent events at Columbine High School. He doesn't have sympathy for the two murderers, but he does see a connection between what happened there and what happened in the New Jersey town he wrote a book about. In both places so much power for the school's athletes made them feel they could treat others badly. The essay explains that popular and admired young men at Glen Ridge could commit a horrible rape and brag about it, because they had come to think of themselves as "omnipotent." They had become celebrities in their high school who could do no wrong. The high school's over-valuing of school athletes sent the message that other types of students "don't count." After publishing his book about what happened in that New Jersey suburb, Lefkowitz received hundreds of letters from people saying how they had felt left out because the school only honored one type of group as leaders. He suggests ways that schools could show all students have value, not just a few cliques. He ends by saying we should use the "catastrophe at Littleton" to take notice of how certain privileged high school groups are given power that can be "potentially devastating" to others.

Sample Student Evaluation of "Don't Further Empower Cliques"

"Don't Further Empower Cliques" is an argument that makes you think. Lefkowitz's purpose is not to make a complete step-by-step argument to prove his overall point. If that's what he was doing, you could say he leaves a lot of things out. He concentrates only on athletes and only briefly mentions the other types of "popular kids" who tend to run schools. He also only concentrates on one school in New Jersey, so someone arguing against him could say he's not giving enough facts about other schools. But he does have a lot of credibility, because he did such a lot of research and wrote a book about what happened in the New Jersey suburban high school. He knows the facts of that case really well. He also heard from a lot of people that said they had similar experiences of being treated like outcasts by the popular cliques. His reasoning about the causes of bad feelings in student outcasts seems good, but he doesn't try to prove that that was the cause of the Columbine massacre. His solutions of making schools be more open to more types of students also seem good. It is a pretty short reading, so he can't get into too much detail. He achieved his purpose of making people think about their own high school experience, even though the school he knows best (Glen Ridge High) may be worse than the average.

My response to the reading was mainly positive, but I did think he exaggerated somewhat. I do think that high school is a hard experience for many, maybe most students. Athletes do get a lot of glory and the cheerleaders who they "get" also get that glory. But in my school, there were other types of cliques that were just as bad—the kids with money, clothes, cars, etc. I can see that there were kids who felt like outcasts, but a lot of us who weren't in those cliques could find ways of getting along, and there were other activities (for me the band) that were encouraged. Still, there was that image in my own mind of the athletes lording it over other kids in the hall. I hated the example of what those athletes did to that girl, and I can hardly believe any athlete in my school would have been that bad. But it was a powerful example. I also liked the way he showed how school authorities tend to prefer certain kinds of students. It's a good thing he wasn't trying to prove that the treatment of the Columbine murderers by athletes was what caused what they did, because that's not at all clear to me. Overall I liked the reading and it did match my high school experience somewhat.

 Form your final thoughts.

Discuss your evaluation of this reading with other students. How did your evaluations compare with the sample student evaluation?

Apply the New Strategy: Make an Evaluation

Now that you understand Strategy 14, put it into practice with another reading. Your instructor may assign one of the Additional Readings in Part VI or ask you to select a reading of your own choice from Part VI or from one of the earlier units in the book.

Chapter 14 Summary

How does Strategy 14 help you *read from the inside out?*

Strategy 14 gives you a chance to put together all you've learned about reading from the inside out throughout this book. From the beginning, you've learned that reading begins with the *inside*—you. Your feelings and ideas about what the writer says make reading come alive for you. You've also learned strategies that increase your comprehension and enjoyment of what you read. **Making an evaluation** asks you to use everything you've learned in order to decide what you think about a reading, based on your objective as well as your subjective consideration of the reading *outside*—the writer's ideas.

How does the *make an evaluation* strategy work?

Making an evaluation shows you how to put together what you've already learned in order to respond as fully as possible to a reading. Here are the two steps for Strategy 14.

STRATEGY 14: MAKE AN EVALUATION

1 Think objectively.

2 Think subjectively.

How is the strategy working for you so far?

1. How do you determine which strategies you need for a particular reading?

2. How easily can you separate your personal views from the objective analysis that is an essential part of an evaluation?

3. How can you imagine using this strategy in other courses?

4. What did you appreciate about using this strategy? What did you dislike?

For more practice with *making an evaluation,*
use the Reading Road Trip CD-ROM or Web site.

PART VI

ADDITIONAL READINGS ON
POPULAR CULTURE AND EVERYDAY LIFE

The readings that follow will give you further practice in using appropriate strategies with other readings on the theme of "Popular Culture and Everyday Life."

READING VI-A PITCHING MESSAGES

JOHN VIVIAN

John Vivian is a professor of mass media at Winona State University in Minnesota. This reading comes from the chapter on advertising in his textbook The Media of Mass Communication *(2002). Vivian discusses the various types of approaches advertisers use to reach audiences.*

Choose appropriate strategies for reading "Pitching Messages." Write down the strategies you've chosen. After finishing the reading, see what others you also needed. Note the study preview that Vivian provides.

STUDY PREVIEW   When the age of mass production and mass markets arrived, common wisdom in advertising favored aiming at the largest possible audience of potential customers. These are called lowest common denominator approaches, and such advertisements tend to be heavy-handed so that no one can possibly miss the point. Narrower pitches, aimed at segments of the mass audience, permit more deftness, subtlety and imagination.

IMPORTANCE OF BRANDS

A challenge for advertising people is the modern-day reality that mass-produced products intended for large markets are essentially alike: Toothpaste is toothpaste is toothpaste. When a product is virtually identical to the competition, how can one toothpaste maker move more tubes?   1

Brand Names

brand: A nongeneric product name designed to set the product apart from the competition.

By trial and error, tactics were devised in the late 1800s to set similar products apart. One tactic, promoting a product as a *brand*° name, aims to make a product a household word. When it is successful, a brand name becomes almost the generic identifier, like Coke for cola and Kleenex for facial tissue.   2

Techniques of successful brand name advertising came together in the 1890s for an English product, Pears' soap. A key element in the campaign   3 was multimedia saturation. Advertisements for Pears' were everywhere—in newspapers and magazines and on posters, vacant walls, fences, buses and lampposts. Redundancy hammered home the brand name. "Good morning. Have you used Pears' today?" became a good-natured greeting among Britons that was still being repeated 50 years later. Each repetition reinforced the brand name.

Brand Image

David Ogilvy: championed brand imaging.

brand image: spin put on a brand name.

David Ogilvy,° who headed the Ogilvy & Mather agency, developed the *brand image*° in the 1950s. Ogilvy's advice: "Give your product a first-class ticket through life."   4

Ogilvy created shirt advertisements with the distinguished Baron Wrangell, who really was a European nobleman, wearing a black eye patch—and a Hathaway shirt. The classy image was reinforced with the accoutrements around Wrangell: exquisite models of sailing ships, antique weapons, silver dinnerware. To some seeing Wrangell's setting, the patch suggested all kinds of exotica. Perhaps he had lost an eye in a romantic duel or a sporting accident.   5

Explaining the importance of image, Ogilvy once said, "Take whiskey. Why do some people choose Jack Daniels, while others choose Grand Dad or Taylor? Have they tried all three and compared the taste? Don't make me laugh. The reality is that these three brands have different images which appeal to different kinds of people. It isn't the whiskey they choose, it's the image. The brand image is 90 percent of what the distiller has to sell. Give people a taste of Old Crow, and tell them it's Old Crow. Then give them another taste of Old Crow, but tell them it's Jack Daniels. Ask them which they prefer. They'll think the two drinks are quite different. They are tasting images."   6

LOWEST COMMON DENOMINATOR

lowest common denominator: messages for broadest audience possible.

Early brand-name campaigns were geared to the largest possible audience, sometimes called an LCD, or *lowest common denominator,*° approach. The term *LCD* is adapted from mathematics. To reach an audience that includes members with IQs of 100, the pitch cannot exceed their level of understanding, even if some people in the audience have IQs of 150. The opportunity for deft touches and even cleverness is limited by the fact they might be lost on some potential customers.   7

unique selling proposition: emphasizing a single feature.

Rosser Reeves: devised unique selling proposition.

LCD advertising is best epitomized in contemporary advertising by USP, short for *unique selling proposition,*° a term coined by *Rosser Reeves*° of the giant Ted Bates agency in the 1960s. Reeves' prescription was simple: Create a benefit of the product, even if from thin air, and then tout   8 the benefit authoritatively and repeatedly as if the competition doesn't have it. One early USP campaign boasted that Schlitz beer bottles were "washed with live steam." The claim sounded good—who would want to drink from dirty bottles? However, the fact was that every brewery used steam to clean reusable bottles before filling them again. Furthermore, what is "live steam"? Although the implication of a competitive edge was hollow, it was done dramatically and pounded home with emphasis, and it sold beer. Just as hollow as a competitive advantage was the USP claim for Colgate toothpaste: "Cleans Your Breath While It Cleans Your Teeth."

Perhaps to compensate for a lack of substance, many USP ads are   9
heavy-handed. Hardly an American has not heard about fast-fast-fast relief from headache remedies or that heartburn relief is spelled R-O-L-A-I-D-S. USP can be unappealing as is acknowledged even by the chairman of Warner-Lambert, which makes Rolaids, who once laughed that his company owed the American people an apology for insulting their intelligence over and over with Bates's USP slogans. Warner-Lambert was also laughing all the way to the bank over the USP-spurred success of Rolaids, Efferdent, Listermint and Bubblicious.

A unique selling proposition need be neither hollow nor insulting, how-   10
ever. Leo Burnett, founder of the agency bearing his name, refined the USP concept by insisting that the unique point be real. For Maytag, Burnett took the company's slight advantage in reliability and dramatized it with the lonely Maytag repairman.

MARKET SEGMENTS

Jack Trout: devised positioning.

positioning: targeting ads for specific consumer groups.

Rather than pitching to the lowest common denominator, advertising   11
executive *Jack Trout*° developed the idea of *positioning*.° Trout worked to establish product identities that appealed not to the whole audience but to a specific audience. The cowboy image for Marlboro cigarettes, for example, established a macho attraction beginning in 1958. Later, something similar was done with Virginia Slims, aimed at women.

Positioning helps to distinguish products from all the LCD clamor and   12
noise. Advocates of positioning note that there are more and more advertisements and that they are becoming noisier and noisier. Ad clutter, as it is called, drowns out individual advertisements. With positioning, the appeal is focused and caters to audience segments, and it need not be done in such broad strokes.

Campaigns based on positioning have included: 13

- Johnson & Johnson's baby oil and baby shampoo, which were positioned as adult products by advertisements featuring athletes.

- Alka-Seltzer, once a hangover and headache remedy, which was positioned as an upscale product for stress relief among health-conscious, success-driven people.

REDUNDANCY TECHNIQUES

Advertising people learned the importance of redundancy early on. To   14
be effective, an advertising message must be repeated, perhaps thousands
of times. Redundancy is expensive, however. To increase effectiveness at
less cost, advertisers use several techniques:

barrages: intensive repetition of ads.

flights: intensive repetition of ads.

waves: intensive repetition of ads.

bunching: short-term ad campaign.

trailing: shorter, smaller ads after campaign is introduced.

- *Barrages.°* Scheduling advertisements in intensive bursts called *flights°* or *waves.°*

- *Bunching.°* Promoting a product in a limited period, such as running advertisements for school supplies in late August and September.

- *Trailing.°* Running condensed versions of advertisements after the original has been introduced, as automakers do when they introduce new models with multipage magazine spreads, following with single-page placements.

- *Multimedia trailing.* Using less expensive media to reinforce expensive advertisements. Relatively cheap drive-time radio in major markets is a favorite follow through to expensive television advertisements created for major events like the Super Bowl.

NEW ADVERTISING TECHNIQUES

Inundated with advertisements, 6,000 a week on network television,   15
double since 1983, many people tune out. Some do it literally with their
remotes. Ad people are concerned that traditional modes are losing effectiveness. People are overwhelmed. Consider, for example, that a major
grocery store carries 30,000 items, each with packaging that screams "buy
me." More commercial messages are put there than a human being can
handle. The problem is ad clutter. Advertisers are trying to address the
clutter in numerous ways, including stealth ads, new-site ads and alternative media. Although not hidden or subliminal, stealth ads are subtle—even
covert. You might not know you're being pitched unless you're attentive,
really attentive.

Stealth Ads

stealth ads: advertisements, often subtle, in nontraditional, unexpected places.

Stealth ads° fit so neatly into the landscape that the commercial pitch   16
seems part of the story line. In 1996 the writers for four CBS television programs, including "Nanny" and "High Society," wrote Elizabeth Taylor into

Ads Everywhere. Joseph Paolo, supervisor of Seaside Heights N.J. Public Works, uses a tractor to rake the beach while towing the Beach N' Billboards Inc. sand ad imprinting machine. The weighted machine was designed with interchangable rubber pads outlining commercial advertisements.

infomercial: program-length broadcast commercial.

'zine: magazine whose entire content, articles and ads, pitches a single product or product line.

their scripts. And there she was, in over two hours of programming one winter night, wandering in and out of sets looking for a missing string of black pearls. Hardly coincidentally, her new line of perfume, Black Pearls, was being introduced at the time.

The gradual convergence of information and entertainment, called infotainment, has a new element: advertising. "Seinfeld" characters on NBC munched Junior Mints. The M&M/Mars candy company bought a role for Snickers in the Nintendo game *Biker Mice from Mars.* In 1997 Unilever's British brand Van den Bergh Foods introduced a video game that stars its Peperami snack sausage. In movies promotional plugs have become a big-budget item. The idea is to seamlessly work the presence of commercial products into a script without a cue—nothing like the hopelessly dated "And now a word from our sponsors." 17

Less subtle is the *infomercial,*° a program-length television commercial dolled up to look like a newscast, live-audience participation show or a chatty talk show. With the proliferation of 24-hour television service and of cable channels, airtime is so cheap at certain hours that advertisers of even offbeat products can afford it. Hardly anybody is fooled into thinking that infomercials are anything but advertisements, but some full-length media advertisements, like Liz Taylor wandering through CBS sitcoms, are cleverly disguised. 18

A print media variation is the *'zine*°—a magazine published by a manufacturer to plug a single line of products with varying degrees of subtlety. 'Zine publishers, including such stalwarts as IBM and Sony, have even been so brazen as to sell these wall-to-wall advertising vehicles at newsstands. In 1996, if you bought a splashy new magazine called *Colors,* you paid $4.50 for it. Once inside, you probably would realize it was a thinly veiled ad for Benetton casual clothes. *Guess Journal* may look like a magazine, but guess who puts it out as a 'zine: The makers of the Guess fashion brand. 19

Stealth advertisements try "to morph into the very entertainment it sponsors," wrote Mary Kuntz, Joseph Weber and Heidi Dawley in *Business* 20

Week. The goal, they said, is "to create messages so entertaining, so compelling—and maybe so disguised—that rapt audiences will swallow them whole, oblivious to the sales component."

New-Site Ads

Ironically, solving the problem of ad clutter by going underground with   21
stealth ads contributes to the clutter. Sooner or later, it would seem, people would also tire of advertising omnipresence. Snapple stickers adorn kiwis and mangoes at the grocery. Sports stadiums named for department stores or other companies, like the Target Center in Minneapolis and the Washington Redskins' FedEx Field, try to weave product names into everyday conversation and the news. Sports events galore bear the names of high-bidding sponsors. How omnipresent can advertising become? Consider the Bamboo lingerie company that stenciled messages on Manhattan sidewalks: "From here, it looks like you could use some new underwear."

Follow-Up Activities   After you've finished reading, use these questions to respond to "Pitching Messages." You may write your answers or prepare them in your mind to discuss in class.

Grab your first impressions.

Respond with your first impressions. Say what you like and dislike; relate your personal experiences to the reading; consider what more you want to know.

Work with new words.

Note that this textbook excerpt reviews important new terms in the margin. However, some additional words may be unfamiliar to you. Use the methods of Strategy 3 to explain what the listed words mean.

1. Use context clues.

    a. generic (paragraph 2) _____

    b. saturation (paragraph 3) _____

    c. covert (paragraph 15) _____

    d. rapt (paragraph 20) _____

    e. oblivious (paragraph 20) _____

2. Use word parts.

    a. subliminal (paragraph 15) _____

    b. proliferation (paragraph 18) _____

    c. omnipresence (paragraph 21) _____

3. Use the dictionary.
   Choose the correct definition of these words as they are used in the context of this reading.

   a. redundancy (paragraph 3) _____

   b. accoutrements (paragraph 5) _____

   c. deft (paragraph 7) _____

   d. stealth (paragraph 15) _____

   e. morph (paragraph 20) _____

4. Select additional words you're unsure of from the reading. Use one of these methods to discover their meaning.

Ask and answer questions.

1. Why is it important to create a brand image, according to David Ogilvy?

2. What is the advantage of advertising campaigns that appeal to the *lowest common denominator?* What are the disadvantages of this type of campaign?

3. What are two methods advertisers use to increase the effectiveness of *redundancy* in order to reduce their costs? How do these methods work?

4. How do stealth ads address advertisers' problems with "ad clutter"? What are two major types of stealth ads? How do these types of ads work?

Inference Questions

5. The *unique selling proposition* (UPS) claim for Colgate toothpaste was that it "Cleans Your Breath While It Cleans Your Teeth." Why did Vivian call that claim "hollow"?

6. How would featuring athletes help Johnson & Johnson position itself as a product for adults?

7. Vivian says in paragraph 15, "Although not hidden or subliminal, stealth ads are subtle—even covert." How different is the definition of covert from hidden? Why does Vivian indicate it is important for ads *not* to be hidden or subliminal?

8. Vivian asks in paragraph 21, "How omnipresent can advertising become?" What other examples can you imagine of places for advertising in addition to the new ones he mentions in that paragraph?

 ## Ask and answer your own questions.

Write two questions based on any of the other information in this reading. Share your questions with others and collaborate on answers.

Make an evaluation.

Think both objectively and subjectively about "Pitching Messages." Thinking objectively, consider how well Vivian fulfilled his purpose in this textbook excerpt of giving a clear and objective explanation of how advertising works. Thinking subjectively, consider how you respond personally to the information in this reading. For example, what is your personal response to the new types of advertising, such as stealth ads?

 Form your final thoughts.

What was your evaluation of this textbook excerpt? Discuss your evaluation of this reading with other students.   ■

READING VI-B   The Argument Culture

Deborah Tannen

Deborah Tannen is a professor of linguistics at Georgetown University in Washington, D.C., and a best-selling author of many books on communication. She is best known for her analysis of the differences between men's and women's conversational styles, the subject of You Just Don't Understand: Women and Men in Conversation *(1990). In this reading, taken from her book* The Argument Culture: Moving from Debate to Dialogue *(1998), she moves beyond gender differences into a broader area of communication.*

Choose appropriate strategies for reading "The Argument Culture." Write down the strategies you've chosen. After finishing the reading, see what others you also needed.

Balance. Debate. Listening to both sides. Who could question these   1
noble American traditions? Yet today, these principles have been distorted. Without thinking, we have plunged headfirst into what I call the "argument culture."

The argument culture urges us to approach the world, and the people   2
in it, in an adversarial frame of mind. It rests on the assumption that opposition is the best way to get anything done: The best way to discuss an idea is to set up a debate; the best way to cover news is to find spokespeople who express the most extreme, polarized views and present them as "both sides"; the best way to settle disputes is litigation that pits one party against the other; the best way to begin an essay is to attack someone; and the best way to show you're really thinking is to criticize.

More and more, our public interactions have become like arguing with   3
a spouse. Conflict can't be avoided in our public lives any more than we can avoid conflict with people we love. One of the great strengths of our society

is that we can express these conflicts openly. But just as spouses have to learn ways of settling their differences without inflicting real damage, so we, as a society, have to find constructive ways of resolving disputes and differences.

The war on drugs, the war on cancer, the battle of the sexes, politicians' turf battles—in the argument culture, war metaphors pervade our talk and shape our thinking. The cover headlines of both *Time* and *Newsweek* one recent week are a case in point: "The Secret Sex Wars," proclaims *Newsweek.* "Starr at War," declares *Time.* Nearly everything is framed as a battle or game in which winning or losing is the main concern.

The argument culture pervades every aspect of our lives today. Issues from global warming to abortion are depicted as two-sided arguments, when in fact most Americans' views lie somewhere in the middle. Partisanship makes gridlock in Washington the norm. Even in our personal relationships, a "let it all hang out" philosophy emphasizes people expressing their anger without giving them constructive ways of settling differences.

SOMETIMES YOU HAVE TO FIGHT

There are times when it is necessary and right to fight—to defend your country or yourself, to argue for your rights or against offensive or dangerous idea or actions. What's wrong with the argument culture is the ubiquity, the knee-jerk nature, of approaching any issue, problem or public person in an adversarial way.

Our determination to pursue truth by setting up a fight between two sides leads us to assume that every issue has two sides—no more, no less. But if you always assume there must be an "other side," you may end up scouring the margins of science or the fringes of lunacy to find it.

This accounts, in part, for the bizarre phenomenon of Holocaust denial. Deniers, as Emory University professor Deborah Lipstadt shows, have been successful in gaining TV air time and campus newspaper coverage by masquerading as "the other side" in a "debate." Continual reference to "the other side" results in a conviction that everything has another side—and people begin to doubt the existence of any facts at all.

The power of words to shape perception has been proved by researchers in controlled experiments. Psychologists Elizabeth Loftus and John Palmer, for example, found that the terms in which people are asked to recall something affect what they recall. The researchers showed subjects a film of two cars colliding, then asked how fast the cars were going; one week later they asked whether there had been any broken glass. Some subjects were asked, "How fast were the cars going when they bumped into each other?" Others were asked, "How fast were the cars going when they smashed into each other?"

Those who read the question with "smashed" tended to "remember" 10 that the cars were going faster. They were also more likely to "remember" having seen broken glass. (There wasn't any.) This is how language works. It invisibly molds our way of thinking about people, actions and the world around us.

In the argument culture, "critical" thinking is synonymous with criti- 11 cizing. In many classrooms, students are encouraged to read someone's life work, then rip it to shreds.

When debates and fighting predominate, those who enjoy verbal spar- 12 ring are likely to take part—by calling in to talk shows or writing letters to the editor. Those who aren't comfortable with oppositional discourse are likely to opt out.

HOW HIGH-TECH COMMUNICATION PULLS US APART

One of the most effective ways to defuse antagonism between two 13 groups is to provide a forum for individuals from those groups to get to know each other personally. What is happening in our lives, however, is just the opposite. More and more of our communication is not face to face, and not with people we know. The proliferation and increasing portability of technology isolates people in a bubble.

Along with the voices of family members and friends, phone lines 14 bring into our homes the annoying voices of solicitors who want to sell something—generally at dinnertime. (My father-in-law startles phone solic- itors by saying, "We're eating dinner, but I'll call you back. What's your home phone number?" To the nonplused caller, he explains, "Well, you're calling me at home; I thought I'd call you at home, too.")

It is common for families to have more than one TV, so the adults can 15 watch what they like in one room and the kids can watch their choice in another—or maybe each child has a private TV.

E-mail, and now the Internet, are creating networks of human connec- 16 tion unthinkable even a few years ago. Though e-mail has enhanced com- munication with family and friends, it also ratchets up the anonymity of both sender and receiver, resulting in stranger-to-stranger "flaming."

"Road rage" shows how dangerous the argument culture—and espe- 17 cially today's technologically enhanced aggression—can be. Two men who engage in a shouting match may not come to blows, but if they express their anger while driving down a public highway, the risk to themselves and others soars.

THE ARGUMENT CULTURE SHAPES WHO WE ARE

The argument culture has a defining impact on our lives and on our   18
culture.

- *It makes us distort facts,* as in the Nancy Kerrigan–Tonya Harding story. After the original attack on Kerrigan's knee, news stories focused on the rivalry between the two skaters instead of portraying Kerrigan as the victim of an attack. Just last month, *Time* magazine called the event a "contretemps"° between Kerrigan and Harding. And a recent joint TV interview of the two skaters reinforced that skewed image by putting the two on equal footing, rather than as victim and accused.

- *It makes us waste valuable time,* as in the case of scientist Robert Gallo, who co-discovered the AIDS virus. Gallo was the object of a groundless four-year investigation into allegations he had stolen the virus from another scientist. He was ultimately exonerated, but the toll was enormous. Never mind that, in his words, "These were the most painful and horrible years of my life." Gallo spent four years fighting accusations instead of fighting AIDS.

- *It limits our thinking.* Headlines are intentionally devised to attract attention, but the language of extremes actually shapes, and misshapes, the way we think about things. Military metaphors train us to think about, and see, everything in terms of fighting, conflict and war. Adversarial rhetoric is a kind of verbal inflation—a rhetorical boy-who-cried-wolf.

- *It encourages us to lie.* If you fight to win, the temptation is great to deny facts that support your opponent's views and say only what supports your side. It encourages people to misrepresent and, in the extreme, to lie.

contretemps: unfortunate occurrence.

END THE ARGUMENT CULTURE BY LOOKING AT ALL SIDES

How can we overcome our classically American habit of seeing issues   19
in absolutes? We must expand our notion of "debate" to include more dialogue. To do this, we can make special efforts not to think in twos. Mary Catherine Bateson, an anthropologist at Virginia's George Mason University, makes a point of having her class compare three cultures, not two. Then, students are more likely to think about each on its own terms, rather than as opposites.

In the public arena, television and radio producers can try to avoid,   20
whenever possible, structuring public discussions as debates. This means avoiding the format of having two guests discuss an issue. Invite three

guests—or one. Perhaps it is time to re-examine the assumption that audiences always prefer a fight.

Instead of asking, "What's the other side?" we might ask, "What are the other sides?" Instead of insisting on hearing "both sides," let's insist on hearing "all sides." 21

We need to find metaphors other than sports and war. Smashing heads does not open minds. We need to use our imaginations and ingenuity to find different ways to seek truth and gain knowledge through intellectual interchange, and add them to our arsenal—or, should I say, to the ingredients for our stew. It will take creativity for each of us to find ways to change the argument culture to a dialogue culture. It's an effort we have to make, because our public and private lives are at stake. 22

Follow-Up Activities After you've finished reading, use these questions to respond to "The Argument Culture." You may write your answers or prepare them in your mind to discuss in class.

Grab your first impressions.

Respond with your first impressions. Say what you like and dislike; relate your personal experiences to the reading; consider what more you want to know.

Work with new words.

Some words in this reading may be unfamiliar to you. Use the methods of Strategy 3 to explain what the listed words mean.

1. Use context clues.

   a. antagonism (paragraph 13) _____

   b. proliferation (paragraph 13) _____

   c. ratchets (paragraph 16) _____

2. Use word parts.

   a. polarized (paragraph 2) _____

   b. partisanship (paragraph 5) _____

   c. predominate (paragraph 12) _____

3. Use the dictionary.
   Choose the correct definition of these words as they are used in the context of this reading.

   a. adversarial (paragraph 2) _____

  b. litigation (paragraph 2) _____

  c. pervade (paragraph 4) _____

  d. ubiquity (paragraph 6) _____

  e. sparring (paragraph 12) _____

4. Select additional words you're unsure of from the reading. Use one of these methods to discover their meaning.

Ask and answer questions.

1. How does Tannen define what she calls the "argument culture"? What are some examples she uses to demonstrate what she means?

2. Why does Tannen say that high-tech communication "pulls us apart"?

3. What are two major consequences Tannen lists to show how the argument culture influences us? Say briefly what example she uses for each one.

4. What solutions does Tannen propose for overcoming the problems caused by our argument culture?

Inference Questions

5. What can you infer about Tannen's praise for one of our society's "great strengths" (paragraph 3): being able to express conflicts openly? Why does she praise open expression of conflict while criticizing our argument culture?

6. What does Tannen mean by saying in paragraph 7 that by always assuming there is another, opposing side for every issue, "you may end up scouring the margins of science or the fringes of lunacy to find it"?

7. Tannen disagrees with the tendency to see "critical" thinking as synonymous with criticizing. What would you infer her definition of critical thinking would be, based on this reading?

8. Why does she catch herself when she uses the word *arsenal* in the last paragraph and change that word to *stew?*

Look for patterns of thought.

Tannen's argument relies a great deal on the use of cause-and-effect reasoning. Find examples of her use of this pattern.

 ## *Ask and answer your own questions.*

Write two questions based on any of the other information in this reading. Share your questions with others and collaborate on answers.

Make an evaluation.

Think both objectively and subjectively about "The Argument Culture." Thinking objectively, consider how well Tannen fulfilled her purpose in pointing out the harmful effects of the "argument culture." One question to keep in mind is how well Tannen follows her own advice. Does she herself introduce some middle ground, or third position, between adversarial argument and nonadversarial argument? Or does she use a fairly traditional argumentative form, focusing on what's wrong with the other side?

Thinking subjectively, consider how you respond personally to the information in this reading. For example, what is your personal response to her example of the classroom in which three cultures were compared, rather than just two?

 Form your final thoughts.

What was your evaluation of this reading? Discuss your evaluation of this reading with other students. ■

READING VI-C MEMO FROM COACH
CHRISTOPHER BUCKLEY

Christopher Buckley is the author of several books written from a funny, ironic perspective, such as Little Green Men, Wry Martinis, *and* Thank You for Not Smoking. *His humorous writing also appears frequently in the* New Yorker *magazine. This reading is a satire—a type of writing that uses irony and humor to expose human faults or weaknesses. In this satire, Buckley takes on the role of coach for a girls' soccer team. Watch for the moment when you can first tell this is no ordinary coach writing to parents.*

Choose appropriate strategies for reading "Memo from Coach." Write down the strategies you've chosen. After finishing the reading, see what others you also needed.

Welcome back! The fall Pixie League soccer season officially kicks off 1 next week, and I'd like to take this opportunity to let you know the schedule and provide guidelines. I'm sure we all agree that, with the Grasshoppers' 1–12 record last season, there's plenty of room for improvement this fall!

With a view to maximizing our performance, this summer I attended 2 the National Conference of Pixie League Coaches, held in King of Prussia, Pa. I did some valuable networking and came away truly "pumped."

PHYSICAL TRAINING

Per my memo last June regarding the summer-training regimen, your 3 nine-year-old daughter should now be able to: (a) run a mile in under five minutes with cinder blocks attached to each ankle (lower body); (b) bench-press the family minivan (upper body); (c) swim a hundred yards in fifty-degree water while holding her breath (wind); (d) remain standing while bowling balls are thrown at her (stamina).

PRACTICE SCHEDULE

Mondays, Wednesdays, Fridays: 5:30 A.M.

Tuesdays, Thursdays: 5:30 P.M.

Sundays: 7 A.M.

Columbus Day Weekend: 7:30 A.M.

Note: Live ammunition will be used at the Thursday practice.

4

VIDEO CRITIQUE OF GAMES

Mondays, 8 P.M. Parents strongly urged to attend. See "Camera Dads" sign-up list (Attachment E). Note: Professional-quality video cameras pre-ferred.

5

GAME SCHEDULE

Saturdays, 8 A.M. Important: Please be sure to have your daughter there *at least two hours before game time* for the pregame strategy briefing and pep rally. Note: As the girls will be biting the heads off live animals, we will need lots of guinea pigs, hamsters, parakeets, etc. See sign-up list (Attachment P). No goldfish, please!

6

HALFTIME SNACKS

Last year, there was some confusion about appropriate nourishment. According to guidelines established by the N.C.P.L.C.'s Committee on Nutrition and Performance, "snacks high in carbohydrates, sucrose, and corn syrup have been demonstrated to provide dramatic short-term meta-bolic gain." So save those low-fat pretzels for your cocktail parties and bring on the Twinkies and Ring Dings. Let's make sure that when the Grasshoppers hit the field they're hoppin'!

7

USE OF STEROIDS

One of the many things I took away from the panel discussions at King of Prussia was that, contrary to medical guidelines, use of anabolic steroids° by preteens is not necessarily a hundred per cent harmful. (See Attachment Q: "New Thinking on Performance Boosters and Mortality.") Grasshopper doctor dad Bill Hughes will discuss the merits of stanozolol versus

8

anabolic steroids: drugs to increase weight and strength.

fluoxymesterone and dispense prescriptions to all interested parents. (Participation encouraged!)

Note: If any Grasshopper parents are planning a vacation in Mexico, please see me about bringing back certain hard-to-get enhancers, like HGH (human-growth hormone) and EPO (erythropoeitin).

PARENTAL INPUT ON PLAYER SUBSTITUTIONS

Much as I appreciate your enthusiasm, it is not helpful if in the middle   9
of a tense game situation you abuse me verbally—or, as one overzealous dad did last season, assault me physically—because I have not sent in your daughter. For this reason, I will be carrying a Taser with me at all times. These anti-assault devices deliver up to fifty thousand volts of electricity, and leave the recipient drooling and twitching for weeks. Though I will make every effort to see that each Grasshopper gets her turn on the field, if you get "in my face" about it don't be "shocked, shocked!" to find your-self flat on your back in need of cardiopulmonary resuscitation.°

cardiopulmonary resuscitation: CPR (procedure for restoring normal breathing after a heart attack).

INJURIES

If your daughter has kept up with the summer-training program, there's   10
no reason she shouldn't be able to finish out a game with minor injuries, such as hairline bone fractures or subdural hematomas.° (Parental support needed!) Remember the Grasshopper motto: "That which does not kill me makes me a better midfielder!"

subdural hematoma: blood clot on the brain.

CHEERLEADING

If the coaches at K. of P. were unanimous about anything, it was the key   11
importance of parental screaming from the sidelines. This not only lets our girls know that Grasshopper parents do not accept failure but also alerts the other team that if they win you will probably "go postal" (kid talk for tem-porary insanity) and try to run them over in the parking lot after the game.

See you Monday morning!

Follow-Up Activities   After you've finished reading, use these questions to respond to "Memo from Coach." You may write your answers or prepare them in your mind to discuss in class.

Grab your first impressions.

Respond with your first impressions. Say what you like and dislike; relate your personal experiences to the reading; consider what more you want to know.

Work with new words: examples of ironic exaggeration.

Most of the words in this reading are probably familiar to you. Take this time to look for specific examples of exaggeration for ironic effect. (See two examples here.) In one column put an example of what you'd expect an ordinary, gung-ho coach to say; in the other column write an example of a ridiculous exaggeration.

Recognizing Irony

Ordinary "Coach Talk"	Exaggeration
". . . daughter should be able to run . . . [for] (lower body)."	". . . a mile under five minutes with cinder blocks attached to each ankle."
"Last year . . . confusion about appropriate nourishment."	". . . bring on the Twinkies and Ring Dings . . . make sure they're hoppin'!"

Ask and answer questions.

1. When do you first become certain this is a satire, not a normal memo?

2. What categories of coaching activities does the memo cover? How do these compare with the normal categories a coach would be involved with?

3. Who is Buckley satirizing? Coaches? Parents? Both? Explain your answer.

4. What is one example of a behavior or attitude that Buckley makes fun of? Explain how he uses ironic exaggeration in that example.

Inference Questions

5. What human weakness (or weaknesses) lies behind the behaviors and attitudes Buckley satirizes?

6. Why do you think Buckley used a team of 9-year-old girls for the coach's team? What difference would it make—if any—if he had used a team of high school football players?

7. What can you infer about Buckley's "message"? How would he, in reality, like adults to support children in playing sports?

 Ask and answer your own questions.

Write two questions based on any of the other information in this reading. Share your questions with others and collaborate on answers.

Make an evaluation.

Think both objectively and subjectively about "Memo from Coach." Thinking objectively, consider how well Buckley fulfilled his purposes for using satire. Keep these questions in mind. First, how much do you think he wanted to simply amuse us? How much did he want to criticize adults obsessed with creating children sports stars? Second, to be effective, his satire depends on making the coach sound believable—until the absurd exaggerations. How effectively did he capture the tone of a real, overly enthusiastic coach? Third, effective satire makes clear the faults that are being exposed. Are those faults made clear in this reading?

Thinking subjectively, consider how you respond personally to irony and satire, in general. For example, do you enjoy comic irony in movies or on television? In addition, think of any personal connections you have with the subject. Do you have any memories of adults getting involved—in positive or negative ways—in the sports you played?

 Form your final thoughts.

What was your evaluation of this satire? Discuss your evaluation of the reading with other students. ■

READING VI-D THE FORMATION OF MODERN AMERICAN MASS CULTURE

JAMES KIRBY MARTIN, RANDY ROBERTS, STEVEN MINTZ, LINDA O. MCMURRY, JAMES H. JONES

James Martin and the four other writers of the history textbook America and Its Peoples: A Mosaic in the Making *(2001) are all university professors of history. Each of these authors has special interests in a certain area of history, such as the history of the family and the history of sports and films in America. This reading is an excerpt from the chapter "Modern Times: 1920–1929." It tells about how much of our current popular culture was born in the 1920s.*

Choose appropriate strategies for reading "The Formation of Modern American Culture." Write down the strategies you've chosen. After finishing the reading, see if there were others you also needed.

Many of the defining features of modern American culture emerged during the 1920s. The best-seller, the book club, the record chart, the radio, the talking picture, and spectator sports all became popular forms of mass entertainment. But the primary reason the 1920s stand out as one of the most important periods in American cultural history is because the decade produced a generation of artists, musicians, and writers who were among the most innovative and creative in the country's history.

MASS ENTERTAINMENT

Of all the new appliances to enter the nation's homes during the 1920s, none had a more revolutionary impact than radio. Sales soared from $60 million in 1922 to $426 million in 1929. The first commercial radio station began broadcasting in 1919, and during the 1920s, the nation's airwaves were filled with musical variety shows and comedies.

Radio drew the nation together by bringing news, entertainment, and advertisements to more than ten million households. Radio blunted regional differences and imposed similar tastes and lifestyles. No other media had the power to create heroes and villains so quickly; when Charles Lindbergh became the first person to fly nonstop across the Atlantic from New York to Paris in 1928, the radio brought his incredible feat into American homes, transforming him into a celebrity overnight.

Radio also brought the nation decidedly unheroic images. The nation's most popular radio show, "Amos 'n Andy," which first aired in 1926 on Chicago's WMAQ, spread vicious racial stereotypes into homes whose white occupants knew little about African Americans. Other minorities fared no better. The Italian gangster and the tightfisted Jew became stock characters in radio programming.

The phonograph was not far behind the radio in importance. The 1920s saw the record player enter American life in full force. Piano sales sagged as phonograph production rose from just 190,000 in 1923 to 5 million in 1929.

The popularity of jazz, blues, and "hillbilly" music fueled the phonograph boom. Novelist F. Scott Fitzgerald called the 1920s the "Jazz Age"— and the decade was truly jazz's golden age. Duke Ellington wrote the first extended jazz compositions; Louis Armstrong popularized "scat" (singing of nonsense syllables); Fletcher Henderson pioneered big band jazz; and trumpeter Jimmy McPartland and clarinetist Benny Goodman popularized the Chicago school of improvisation.

The blues craze erupted in 1920, when a black singer named Mamie   7
Smith released a recording called "Crazy Blues." The record became a sensation, selling 75,000 copies in a month and a million copies in seven
months. Recordings by Ma Rainey, the "Mother of the Blues," and Bessie
Smith, the "Empress of the Blues," brought the blues, with its poignant and
defiant reaction to life's sorrows, to a vast audience.

"Hillbilly" music broke into mass culture in 1923, when a Georgia   8
singer named "Fiddlin' John" Carson sold 500,000 copies of his recordings.
"Country" music's appeal was not limited to the rural South or West; city
people, too, listened to country songs, reflecting a deep nostalgia for a simpler past.

The single most significant new instrument of mass entertainment was   9
the movies. Movie attendance soared, from 50 million patrons a week in
1920 to 90 million weekly in 1929. Americans spent 83 cents of every entertainment dollar going to the movies—and three-fourths of the population
went to a movie theater every week.

During the late teens and 1920s, the film industry took on its modern   10
form. In cinema's earliest days, the film industry was based in the nation's
theatrical center—New York. By the 1920s, the industry had relocated to
Hollywood, drawn by cheap land and labor, the ready accessibility of varied
scenery, and a climate ideal for year-round filming. Each year, Hollywood
released nearly 700 movies, dominating worldwide film production. By
1926, Hollywood had captured 95 percent of the British and 70 percent of
the French markets.

A small group of companies consolidated their control over the film   11
industry and created the "studio system" that would dominate film production for the next thirty years. Paramount, 20th-Century Fox, MGM, and
other studios owned their own production facilities, ran their own worldwide distribution networks, and controlled theater chains committed to
showing their companies' products. In addition, they kept certain actors,
directors, and screenwriters under contract.

The popularity of the movies soared as films increasingly featured   12
glamour, sophistication, and sex appeal. New kinds of movie stars appeared:
the mysterious sex goddess, personified by Greta Garbo; the passionate hot-
blooded lover, epitomized by Rudolph Valentino; and the flapper, with her
bobbed hair and skimpy skirts. New film genres also debuted, including
swashbuckling adventures, sophisticated comedies, and tales of flaming
youth and the new sexual freedom. Americans flocked to see Hollywood
spectacles such as Cecil B. DeMille's *Ten Commandments* (1923) with its
"cast of thousands" and dazzling special effects.

Like radio, movies created a new popular culture, with common speech,   13
dress, behavior, and heroes. And like radio, Hollywood did its share to rein-

force racial stereotypes by denigrating minority groups. The radio, the electric phonograph, and the silver screen all molded and mirrored mass culture.

SPECTATOR SPORTS

Spectator sports attracted vast audiences in the 1920s. The country yearned for heroes in an increasingly impersonal, bureaucratic society, and sports, as well as the film industry, provided them. Prize fighters like Jack Dempsey became national idols. Team sports flourished, but Americans focused on individual superstars, people whose talents or personalities made them appear larger than life. Knute Rockne and his "Four Horsemen" at Notre Dame spurred interest in college football, and professional football began during the 1920s. In 1925, Harold "Red" Grange, the "Galloping Ghost" halfback for the University of Illinois, attracted 68,000 fans to a professional football game at Brooklyn's Polo Grounds. 14

Baseball drew even bigger crowds than football. The decade began with the sport mired in scandal. In 1920, three members of the Chicago White Sox told a grand jury that they and five other players had thrown the 1919 World Series. As a result of the "Black Sox" scandal, eight players were banished from the sport. But baseball soon regained its popularity, thanks to George Herman ("Babe") Ruth, the sport's undisputed superstar. Up until the 1920s Ty Cobb's defensive brand of baseball, with its emphasis on base hits and stolen bases, had dominated the sport. Ruth transformed baseball into the game of the home-run hitter. In 1921, the New York Yankee slugger hit 59 home runs—more than any other team combined. In 1927, the "Sultan of Swat" hit 60. 15

LOW-BROW AND MIDDLE-BROW CULTURE

"It was a characteristic of the Jazz Age," novelist F. Scott Fitzgerald wrote, "that it had no interest in politics at all." What, then, were Americans interested in? Entertainment was Fitzgerald's answer. Parlor games like Mah Jong and crossword puzzles became enormously popular during the 1920s. Americans hit golf balls, played tennis, and bowled. Dance crazes like the fox trot, the Charleston, and the jitterbug swept the country. 16

pulp fiction: magazine or book printed on cheap paper.

New kinds of pulp fiction° found a wide audience. Edgar Rice Burroughs' *Tarzan of the Apes* became a runaway best-seller. For readers who felt concerned about urbanization and industrialization, the adventures of the lone white man in "dark Africa" revived the spirit of frontier individualism. Zane Grey's novels, such as *Riders of the Purple Sage,* enjoyed even greater popularity, with their tried but true formula of romance, action, and a moralistic struggle between good and evil, all in a western setting. 17

Other readers wanted to be titillated, as evidenced by the boom in   18
"confession magazines." Urban values, liberated women, and Hollywood
films had all relaxed Victorian standards. Confession magazines rushed to
fill the vacuum, purveying stories of romantic success and failure, divorce,
fantasy, and adultery. Writers survived the censors' cut by placing moral
tags at the end of their stories, in which readers were advised to avoid similar mistakes in their own lives.

Readers too embarrassed to pick up a copy of *True Romance* could   19
read more urbane magazines such as *The New Yorker* or *Vanity Fair,* which
offered entertainment, amusement, and gossip to those with more sophisticated tastes. They could also join the Book-of-the-Month Club or the
Literary Guild, both of which were founded during the decade.

THE AVANT-GARDE

Few decades have produced as many great works of art, music, or liter-   20
ature as the 1920s. At the decade's beginning, American culture stood in
Europe's shadow. By the decade's end, Americans were leaders in the
struggle to liberate the arts from older canons of taste, form, and style. It was
during the twenties that Eugene O'Neill, the country's most talented drama-
tist, wrote his greatest plays, and that William Faulkner, Ernest Hemingway,
F. Scott Fitzgerald, and Thomas Wolfe published their first novels.

American poets of the 1920s—such as Hart Crane, e.e. cummings,   21
Countee Cullen, Langston Hughes, Edna St. Vincent Millay, and Wallace
Stevens—experimented with new styles of punctuation, rhyming, and
form. Likewise, artists like Charles Demuth, Georgia O'Keeffe, and Joseph
Stella challenged the dominant realist tradition in American art and pio-
neered nonrepresentational and expressionist art forms.

The 1920s marked America's entry into the world of serious music. It   22
witnessed the founding of fifty symphony orchestras and three of the
country's most prominent music conservatories—Julliard, Eastman, and
Curtis. The decade also produced America's first great classical com-
posers—including Aaron Copland and Charles Ives—and witnessed George
Gershwin create a new musical form by integrating jazz into symphonic
and orchestral music.

World War I had left many American intellectuals and artists disillu-   23
sioned and alienated. Neither Wilsonian idealism° nor Progressive reform-
ism° appealed to America's postwar writers and thinkers, who believed that
the crusade to end war and to make the world safe for democracy had been
a senseless mistake.

During the 1920s, many of the nation's leading writers exposed the shal-   24
lowness and narrowmindedness of American life. The United States was a

Wilsonian idealism: refers
to Woodrow Wilson, U.S.
president during World War I.
Progressive reformism:
political movement empha-
sizing social progress for the
poor and underprivileged.

nation awash in materialism and devoid of spiritual vitality, a "wasteland," wrote the poet T. S. Eliot, inhabited by "hollow men." No author offered a more scathing attack on middle-class boorishness and smugness than Sinclair Lewis, who in 1930 became the first American to win the Nobel Prize for Literature. In *Main Street* (1920) and *Babbitt* (1922) he satirized the narrow-minded complacency and dullness of small-town America, while in *Elmer Gantry* (1922) he exposed religious hypocrisy and bigotry.

As editor of *Mercury* magazine, H. L. Mencken wrote hundreds of essays   25 mocking practically every aspect of American life. Calling the South a "gargantuan paradise of the fourth rate," and the middle class the "booboisie," Mencken directed his choicest barbs at reformers, whom he blamed for the bloodshed of World War I and the gangsters of the 1920s. "If I am convinced of anything," he snarled, "it is that Doing Good is in bad taste."

The writer Gertrude Stein defined an important group of American intel-   26 lectuals when she told Ernest Hemingway in 1921, "You are all a lost generation." Stein was referring to the expatriate novelists and artists who had participated in the Great War only to emerge from the conflict convinced that it was an exercise in futility. In their novels, F. Scott Fitzgerald and Hemingway foreshadowed a philosophy now known as "existentialism"—which maintains that life has no transcendent purpose and that each individual must salvage personal meaning from the void. Hemingway's fiction lionized toughness and "manly virtues" as a counterpoint to the softness of American life. In *The Sun Also Rises* (1926) and *A Farewell to Arms* (1929) he emphasized meaningless death and the importance of facing stoically the absurdities of the universe. In the conclusion of *The Great Gatsby* (1925), Fitzgerald gave pointed expression to an existentialist outlook: "so we beat on, boats against the current, borne back ceaselessly into the past."

THE SEX DEBATE

"If all girls at the Yale prom were laid end to end, I wouldn't be surprised,"   27 sighed Dorothy Parker, the official wit of New York's smart set. Parker's quip captured the public's perception that America's morals had taken a nosedive. Practically every newspaper featured articles on prostitution, venereal disease, sex education, birth control, and the rising divorce rate.

City life nurtured new sexual attitudes. With its crowded anonymity,   28 urban culture eroded sexual inhibitions by relaxing community restraints on individual behavior. Cities also promoted secular, consumer values, and city people seemed to tolerate, if not welcome, many forms of diversity.

While cities provided the ideal environment for liberalized sexual   29 values, Sigmund Freud provided the ideal psychology. A Vienna physician, Freud revolutionized academic and popular thinking about human behavior

The image of the "flapper," who bobbed her hair, bared her knees, and smoked and drank in public, alarmed a public still clinging to Victorian codes of morality.

by arguing that unconscious sexual anxieties cause much of human behavior. Freud also explained that sexual desires and fears develop in infancy and stay with people throughout their lives. During the 1920s, Freud's theories about the sexual unconscious were widely debated by physicians, academics, advice columnists, women's magazine writers, and preachers.

The image of the "flapper"—the liberated woman who bobbed her hair, painted her lips, raised her hemline, and danced the Charleston—personified the public's anxiety about the decline of traditional morality. In the 1950s Alfred C. Kinsey, a sex researcher at Indiana University, found that women born after 1900 were twice as likely to have had premarital sex as their mothers, with the most pronounced changes occurring in the generation reaching maturity in the early 1920s.   30

Sexual permissiveness had eroded Victorian values, but the "new woman" posed less of a challenge to traditional morality than her critics feared. Far from being promiscuous, her sexual experience before marriage was generally limited to one or two partners, one of whom she married. In practice, this narrowed the gap between men and women and moved society toward a single standard of morality. Instead of turning to prostitutes, men made love with their sweethearts, who in many instances became their wives.   31

Follow-Up Activities   After you've finished reading, use these questions to respond to "The Formation of Modern American Culture." You may write your answers or prepare them in your mind to discuss in class.

Grab your first impressions.

Respond with your first impressions. Say what you like and dislike; relate your personal experiences to the reading; consider what more you want to know.

Work with new words.

Some words in this reading may be unfamiliar to you. Use the methods of Strategy 3 to explain what the listed words mean.

1. Use context clues.
    a. nostalgia (paragraph 8) _____
    b. epitomized (paragraph 12) _____
    c. purveying (paragraph 18) _____
    d. transcendent (paragraph 26) _____

2. Use word parts.
    a. denigrating (paragraph 13) _____
    b. urbane (paragraph 19) _____
        Use the context to see how *urbane* relates to the word *urban*.
    c. alienated (paragraph 23) _____
    d. expatriate (paragraph 26) _____
    e. lionized (paragraph 26) _____

3. Use the dictionary.
    Choose the correct definition of each word as it is used in the context of this reading.
    a. innovative (paragraph 1) _____
    b. poignant (paragraph 7) _____
    c. complacency (paragraph 24) _____
    d. bigotry (paragraph 24) _____
    e. stoically (paragraph 26) _____

4. Select additional words you're unsure of from the reading. Use one of these methods to discover their meaning.

Ask and answer questions.

1. What three features of modern American life were introduced in the 1920s? Explain briefly the influence on the American public of *one* of these features.

2. Why did America "yearn for heroes" during this decade? How did spectator sports meet Americans' need for heroes?

3. What kind of reading appealed to a 1920s mass audience—the low-brow audience? What types of magazines appealed to more sophisticated readers—the high-brow audience?

4. The authors tell us that World War I "left many American intellectuals and artists disillusioned." Choose one of the disillusioned writers, and explain briefly what his or her writing dealt with.

5. What were the causes of the changed sexual attitudes of the 1920s? How did the flapper reflect those changed attitudes?

Inference Questions

6. How would radio programs such as *Amos 'n Andy* promote racial or ethnic stereotypes?

7. Why had American culture "stood in Europe's shadow" at the beginning of the decade?

8. Why did the "new woman" of the 1920s "pose less of a challenge to traditional morality than her critics feared"?

 Ask and answer your own questions.

Write two questions based on any of the other information in this reading. Share your questions with others and collaborate on answers.

Make an evaluation.

Think both objectively and subjectively about "The Formation of Modern American Culture." Thinking objectively, consider how well the authors fulfilled their purpose in this textbook excerpt of giving a clear and objective history of the importance of the 1920s in the development of modern American culture. Thinking subjectively, consider how you respond personally to the information in this reading. For example, what parts of the history of this decade do you find most interesting? Which least interesting? Does your choice depend on your prior interests, on the way the part was presented, or both?

 Form your final thoughts.

What was your evaluation of this textbook excerpt? Discuss your evaluation of the reading with other students.   ■

PART VI REVIEW
ANALYZING AND EVALUATING

Now that you've completed Part VI, think over what you've read about the role popular culture plays in people's lives. Then review the two strategies introduced in this part and see how they work throughout the reading process.

Linking Ideas on the Theme: Popular Culture and Everyday Life

 Respond to the readings in Part VI by linking ideas on the theme of "Popular Culture and Everyday Life." Answer these questions in writing or in discussion with others.

1. Some of these writers take a historical perspective, looking at earlier media and its impact on the culture of its time. Compare two of these readings, showing what they have in common as well as how they differ.

2. Choose two authors who focus on our current media's effect on our image of ourselves and our relationships with others. Say what the two readings have in common as well as how they differ.

3. Music is an important part of what is known as "youth culture." Find ways of linking the ideas found in two of the readings on either of those topics.

4. You may think of yet another way of linking two readings on this theme. Say what the two readings have in common as well as how they are different.

5. Try linking ideas from one or two of these readings with ideas in something else you've read—including something in an earlier part of this book—or with a movie or TV program you've seen.

6. Take notes for the personal part of an evaluation you might write on a reading you have strong feelings about, either positive or negative. Share this part of your evaluation of the writing with others. How similar or different were their personal responses? Then discuss what you might want to include in the *objective* part of the evaluation. What did you learn about the difference between the personal and the objective parts of an evaluation?

Using Strategies throughout the Reading Process

Strategy 13: **Analyze the Information**

Strategy 14: **Make an Evaluation**

You have seen how the strategies in Part VI incorporate the earlier strategies for predicting, comprehending, summarizing, and interpreting a reading. These new strategies help you put together the strategies you have learned and use them for a careful consideration of a reading.

Use the chart on the next page as a reminder of how a strategy helps you at each of the three stages: Get Started, Read, Follow Up. The new strategies are highlighted.

How Have the Strategies Worked for You?

Here is your last chance in this book to evaluate the strategies. But as you continue reading for your college courses, keep asking yourself these same kinds of questions, so you can continue using the strategies in ways that work best for you.

First, look back at what you wrote about the strategies at the end of Part V. What differences would there be in your answers to those questions now?

Next, answer the following questions to help you evaluate Strategies 13 and 14. Finally, compare notes with other students, and ask your instructor for ideas on how to get more out of the strategies.

1. How have the strategies helped you to read from the inside out?

   _____

   _____

   _____

2. Which strategies would you say have made the biggest difference in your overall understanding of what you read? Which ones have added to your enjoyment?

   _____

   _____

   _____

3. Think about the courses you're likely to take next term. Which strategies do you think you'll need to do well with the types of reading in those courses?

   _____

   _____

   _____

**STRATEGIES
THROUGH PART VI**

1. Check in
2. Respond
3. Work with new words
4. Get an overview
5. Ask questions
6. Find and mark main ideas
7. Look for patterns of thought
8. Make inferences
9. Map main ideas
10. Write a summary
11. Find meaning in metaphors
12. Determine the writer's purpose
13. Analyze the information
14. Make an evaluation

GET STARTED   Begin with strategies that help you think about the subject and find out about what the writer will say.

- Check in
- Get an overview
- Ask questions
- Determine the writer's purpose

READ   Use strategies that help you read with greater understanding, interpret the language, and respond with your own questions and ideas.

- Respond
- Work with new words
- Find meaning in metaphors
- Ask questions
- Find and mark main ideas
- Look for patterns of thought
- Make inferences
- Determine the writer's purpose

FOLLOW UP   End with strategies that help you look more closely at the language and ideas in the reading, assess your understanding, and respond in a thoughtful way.

- Work with new words
- Respond
- Find meaning in metaphors
- Ask questions
- Find and mark main ideas
- Look for patterns of thought
- Make inferences
- Map main ideas
- Write a summary
- Determine the writer's purpose
- Analyze the information
- Make an evaluation

PART VI REVIEW

4. For the strategies you're still less sure of, what specific things can you do to make them more effective?

_____

_____

_____

5. What is the most important idea about reading that you will take with you from this book? What made the deepest and most meaningful impression on you? What did this book do to change your attitude and practice of reading?

_____

_____

_____

GLOSSARY

annotating: writing notes in the margin to supplement underlining

argument: reasoning that persuades you to believe something or do something

assumptions: ideas we take for granted, based on our previous beliefs and experience

bias: leaning to one or another side of a debatable question; emotional involvement

complete sentence: sentence that has a subject and verb and expresses a complete thought

connotation (connotative meaning): the cluster of specialized associations that accompany a word

context: surroundings in which you find a word

credible argument: believable argument in terms of kinds of support and reasoning

denotation (denotative meaning): literal meaning of a word

description: account that shows what someone or something looks like

etymology: origin and history of a word

evidence: piece of information that furnishes some proof that what the writer argues is true

exposition: writing that explains something or informs

fact: statement that can be verified or proven

figurative language: nonliteral comparison, often highly visual

general: refers to a large category that includes several items (for example, fruit)

general reader: someone who has no special background in a subject

headnotes: notes before a reading about the author and the reading

imply: suggest meaning by using certain words, details, or other evidence

infer (make inferences): make connections and draw logical conclusions based on evidence

intended audience: the people a writer wants to reach

irony: use of words to convey meaning that is opposite to—or very different from—the literal meaning journal or reading log: place for writing personal responses to a reading

linking ideas: seeing relationships between ideas in different readings or other sources

literal: the ordinary or primary meaning of a word; *rusty nail* uses the literal meaning of *rusty*; *rusty pianist* uses its metaphorical meaning

main idea: general idea about a topic; it supports the overall point

map: cluster or boxed grouping of the overall point and main ideas in a reading

margin notes: marks or very brief notes in the margin showing reader's personal response

metaphor: implied comparison that does not use *like* or *as*

metaphorical expression: figure of speech that heightens the effect and meaning of language

narration: writing that tells a story

objective: neutral; free from emotional attachment to one side or the other

opinion: statement that cannot be proven or disproven, but may be valuable support

outline: vertical listing, with indents, that shows the relationship of ideas—the overall point and main ideas—in a reading

overall point: writer's most important message that covers—or includes—all the other ideas in the reading

overall-point question: question that asks about the writer's overall point; it is an umbrella question because it covers all the ideas in the reading

overview: general sense of an entire subject, indicating what will be important in a reading

paraphrase: translation of others' words into one's own words

patterns of thought: structures we use to think, such as reasons or examples

personal preferences: opinions based only on what one likes

perspective: way of looking at a subject; one's position on it

predicting: using all the elements in the reading to see what to expect

prefix: word part that comes at the beginning of a word; it shows such information as direction (in, out, under) and number

purpose: writer's reasons for writing

reading cues: parts of the reading, such as the title, headings, introduction, and conclusion, that point to important information

reliable information: information you can rely on or trust to be fair, accurate, and complete

review: go over again to study and remember

root: word part that gives the core meaning of a word

sarcasm: ironic use of a term to mean its opposite

simile: specific kind of metaphorical expression that uses *like* or *as* to make an explicit comparison

skimming: high-speed reading just to grasp the broad outlines of a reading

specific: refers to a particular type or part within the larger category (for example, type of fruit, including bananas, grapes, apples)

subjective: having emotional involvement or bias (leaning) to one side or the other

suffix: word part that comes at the end of a word: it shows the word's part of speech (verb, noun, adjective, adverb)

summary: brief—usually one paragraph—restatement of main ideas

support: information used to explain or clarify the overall point or a main idea

supporting idea: more specific idea that supports a main idea

sweeping generalizations: general statements that seem overly inclusive

synonym: word that has the same meaning

tone: written expression showing writer's attitude or mood

topic: what a main part of a reading is about

transition: word or phrase that serves as a bridge from one thought to another

ADDITIONAL QUESTIONS FOR

READING FROM THE INSIDE OUT

This section of the book gives you and your instructor additional ways to make sure you've understood a reading and learned some of the new words the reading's author used. For each reading you'll find five multiple-choice comprehension questions. Starting with Reading 6, after you've been introduced to **working with new words,** you'll also find five multiple-choice vocabulary questions for each reading.

Chapter 1

Reading 1: I Do Not Like to Read—Sam-I-Am!

Comprehension questions.

Choose the answer that best completes each statement.

_____ 1. When she began the first grade, Grabiner was behind the other children in reading because she

    a. had been laughed at by the children in her previous school.

    b. did not like books.

    c. had gone to a school that emphasized learning about revolutions.

    d. had gone to a school that emphasized enjoying learning.

_____ 2. Grabiner kept her eyes closed tight or squinted

    a. because she needed glasses.

    b. to keep herself from reading words.

    c. to keep from seeing the pictures of Dick and Jane and Spot.

    d. to let her parents know how unhappy she was.

_____ 3. Even though Grabiner enjoyed having her father read to her at night, she didn't like reading partly because she

    a. didn't like sitting still long enough to read.

    b. preferred doing things such as shopping at the supermarket with her mother, instead of just reading about it.

    c. didn't like the books she had to read at school.

    d. had to look at books by herself when her father was out of town.

_____ 4. Grabiner finally realized she could enjoy reading when she

    a. recognized words on the page of *Green Eggs and Ham* by accident.

    b. read a book during recess one day at school.

    c. found *Green Eggs and Ham* by reading the title.

    d. found the words she was reading were different from the ones her parents said.

_____ 5. We can assume from the reading that the main reason Grabiner got over her dislike of reading was that

    a. being in the lowest reading group gave her the reading skills she needed.

    b. she'd had good experiences with books every night when her parents read to her.

    c. she got the glasses she needed in order to read comfortably.

    d. her parents rewarded her with special treats for learning to read.

Reading 2: The Voice You Hear When You Read Silently

Comprehension questions.

Choose the answer that best completes each statement.

_____ 1. The "voice" in the poem refers to

    a. the remembered voice of the person who first read to you.

    b. your own voice as you whisper the words to yourself.

    c. your own thoughts as you read.

    d. someone reading the poem aloud to you.

_____ 2. Lux says this voice is "not the sound your friends know/ or the sound of a tape played back."

    a. This voice is only in your own mind.

    b. You don't sound the same to your friends or yourself when you're reading instead of just talking.

    c. Everyone thinks their tape-recorded voice sounds different from the voice they hear when they talk.

    d. This voice is not really yours, but a voice you remember from childhood.

_____ 3. "The dark cathedral of your skull" in lines 11–12 refers to

    a. a library with a large, quiet space that allows your mind to concentrate on what you're reading.

    b. the unique, almost sacred space inside your mind.

    c. a spirit of gothic darkness that can take over your mind.

    d. your imagination, brightly colored like the stained glass of a cathedral.

_____ 4. Lux uses the example of the word *barn* in the poem in order to

    a. show us a vivid picture of the barn he grew up with.

    b. indicate the importance of getting background so you can picture things as you read.

    c. demonstrate that a barn can be as good a place to read as a library or cathedral.

    d. demonstrate that each of us has our own special associations with a word as we read it.

_____ 5. This poem demonstrates the importance of the *reader* in the reading process by

    a. describing the reader as a viewer of word pictures.

    b. encouraging the reader to read the writer's words aloud.

    c. showing that as a reader, you need to put aside any previous ideas you've had in order to acquire new ideas.

    d. showing that as a reader, you bring your own unique experience to each piece of writing you read.

Chapter 2

Reading 3: Forbidden Reading

Comprehension questions.

Choose the answer that best completes each statement.

_____ 1. Plantation owners tried to keep their slaves from reading or teaching others to read by

    a. keeping all reading material hidden and locked away.

    b. whipping them or even hanging them.

    c. whipping them or selling them to other masters.

    d. threatening them with the branding iron.

_____ 2. One of the slaves praised his master's son's reading of a Bible passage and asked him to read it over and over. Doing this was an example of

    a. an attempt to flatter the master's son, so he would break the rules and teach the slave to read.

    b. an attempt to keep the boy reading, so the slave could put off doing his hard labor as long as possible.

    c. a device that allowed the slave to learn to read without being caught.

    d. a device for learning Bible passages in order to say them in times of trouble.

_____ 3. It's possible to teach yourself to read whole books just by learning the alphabet and a few words because

    a. when you know how to sound out a few words in English, you can figure out the system for sounding out all English words.

    b. each letter of the alphabet has a unique shape that allows you to remember it when you see it in words.

    c. books for beginners have very few words and therefore require learning only a small number of words.

    d. when you know how to sound out a few words in English, you can memorize those words and skip over the other words.

_____ 4. Frederick Douglass was motivated to learn to read first when he heard his mistress reading the Bible aloud and then when

    a. his mistress refused to help him.

    b. his mistress praised him for learning to spell words of three and four letters.

    c. his master tried to keep him from learning.

    d. he was able to see the alphabet blocks of his mistress's baby.

_____ 5. Slave owners were afraid to have slaves learn to read because they knew that

    a. once you can read, you have access to knowledge, and through knowledge you gain power.

    b. once you can read, you become more involved in stories and fantasy that lead you away from working hard.

    c. slaves did not have the mental capacity to learn to read.

    d. slaves might learn to read in their native African languages and be better able to communicate with one another.

Reading 4: Teaching My Grandmother to Read

Comprehension questions.

Choose the answer that best completes each statement.

_____ 1. Frisina's grandmother wanted to come to the United States all by herself at age 14 because

    a. her life in Greece promised only hard work and poverty, and she thought everyone could get rich in America.

    b. she was expected to marry at 14, and she wanted to escape the arranged marriage.

    c. she had to take care of her brother and sister and thought she could give them better care by sending back money to them from America.

    d. she felt she could return to Greece if things didn't work out, which is why she gave her gold earrings to her cousin for safekeeping.

_____ 2. Frisina's grandmother met with disappointments and difficulties that were typical of immigrants' experiences. These included

    a. being forced to go to school and learn English.

    b. finding pieces of bouquets and trying to sell these flowers to strangers.

    c. being labeled a foreigner and restricted by city law to staying in her own neighborhood.

    d. having to work hard just to have money to eat and having no time for school.

_____ 3. Frisina is most grateful for what she had learned from her grandmother about

    a. covering trees with tar paper.

    b. cooking without a recipe.

    c. the ways of immigrant life in a brand-new culture.

    d. the ways of her ethnic heritage.

_____ 4. During these reading lessons, Frisina's grandmother

    a. became upset when Frisina laughed at her pronunciation mistakes.

    b. laughed hard at her own pronunciation mistakes.

    c. wanted to give up trying when she still couldn't read the newspaper.

    d. became upset when Frisina wanted to stop and go back to telephone gossiping.

_____ 5. Both the author and her grandmother felt the importance of these reading lessons, because the lessons

    a. finally allowed her grandmother to sit comfortably with a newspaper or magazine.

    b. were evidence that her grandmother was more intelligent than people had given her credit for.

    c. were evidence of the love the author felt for her grandmother.

    d. finally allowed her grandmother to give up the crocheting she had had to do for so many years.

Chapter 3

Reading 5: Where English Words Come From

Comprehension questions.

Choose the answer that best completes each statement.

_____ 1. Words such as *child*, *eat*, *fight*, and *sleep*

     a. come from two ancient languages, Greek and Latin.

     b. came into the language because of the French invasion in 1066.

     c. were first spoken in the English of a thousand years ago.

     d. were first spoken in the English of Shakespeare's day.

_____ 2. After the French invasion in 1066, English changed because

     a. so many new words came into the language from the French words used by the French ruling classes.

     b. so many peasants were forced to leave England to work in France.

     c. everyone in England was forced to speak French.

     d. Old English was not considered up to date enough for the French ruling classes.

_____ 3. According to the reading, slang is

     a. prohibited from being included in the dictionary.

     b. the source of problems in communication.

     c. constantly changing and therefore cannot be included in the dictionary.

     d. the source of many new words included in the dictionary.

_____ 4. The English language continues to incorporate new words in many different ways. Which one of the following is **not** one of these ways?

     a. New words from slang become part of mainstream English.

     b. New words are created by an official committee of English and American lexicographers.

     c. New words come from Asia and Africa, as well as Europe.

     d. New words come from recent developments in technology.

_____ 5. Based on this reading, you can assume there are so many words of Greek and Latin origin in your textbooks because

a. Greek and Latin words provide the best structures for creating new words.

b. for centuries Greek and Latin were the languages of scholarship and learning.

c. for centuries Greeks and Romans wrote most of the books used in the universities of Europe.

d. even today, university professors write their textbooks in Greek or Latin before translating them into English.

Chapter 4

Reading 6: What Deprived Children Tell Us about Human Nature

Vocabulary questions.

Using the methods of Strategy 3, choose the correct definition of each italicized word as it is used in the context of this reading.

_____ 1. how much from *nurture* (paragraph 7):

a. nourishment   c. heredity

b. social environment   d. discipline

_____ 2. their *controversial* idea (paragraph 11):

a. debatable   c. standard

b. disagreeable   d. irritable

_____ 3. follow social *norms* (paragraph 15):

a. tastes   c. medians

b. averages   d. customs

_____ 4. close *bonds* with others (paragraph 15):

a. agreements   c. constraints

b. adhesives   d. attachments

_____ 5. impossible to *compensate for* (paragraph 18):

a. overbalance   c. make up for

b. improve   d. pay damages for

Comprehension questions.

Choose the answer that best completes each statement.

_____ 1. Isabelle was able to catch up with her peers in her intellectual and social development; Genie, however, remained severely limited both intellectually and socially because

    a. she had less natural intelligence than Isabelle.

    b. at 13, she had already missed the critical period for language and social development.

    c. lack of proper food caused lasting physical and mental problems.

    d. the training she received was not as intensive and thorough as Isabelle's.

_____ 2. In the 1930s, the "commonsense" idea about the reason for orphanage children's low intelligence and poor social skills was that

    a. they needed better nutrition and exercise.

    b. they needed better training and education.

    c. they lacked human love and contact.

    d. they were born with lower intelligence and an inability to interact with others.

_____ 3. When the women in the institution for the mentally retarded spent time holding and playing with the orphaned babies, those babies grew into adults who

    a. succeeded in school and lived normal lives.

    b. had minimal schooling and were happy with low-level jobs.

    c. sounded and acted like the retarded women who had cared for them.

    d. dedicated their lives to helping other orphaned babies.

_____ 4. The Harlows' experiment showed that, like human children, young animals' social development depends most on

    a. good nutrition.

    b. a quiet, protected environment.

    c. close physical contact with a mother or mother substitute.

    d. frequent pretend fights with their peers.

_____ 5. Henslin tells us that "society makes us human." He supports his statement by showing that children raised in isolation

    a. can survive even under horrifying conditions.

    b. are unable to learn adequate language or to interact normally with others.

    c. depend on the rest of society to get along in life.

    d. must have superior intelligence in order to make up for being isolated.

Reading 7: The Good Person

Vocabulary questions.

Using the methods of Strategy 3, choose the correct definition of each italicized word as it is used in the context of this reading.

_____ 1. certain *secular* values (paragraph 1):

    a. not specifically religious   c. occurring once in a century

    b. sophisticated   d. spiritual

_____ 2. the *rhetoric* of goodness (paragraph 8):

    a. study of rules of speech   c. pretense

    b. public speaking   d. skill in using speech

_____ 3. *priggish*, all too full of yourself (paragraph 10):

    a. delicate   c. plodding

    b. self-satisfied   d. dull

_____ 4. ethical *speculation* (paragraph 7):

    a. thinking   c. hearing rumors

    b. taking business risks   d. anecdote

_____ 5. *glean* from it a message (paragraph 3):

    a. pick over in search of relevant ideas

    b. gather grain

    c. shine

    d. erase from memory

Comprehension questions.

Choose the answer that best completes each statement.

_____ 1. The children related the message of the story "Starry Time" to their own lives by

    a. bringing items to school to share with others.

    b. asking their parents to be more generous to others.

    c. wondering what they would be willing to share with others.

    d. deciding that no one could be as good as Stella was.

_____ 2. Coles's heading "Words into Action" refers to his idea that

    a. words are harder to remember than actions.

    b. it's easier to list qualities that make up goodness than to act them out in daily life.

    c. it's easier to act like a good person than to really be one.

    d. turning nouns into verbs teaches children about grammar.

_____ 3. In paragraph 10, Coles compares the boy's description of being good to the myth of Sisyphus because

    a. you can never give a person something without that person wanting even more from you.

    b. being good is a constant struggle and it's always possible to backslide.

    c. being good is like rolling a rock that's too heavy for you.

    d. human beings are condemned to fail at being good.

_____ 4. Under the heading "A Good Person" Coles defines good children as those who

    a. sincerely believe in the desirability of goodness but understand that life doesn't always allow you to be good.

    b. understand the ideas of goodness and realize the importance of holding on to these abstract ideas.

    c. understand the Golden Rule and can help others to understand its meaning.

    d. sincerely believe in the desirability of goodness and understand that goodness must be lived through one's actions.

_____ 5. The 13-year-old boy referred to in paragraphs 9–10 comes to the realization that "a good guy" could ruin everything by calling attention to himself; that's a problem because then he

    a. starts pretending to be good, instead of really being good.

    b. can become so involved in self-congratulation that he starts doing bad things.

    c. can become more involved in self-congratulation than in actually doing good.

    d. only cares about pointing out the faults of others.

Chapter 5

Reading 8: How Babies Use Patterns to See

Vocabulary questions.

Using the methods of Strategy 3, choose the correct definition of each italicized word as it is used in the context of this reading.

_____ 1. *detection* of fine-grained detail (paragraph 4):

    a. acknowledgment   c. solution

    b. recollection   d. recognition

_____ 2. missing as much as two-thirds of their *contour* (paragraph 8):

    a. circle   c. surrounding details

    b. outline   d. drawing

_____ 3. infants *extract* meaningful patterns (paragraph 8):

    a. add   c. draw out

    b. separate   d. mine

_____ 4. pausing . . . to look at each *salient* part (paragraph 5):

    a. standing out   c. excellent

    b. central   d. hard to see

_____ 5. a *succession* of partial views (paragraph 8):

    a. sequence   c. chain

    b. type   d. accomplishment

Comprehension questions.

Choose the answer that best completes each statement.

_____ 1. Very young infants prefer to look at black-and-white checkerboards with a few large squares instead of the checkerboard with many small squares because they

a. see only the central squares of the checkerboard.

b. haven't learned to appreciate contrast.

c. can't tell the difference between curved and straight lines.

d. can't see the fine detail in the smaller checkerboard.

_____ 2. Figure 5.2 tells you that when a newborn looks at a pattern, such as a geometric shape or a human face, the baby

a. examines the internal features.

b. stares at a point beyond the shape or face.

c. stares at a single point on the shape or face.

d. blinks several times a second.

_____ 3. The ability of 4-month-old babies to perceive subjective boundaries that are not really present comes from their learning

a. to scan an entire border of a shape.

b. to see more contrast.

c. to use their imagination.

d. to detect pattern organization.

_____ 4. By the end of the first year, babies can

a. figure out the shape of an object even when only shown incomplete views of it.

b. figure out the shape of an object when its image is flashed only once.

c. use a light to create original shapes.

d. use contrast sensitivity to figure out the shape of an object.

_____ 5. Based on the reading, we can assume a newborn would prefer to look at a circle that is painted

a. in one pastel color, such as pink or baby blue.

b. with broad black-and-white stripes.

c. in one bright color, such as red or yellow.

d. with tiny white dots all over a black background.

Reading 9: talking back

Vocabulary questions.

Using the methods of Strategy 3, choose the correct definition of each italicized word as it is used in the context of this reading.

_____ 1. write using the *pseudonym* (paragraph 14):

    a. false front   c. stage name

    b. falsehood   d. pen name

_____ 2. in *retrospect* (paragraph 15):

    a. looking back   c. looking within

    b. summing up   d. admiring

_____ 3. learned to be *vigilant* (paragraph 9):

    a. reckless   c. painstaking

    b. sensible   d. on your guard

_____ 4. *legacy* of defiance (paragraph 14):

    a. gift given in a will   c. donation

    b. something passed on   d. payment
       from ancestors

_____ 5. legacy of *defiance* (paragraph14):

    a. wickedness   c. act of challenging authority

    b. bad behavior   d. act of risking one's life

Comprehension questions.

Choose the answer that best completes each statement.

_____ 1. In the black, small-town, southern community of hooks's childhood,

    a. men dominated in the church, but women were the authorities in the home.

    b. women were not allowed in the men's church, but preached and worshipped in their own church.

    c. women spoke a different language in the home, so they would not be understood by the men.

    d. women had no role in establishing rules for behaving in everyday life.

_____ 2. "The right speech of womanhood" that hooks was supposed to learn as a child is

    a. speaking out for women's rights.

    b. talking that can be ignored by others.

    c. talking in a special code only to other women.

    d. dialogue between equals.

_____ 3. Too much talking back for a female might bring both

    a. scolding and ridicule.

    b. physical punishment and the threat that she'll be turned out of the home.

    c. ruin to her family and the threat she will end up crazy.

    d. physical punishment and the threat she will end up crazy.

_____ 4. As a girl, hooks turned to writing because

    a. she had a great-grandmother who was a writer.

    b. she needed to write to others who might help her.

    c. she wanted to try to capture what she heard and to ask the questions she wasn't supposed to ask.

    d. she wanted to practice writing so she could one day become a writer.

_____ 5. Based on what you've read and on what you know about the segregated South of the 1950s, why would hooks's parents feel that children had to learn to be quiet and obedient above all else? The answer is probably that

    a. black people still felt fearful about doing or saying anything that could anger white people.

    b. the parents and grandparents themselves had been taught that disobedient children might grow up to be crazy.

    c. black people were moving to northern cities and wanted to take with them their traditional ways of raising children.

    d. black people were beginning to demand their civil rights, and they wanted their children to know how to speak without getting into trouble.

Chapter 6

Reading 10: How the Self-Concept Develops

Vocabulary questions.

Using the methods of Strategy 3, choose the correct definition of each italicized word as it is used in the context of this reading.

_____ 1. *accolades* of her friends (paragraph 5):

      a. credits   c. great compliments

      b. expressions of surprise   d. expressions of adoration

_____ 2. *adhering* to cultural rules (paragraph 10):

      a. admitting   c. disregarding

      b. cementing   d. holding on

_____ 3. roles they *assume* (paragraph 9):

      a. suppose   c. imagine

      b. take on   d. fake

_____ 4. as we *alluded* to earlier (paragraph 8):

      a. related   c. submitted

      b. referred   d. passed on

_____ 5. thought of herself as a *"maverick"* (paragraph 12):

      a. individualist   c. unbranded range animal

      b. revolutionary   d. untamed

Comprehension questions.

Choose the answer that best completes each statement.

_____ 1. Our self-concept is influenced most by

      a. our current relationships with peers.

      b. our early experiences with teachers.

      c. our early experiences with peers.

      d. our early experiences with parents and siblings.

_____ 2. If someone has been harshly criticized as a child,

    a. he or she will not be able to gain a good self-concept as an adult.

    b. it takes a lot of work to gain a good self-concept.

    c. it makes the person tougher and thus strengthens the person's self-concept.

    d. it means the parents were treated the same way as children.

_____ 3. Our awareness of who we are is often connected with groups we associate with; these are groups that

    a. we are born into or choose on our own.

    b. we choose after we've learned to know what we think is important to us.

    c. we have to work hard to join.

    d. we are born into or have friends or family as members.

_____ 4. Self-reflexiveness shapes our self-concept by

    a. changing what we think of ourselves to better reflect societal norms and conventions.

    b. giving us a chance to adapt to other people's concept of us.

    c. allowing us to describe who we are as we observe ourselves doing things.

    d. allowing us to do things by instinct, as if by reflex.

_____ 5. Based on the information about gender roles in the reading, you could assume that

    a. babies are born with a strong awareness of gender roles.

    b. from birth on, parents exert a powerful influence on a child's awareness of gender roles.

    c. as we grow into adult men and women, our self-concept is less and less dependent on strong identification with a gender role.

    d. until the age of 3, children have no awareness of gender roles.

Reading 11: School Is Bad for Children

Vocabulary questions.

Using the methods of Strategy 3, choose the correct definition of each italicized word as it is used in the context of this reading.

_____ 1. *goldbrick* (paragraph 4):

    a. shirk responsibility   c. create wealth

    b. create something worthless   d. work hard

_____ 2. *miseducation* (paragraph 15):

    a. higher education   c. missed opportunities

    b. poor teaching   d. absences from school

_____ 3. *compulsory* (paragraph 8):

    a. protective   c. essential

    b. important   d. enforced

_____ 4. *exploitation* (paragraph 8):

    a. development   c. manipulation

    b. utilization   d. management

_____ 5. *charade* (paragraph 7):

    a. reproduction   c. fake situation

    b. guessing game   d. make-believe

Comprehension questions.

Choose the answer that best completes each statement.

_____ 1. Holt gives several important *negative* lessons that he says school teaches children from the very beginning. Which of these is **not** one of those negative lessons?

    a. Getting correct answers from children is the school's main concern.

    b. Learning for its own sake is more important than getting good grades.

    c. Appearing to be busy and productive is what counts.

    d. Teachers are not there to answer children's questions.

_____ 2. Holt says that "school is a long lesson in how to turn yourself off" because

    a. the only way children can get correct answers is by ignoring what their peers are doing.

    b. the only way children can hold on to their individual interests is by escaping into their own daydreams.

    c. children ignore what interests them in order to do well in school.

    d. children are not allowed to turn on the electronic games they like to play.

_____ 3. Holt knows people would object to his proposals for abolishing required schooling. One answer he gives to answer these objections is that schools would have to

    a. improve in order to attract children to come.

    b. get jobs for children that would pay them to go to schools.

    c. improve their monitoring to tell which children were not attending.

    d. encourage teachers and students to become friends.

_____ 4. Holt says that children can learn on their own, without teachers giving them lessons and grades. He supports his idea by saying that if left alone, children

    a. compare what they do with what they see more skilled people doing.

    b. become more sensitive to their own needs and fear being judged by teachers.

    c. get answers in such subjects as math and science by trial and error.

    d. become dependent on the experts they come in contact with.

_____ 5. Holt says in the second-to-last paragraph that "the most important questions of our time are not *in* the curriculum, not even in the hot-shot universities. . . ."Given Holt's concerns in this reading, we can assume that one of these "most important questions" would be

    a. How can we have a well-trained work force for our future economy?

    b. What technologies can be used in schools to improve children's learning?

    c. What historical events led to the adoption of compulsory school attendance?

    d. How can we get along well with others in our families, in our neighborhoods, and in our larger communities?

Chapter 7

Reading 12: Optimism: The Great Motivator

Vocabulary questions.

Using the methods of Strategy 3, choose the correct definition of each italicized word as it is used in the context of this reading.

_____ 1. *surmounting* these challenges (paragraph 9):

    a. overdoing   c. overcoming

    b. suffering   d. suppressing

_____ 2. falling into *apathy* (paragraph 3):

    a. lack of interest   c. pity

    b. laziness   d. lack of ability

_____ 3. a too-*naïve* optimism (paragraph 3):

    a. sophisticated   c. stupid

    b. inexperienced   d. sad

_____ 4. *tempered* by experience (paragraph 9):

    a. irritated   c. moderated

    b. enraged   d. characterized

_____ 5. not a fixed *property* (paragraph 10):

    a. quality   c. material possession

    b. piece of real estate   d. ground

Comprehension questions.

Choose the answer that best completes each statement.

_____ 1. Biondi rebounded from the bad news about his performance, whereas his teammates did not because

　　a. he had trained more consistently and was therefore stronger.

　　b. he had a healthier attitude that allowed him to learn from his mistakes.

　　c. he had better luck in the successive events than his teammates did.

　　d. his too-naïve optimism gave him the illusion that he couldn't fail.

_____ 2. Martin Seligman's study of incoming freshmen at the University of Pennsylvania showed that success in college

　　a. depends on your having a good explanatory style for convincing professors to raise your grade when necessary.

　　b. comes from being highly motivated no matter what level of ability or talent you have.

　　c. depends on a combination of high SAT scores and good high school grades.

　　d. comes from a combination of reasonable intelligence and the ability to keep going after experiencing defeat.

_____ 3. You can strengthen your self-efficacy by

　　a. becoming competent in any endeavor, which in turn allows you to avoid making mistakes.

　　b. making yourself more efficient by organizing your activities and practicing more self-discipline.

　　c. becoming more competent in any endeavor, which in turn gives you the confidence to take on greater challenges.

　　d. being willing to say no to new things you have never tried before.

_____ 4. Goleman shows that optimism is "an emotionally intelligent attitude" because

    a. optimists analyze a failure to see what specific things they
could do better next time, whereas pessimists assume there is
nothing they can do to improve.

    b. optimists overlook their failures and pretend they didn't happen,
whereas pessimists dwell on the things they can do to improve.

    c. pessimists, in general, tend to have lower intelligence than
optimists and to do more poorly on tests than optimists do.

    d. optimists don't expect to face any failures and therefore they
are usually able to avoid disappointment.

_____ 5. You can assume from this reading that one of the following
people would be an example of a "too-naïve" optimist:

    a. A student in first-year chemistry expects to get a higher grade
on her next test by going to the campus tutoring center.

    b. An insurance salesman expects to find a certain percentage of
his clients in a good mood.

    c. An artist expects to sell some of the paintings that were
chosen for a local art show.

    d. A 16-year-old skater who just started skating two months ago
expects to enter the Olympics next year.

Reading 13: How Conscious Is Thought?

Vocabulary questions.

Using the methods of Strategy 3, choose the correct definition of each italicized word as it is used in the context of this reading.

_____ 1. they rely on *intuition* (paragraph 3):

a. payment for college	c. quick and ready insight
b. feelings of extrasensory perception	d. foreboding

_____ 2. this sort of mental *inertia* (paragraph 6):

a. laziness	c. exhaustion
b. energy	d. solidity

_____ 3. guides you toward a . . . *hypothesis* (paragraph 4):

a. overactivity	c. logic
b. theory	d. instinct

_____ 4. feel like a sudden *revelation* (paragraph 4):

    a. sudden victory   c. surprising confession

    b. surprising discovery   d. unlikely description

_____ 5. *cognitive* psychologists have . . . devoted . . . study (paragraph 9):

    a. having to do with animal behavior

    b. having to do with sexual desire

    c. having to do with how we think

    d. having to do with how we experience emotion

Comprehension questions.

Choose the answer that best completes each statement.

_____ 1. We can handle automatic routines, such as knitting, driving a car, and typing, "without thinking," because our mind can perform "subconscious processes." These subconscious processes

    a. require us to do more than one thing at one time.

    b. require our constant attention.

    c. are those that deal with childhood experiences.

    d. can be brought into consciousness when necessary.

_____ 2. Nonconscious processes are defined as those which

    a. remain outside our awareness.

    b. babies are born with, but lose within the first three years.

    c. can easily be brought into consciousness.

    d. are performed as we sleep.

_____ 3. The authors tell us that intuition probably goes through two stages. In the first stage, a problem sets off certain memories and/or knowledge in your mind that you're not yet aware of and leads you to a hunch. In the second stage,

    a. you lose consciousness and wait for the solution to come to you.

    b. your thinking becomes more conscious as a possible solution presents itself.

    c. you work out the solution using pencil and paper.

    d. your memory of the correct answer becomes clear to you.

_____ 4. According to Ellen Langer, *mindlessness* is a kind of "mental inertia." She says that mindlessness causes problems because it keeps people from

a. seeing they can accomplish more tasks by learning to do them without engaging all parts of their mind.

b. noticing when something in a familiar situation has changed and thus requires them to change their behavior.

c. understanding that they must become conscious of each part of the tasks they take on in daily life.

d. focusing on their feelings and emotions rather than relying so much on mental activities.

_____ 5. Three of the four following activities are ones that people often do "mindlessly." Which is the *one* activity most people would **not** do "mindlessly"?

a. brush teeth

b. drive a car

c. give an oral report in front of a class

d. copy notes from the blackboard

Chapter 8

Reading 14: A Letter to My Teacher

Vocabulary questions.

Choose the phrase that best expresses the special connotation of each italicized word as it is used in this reading.

_____ 1. I didn't need the *agony* of a presentation (paragraph 8):

a. shows how much she looks forward to the presentation

b. shows how terrified she feels at having to give a presentation

c. demonstrates her annoyance at having to do the assignment

d. shows how unwilling she is to do the presentation

_____ 2. Becoming a student was a great *scheme* (paragraph 4):

a. indicates her sense that she is fooling others about her abilities

b. indicates her confidence in herself as a student

c. shows her cleverness in preparing for college

d. shows her willingness to admit she is a liar

_____ 3. But I was already halfway down the hall to the bathroom where I promptly *lost my lunch* (paragraph 6):

    a. gives the sentence a bitter, almost angry feeling

    b. gives the sentence a sad, almost tragic feeling

    c. contributes to the formal, somewhat academic expression in her writing

    d. contributes to the vivid and informal expression in her writing

_____ 4. I'd *scraped together* enough credits (paragraph 14):

    a. emphasizes how hard it was to get the credits

    b. emphasizes how dangerous it was to get the credits

    c. shows her impatience with the academic system

    d. shows her confidence in dealing with the academic system

_____ 5. I *steamed* out of the classroom (paragraph 19):

    a. is used instead of "walked" to show how hot it was

    b. is used instead of "walked" to show her anger

    c. contributes to the formal, somewhat academic expression in her writing

    d. contributes to the sad, depressed feeling in her writing

Comprehension questions.

Choose the answer that best completes each statement.

_____ 1. Boyes decided to take her first college course primarily because

    a. she was tired of working two jobs.

    b. she found an interesting course in the catalog she'd fished out of the trash.

    c. she could get health insurance for herself and her children.

    d. she wanted to prove the statisticians wrong about her not belonging in college.

_____ 2. Her teacher's enthusiasm made Boyes want to stay in her class, even though her teacher

    a. demanded too much homework.

    b. was boring and repetitive.

    c. was nervous and inexperienced.

    d. relied too much on student presentations.

_____ 3. For her first oral presentation, Boyes avoided speaking in front of the class by taping her talk. For her second presentation,

    a. she played a tape of Lucretia Mott speaking to a crowd of Quakers.

    b. she had to be herself, no tape, no taking on a persona.

    c. she was too nervous to speak and had to leave the classroom.

    d. she pretended to be the person she was talking about.

_____ 4. You could summarize the most important improvements her teacher made in her teaching by the third course Boyes took with her by saying that

    a. she knew her students and engaged them in ongoing discussions.

    b. she had control over the class and prevented any whispering and sleeping.

    c. she gave up student oral presentations in favor of her own well-organized lectures.

    d. she made more demands on her students and expected class discussions to last long after the official end of class.

_____ 5. From the way Boyes handled the first two oral presentations, you can infer that

    a. she had been physically abused by her father for not doing an oral presentation in high school.

    b. she was clever and resourceful in meeting the demands of a course.

    c. she really was an imposter in the classroom.

    d. she was unable to fulfill the assignments and wasn't yet ready for college.

Reading 15: Why Men Don't Last

Vocabulary questions.

Using the methods of Strategy 3, choose the correct definition of each italicized word as it is used in the context of this reading.

_____ 1. he was a *dogged* exerciser (paragraph 1):

    a. companionable   c. aggressive

    b. determined   d. canine

_____ 2. *dispelling* the mood (paragraph 5):

    a. forgetting

    b. casting spells

    c. cheering up

    d. clearing away

_____ 3. men get *enamored of* the action (paragraph 13):

    a. stolen by

    b. rejected by

    c. disgusted by

    d. captivated by

_____ 4. feel powerful and *omnipotent* (paragraph 13):

    a. able to eat anything

    b. unable to perform sexually

    c. unstoppable

    d. violent

_____ 5. the *polarized*, weak-strong imagery (paragraph 18):

    a. opposite

    b. cold

    c. north-south

    d. dissimilar

Comprehension questions.

Choose the answer that best completes each statement.

_____ 1. In some ways men take better care of themselves than women do; they

    a. turn inward and ruminate, rather than expressing their emotions.

    b. are less likely to be overweight, to die of a chronic disease, or to die in a traffic accident.

    c. exercise more, are less likely to be overweight, and suffer from fewer chronic diseases.

    d. exercise more, are less likely to abuse alcohol or drugs, and suffer from fewer chronic diseases.

_____ 2. The fact that men are four times as likely to die from suicide as women is used as one piece of evidence to show

    a. men's tendency to "self-destruct."

    b. the greater numbers of suicide attempts made by men than by women.

    c. men's ability to take better care of themselves than women do.

    d. men's tendency to distract themselves by acting rather than thinking.

_____ 3. In paragraphs 11 through 14, Angier explains the theory that men die earlier than women do because they are greater risk takers. Then she criticizes that theory by saying that

    a. men who complete a suicide attempt tend to fit a personality profile that is relatively high on the "openness-to-experience" scale.

    b. men outnumber women in the use of alcohol and drugs that numb pain and provide escape from anxiety.

    c. men outnumber women in using food to self-medicate and avoid uncomfortable feelings.

    d. there is a negative stigma attached to men who fail at a suicide attempt.

_____ 4. Dr. William S. Pollock blames "the persistent image of the dispassionate, resilient, action-oriented male—the Marlboro Man" for many of men's self-destructive tendencies. He says this image

    a. is responsible for the great rise in lung cancer caused by smoking.

    b. limits the ways in which boys and men are allowed to experience and express their feelings.

    c. takes away a boy's or man's ability to experience any feelings.

    d. teaches them that the only response to any difficult situation is to consider suicide.

_____ 5. Dr. Pollock implies that boys and men would be better off if they could express a wider range of emotions because

    a. they would be able to rely on women more.

    b. they would be more able to treat women as equals.

    c. they would be more able to display the bravado our culture demands of them.

    d. they would be able to ask for help when they need it.

Chapter 9

Reading 16: Why People Don't Help in a Crisis

Vocabulary questions.

Using the methods of Strategy 3, choose the correct definition of each italicized word as it is used in the context of this reading.

_____ 1. her *assailant* takes half an hour to murder her (paragraph 1):

    a. accomplice   c. enemy

    b. attacker   d. gang

_____ 2. the studied *nonchalance* of patients (paragraph 15):

    a. lack of concern   c. informality

    b. anxiety   d. lack of desire

_____ 3. experimental evidence *corroborates* this (paragraph 11):

    a. confirms   c. settles

    b. corrects   d. disputes

_____ 4. if he is to *intervene* in an emergency (paragraph 9):

    a. intrude   c. get out of

    b. escape   d. get involved

_____ 5. to test this *diffusion*-of-responsibility theory (paragraph 21):

    a. shattering   c. spreading

    b. escaping   d. thinning out

Comprehension questions.

Choose the answer that best completes each statement.

_____ 1. Before the research done by Darley and Latané, the explanations given about why people don't help in a crisis included the fact that

    a. we now live in such large urban areas that crime can easily go undetected.

    b. television violence has caused people to become insensitive to the needs of others.

    c. bystanders to emergencies are different from the rest of us.

    d. we now live in such large urban areas that we lose our sense of connection with others.

_____ 2. A person is less likely to even notice there is an emergency if he or she is in a crowd rather than being alone because

a. everyone is trying to appear more calm and more unconcerned than they are feeling in order not to seem foolish for being too anxious.

b. everyone has become so alienated by today's urban society that they ignore any crisis around them.

c. with so many people in the way, it's difficult to see the details of what is going on.

d. everyone is trying to appear more calm and unconcerned than they are feeling in order not to avoid helping out.

_____ 3. The diffusion-of-responsibility theory is based on the idea that

a. people have lost their sense of responsibility as a result of their poor upbringing.

b. the presence of others makes a person feel that he or she doesn't need to help because someone else in the group will.

c. the presence of others makes a person feel embarrassed to show any concern or anxiety.

d. people would rather escape responsibility than face it.

_____ 4. The people who failed to report that an individual they heard on tape was apparently having a seizure

a. were more upset than the people who did report the emergency.

b. were callous and unconcerned about what they had heard.

c. showed few signs of concern or nervousness about what they had heard.

d. were examples of the unconcerned, depersonalized *homo urbanus*.

_____ 5. We can infer from the final paragraph that the purpose of the authors in writing is to show that

a. we must begin training our children to take care of themselves because they can't expect help from others.

b. the influence of the crowd can give us confidence and strength when we're facing an emergency.

c. we can resist the influence of the crowd and help out in an emergency.

d. we can resist the influence of the crowd and keep from looking foolish in an emergency.

Reading 17: Mother Tongue

Vocabulary questions.

Using the methods of Strategy 3, choose the correct definition of each italicized word as it is used in the context of this reading.

_____ 1. I should *hone* my talents (paragraph 19):

    a. center in on   c. prepare

    b. whet   d. perfect

_____ 2. carefully *wrought* grammatical phrases (paragraph 3):

    a. inflicted   c. formed

    b. spelled   d. twisted

_____ 3. her *impeccable* broken English (paragraph 13):

    a. unsoiled   c. unpronounceable

    b. embarrassing   d. flawless

_____ 4. find out about a *benign* tumor (paragraph 14):

    a. kindly   c. benevolent

    b. harmless   d. cancerous

_____ 5. the most *bland* combinations of thoughts (paragraph 16):

    a. dull and boring   c. second rate

    b. exciting and new   d. lacking in salt

Comprehension questions.

Choose the answer that best completes each statement.

_____ 1. The "different Englishes" Amy Tan tells us about in this reading include all of the following except

    a. the baby talk she uses with little children.

    b. the way she speaks with her mother.

    c. the way she writes her books.

    d. the way she speaks to business professionals.

_____ 2. She sees problems with the term *limited English* for the kind of English her mother speaks because

    a. the term doesn't convey the richness and complexity of her mother's speech.

    b. the term doesn't convey the severe difficulties her mother has had with English.

    c. *limited* implies that her mother can never improve her English.

    d. *limited* applies to the English of all immigrants, so it doesn't convey the way the Chinese learn to speak the language.

_____ 3. Her experiences translating for her mother taught her that if you speak limited English,

    a. stockbrokers and medical personnel are particularly insensitive to limited English speakers.

    b. you will win friends because of your charming accent.

    c. people don't take you as seriously as if you speak "perfect" English.

    d. people will automatically refuse to do business with you.

_____ 4. Tan had a slow start in writing fiction partly because her schools

    a. expected her to excel in English and criticized her when she did not.

    b. did not allow her to take tests with fill-in the blank sentence completions.

    c. expected her to do well in math and science, not in English.

    d. encouraged her to learn to write in Chinese rather than English.

_____ 5. From what Tan tells us we can infer that

    a. she is still bitter about the disgrace she felt when translating for her mother.

    b. she now looks back with fondness and values what her mother gave her as she grew up.

    c. she has learned to get over caring about what her mother thinks of her.

    d. she has decided that she would rather write just for her mother and ignore a wider reading public.

Chapter 10

Reading 18: Police and the Community

Vocabulary questions.

Using the methods of Strategy 3, choose the correct definition of each italicized word as it is used in the context of this reading.

_____ 1. are viewed as *deviant* (paragraph 6):

      a. remarkable   c. clever

      b. abnormal   d. criminal

_____ 2. more *affluent* neighborhoods (paragraph 14):

      a. mainstream   c. underprivileged

      b. valuable   d. prosperous

_____ 3. *permissive* law enforcement (paragraph 10):

      a. lax   c. lazy

      b. accommodating   d. bureaucratic

_____ 4. *adherents* of the Santaría religion (paragraph 6):

      a. campaigners   c. believers

      b. possessors   d. opponents

_____ 5. crime prevention can be *enhanced* (paragraph 12):

      a. diminished   c. imagined

      b. improved   d. included

Comprehension questions.

Choose the answer that best completes each statement.

_____ 1. According to this reading, during the last quarter century, police work has become more complicated because of

      a. new types of technology.

      b. the lack of competent instructors in police academies.

      c. the growth of the suburbs throughout the United States.

      d. changes in the racial and ethnic makeup of the United States.

_____ 2. There are often problems of communication between the police and racial and ethnic minorities because

    a. the police have stereotypes about the minorities.

    b. the minorities have stereotypes about the police.

    c. both the police and the minorities have learned to avoid stereotyping.

    d. both the police and the minorities hold on to stereotypes about one another.

_____ 3. One main challenge for the police in developing effective working relations with new immigrants involves

    a. getting the children of immigrants to go to school and learn English.

    b. learning about new immigrants' cultural practices so they can adapt them for American holidays and celebrations.

    c. dealing with strange cultural practices that are considered normal in the immigrants' homeland.

    d. dealing with strange cultural practices the immigrants must learn in order to become Americans.

_____ 4. A major reason why people in inner-city neighborhoods tend to resent the police is because they feel

    a. the police abuse the residents instead of protecting them.

    b. the police fail to learn new languages spoken by the immigrants who live there.

    c. the police are always there to arrest a wrongdoer, but don't turn up in court to testify against him or her.

    d. the police are rarely seen in these inner-city neighborhoods.

_____ 5. The authors say that "treating people according to stereotypes, rather than as individuals, creates tensions that harden negative attitudes." This statement implies that it would ease these tensions if there were

    a. less contact between individuals from hostile groups so they can avoid hurting one another.

    b. more contact between individuals from hostile groups so they could get to know each other as individuals.

    c. more contact between individuals from hostile groups so they could confirm the stereotypes they already had.

    d. less contact between people from hostile groups to allow time away from one another to heal the differences.

Reading 19: Don't Let Stereotypes Warp Your Judgments

Vocabulary questions.

Using the methods of Strategy 3, choose the correct definition of each italicized word as it is used in the context of this reading.

_____ 1. *perpetuated* in the advertisements we read (paragraph 8):

    a. put an end to   c. kept alive

    b. enabled   d. appropriated

_____ 2. formed rigid *preconceptions* (paragraph 11):

    a. methods of prevention   c. guesses

    b. prejudices   d. beginnings

_____ 3. *inimitable* and independent fashion (paragraph 12):

    a. incomparable   c. enviable

    b. superior   d. reproducible

_____ 4. *delve* into the main asset of a telephone stock swindler (paragraph 4):

    a. skim over   c. burrow

    b. fumble around   d. look deeply

_____ 5. he stands triumphantly *vindicated* (paragraph 11):

    a. guiltless   c. justified

    b. wronged   d. victorious

Comprehension questions.

Choose the answer that best completes each statement.

_____ 1. In the study conducted with Columbia and Barnard students, the students' opinions about the girls in the photos depended on whether a girl had an ethnic or an "American" name attached to her photo. This study shows that

    a. the students who observed these photos had themselves been stereotyped by others.

    b. stereotypes have the power to affect the way we see people.

    c. stereotypes help us see the characteristics of certain groups of people.

    d. the girls with ethnic backgrounds had less attractive names than American girls have.

_____ 2. The main reason Heilbroner gives for the power of stereotypes to influence our thinking is that

    a. they help us make sense of the complex and confusing world around us.

    b. they make us feel more confident about our opinions of others.

    c. they make us able to understand jokes made about certain groups.

    d. they show us the exceptions that prove the rule.

_____ 3. Heilbroner thinks it is not only harmful to the other person when you stereotype him or her, it is harmful to *you* because

    a. you start to see everyone as a dangerous enemy.

    b. you hurt yourself when you do harm to others.

    c. you lose your ability to be yourself and think in an independent way.

    d. you lose your ability to classify people into useful categories.

_____ 4. Heilbroner ends this reading by telling us how to avoid being too influenced by stereotypes. All of the following are guidelines he gives **except**

    a. become more aware of the standardized pictures in our heads.

    b. become suspicious when we think an exception has "proven" the rule.

    c. be careful of making generalizations about people.

    d. become more aware of the exception that "proves" the rule.

_____ 5. Heilbroner says in paragraph 15, "Often we do not even know that we have let a stereotype lapse until we hear someone saying, 'all so-and-so's are like such-and-such,' and we hear ourselves saying, 'Well—maybe.'" He means by this statement that

    a. it takes several different experiences with individuals from a group to make us certain we can know the group's characteristics.

    b. you have to agree with someone else when they tell you their stereotype about a group.

    c. it is impossible to let go of stereotypes because we keep hearing ourselves saying we believe they're true.

    d. it takes several different experiences with individuals from a group to realize our view of the group has been modified.

Chapter 11

Reading 20: Terror Unlimited

Vocabulary questions.

Using the methods of Strategy 3, choose the correct definition of each italicized word as it is used in the context of this reading.

_____ 1. tossed it over the *precipice* (paragraph 13):

    a. rock face   c. edge

    b. mountain   d. prow of a ship

_____ 2. no way to recover from this *calamity* (paragraph 23):

    a. disaster   c. fall

    b. panic   d. mistake

_____ 3. possessed by a sense of *vertigo* (paragraph 10):

    a. dread   c. fear of heights

    b. dizziness   d. weakness

_____ 4. it was *visceral* (paragraph 10):

    a. logical   c. gut level

    b. mortal   d. intuitive

_____ 5. sense of *imminent* insanity (paragraph 11):

    a. on the horizon   c. under consideration

    b. on the table   d. about to happen

Comprehension questions.

Choose the answer that best completes each statement.

_____ 1. The idea for the particular episode when Cahill was asked to be on the proposed ABC talk show, called *Stories*, was that the guests would tell

    a. stories of their bouts with panic disorders.

    b. tales of experiences with flying saucers.

    c. tales of daring adventure.

    d. stories of being forest rangers in national parks.

_____ 2. Cahill agrees to tape the show and put himself through the "worst case of stage fright in television history" because

    a. he desperately needed the money, since his panic disorder had kept him from working.

    b. he hoped to overcome his fears by facing them directly.

    c. he had always wanted to work with the TV host Hugh Downs.

    d. he wanted to get exposure on television for his book about ascending El Capitan in Yosemite.

_____ 3. When he says he and his photographer companion were going to "yo-yo" El Capitan, Cahill means they would

    a. rappel first, then climb back up the cliff wall.

    b. use a bungee cord attached to the top of the cliff wall to bounce up and down.

    c. use special climbing equipment nicknamed "yo-yos" to keep themselves attached to each other during the climb.

    d. climb the cliff wall first, then rappel back down.

_____ 4. The principal danger Cahill had tried to avoid by running the long rope through the carabiner that held his seat harness together was

    a. the climber would lose his footing and fall to his death.

    b. the climber's companion would be unable to stay connected to him and help him up to the summit.

    c. the climber would fall backward and end up hanging upside down.

    d. the rope would get sawed in half by the sharp granite rock and snap in two.

_____ 5. Cahill explains the fear that came from his panic disorder felt worse than real physical fear because

    a. when facing a real life-or-death situation, there is almost always something you can do.

    b. when dealing with uncontrolled anxiety you must avoid other people.

    c. real life-or-death situations cause such terror that you forget all your imaginary fears.

    d. a diagnosed panic disorder requires taking medication that may produce dangerous side effects.

Chapter 12

Reading 21: A Global Green Deal

Vocabulary questions.

Using the methods of Strategy 3, choose the correct definition of each italicized word as it is used in the context of this reading.

_____ 1. poverty *alleviation* (paragraph 2):

    a. progress   c. upturn

    b. expansion   d. lessening

_____ 2. other environmental *abominations* (paragraph 13):

    a. hostilities   c. crises

    b. outrages   d. activists

_____ 3. too many *entrenched* interests (paragraph 10):

    a. well-established   c. preset

    b. variable   d. shallow

_____ 4. while benefiting from *subsidies* (paragraph 11):

    a. financial support   c. scholarships

    b. donations   d. advantages

_____ 5. *redundant* German coal miners (paragraph 14):

    a. extravagant   c. surplus

    b. moderate   d. traditional

Comprehension questions.

Choose the answer that best completes each statement.

_____ 1. According to Hertsgaard, world poverty is central to our environmental problems because

    a. poor people don't have the education they need in order to take care of the environment.

    b. the wealthier nations will send the poorer nations shoddier goods that cause more environmental pollution.

    c. as poor people in the rest of the world seek to improve their lives, the increased production of consumer goods will cause even more damage to the environment.

    d. the demands of poor people in the rest of the world will cause wars, resulting in more environmental damage.

_____ 2. Hertsgaard uses several examples to show that increased efficiency can help the environment *and* be good for business. All these are examples he uses **except**

    a. better lighting and insulation.

    b. efficient windows and use of solar energy.

    c. wind power for generating electricity.

    d. a super-refrigerator.

_____ 3. According to Hertsgaard, the U.S. government could promote increased efficiency in automobiles by

    a. buying only hybrid-electric or hydrogen-fuel-cell cars for official government use.

    b. demanding more fuel-efficient sport utility vehicles.

    c. encouraging auto manufacturers to produce more green-colored cars to symbolize their commitment to the environment.

    d. buying only older cars rather than adding to the wasteful production of new cars.

_____ 4. Hertsgaard calls the Green Deal "revenue neutral," but some people would still oppose it, including

    a. people who do not believe in any kind of government subsidies.

    b. people and corporations who benefit from the way things currently work.

    c. people and corporations who fear they would fail to get government contracts.

    d. people who view environmentalists as dangerous extremists.

_____ 5. At the end of the article, Hertsgaard emphasizes that this plan is a way to buy time until we can make more "deep-seated" changes. Underlying all these changes is this most important change in attitude:

    a. recognizing that environmentalism is only one factor in determining how we create a just society.

    b. understanding the importance of educating our youth in the science and technology needed to solve our environmental problems.

    c. seeing that all human beings deserve the comfortable life we have in the United States.

    d. seeing human beings as just one part of the fragile system of life on earth.

Reading 22: Infernal Paradise

Vocabulary questions.

Using the methods of Strategy 3, choose the correct definition of each italicized word as it is used in the context of this reading.

_____ 1. *infernal* paradise (title):

     a. inside   c. heavenly

     b. hellish   d. deadly

_____ 2. the earth had . . . *disgorged* its contents (paragraph 2):

     a. poured out   c. banished

     b. driven out   d. gagged on

_____ 3. owns *adjacent* land (paragraph 11):

     a. scenic   c. far-off

     b. public   d. neighboring

_____ 4. the sharp *perimeter* of cliffs (paragraph 1):

     a. boundary   c. straight line

     b. passage   d. frontier

_____ 5. the strange *topography* of Haleakala Crater (paragraph 3):

     a. staging   c. landscape

     b. volcano   d. climate

Comprehension questions.

Choose the answer that best completes each statement.

_____ 1. It was very hard for Kingsolver to judge distances on her walk down the volcanic crater because

     a. the trail was so steep and curved, she could hardly see what was coming.

     b. it was an empty land, with no familiar landmarks, so a spot on the trail ahead could be a person or a huge boulder.

     c. the high temperatures made the heat give off mirages that confused the eye.

     d. the lava was still flowing, and its curving paths caused confusion to the onlooker.

_____ 2. In paragraph 4, Kingsolver says that Hawaii's natural history is made up of a series of "unceasing invasions." During the very first of these invasions,

  a. the native plants and animals were crowded out by species from other parts of the world.

  b. the fragile plant and animal species that had existed underwater were quickly taken over by species from other islands.

  c. plants or animals arrived over sea or on the wind, and a few were able to survive on the islands' bare rock.

  d. Europeans brought plant and animal species from Europe.

_____ 3. Haleakala Crater still looks much as it did two thousand years ago because it is protected as national parkland and also because

  a. the landscape there is not good for growing pineapples and orchids.

  b. the federal and state governments have spent millions to restore the landscape there.

  c. the slopes of the crater are so steep that they can only support a few types of native plants.

  d. feral pigs and rats can't get to the plants that grow there.

_____ 4. According to Kingsolver, Hawaii has been losing its native species of plants at such a high rate that

  a. you can now visit Hawaii and never see a single native Hawaiian plant.

  b. botanists are now trying to classify the species that have already been lost.

  c. researchers were called in to see what could be done to stop this mass plant extinction.

  d. tourists are required to prove they have no native plants, such as the silversword, in their suitcases.

_____ 5. Kingsolver tells of a creature in paragraph 10 "that walked upright and killed whenever it found an easy mark." *Creature* here refers to

  a. an egg-eating rodent.

  b. an ape.

  c. a human being.

  d. a nēnē goose.

Chapter 13

Reading 23: Hip-Hop Nation

Vocabulary questions.

Using the methods of Strategy 3, choose the correct definition of each italicized word as it is used in the context of this reading.

_____ 1. what is musically *palatable* (paragraph 12):

     a. disgusting   c. charming

     b. edible   d. acceptable

_____ 2. the violence and *misogyny* (paragraph 13):

     a. anti-authoritarianism   c. anti-rape message

     b. anti-woman feeling   d. anti-youth message

_____ 3. the *genre's* political content (paragraph 14):

     a. genius   c. leader

     b. musician   d. type

_____ 4. rap's *entrepreneurial* spirit (paragraph 5):

     a. imaginative   c. commercial

     b. entertaining   d. end user

_____ 5. ads are becoming *stealthier* (paragraph 6):

     a. sneakier   c. more relaxed

     b. sexier   d. more violent

Comprehension questions.

Choose the answer that best completes each statement.

_____ 1. According to Farley, Madison Avenue has

     a. played a large part in the rise of hip-hop culture.

     b. neglected hip-hop in favor of more mainstream music.

     c. excited hip-hop fans who love having their own culture sold back to them.

     d. lost millions of dollars in trying to promote hip-hop culture.

_____ 2. Clive Campbell, also known as Kool Herc, made some innovations that gave hip-hop its start. His crucial innovation was to

   a. do dance moves that included spinning on his head and shoulders.

   b. use two turntables to create harmony out of the two songs being played.

   c. charge money for after-school parties held in a rec room.

   d. recite rhymes over the "break," or instrumental part of the records he was playing.

_____ 3. Grandmaster Flash improved on what Kool Herc had done by

   a. using break dancers, called b-boys, who danced during the break in the music.

   b. inventing "scratching"—spinning a record back and forth to create a scratchy sound.

   c. introducing violent anti-woman and anti-police rap lyrics.

   d. wearing harem-style balloon pants that gave rap its early, characteristic style.

_____ 4. Farley believes the violence and exploitation of women in much of rap music is

   a. damaging to the youth of our society.

   b. a necessary part of the political message of this type of music.

   c. no longer a major part of what we hear in today's rap music.

   d. a part of the traditions of American popular culture.

_____ 5. When Bob Law says, in paragraph 14, "It's just, 'Give me a piece of the action,'" he means

   a. the main concern for today's rap musicians is to encourage social activism and challenge governmental authority.

   b. rap musicians of today are more interested in getting rich and famous than in making a political statement.

   c. more and more rap musicians are getting in trouble with the law.

   d. young, would-be rap musicians are apt to get involved in gambling.

Reading 24: Buy This 24-Year-Old and Get All His Friends Absolutely Free

Vocabulary questions.

Using the methods of Strategy 3, choose the correct definition of each italicized word as it is used in the context of this reading.

_____ 1. the most precious *commodity* for advertisers (paragraph 2):

    a. product

    b. favor

    c. medium

    d. assistance

_____ 2. longer *prenuptial* agreements (paragraph 9):

    a. before marriage

    b. before birth

    c. before legislation

    d. before buying

_____ 3. they want "very *chic* shows . . ." (paragraph 6):

    a. well-dressed

    b. feminine

    c. stylish

    d. traditional

_____ 4. a *sinister* ad for a Website (paragraph 7):

    a. horrifying

    b. abnormal

    c. imaginative

    d. disturbing

_____ 5. emphasis on the *affluent* (paragraph 11):

    a. influential

    b. wealthy

    c. young

    d. inner city

Comprehension questions.

Choose the answer that best completes each statement.

_____ 1. According to the reading, the Oscar ceremony is known as the Super Bowl for women because

    a. advertisers introduce clever new ads during the Oscar ceremony commercial breaks, just as they do during the Super Bowl commercial breaks.

    b. the Oscar ceremony can deliver well over half of the nation's women to advertisers.

    c. over half of the audience who watches the Oscar ceremony is female.

    d. women bet on which actors will win Oscars in the same way that men bet on which team will win the Super Bowl.

_____ 2. In paragraph 3, Kilbourne says, "The primary purpose of the mass media is to sell audiences to advertisers." The most direct way that media producers sell audiences to advertisers is by

    a. getting consumers to buy their products.

    b. making popular radio and television programs and producing best-selling magazines and newspapers.

    c. placing ads in advertising and industry publications.

    d. developing strong relationships between the advertising departments of TV, radio, and print media and their potential advertisers.

_____ 3. Of the following people, the one *most* likely to find out that one of his or her favorite television programs is being canceled is

    a. an unmarried 34-year-old.

    b. a 40-year-old living in a rural area.

    c. an 18-year-old living in a city.

    d. a 30-year-old suburbanite.

_____ 4. One of the effects of the current advertising practices as Kilbourne describes them is that

    a. poor people are barely visible in our media.

    b. people between the ages of 18 and 24 are rarely seen in our media.

    c. children's TV programming has become more violent.

    d. more and more famous people refuse to endorse products.

_____ 5. In paragraph 6, Kilbourne says, "The target audience that appeals to advertisers is becoming more narrow all the time." She says this is because advertisers want to reach people who have money to spend and who

    a. are mature enough to see through the exaggerated messages that advertisements make.

    b. make the decisions about when to purchase big household items.

    c. are mature enough to want to keep to the brands they are used to.

    d. are young enough so advertisers can imprint their company's brand name on them as early as possible.

Chapter 14

Reading 25: Don't Further Empower Cliques

Vocabulary questions.

Using the methods of Strategy 3, choose the correct definition of each italicized word as it is used in the context of this reading.

_____ 1. vent their *grievances* (paragraph 1):

      a. errors   c. sorrows

      b. complaints   d. demonstrations

_____ 2. quick to *venerate* kids (paragraph 9):

      a. despise   c. benefit from

      b. spare   d. honor

_____ 3. *carnage* at Columbine High (paragraph 1):

      a. suicide   c. bloodbath

      b. tragedy   d. terror

_____ 4. school's unqualified *adulation* (paragraph 6):

      a. idolization   c. discipline

      b. acceptance   d. affection

_____ 5. unsocial or *iconoclastic* (paragraph 9):

      a. withdrawn   c. revolutionary

      b. unacceptable   d. angry

Comprehension questions.

Choose the answer that best completes each statement.

_____ 1. The people Lefkowitz interviewed in the New Jersey suburb told him they thought the young men boasted at school about raping the young retarded woman because

      a. they had watched so much media violence, they had lost any sense of right and wrong.

      b. they had come to feel all-powerful because the school and parents had treated them like special celebrities for so long.

      c. they were as retarded as the young woman and didn't think what they'd done was wrong.

      d. underneath their boasting, they felt tremendous guilt and wanted people to find out so they would be punished.

_____ 2. The assemblies at Glen Ridge High School

    a. honored their athletes far more than their good students.

    b. were held for special lectures to try to prevent what had happened to the retarded woman from happening again.

    c. honored their good students far more than their athletes.

    d. were held to celebrate the individuality and diversity of all its students.

_____ 3. Lefkowitz says the kind of student that schools tend to value most is

    a. aggressive, arrogant, and intensely competitive.

    b. studious, obedient, and well organized.

    c. imaginative, creative, and artistic.

    d. well rounded, friendly, and diligent.

_____ 4. One of Lefkowitz's suggestions for making other students—those not in the favored cliques—feel more valued by schools would be to

    a. help underachieving students succeed by improving tutoring and counseling services.

    b. get all students involved in intellectual and artistic endeavors as well as athletic activities.

    c. honor achievements that are intellectual and artistic as well as athletic.

    d. develop classes for improving peer social interactions.

_____ 5. Lefkowitz says highly valued athletes at a school like Glen Ridge get away with behaviors that others would have been punished for. The most likely of these behaviors would be

    a. hitting a teacher.

    b. selling drugs on school grounds.

    c. bringing a gun to school.

    d. cheating on a test.

Part II Additional Readings

Reading II-A: Think Big

Vocabulary questions.

Using the methods of Strategy 3, choose the correct definition of each italicized word as it is used in the context of this reading.

_____ 1. spend your life on *skid row* (paragraph 16):

    a. the last row in the classroom

    b. a dangerous place, prone to landslides

    c. a rundown place for drunks and the homeless

    d. a small, cramped row house

_____ 2. went through . . . *trauma* (paragraph 20):

    a. ordeal   c. horror

    b. damage   d. injury

_____ 3. *tenement* building (paragraph 20):

    a. two-story   c. public housing

    b. antiquated   d. skyscraper

_____ 4. I tried to appear *indifferent* (paragraph 58):

    a. undistinguished   c. uncaring

    b. unexceptional   d. unconcerned

_____ 5. everyone *acknowledged* as the smartest kid (paragraph 67):

    a. admitted   c. resented

    b. recognized   d. envied

Comprehension questions.

Choose the answer that best completes each statement.

_____ 1. Carson got off to a bad start in his fifth grade class because

    a. he had had poor teaching in his previous school, and he was upset over his parents' recent separation.

    b. he was so shy and afraid of speaking in class, he never answered the teacher.

    c. he felt he was so much in his older brother's shadow that he didn't want to try to do well.

    d. he had been known as the "dumbest kid in class" in his previous school, and he had come to accept the label.

_____ 2. In order to improve Carson's and his brother's school performance, their mother made them read two library books a week in
addition to requiring them to

a. stop watching any TV.

b. watch only two TV programs a week.

c. cut back on their TV viewing and get all their homework done
before watching any TV.

d. go to the after-school program and watch the educational TV
programs provided there.

_____ 3. Carson's mother was able to get her boys to follow her strict plan
because

a. she promised them they would move back to their old house if
they did what she said.

b. the boys were afraid they would be severely beaten if they
didn't do what their mother told them to do.

c. they had been aware they were failing, and they were eager to
follow a plan designed to improve their learning.

d. the boys took it for granted they would obey what their
mother told them to do.

_____ 4. Carson began to realize his reading could be of practical use as
well as being entertaining when

a. he was able to fix the kitchen sink for his mother by reading a
simple book about plumbing.

b. he finally got a good grade on his reading test.

c. he could help his older brother learn the names of rocks they
found along the railroad tracks.

d. he was able to tell the class what he'd learned about obsidian
from reading books about rocks.

_____ 5. From the reading, you can assume that Carson's mother was

a. uncertain of how to help her sons improve in school because
of her own limited education.

b. certain of her plan to help her boys improve in school because
it had come to her through prayer.

c. unreasonably strict, using harsh physical punishment to get
the boys to follow her plan.

d. compassionate and flexible, allowing her boys to follow their
own version of her plan for helping them improve in school.

Reading II-B: Does Media Violence Desensitize Children to Violence?

Vocabulary questions.

Using the methods of Strategy 3, choose the correct definition of each italicized word as it is used in the context of this reading.

_____ 1. scientists who study *arousal* (paragraph 5):

   a. fear   c. taking away

   b. impression   d. stimulation

_____ 2. *desensitize* (title):

   a. make one descend

   b. make one more violent

   c. make one less sensitive

   d. make one more sensitive

_____ 3. treat individuals with *phobias* (paragraph 10):

   a. panic disorder

   b. feelings of depression

   c. irrational fears

   d. fear of high places

_____ 4. heart rate and the speed of intervention . . . were . . . *correlated* (paragraph 14):

   a. corrected   c. unrelated

   b. connected   d. partnered

_____ 5. *genocide* still comes . . . on our nightly news (paragraph 15):

   a. deliberate extermination of a whole racial or ethnic group

   b. bloodbath caused by a mass murderer

   c. dying out of a whole racial or ethnic group

   d. mass suicide

Comprehension questions.

Choose the answer that best completes each statement.

_____ 1. In paragraph 4 Levine tells us that graduate student research assistants needed to be taught how to identify aggressive acts because

a. media violence has become so routine that normal people don't always recognize pushing, shoving, or hitting as aggression.

b. graduate students are under such pressure that their own aggressive thoughts prevent them from looking objectively at what would normally be called aggression.

c. pushing, shoving, or hitting are not defined by the researchers as real acts of aggression.

d. the graduate students had spent most of their childhood and adolescence reading books and studying and were unfamiliar with normal childhood acts of aggression.

_____ 2. A psychologist who helps a person overcome an unreasonable and deep-seated fear may

a. help the person see the irrationality of their fears.

b. use a process of gradually exposing the person to the frightening stimulus.

c. help the person forget the fear by substituting good thoughts and feelings.

d. place the person in a situation that will shock them out of their fear.

_____ 3. In the study described in paragraphs 11 and 12, two groups of children watched television violence. The study showed all of the following except

a. the heavy TV viewers were less anxious after seeing aggressive acts than the light TV viewers.

b. the light TV viewers were less anxious after seeing aggressive acts than the heavy TV viewers.

c. the light TV viewers were more aroused than the heavy viewers even during nonviolent segments of the boxing movie.

d. it was harder for the light TV viewers to recover from having seen the TV violence.

_____ 4. Researchers Ronald Drabman and Margaret Thomas studied children's capacity to show care and concern for others. In this study they found that

a. children who grow up in households where parents fight a lot are likely to ignore the fighting that other children do.

b. after watching TV violence children are likely to seek help from an adult when they see other children fighting.

c. children who come from stable, loving households are likely to be less influenced by TV violence than those who come from unstable homes.

d. children who are exposed to more violent TV programming may be more likely to think that fighting is a normal way to resolve conflict.

_____ 5. Levine suggests that one result of our becoming less sensitive to violence is that we

a. are more likely to become aggressive with others when we become impatient over minor annoyances.

b. may be less likely to fear blood and gore, and so be better equipped to help out in a medical emergency.

c. may be less likely to recognize an emergency situation when it comes up in real life.

d. become more withdrawn and depressed because of our lack of trust of others.

Reading II-C: Powder

Vocabulary questions.

Using the methods of Strategy 3, choose the correct definition of each italicized word as it is used in the context of this reading.

_____ 1. and she *relented* (paragraph 2):

a. admitted defeat   c. begged to differ

b. gave in   d. stood firm

_____ 2. bitter, blinding *squalls* (paragraph 2):

a. screams   c. flakes

b. gusts   d. ice patches

_____ 3. now you're an *accomplice* (paragraph 19):

    a. champion   c. soul mate

    b. buddy   d. partner in crime

_____ 4. my father would *wheedle* (paragraph 33):

    a. sing   c. coax

    b. chatter   d. inform

_____ 5. all persuasion, no *coercion* (paragraph 34):

    a. force   c. meanness

    b. harassment   d. influence

Comprehension questions.

Choose the answer that best completes each statement.

_____ 1. The first half of the story shows the following strengths and weaknesses that seem characteristic of the father:

    a. amusing and loving toward his son, but lacking in intelligence and common sense.

    b. devoted husband and father, but devious and prone to illegal activity.

    c. fun loving, devoted to his son, but immature, impulsive.

    d. intelligent and responsible, but with a cruel streak.

_____ 2. When his father says to the boy, "Now, you're an accomplice . . . we go down together,"

    a. he is being sarcastic with his son in order to get back at the boy for wanting to be home with his mother on Christmas Eve.

    b. he is just kidding with his son, knowing the boy is a little afraid to go against what the state trooper told them.

    c. he is gently warning the boy that there may be serious trouble ahead.

    d. he is trying to make his son feel bad by scaring him that there will be trouble ahead.

_____ 3. The fact that the father is driving this particular car is important in portraying his character because it shows that

    a. the immediate pleasure of driving a wonderfully made, expensive sports car is more important to him than keeping his promise to sell it.

    b. the father hopes his son will learn to drive the way he does.

    c. the father often needs to have a car that handles extremely well in order to get away from the police.

    d. the father has been careful and wise to keep a car that handles well in snowy conditions.

_____ 4. Because one of the main strengths of the son is to "think ahead," he

    a. becomes resigned to being caught by the state troopers, and so begins to relax.

    b. becomes more and more anxious about being caught by the state troopers.

    c. thinks about what his mother will say when they get home late.

    d. worries about how he'll get his homework assignments done, since he and his father will get home so late.

_____ 5. The final paragraph of the story shows

    a. the fear and anxiety the boy feels about driving through "the unbroken surface of the snow."

    b. the author creating a magical ending for the story, when the car turns into a boat that can go downhill in the snow.

    c. the admiration and love the boy has for his father and the pleasure he takes in being driven through the snow.

    d. the love and sadness the boy feels for his father, knowing that soon after this Christmas Eve, his mother will split up with his father.

Part III Additional Readings

Reading III-A: Stress Management and Wellness

Vocabulary questions.

    Using the methods of Strategy 3, choose the correct definition of each italicized word as it is used in the context of this reading.

_____ 1. emotional *arousal* (paragraph 10):

  a. fear   c. enthusiasm

  b. impression   d. stimulation

_____ 2. exercise *enhances* well-being (paragraph 16):

  a. creates   c. visualizes

  b. demonstrates   d. improves

_____ 3. these are called *psychosomatic* (paragraph 8):

  a. imaginary   c. mental and emotional

  b. physical   d. intellectual and artistic

_____ 4. their *euphoric* . . . effect (paragraph 15):

  a. wound-up   c. exhilarating

  b. depressing   d. fascinating

_____ 5. this is an interesting *paradox* (paragraph 49):

  a. puzzling contradiction   c. half-hearted effort

  b. untrue statement   d. great comfort

Comprehension questions.

  Choose the answer that best completes each statement.

_____ 1. *Stress reactivity* is defined as the physical reaction to a stressor that causes several changes in the body. All of the following are physical changes that stress causes except:

  a. you perspire under the arms and on the forehead.

  b. your breathing becomes more rapid and shallow.

  c. your vision becomes blurred.

  d. your heart beats faster.

_____ 2. According to the model of stress discussed in this chapter, once a life situation is perceived as distressing, the first level of stress is

  a. physiological arousal.

  b. emotional arousal.

  c. negative consequences.

  d. psychosomatic illness.

_____ 3. Exercise is especially helpful in managing stress because

    a. it can take away stress at every level on the stress model.

    b. it enhances your body image so you can relax about your appearance.

    c. it gives you a bigger appetite for more nutritious foods.

    d. it can be done no matter what life situation you are facing.

_____ 4. The relaxation techniques described in the chapter are all ways for you to

    a. use stretching or weight lifting to relax the muscles throughout your body.

    b. use the mind to influence the body or the body to influence the mind.

    c. use the right equipment and techniques for massaging your muscles.

    d. develop the self-esteem that is the basis for having a relaxed attitude toward life.

_____ 5. The most harmful characteristic of people who are Type A personalities is

    a. anxiety.   c. depression.

    b. competitiveness.   d. hostility.

Reading III-B: Learning the River

Vocabulary questions.

Using the methods of Strategy 3, choose the correct definition of each italicized word as it is used in the context of this reading.

_____ 1. was sure to *subside* (paragraph 4):

    a. settle down   c. collapse

    b. build up   d. immerse

_____ 2. even *remorseful* (paragraph 4):

    a. pathetic   c. shameful

    b. regretful   d. sad

_____ 3. of all the *eluding* . . . objects (paragraph 13):

    a. breaking   c. escaping

    b. annoying   d. challenging

_____ 4. a *conspicuous* dead tree (paragraph 13):

     a. plain   c. fine-looking

     b. ancient   d. noticeable

_____ 5. *merged* into the general forest (paragraph 13):

     a. escaped   c. grown

     b. mingled   d. blended

Comprehension questions.

Choose the answer that best completes each statement.

_____ 1. When Twain says he didn't know Walnut Bend had "any partic-ular shape," Mr. Bixby got so mad that

     a. his gun went off accidentally.

     b. he told Twain he was fired.

     c. he used every swear word he could think of.

     d. he went off to do some shooting practice to get over his anger.

_____ 2. Mr. Bixby explains to Twain that it's actually an advantage the shapes he sees along the river change "every three seconds" because

     a. the changing shapes keep the pilot from getting bored and losing concentration.

     b. if the shapes changed more slowly, they could be confused with other steamboats approaching.

     c. by knowing exactly how and where the shape will change, you can know where to steer the boat.

     d. when one shape splits into two parts, you can steer the boat between the two parts.

_____ 3. Once Twain learns the shape of the river, he is shocked to find out Mr. Bixby has yet another type of information that must be memorized. He must also know

     a. the speed of the current at each point.

     b. the depth of the water at each point.

     c. the speed of each steamboat as it approaches the boat he is on.

     d. the names of each farm and plantation along the river.

_____ 4. When Twain finds out he must learn this new type of information, he says

    a. he'd have to be a miracle worker and a genius to be able to learn all that.

    b. he might as well become a stage magician and leave the steamboat business.

    c. he might as well try to become a famous painter and artist as learn all that.

    d. he's not strong enough to carry all the books he'd need to learn all that.

_____ 5. From what we see of Mr. Bixby in this excerpt, we can see he's the kind of teacher who is basically

    a. mean spirited and determined to make his apprentice feel bad.

    b. lazy and determined to make his apprentice do all the work.

    c. bad tempered and unwilling to apologize when he loses control of his temper.

    d. good hearted and dedicated to getting his apprentice to learn.

Part IV Additional Readings

Reading IV-A: Traveling

Vocabulary questions.

Choose the phrase that best expresses the unusual way the italicized words are used in this reading.

_____ 1. "A white man was standing right beside her, but on the other side of *the invisible absolute racial border.*" (paragraph 13):

    a. the unseen line, known as the Mason-Dixon line, that divided the North and the South

    b. the mental line drawn because of prejudice against black people

    c. the border between Mexico and the United States

    d. the line in the bus dividing the black section from the white section

_____ 2. "[T]he movement of the passengers was *like a tide that sometimes ebbed and now seemed to be noisily rising.*" (paragraph 12):

  a. the bus traveled on a road that passed by the shoreline where the ocean's waves could be seen rising and falling

  b. the passengers would become sleepy and quiet and then wake up and get noisy

  c. the bus driver controlled the black passengers by sending them to the back, but then they would start demanding to come forward

  d. the numbers of passengers seemed to dwindle and now were on the increase

_____ 3. "Lady, I wouldn't of *touched that thing with a meat hook.*" (paragraph 13):

  a. the white man reveals his shameless prejudice by his brutal remark about the baby

  b. the white man tries to protect the baby from being harmed by a dangerous instrument

  c. the narrator reveals her attempt to aid the young black mother by telling her to stay away from that prejudiced white man

  d. the young black mother agrees with the narrator that she must keep her baby from getting harmed by the white man

_____ 4. "Oh, this *world will end in ice*" (paragraph 14) refers to Robert Frost's poem "Fire and Ice" that begins, "Some say the world will end in fire/Some say in ice." Paley says the world will end in ice because

  a. after hearing what the man said to her, she feels the cold, bitter hatred in his heart

  b. after being on the unheated bus for hours, she feels the bitter cold of the winter weather

  c. after hearing the baby cry, she realizes the cold, hard world this baby will face

  d. after leaving the bus, she slips on the ice

_____ 5. "I told them: how it happened on just such a journey . . . that I first knew my *grandson.*" (paragraph 20):

    a. her daughter and grandson had traveled with her on her trip down south

    b. when she was on her bus trip, she fell asleep and dreamed of having a black grandson one day

    c. her daughter's son, by a black father, reminds her of the black baby she held on the bus

    d. her grandson became a civil rights activist because of hearing about the prejudice she encountered on that bus trip

Comprehension questions.

Choose the answer that best completes each statement.

_____ 1. The time periods of this reading are

    a. the 1920s, the 1930s, and the 1940s.

    b. the 1920s, the 1940s, and the 1990s.

    c. the 1920s and the 1940s.

    d. the 1940s and the 1990s.

_____ 2. Paley's mother was supposed to change seats once the bus got to Washington because

    a. she was getting out at the next stop and needed to make room for incoming passengers.

    b. she was seen as being too friendly with black people and would have to be separated from them.

    c. she was sitting in the back of the bus, where only black people were supposed to sit.

    d. she hadn't paid for a first-class seat.

_____ 3. On her own bus trip, Paley was going

    a. back to New York to see her grandson.

    b. to Miami Beach to see her husband who was in the military.

    c. to Virginia to see her brother who was in the military.

    d. to South Carolina or Georgia depending on where the military had sent her husband.

_____ 4. When Paley was on the bus trip and held the young mother's baby on her lap,

    a. she felt uncomfortable at first about holding a baby of a different race.

    b. the baby cried, so she had to give him back to his mother.

    c. the baby reminded her of holding her younger brother when he'd been small.

    d. she thought about what it would be like to hold her own baby.

_____ 5. The most obvious qualities we see in both Paley's mother and Paley in this reading are

    a. creativity, intelligence, and imagination.

    b. efficiency, intelligence, and broadmindedness.

    c. resilience, determination, and practicality.

    d. compassion, courage, and broadmindedness.

Reading IV-B: Managing Workforce Diversity

Vocabulary questions.

Using the methods of Strategy 3, choose the correct definition of each italicized word as it is used in the context of this reading.

_____ 1. treat everyone *equitably* (paragraph 3):

    a. fairly   c. logically

    b. efficiently   d. sensibly

_____ 2. *diversify* their workforces (paragraph 4):

    a. spread out   c. make bigger

    b. specialize   d. get more variety

_____ 3. be *scrupulously* fair (paragraph 4):

    a. thoroughly   c. minimally

    b. morally   d. absurdly

_____ 4. there is no *consensus* yet (paragraph 5):

    a. cooperation   c. negotiation

    b. agreement   d. confrontation

_____ 5. there are sometimes *repercussions* (paragraph 6):

    a. impressions   c. consequences

    b. achievements   d. suggestions

Comprehension questions.

Choose the answer that best completes each statement.

_____ 1. In addition to gender, race, and ethnicity as categories of difference, the authors also mention

   a. people of different educational backgrounds and intellectual abilities.

   b. people from different parts of the country who have different accents.

   c. people from other countries who need special work visas.

   d. people of different ages and physical abilities.

_____ 2. One reason that organizations find it advantageous to have a diverse workforce is

   a. they can reach a wider range of consumers.

   b. they can get cheaper labor.

   c. workers from different groups can share their customs and traditions with one another.

   d. workers from different groups can be pitted against each other during battles between management and workers.

_____ 3. In reporting on the progress U.S. companies are making toward greater diversity of their workforce, the authors say that

   a. most companies have made good headway on diversifying their workforce.

   b. there are new general guidelines about how to diversify that companies must follow.

   c. most companies have diversified so well that white males are very concerned about their jobs.

   d. very few companies have successfully diversified their workforce.

_____ 4. The purpose of diversity training is to

   a. help employees from diverse groups learn to blend in with the attitudes and behaviors of the corporate culture.

   b. let employees from diverse groups get specialized training in new technologies.

   c. improve employees' understanding of differences in attitudes and behaviors among the people they work with.

   d. help managers hire the best people from diverse groups.

_____ 5. The reason some diversity training programs have negative repercussions may be that they have focused too much on

    a. issues such as race or gender.

    b. the backlash against women.

    c. ending affirmative action.

    d. integrating training into daily routines.

Reading IV-C: Perhaps the World Ends Here

Vocabulary questions.

Choose the phrase that best expresses the unusual way the italicized words are used in this reading.

_____ 1. *The world begins at a kitchen table.* No matter what, we must eat to live. (stanza 1):

    a. The world of a child begins when it can leave its mother and start eating at a table with grownups.

    b. A kitchen table may be all the furniture people need, since eating meals is such an important thing we do at home.

    c. As human beings come into the world by being born on a table, and when we die we are prepared for burial on a table.

    d. Our world as human beings depends on gathering together, helping one another, and feeding one another.

_____ 2. *Wars have begun and ended at this table.* (stanza 8):

    a. During wartime, people could hide under the table to protect themselves during bombing raids.

    b. High-level talks about war and peace are carried out by government officials sitting around a table.

    c. People sat around the table discussing what to do to defend themselves against enemies and how to make peace with enemies.

    d. People sat around arguing about who should be the one to inherit the table.

_____ 3. *Our dreams drink coffee with us as they put their arms/ around our children.* (stanza 6):

    a. We imagine the lovers of our dreams coming to live with us, drinking coffee in the morning and helping care for the children.

    b. As we sit drinking coffee, ghosts from the past come back to watch over the children.

    c. While we sit around the table drinking coffee, we share our hopes and dreams for our children with one another.

    d. As we sit at the table drinking our morning coffee, we remember dreaming about our children during the night.

_____ 4. *They* [our dreams] *laugh with us.* (stanza 6):

    a. They are ghosts who play humorous tricks on us.

    b. They are like kindly parents smiling down on us.

    c. They are like demanding teachers making fun of us.

    d. They are like former friends who have been jealous of us and can now laugh at our problems.

_____ 5. *This table has been a house in the rain, an umbrella in the sun* (stanza 7):

    a. The table is brought out in the summertime for children to play house with it.

    b. The table is the last protection in a bombed-out house.

    c. Sharing food around the table makes people forget they are living in a harsh climate.

    d. The sense of community and support found from people gathering around the table sustains us through all kinds of situations.

Comprehension questions.

Choose the answer that best completes each statement.

_____ 1. When Harjo says that children are given instructions at the table about "what it means to be human," she means

    a. parents show children that providing food for others is a basic way of expressing love and generosity.

    b. parents talk to their children at the table about how to get along with others and how to express themselves well.

    c. children learn how to get along with others as they play around the table and begin joining in conversation with adults and other children.

    d. children learn table manners as early as possible, so they can join the adults' conversation around the table.

_____ 2. Men and women are "made" at the table because young people

    a. learn to enter into adult relationships through sharing hopes, discussing problems, finding solutions.

    b. learn how to hold their own in an argument and become independent thinkers.

    c. start flirting with one another at the table as a preliminary to dating.

    d. use the kitchen table as a place to do their homework.

_____ 3. The table is a place "to hide in the shadow of terror" or "a place to celebrate a terrible victory" because

    a. it provides a strong barrier against falling debris and can stand up against wild victory celebrations.

    b. your family and friends who gather around the table support you in bad times as well as good times.

    c. people can hide their feelings by eating and drinking at the table instead of having to talk about what's going on.

    d. eating well gives us strength to face our troubles and pleasure when our troubles are over.

_____ 4. From what we see in the poem, we could assume the home life referred to includes all of the following except

    a. considerable wealth.

    b. a rural setting.

    c. a large family.

    d. respect for traditional customs.

_____ 5. Part of the meaning of the last stanza of the poem (stanza 11) is that

    a. we must recognize the sweetness of life or it will be taken away from us.

    b. we don't want to die having been so wrapped up in our own laughter and tears that we don't think of the others "at the table" with us.

    c. we only appreciate the gifts of life when we no longer have them.

    d. we most fully appreciate all the gifts of life by sharing them with others.

Part V Additional Readings

Reading V-A: Imprinting: A Form of Learning

Vocabulary questions.

Using the methods of Strategy 3, choose the correct definition of each italicized word as it is used in the context of this reading.

_____ 1. learn the *traits* (paragraph 2):

    a. characteristics   c. tricks

    b. treatments   d. environments

_____ 2. eggs that were artificially *incubated* (paragraph 2):

    a. warmed   c. fertilized

    b. sat on   d. brewed

_____ 3. *stimulus* for the innate following response (paragraph 4):

    a. desire   c. ability

    b. inspiration   d. impulse

_____ 4. stimulus for the *innate* following response (paragraph 4):

    a. unusual   c. likely

    b. inborn   d. biological

_____ 5. the local *embellishments* (paragraph 7):

    a. environments   c. added extras

    b. basic outlines   d. decorations

Comprehension questions.

Choose the answer that best completes each statement.

_____ 1. Konrad Lorenz devised an experiment to

    a. see how the following response is developed in certain young animals.

    b. test the ability of humans to influence the young of another species.

    c. test the ability of humans to artificially incubate geese.

    d. determine what happens when young animals are trained after the critical period for learning has passed.

_____ 2. *Imprinting* is defined as a kind of learning that occurs over a relatively brief period of time during which the baby animal learns

    a. to identify who its parent is.

    b. to mark out its own territory.

    c. to make embellishments in the innate patterns of its species.

    d. to make a specific response to certain aspects of the environment.

_____ 3. The goslings regarded Lorenz as "one of their own" because

    a. he was the figure they first encountered during the critical period for imprinting.

    b. after rescuing them when their mother died, he hand-fed them.

    c. they left their mother for Lorenz because he was the largest figure they saw during the critical period for imprinting.

    d. they were raised by Lorenz's lab technicians and so their preference was for male humans.

_____ 4. The jackdaw's actions showed how it had learned species identification when it would

    a. follow Lorenz around the barnyard.

    b. reject all the female jackdaws in the area.

    c. try to feed Lorenz some wormy pulp.

    d. "courtship feed" a female jackdaw.

_____ 5. If white-crowned sparrows are not exposed to the song of their species during the critical period,

    a. they will not learn to sing at all.

    b. they will sing normally, since the songs are an innate pattern in that species.

    c. they will become isolated from other birds and go into a decline.

    d. they will produce abnormal songs, lacking in finer details.

Reading V-B: The Gorilla's Embrace

Vocabulary questions.

Using the methods of Strategy 3, choose the correct definition of each italicized word as it is used in the context of this reading.

_____ 1. mastered at least the *rudiments* (paragraph 4):

      a. facts   c. details

      b. basics   d. fine points

_____ 2. the rudiments of baboon *propriety* (paragraph 4):

      a. behavior   c. friendliness

      b. good manners   d. biology

_____ 3. *somber* adult males (paragraph 5):

      a. dull   c. solemn

      b. sad   d. gloomy

_____ 4. some small comfort from my *proximity* (paragraph 8):

      a. estimate   c. nearness

      b. behavior   d. distance

_____ 5. this exploration was . . . *poignant* (paragraph 9):

      a. upsetting   c. charming

      b. tragic   d. touching

Comprehension questions.

Choose the answer that best completes each statement.

_____ 1. The work Smuts does is defined as "scientific research" because

      a. she documents every type of animal behavior by recording, filming, and note taking.

      b. it is designed to gain objective information about the animals' lives that other scientists using the same methods would be likely to find.

      c. it is designed to allow her to bring the animals out of the wilds and into a scientific laboratory.

      d. she brings her equipment from her scientific laboratory into the animals' environment.

_____ 2. It was hard to retain a completely detached, neutral view of the baboons she was studying because

    a. the baboons expected her to join with them as a part of their social organization.

    b. sometimes the baboons became too aggressive and threatened to attack her.

    c. she sometimes found the baboons' behavior too disgusting.

    d. the baboons frustrated her because they kept running away from her.

_____ 3. The main lesson Smuts gains from the gorilla's embrace was

    a. how surprisingly sweet the breath of a gorilla could be.

    b. how impossibly long the arms of a gorilla are as they wrapped around her.

    c. how much intimacy and respect there can be between a "wild" animal and a human being.

    d. how little cause she had for feeling terrified of the gorilla.

_____ 4. Smuts had proof of how well the baboons got to know and trust her as an individual human being when

    a. she visited the same group five years later and they accepted her while running away from the fellow scientist they'd never seen before.

    b. a female baboon came up to her and embraced her.

    c. she would return after trips into town with a fellow scientist and they would run away from him but greet her warmly.

    d. she fell asleep among them, and they covered her with leaves.

_____ 5. Smuts's fundamental belief about the way we should interact with animals is that we should

    a. look for the human attributes in them.

    b. train them so the human attributes in them can be developed.

    c. accept them as the independent, wild creatures they are.

    d. treat them like individuals, using the care and respect we would like to be treated with ourselves.

Reading V-C: Víctor

Vocabulary questions.

Underline the metaphor or simile in each of these sentences from the reading.

1. Víctor lifts his unbuttoned shirt over his head. He hides underneath it [the shirt] like the lizard under the frond of the elephant fern. (paragraph 4)

2. [She] speaks Spanish as if she were worried there might be a little stone in among the words that will crack her mouthful of white teeth. Each word is carefully spoken and cleanly finished before the next one starts. (paragraph 7)

3. "You know better," his father agrees. Víctor recognizes the look that says, You have put your foot down beside a wasp nest. Watch out. (paragraph 25)

4. Víctor feels silence tingling the inside of his mouth—as if he had taken a bite of the bejuco de gato and his tongue had gone numb. (paragraph 42)

5. The day is waning and there is still so much to show. The bamboo knock against one another like knuckles rapping on a desk asking for attention. (paragraph 54)

Stories depend a great deal on implied meanings, so most of these questions require making some inferences.

Comprehension questions.

Choose the answer that best completes each statement.

_____ 1. This visitor to the national park is different from the other turistas that Don Bernardo and Víctor have been used to because

  a. she is from the United States and does not speak Spanish well, so she doesn't understand much of what they say.

  b. she was sent to find out how good a director of parks Don Bernardo is.

  c. she just wants to take home some beautiful orchids or bromeliads.

  d. she is not just coming to see the beautiful flowers and birds; she wants to "do good" by assessing Víctor's education.

_____ 2. What is the most likely reason this turista keeps missing what Víctor is trying to show her?

a. She is too full of her own ideas about what is important to be able to look and listen carefully to what she's being shown.

b. Her purpose in coming was to tutor Víctor, not to see the forest.

c. She is too distracted by her fears about getting stung by the wasps she's been warned about.

d. She is too busy trying to get Víctor to pick her some flowers.

_____ 3. The association between wasps and the campana flower is first mentioned

a. early in the story, when the lady sees it as the first flower she wants to know about.

b. in the middle of the story, when the lady decides to take the path to the river.

c. later in the story, when the lady and Don Bernardo are discussing illiteracy by the river.

d. near the end of the story, when Víctor tries to warn the lady not to climb up an overgrown mule track.

_____ 4. A typical way for Víctor to react to being put on the spot about his lack of school knowledge is to

a. run away from the lady.

b. try to make her laugh by joking about the names of plants.

c. find a flower to cut down for the lady.

d. point out another plant, flower, or bird.

_____ 5. Remember that the term *irony* refers to the use of words to convey meaning that is opposite to—or very different from—the literal meaning. There is irony in the last sentence of the story, when Víctor runs to get the book of things "he has tried to teach [the lady] about the rain forest" because the well-educated lady

a. was really the one who could have taught Víctor what he would need to survive in the modern world.

b. was a rain forest expert who had come to teach Don Bernardo techniques for conserving the forest.

c. knew only book learning and was therefore unable to learn from what an illiterate boy, Víctor, could have taught her.

d. had been "taught" a harsh lesson by Víctor when he made the wasps attack her.

Part VI Additional Readings

Reading VI-A: Pitching Messages

Vocabulary questions.

Using the methods of Strategy 3, choose the correct definition of each italicized word as it is used in the context of this reading.

_____ 1. the *generic* identifier (paragraph 2):

     a. specific   c. common

     b. necessary   d. critical

_____ 2. the *proliferation* of 24-hour television service (paragraph 18):

     a. demand   c. entertainment

     b. spreading   d. nuisance

_____ 3. *stealth* advertisements (paragraph 20):

     a. sneaky   c. expensive

     b. annoying   d. imaginative

_____ 4. *oblivious* to the sales component (paragraph 20):

     a. forgetful   c. inconsiderate

     b. unaware   d. conscious

_____ 5. tire of advertising *omnipresence* (paragraph 21):

     a. blaring noise   c. everywhere, all the time

     b. deception and lies   d. enormous power

Comprehension questions.

Choose the answer that best completes each statement.

_____ 1. According to David Ogilvy, it is important to create a brand image because it

     a. helps people choose a distinctive product among others like it; find a special product.

     b. makes companies imagine new products that people would like to buy.

     c. helps keep a healthy competition among similar products.

     d. makes a product seem special while being the same as others like it.

_____ 2. The ad for the lonely Maytag repairman that dramatized the company's slight advantage in reliability was an example of

   a. the unique selling proposition (USP) with a hollow claim.

   b. the unique selling proposition (USP) that really had a unique point.

   c. a campaign to appeal to the lowest common denominator.

   d. a campaign based on positioning to blue-collar workers.

_____ 3. Two methods that advertisers use to increase the effectiveness of redundancy are

   a. trailing and positioning.

   b. barrages and bunching.

   c. cluttering and posting.

   d. positioning and targeting.

_____ 4. The *unique selling proposition* (USP) claim for Colgate toothpaste was that it "Cleans Your Breath While It Cleans Your Teeth." Vivian calls that a "hollow" claim because

   a. it creates a claim out of thin air and says it repeatedly as if the competition doesn't have it.

   b. it creates a product from scratch and advertises it before it's fully developed.

   c. the benefits of the product are so exaggerated as to have almost no basis in fact.

   d. the claims are made about defective, or "hollow," products.

_____ 5. Advertisers are trying new methods, such as stealth ads and alternative media, to try to deal with

   a. ad clutter.

   b. the proliferation of 24-hour television service.

   c. the lowest common denominator.

   d. the ethical problems involved in advertising.

Reading VI-B: The Argument Culture

Vocabulary questions.

Using the methods of Strategy 3, choose the correct definition of each italicized word as it is used in the context of this reading.

_____ 1. an *adversarial* frame of mind (paragraph 2):

     a. unfriendly   c. approachable

     b. argumentative   d. dangerous

_____ 2. war metaphors *pervade* our talk (paragraph 4):

     a. spread through   c. go around

     b. attack   d. include

_____ 3. debates and fighting *predominate* (paragraph 12):

     a. fail   c. take the lead

     b. take place   d. oppress

_____ 4. enjoy verbal *sparring* (paragraph 12):

     a. questioning   c. gossiping

     b. rattling   d. arguing

_____ 5. the *proliferation* . . . of technology (paragraph 13):

     a. demand   c. spreading

     b. entertainment   d. nuisance

Comprehension questions.

Choose the answer that best completes each statement.

_____ 1. The problem with our "argument culture," according to Tannen, is that it portrays issues as two-sided debates that

     a. give unfair advantage to one side.

     b. allow only two people to have their say.

     c. have to follow strict debating format.

     d. don't allow room for a middle ground.

_____ 2. According to Tannen, the main reason high-tech communication "pulls us apart" is that

    a. it increases the anonymity between the sender and receiver of information.

    b. it frustrates communication because of the constant technical breakdowns.

    c. there is a growing split between those people who have the latest high-tech devices and those who don't.

    d. it allows so many annoying interruptions—often during dinner—that we want to withdraw from having communication with anyone.

_____ 3. Tannen says one of the consequences of our argument culture is that it encourages us to lie. She says this because

    a. people are so overwhelmed by hearing arguments that they've become too confused to know the difference between telling the truth and lying.

    b. people want to win so badly, they are willing to misrepresent facts or even lie.

    c. arguing in order to triumph in a debate causes us to lose sight of the truth, and we lie without even realizing it.

    d. people lose control of their temper during fierce arguments and are later so ashamed of their behavior that they feel they must lie about it.

_____ 4. The main way to overcome the problems caused by our argument culture is to

    a. give people more time to think about issues before expecting them to take a stand one way or the other.

    b. open up discussions to more than just two opposing sides.

    c. provide clear ground rules that give a fair hearing to both sides.

    d. make sure a neutral third party is in any discussion.

_____ 5. In paragraph 22, Tannen changes her wording from "add them to our arsenal" to "the ingredients for our stew." She makes the change because she wants to demonstrate the need to

    a. give women more of a voice in public discourse by using more kitchen metaphors.

    b. avoid clichés and use more creative metaphors.

    c. find new metaphors other than sports and war.

    d. replace sports and war metaphors with metaphors from the kitchen.

Reading VI-C: Memo from Coach

Instead of answering vocabulary questions, do the exercise for this reading under "Work with new words: examples of ironic exaggeration" on page 407.

Comprehension questions.

Choose the answer that best completes each statement.

_____ 1. You first become certain this is a satire, not a normal memo, when the coach says

    a. The fall Pixie League soccer season officially kicks off next week.

    b. I did some valuable networking and came away truly "pumped."

    c. your 9-year-old daughter should now be able to [a] run a mile in under five minutes with cinder blocks attached to each ankle (lower body).

    d. Note: Live ammunition will be used at the Thursday practice.

_____ 2. The memo covers normal categories of coaching activities. All of the following are included in the categories in the memo **except**

    a. sportsmanship.　　　　c. nutrition.

    b. practice schedule.　　　d. drugs.

_____ 3. Satire is a form of irony. But the coach Buckley has created in his satire doesn't use an ironic tone. Instead, the coach's tone is

    a. serious.　　　　　　　　c. humorous.

    b. enthusiastic.　　　　　　d. informative.

_____ 4. An example of a real behavior or attitude that Buckley makes fun of is

    a. children dreaming of become superathletes.

    b. parents wanting the best for their children.

    c. coaches' poor writing ability.

    d. parents putting undue pressure on their children to excel.

_____ 5. It's probable that Buckley used 9-year-old girls for the coach's team instead of high school football players because

    a. he knew more about coaching for girls' teams.

    b. they add to the absurd contrast between what the players were being told to do and what they would actually be able to do.

    c. he wanted to appeal to women readers, since they are generally more sensitive to irony.

    d. they would have more appeal to the reader because they're little and cute.

Reading VI-D: The Formation of Modern American Mass Culture

Vocabulary questions.

Using the methods of Strategy 3, choose the correct definition of each italicized word as it is used in the context of this reading.

_____ 1. the most *innovative* and creative (paragraph 1):

    a. ground-breaking   c. up-to-the-minute

    b. imaginative   d. modern

_____ 2. *poignant* and defiant reaction (paragraph 7):

    a. upsetting   c. charming

    b. tragic   d. touching

_____ 3. *nostalgia* for a simpler past (paragraph 8):

    a. sadness   c. remembrance

    b. longing   d. rejection

_____ 4. read more *urbane* magazines (paragraph 19):

    a. crude   c. sophisticated

    b. well-designed   d. tasteful

_____ 5. no *transcendent* purpose (paragraph 26):

    a. tender

    b. apparent

    c. expressive

    d. uplifting

Comprehension questions.

Choose the answer that best completes each statement.

_____ 1. Three features of modern American life were introduced in the 1920s. They were

    a. the phonograph, the vacuum cleaner, and the washing machine.

    b. radio, the phonograph, and the movies.

    c. radio, television, and the telephone.

    d. the movies, television, and computers.

_____ 2. America longed for heroes during this decade because

    a. families had lost so many of their young men during World War I.

    b. the society had grown more impersonal and bureaucratic.

    c. the country was at war.

    d. they needed inspiration to carry on with the hard work most Americans did.

_____ 3. The reading that appealed to a 1920s mass audience—the low-brow audience—included

    a. new styles of poetry.

    b. early forms of science fiction.

    c. self-help books.

    d. confession magazines.

_____ 4. The emergence of the flapper of the 1920s reflected the decade's

    a. changed attitudes about sex.

    b. return to the traditional role for women.

    c. oppression of women at home and in the workplace.

    d. experimentation with legalized prostitution.

_____ 5. Radio programs such as *Amos 'n Andy* promoted racial or ethnic stereotypes because

    a. prejudiced white and nonethnic actors played all the roles on these programs.

    b. people who owned radios tended to be more prejudiced than those in the general population.

    c. the radio programs portrayed caricatures of people from these groups rather than real people.

    d. the programs were intended as propaganda that would support both real and de facto segregation.

BIBLIOGRAPHY

Abbey, Edward. *The Journey Home.* New York: Dutton Signet, 1977.

Ackerman, Diane. *A Natural History of the Senses.* New York: Random House, 1990.

Allen, R. J., and D. Hyde. *Investigations in Stress Control,* 101–105. Minneapolis: Burgess, 1980.

Alvarez, Julia. "Víctor." In *Off the Beaten Path: Stories of Place,* edited by Joseph Barbato and Lisa Weinerman Horak, 243–248. New York: North Point Press, 1998.

Angier, Natalie. "Why Men Don't Last." *New York Times,* February 17, 1999.

Banks, M. S., and P. Salapatek. "Infant Visual Perception." In *Handbook of Child Psychology: Vol. 2. Infancy and Developmental Psychobiology,* 4th ed., edited by M. M. Haith and J. J. Campos, 504. New York: Wiley, 1983.

Beebe, Steven A., Susan J. Beebe, and Diana K. Ivy. *Communication: Principles for a Lifetime.* Boston: Allyn & Bacon, 2001.

Berk, Laura E. *Child Development,* 5th ed. Boston: Allyn & Bacon, 2000.

Boyes, Kate. "Letter to My Teacher." In *Fortitude: True Stories of True Grit,* edited by Malinda Teel. New York: Red Rock Press, 2000.

Buckley, Christopher. "Memo from Coach." *New Yorker,* January 1998.

Cahill, Tim. "Terror Unlimited." *Outside,* August 1999.

Campbell, Neil A., Lawrence G. Mitchell, and Jane B. Reece. *Biology: Concepts and Connections,* 3rd ed. New York: Benjamin Cummings, 2000.

Carson, Ben. *Think Big.* Grand Rapids, MI: Zondervan, 1992.

Cole, George F., and Christopher E. Smith. *Criminal Justice in America,* 2nd ed. Belmont, CA: Wadsworth, 1999.

Coles, Robert. *The Moral Intelligence of Children.* New York: Random House, 1997.

Darley, John M., and Bibb Latané. "Why People Don't Help in a Crisis." *Psychology Today,* December 1968, 2, 54–57, 70–71.

Ebert, Ronald J., and Ricky W. Griffin. *Business Essentials,* 3rd ed. New York: Prentice Hall, 2000.

Egan, Timothy. "When to Campaign with Color." From the series "How Race Is Lived in America." *New York Times,* June 20, 2000.

Ehrlich, Gretel. *The Solace of Open Spaces.* New York: Penguin, 1986.

Farley, Christopher John. "Hip-Hop Nation." *Time,* February 8, 1999.

Frisina, Ellen Tashie. "See Spot Run: Teaching My Grandmother to Read." In *The Short Prose Reader,* 9th ed., edited by Gilbert H. Muller, Harvey S. Wiener, and Igor Webb. New York: McGraw-Hill, 2000.

Goleman, Daniel. *Emotional Intelligence: Why It Can Matter More Than IQ.* New York: Bantam, 1995.

Grabiner, Rebecca. "I Do Not Like to Read, Sam-I-Am." *University of Chicago Magazine,* February 1997.

Greenberg, Jerrold S., and George B. Dintiman. *Wellness: Creating a Life of Health and Fitness.* Boston: Allyn & Bacon, 1997.

Harjo, Joy. *The Woman Who Fell From the Sky.* New York: Norton, 1994.

Heilbroner, Robert L. "Don't Let Stereotypes Warp Your Judgments." *Reader's Digest.*

Henretta, James A., David Brody, Susan Ware, and Marilynn S. Johnson. *America's History,* Vol. 2, 4th ed. New York: Bedford/St. Martin's, 2000.

Henslin, James M. *Essentials of Sociology: A Down-to Earth Approach,* 3rd ed. Boston: Allyn & Bacon, 2000.

Hertsgaard, Mark. "A Global Green Deal." *Time,* Special Edition, Earth Day 2000.

Holt, John. "School Is Bad for Children." *The Saturday Evening Post,* February 8, 1969.

hooks, bell. *talking back: thinking feminist, thinking black.* Cambridge, MA: South End Press, 1989.

James, William. "The Energies of Men." *Science,* N.S. 25 (No. 635, 1907), 321–332.

Kilbourne, Jean. *Can't Buy My Love: How Advertising Changes the Way We Think and Feel.* New York: Touchstone, 1999.

Kingsolver, Barbara. *High Tide in Tucson: Essays from Now or Never.* New York: HarperCollins, 1995.

Lefkowitz, Bernard. "Don't Further Empower Cliques." *Los Angeles Times,* May 2, 1999.

Levine, Madeline. *See No Evil: A Guide to Protecting Our Children from Media Violence.* San Francisco: Jossey-Bass, 1998.

Lewis, Richard, ed. *Miracles: Poems by Children of the English-Speaking World*. New York: Bantam, 1966.

Lopez, Barry. "A Reflection on White Geese." In *The Best of* Outside, edited by the editors of *Outside* Magazine, 307–317. New York: Vintage, 1997.

Lux, Thomas. *New and Selected Poems*. New York: Houghton Mifflin, 1997.

Manguel, Alberto. *A History of Reading*. New York: Viking, 1996.

Martin, James Kirby, Randy Roberts, Steven Mintz, Linda O. McMurry, and James H. Jones. *America and its Peoples: A Mosaic in the Making*, 4th ed. New York: Addison Wesley Longman, 2001.

McKibben, Bill. *The End of Nature*. New York: Random House, 1989.

Merck drug advertisement. *New York Times Magazine*, December 9, 2001.

Paley, Grace. "Traveling." *New Yorker*, September 8, 1997.

Powell, Kevin. An interview conducted by Tony Karon. Time.com (*The Sampler*), September 22, 2000.

Salapatek, P. "Pattern Perception in Early Infancy." In *Infant Perception: From Sensation to Cognition*, edited by L. B. Cohen and P. Salapatek, 201. New York: Academic Press, 1975.

Smuts, Barbara. "The Gorilla's Embrace." *Whole Earth*, Summer 1999, 10–13.

Tan, Amy. "Mother Tongue." *The Threepenny Review*, Fall 1990.

Tannen, Deborah. "The Argument Culture." *USA Today*, March 1, 1998.

Vivian, John. *The Media of Mass Communication*, 6th ed. Boston: Allyn & Bacon, 2002.

Wade, Carole, and Carol Tavris. *Psychology*, 6th ed. New York: Prentice Hall, 2000.

Wallace, Robert A. *Biology: The World of Life*, 7th ed. New York: Addison Wesley Longman, 1997.

Wolff, Tobias. *The Night in Question: Stories*. New York: Knopf, 1996.

Zocor advertising supplement. *New York Times Magazine*, December 9, 2001.

CREDITS

Page	Literary credits
6	"I Do Not Like to Read, Sam-I-Am!" by Rebecca Grabiner, originally appeared in the *University of Chicago Magazine*. Copyright © 1997 by Rebecca Grabiner.
4, 9	"The Voice You Hear When You Read Silently" from *New & Selected Poems* by Thomas Lux. Copyright © 1997 by Thomas Lux. Reprinted by permission of Houghton Mifflin Company. All rights reserved. Previously published in *The New Yorker*.
16	"Forbidden Reading" from *A History of Reading* by Alberto Manguel. Copyright © 1996 by Alberto Manguel. Used by permission of Penguin, a division of Penguin Putnam Inc.
21	"'See Spot Run': Teaching My Grandmother to Read," copyright © 1988 by Ellen Tashie Frisina. Ellen Tashie Frisina is a journalism professor at Hofstra University. Reprinted by permission of author.
59	These poems were first published in *Miracles: Poems by Children of the English-Speaking World*, edited by Richard Lewis. Copyright © 1966 by Richard Lewis.
65	"What Deprived Children Tell Us about Human Nature" from James M. Henslin, *Essentials of Sociology: A Down-to-Earth Approach*, Fourth Edition. Copyright © 2000 by Allyn & Bacon. Reprinted by permission.
72	"The Good Person" from *The Moral Intelligence of Children* by Robert Coles. Copyright © 1997 by Robert Coles. Used by permission of Random House, Inc.
86	"How Babies Use Patterns to See" from *Child Development*, Fifth Edition, by Laura E. Berk. Copyright © 2000 by Allyn & Bacon. Reprinted by permission. Figure 5.1 adapted from M. S. Banks and P. Salapatek, 1983, "Infant Visual Perception" in M. M. Haith and J. J. Campos (eds), *Handbook of Child Psychology: Vol. 2. Infancy and Developmental Psychobiology*, Fourth Edition, New York: Wiley, p. 504. Copyright © 1983 by John Wiley & Sons. Reprinted by permission of John Wiley & Sons, Inc. Figure 5.2 from "Pattern Perception in Early Infancy" by P. Salapatek in *Infant Perception: From Sensation To Cognition, Basic Visual Processes*, Volume 1,

permission of Pearson Education, Inc. Table "Physical Stress Symptoms Scale" from *Investigations in Stress Control*, by R. J. Allen and D. Hyde, 1980, Minneapolis: Burgess, pp. 101–105.

224   "Learning the River" by Mark Twain from *Mississippi Writings* (New York: The Library of America, 1982), pp. 274–279. Originally published in 1883.

238   "Why People Don't Help in a Crisis" by John M. Darley and Bibb Latané. *Psychology Today*, December 1968, 2, 54–57, 70–71. Reprinted with permission from *Psychology Today* Magazine. Copyright © 1968 by Sussex Publishers.

249   "Mother Tongue" copyright © 1990 by Amy Tan. First appeared in *The Threepenny Review*. Reprinted by permission of the author and the Sandra Dijkstra Literary Agency.

259   "Police and the Community" from *Criminal Justice in America, Second Edition*, by George F. Cole and Christopher E. Smith. Copyright © 1999. Reprinted with permission of Wadsworth, an imprint of the Wadsworth Group, a division of Thomson Learning. Fax 800-730-2215.

269   "Don't Let Stereotypes Warp Your Judgments" by Robert L. Heilbroner, was first published in *Reader's Digest*. Reprinted by permission of the author.

277   "Traveling" by Grace Paley, was first published in *The New Yorker*. Copyright © 1997 by Grace Paley.

282   "Managing Workforce Diversity" in *Business Essentials*, Third Edition by Ronald J. Ebert and Ricky W. Griffin. Copyright © 2000. Reprinted by permission of Pearson Education, Inc., Upper Saddle River, NJ.

287   "Perhaps the World Ends Here" from *The Woman Who Fell from the Sky* by Joy Harjo. Copyright © 1994 by Joy Harjo. Used by permission of W. W. Norton & Company, Inc.

303   "Terror Unlimited" by Tim Cahill, originally appeared in *Outside*. Copyright © 1999 by Tim Cahill.

319   "A Global Green Deal" by Mark Hertsgaard, originally appeared in *Time*. Copyright © 2000 by Time Inc. Reprinted by permission.

325   "Infernal Paradise" from *High Tide in Tucson: Essays From Now or Never*, by Barbara Kingsolver. Copyright © 1995 by Barbara Kingsolver. Reprinted by permission of HarperCollins Publishers Inc.

INDEX